Kate Nowicki
Seattle
1977

AREA HANDBOOK

for

SAUDI ARABIA

Coauthors
First Edition

Norman C. Walpole
Alexander J. Bastos
Frederick R. Eisele
Allison Butler Herrick
Howard J. John
Tura K. Wieland

Research completed December 1970

Second Edition

Published 1971

(This pamphlet supersedes DA Pam 550-51, December 1966)

DA Pam 550-51

Library of Congress Catalog Card Number: 67-5743

For sale by the Superintendent of Documents, U.S. Government Printing Office
Washington, D.C. 20402 - Price $6.50
Stock Number 008-020-00383-2
Catalog Number D 101.22:550-51/2

FOREWORD

This volume is one of a series of handbooks prepared by Foreign Area Studies (FAS) of The American University, designed to be useful to military and other personnel who need a convenient compilation of basic facts about the social, economic, political, and military institutions and practices of various countries. The emphasis is on objective description of the nation's present society and the kinds of possible or probable changes that might be expected in the future. The handbook seeks to present as full and as balanced an integrated exposition as limitations on space and research time permit. It was compiled from information available in openly published material. An extensive bibliography is provided to permit recourse to other published sources for more detailed information. There has been no attempt to express any specific point of view or to make policy recommendations. The contents of the handbook represent the work of the authors and FAS and do not represent the official view of the United States government.

An effort has been made to make the handbook as comprehensive as possible. It can be expected, however, that the material, interpretations, and conclusions are subject to modification in the light of new information and developments. Such corrections, additions, and suggestions for factual, interpretive, or other change as readers may have will be welcomed for use in future revisions. Comments may be addressed to:

> The Director
> Foreign Area Studies
> The American University
> 5010 Wisconsin Avenue, N.W.
> Washington, D.C. 20016

PREFACE TO THE SECOND EDITION

The research on the first edition of the *Area Handbook for Saudi Arabia* that was published in December 1966 was completed in December 1965. Since that time the country has experienced relatively modest changes in its social, economic, and political structure, although there have been significant expansions in the fields of education, medical services, and related social welfare matters. These changes, however, have not markedly altered the basic society, the form of government, and the conduct of life.

In late 1970, therefore, the decision was made to publish a second edition of the handbook without revision but with a new section entitled "Summary of Events: January 1966—December 1970." This new section was completed on December 30, 1970, by a team composed of Beryl L. Benderly, William W. Cover, and Gordon C. McDonald, with Richard F. Nyrop as chairman. In addition, Joanne M. Jarvis drafted important sections and participated in the research effort. The text of the first edition was written by Alexander J. Bastos, Frederick R. Eisele, Allison Butler Herrick, Howard J. John, and Tura K. Wieland under the chairmanship of Norman C. Walpole.

In preparing the new section, the authors followed the transliteration system recommended by the Library of Congress in the spelling of Arabic words and names, with the exception that no diacritical markings or other symbols were used. The place names used are those established for Saudi Arabia by the United States Board of Geographic Names in July 1961. In some instances a name established by the board, for example, Makkah, is shown in parentheses, but the more familiar name, Mecca, is used thereafter. The reader will notice that the spelling of place names in the summary may vary from that in the original text because of the different sources used.

Data on Saudi Arabia remain sparse and open to question. Neither the population nor the size of the country, for example, has been established with any degree of precision, and in 1970 the population estimates ranged from 3.4 million to 7.7 million. Reliable information on family life and other social indicators is equally subject to error and uncertainty. Economic statistics and descriptions should be taken as approximations rather than as final reports, with the exception of data on oil production and revenues, which are believed to be reliable.

SUMMARY OF EVENTS:
JANUARY 1966–DECEMBER 1970

In the 1966–70 period the Kingdom of Saudi Arabia continued to follow trends established during the preceding two decades. Economic growth and moderate but steady improvements in social services and living standards had become the normal year-to-year pattern, sustained by orderly growth in petroleum revenues. The importation of Western technologists, builders, and teachers continued. Nevertheless, there were no rapid changes in social or political attitudes and structures. Family connections, Islamic law, and long-established tradition continued as the dominant forces in society and government.

Petroleum production increased by 1970 to about 1.1 billion barrels annually. Oil income to the government of King Faisal (King Faisal Ibn Abd al Aziz al Faisal al Saud, in power since 1964) approached the equivalent of US$1 billion annually, constituting about 85 percent of government income and 90 percent of its foreign exchange.

Revenues are dispensed as determined by the Faisal government, which includes many senior officials who are either sons of the late King Abd al Aziz Ibn Saud, who founded the kingdom and ruled until 1953, as is King Faisal, or close relatives. Combined with an adherence to traditional social values, the king has shown a willingness to accept technology, education, and some forms of economic and social change among Saudi Arabian citizens.

The increasing number of foreign scientists, technicians, and teachers brought into the country during the 1960s—in some instances with the help of the United Nations—worked on programs and projects ranging throughout the spectrum of economic and social development. The influx of oil revenue and overall economic growth also provided jobs, trading opportunities, and other means of gaining a livelihood for about 300,000 non-Saudis living in the country in 1970. The majority of these came from the peripheral states and the Arab states adjacent to or near northern Saudi Arabia, but there were also technicians, teachers, and businessmen from Europe and elsewhere. Meanwhile, an estimated 40 to 50 percent of the Saudi population continued their traditional life as nomadic herdsmen, almost entirely outside the wage-earning or business economy. Half of this group, more than one-fourth of the total national population, depended primarily on camel herding for their livelihood.

By fiscal year 1969/70 the gross national product (GNP) was estimated at over SR12 billion annually (4.5 Saudi riyals equal US$1). The national budget for fiscal year 1970/71 was projected at about SR6.4 billion, of which about 50 percent was to be devoted to development and more than 30 percent, to defense. During the late 1960s the GNP grew at almost 10 percent per year, one of the highest rates in the world.

Educational budgets and total student enrollment both increased by about 70 percent during the late 1960s, continuing the rapid growth trend of the previous decade. About 10 percent of the national budget was devoted to education. An important change in traditional attitudes is dramatized by the increase in publicly supported elementary schools for girls. The first such school was opened in 1960, and the number of students grew rapidly. Education was free to all students at all levels from elementary school to upper-level university courses, including the expenses incurred by about 2,000 students in various Middle Eastern, European, and American universities.

Intentionally or otherwise, other government programs in addition to education were bringing moderate social changes to some segments of the population. State lands were being distributed to Bedouin tribesmen and others to encourage them to become sedentary farmers rather than nomadic herdsmen. Other agriculture-related projects were being directed toward self-sufficiency in food for the entire nation.

The General Petroleum and Mineral Organization (Petromin), an autonomous private organization sponsored by the government, was the most important organization involved in the development of the economy, particularly the development of petroleum processing and related industries. Through Petromin, the government regularly channeled some of its oil revenues into construction and development projects and the training of personnel to establish policies and manage current and future development, thus reducing the need for foreign managers and advisers. The Petromin staff grew from 30 in 1962 to 3,000 in 1970. Among Petromin's many projects, large and small, were the construction of oil refineries by foreign companies, arranged by Petromin, and the programming of production of basic chemicals and construction materials.

Diversification of the economy continued in late 1970 to be one of the major goals of the Faisal government, whose planners hope to reduce the extremely heavy dependence upon crude petroleum revenues. Although it was establishing the usual basis for an industrial sector, including roads, power plants, factories, refineries, and communication nets, the government was also supporting agricultural research—seeking eventual self-sufficiency in food—and was continuing a search for minerals other than petroleum. Until the 1960s the traditional economy had been dependent almost entirely upon government funds for the creation or development of new industrial or commercial ventures. By 1970, however, private investors were responsible for almost one-half of gross capital formation, and private investment was reportedly growing at the rate of about 9 percent per year.

Commercial bank deposits and the banking system in general were also growing at a rate of about 10 percent annually. The Agricultural Bank had been active since 1965; an industrial bank was to be formally initiated in 1971; and other types of banks were in the planning stage. The discovery in 1970 of additional reserves of crude oil indicated that the nation would continue to have the funds for impressive economic growth.

SOCIAL CHANGES

In late 1970 social and ethnic relations were largely unchanged. During the late 1960s the kingdom, nevertheless, had realized significant progress in education, communications, and welfare, which collectively carry a significant potential for social change.

One such step was taken in April 1967 when the Ministry of Information inaugurated television broadcasts aimed at the Saudi population. From the original two hours daily, service has expanded to six hours of news, commentary, variety shows, and educational and religious programs. Television represents a significant departure from certain traditions in Saudi life; until it was introduced, no portrayal of the human form was permitted. Television's ability to transmit religious teachings won over conservative leaders.

Approximately 70 percent of the programming is of local origin; about half of the imported programs—primarily adventures, comedies, westerns, and sports events—originate in the United States. Censorship assures that the foreign programs do not offend Saudi sensibilities; references to alcohol, promiscuity, gambling, and non-Islamic religions, as well as unseemly violence, are deleted. Observers have noted the influence of foreign customs and values presumed to be felt in local life. Increasingly, men are seen walking in the markets with their wives and families. Family evenings around the television set are beginning to supplant the traditional all-male socializing.

A minimal exposure to foreign cultures is one byproduct of television; another is broadened educational opportunities for home-bound women. The authorities have taken advantage of the new opportunity to present programs on maternal and child health, food preparation, housekeeping, and self-improvement for women. In keeping with tradition, however, Saudi women never appear on television; at most, their hands may be shown during a cooking demonstration.

The number of sets in the country is variously estimated at between 12,000 and 75,000. In 1970 the Saudi Arabian Government Television Service maintained stations at Riyadh (Ar Riyad), Jiddah (Juddah), Medina (Madinah), Damman, Qasim, and Taif. In addition, the Arabian American Oil Company (Aramco) maintained a television station at Dhahran (Zahran) for its employees, broadcasting in both English and Arabic. The country was receiving technical aid from several foreign broadcasting organizations, and Saudis were studying television techniques abroad as well.

Radio broadcasting has also undergone expansion, especially in the realm of broadening international contacts. The government radio international service at Jiddah carried news, commentary, and variety programs on seven frequencies in seven languages. In mid-1970 consideration was being given to the establishment of ground stations for communication with the Atlantic Ocean and Indian Ocean communications satellites. The Ministry of Information also began subscribing to Agence France Presse, the French news service, and in late 1970 the ministry claimed to be receiving news from all important foreign news services. In June 1970 a radio-television cooperation agreement was signed with the government of Tunisia.

The domestic radio service of the ministry broadcasts from Jiddah on three shortwave and three mediumwave transmitters and from Riyadh on five shortwave and five mediumwave transmitters. A powerful new radio station under construction near Riyadh, scheduled for completion in 1971, was slated to include four new 350-kilowatt transmitters, a large antenna, and several 4000-kilowatt generators. The project, which will include eleven studios, is designed to transmit four programs simultaneously. Government sources in 1970 estimated a total of 1 million radio sets, many of which were said to belong to nomadic Bedouin. Since the 1967 Arab-Israeli War, a locally produced program "With the Fedayeen" has been transmitted on the domestic services.

In late 1970 the press continued to function under the system established by the government. Several new periodicals had begun publication since 1965, including a monthly that was founded in 1966 and was edited by a woman.

Significant strides have been taken in education, health, and welfare as well. From 1964 to 1969 the education budget increased by 47 percent; the 1968/69 budget alone was approximately 25 percent greater than the budget of the preceding year. During this five-year period new schools were built at the average rate of 121 per year; their number increased by 46 percent. The student population in primary, secondary, and higher education rose by 85 percent, 148 percent, and 124 percent, respectively. Adult education also increased rapidly.

Progress in girls' education has been especially striking. At the end of the five-year period three times as many girls were attending primary schools, and eleven times as many were enrolled in postprimary schools. In 1969 the enrollment in girls' primary schools increased by 19 percent, and that of secondary schools, by 54 percent; the number of institutions also increased by 54 percent. More than 250,000 boys attended school in 1969, and female students numbered more than 100,000. At least a dozen more schools for girls were scheduled to open in 1970 and 1971.

The first vocational training center in the kingdom was opened at Riyadh in 1963 under the auspices of the Ministry of Labor and Social Affairs. Between 1966 and 1968 centers were opened in Jiddah, Buraidah, Dammam, and al Jawf. There were 656 students in 1968. These centers offer training in air-conditioning and refrigeration equipment maintenance, plumbing, and auto mechanics, as well as other technical subjects. In addition, in fiscal year 1968/69 the Ministry of Education established four technical intermediate schools at Jiddah, Medina, Riyadh, and al Hufuf, which enrolled 413 postprimary students. The Royal Vocational Institute at Riyadh, for the training of students who have completed intermediate studies in some thirty technical subjects, was organized in 1968 and enrolled 252. The ministry expects that this institution will eventually enroll 1,000 day and 2,000 evening students.

Several new programs in higher education have been inaugurated in recent years. Among them are the English Language Institute, the Higher Juridical Institute, and a master's degree program in Islamic studies. In 1969 a medical school was established which enrolled thirty-five students and whose faculty had been trained in cooperation with the University of London. In addition, some 2,000 students were being supported by the government in advanced studies abroad, many of them in medical training programs.

The founding of a medical college was one of a series of advances in health care realized since 1965. In 1966 there were 5,952 hospital beds, or 1 for every 1,150 persons; physicians numbered 525 in the same year, or 1 for each 13,090 persons. From 1964 to 1969, however, the number of hospital beds increased 22 percent; hospitals, 19 percent; and dispensaries and health centers, approximately 30 percent. During the same period the number of physicians more than doubled, as did that of nurses of both sexes and of midwives; the number of pharmacists more than tripled. Other public health programs in progress in 1970 included plans for a public health laboratory, a blood bank, and water projects in Mecca (Makkah) and Riyadh.

Public health programs have been steadily increasing in effectiveness. Among those programs in progress in 1970 were large-scale attacks on malaria and tuberculosis. In addition to the health of its own citizens, the country faces an annual public health crisis during the Muslim pilgrimage season. The number of pilgrims from abroad has been increasing rapidly. In the Muslim year 1384 (1964–65) they numbered 283,319; by 1389 (1969–70), 406,295 joined the pilgrimage. During the 1969 pilgrimage, eleven active cases of smallpox were discovered among foreign pilgrims entering Saudi Arabia. In keeping with Saudi public health practices, they were removed to government quarantine stations for treatment and isolation. Ten of the patients recovered, and one died. Because of prompt action, however, there was no further outbreak of smallpox in the country, among either citizens or pilgrims.

In addition to modernizing social facilities, King Faisal hopes to modernize the way of life of his nomadic subjects. An extensive plan has been drawn up to develop certain desert areas as arable land and eventually to settle 57,000 Bedouin families as sedentary agriculturalists. Various contracts for agricultural development were being arranged with foreign specialists and development companies. For example, in 1969 the Ministry of Agriculture and Water contracted with a Swiss consulting firm to develop cropland and eventually to turn the land over to newly trained former nomads.

Despite some effects, economic development and change by 1970 had not been accompanied by changes of comparable magnitude in the basic political and social outlook. The government remains traditional and paternalistic in character; the Islamic system, however, contains within itself its own strong factor of egalitarianism, and individual rights in this system, especially the right to present grievances and receive prompt attention, are well defined.

The rapid expansion of education, industry, and communications raised multiple problems concerned with law, the generation of wealth, and social justice in relation to the traditional ideology. The government, recognizing the need to prepare for change, sought to identify with, but also to control and channel, these new forces in the general interest. For example, in commenting on the government's expenditures under the national social security program begun in 1964, King Faisal noted that the goal of the program was to promote both individual and collective self-help and productivity. As reported on August 16, 1970, he added: "The Kingdom of Saudi Arabia is a Muslim state that believes in social justice and endeavors to achieve it. Social security is an important pillar of social justice."

POLITICAL DEVELOPMENTS

The Governmental and Political System in 1970

Despite substantial changes elsewhere in the Middle East resulting from intra-Arab tensions and the stresses of the Arab-Israeli confrontation, the government of Saudi Arabia continued to exhibit in late 1970 the high degree of stability prevailing since King Faisal was proclaimed monarch on November 2, 1964. The governmental and political system was little changed since 1965 and had showed itself able to conduct the nation successfully through the intervening years under King Faisal's policy of guided and gradual modernizing development.

In the national society the integration of church, state, and social forms continued to prevail, and the king's position continued to be the focus of all lines of power. Following traditional practices, he is, at once, the head of state in Western terms; the sheikh of sheikhs in the ancient pattern of Arab social structure; the *imam* of the faith, or supreme Islamic religious leader; and commander in chief of the armed forces and police. Assisted by the Council of Ministers, appointed by and responsible to him, and an extensive government service, he exercises authority within the framework of Arab tradition and the *sharia*, the Islamic law of the Quran, as supplemented in recent years by decree law.

King Faisal, in addition to being head of state, continued in 1970 as prime minister and working executive head of the government. He also acted as his own foreign minister, assisted by a minister of state for foreign affairs. In the absence of a legislative body, the Council of Ministers functioned as the instrument of royal authority in legislative as well as executive matters. There were fourteen ministries in late 1970.

In addition to the king as prime minister, the Council of Ministers was composed of two deputy prime ministers and the respective ministers, all appointed by him. With the exception of the offices of second deputy prime minister, minister of state for foreign affairs, and minister of justice, the organization of the council was the same as in 1965. Crown Prince Khalid Ibn al Aziz al Saud held the office of first deputy prime minister, and Prince Fahd Ibn Abd al Aziz al Saud was second deputy prime minister and minister of interior.

The courts, with Islamic judges organized and appointed under Faisal's central role as *imam*, continued to dispense justice and administer judicial functions under the *sharia*. Two types of litigation prevail: public right actions, comparable to criminal law in Western terminology; and private right actions, comparable to civil and equity law. At the head of the system, below the king, is the grand *mufti* (leader) or chief *qadi* (judge). The Higher Juridical Institute, established in 1965, provides three extra years of study for selected graduates of the *sharia* college. The institute enables Islamic jurists to study intensively the religious-legal problems confronting the kingdom because of modern development and to make recommendations for their solution.

After 1962 budgetary provision was made for a ministry of justice to administer the body of accumulating decree law and ministerial regulations necessitated by the new economic and technological situations and to coordinate this law with the *sharia* administration. This ministry was not immediately organized, however, but developed slowly. On September 23, 1970, by royal order, Sheikh Muhammad bin Ali al Harkan was appointed minister of justice. The relationship of this new ministry to the office of the chief *qadi* and, in turn, of both these offices to the Council of Ministers, was not clear in late 1970. It appeared that the role of the chief *qadi* was merged with that of the minister of justice, who would sit with the Council of Ministers. The role of grand *mufti* was being assumed by a council of *muftis*.

Political parties were not authorized, and public offices were not elective. Although some agitation for change has been manifested in this regard, the Saudi society at large continued to be conservative, tribal oriented, and committed to the well-understood Islamic system.

The monarchy itself is not hereditary. It is limited by the *sharia*, and designation to the throne is made by the royal family's choice, sanctioned by the *ulema* (the body of leading Islamic scholars). This designation rests upon a consensus of support among a wide base of established sociopolitical segments: the ruling family itself, the principal tribal sheikhs, the Council of Ministers, the *ulema*, and the armed forces. Prince Khalid, half-brother of King Faisal, was formally named as crown prince by Faisal in March 1965, and this designation was supported by the consensus. In the event of the king's demise, a consensus would again be sought to confirm the succession.

Provincial and municipal government patterns in 1970 were essentially unchanged from 1965; tribal affairs and local government in the small villages remained close to traditional forms. The village or tribal sheikh, chosen by a local consensus resembling, in microcosm, that at the national level, is confirmed by the provincial governor. Local leadership remains dependent, however, upon continued support of the population. This means that the headman must act in the general interest of the people and within the system.

Substantial internal revolutionary forces had not emerged in late 1970. Most of the population apparently continued to regard the Islamic state, under King Faisal, as the natural way of political expression and accepted his policy of gradual, adaptive modernization. Some dissatisfaction existed with the pace of modernization and the conservatism of some of the Islamic clergy, but active dissent took the political form of small groups of subversive conspirators rather than a widely based movement.

Foreign Relations

In 1970 Faisal continued his government's active membership in the United Nations and the League of Arab States. Foreign policy continued to be independent and was aimed at preserving the country's paramount position in the Arabian peninsula and its prestige in the Arab and Muslim worlds as protector of the holy places.

The country played a leading role in regional affairs; its foreign policy was heavily oriented toward the other Arab states and the defense of Arab interests. In 1966 Faisal made extensive use of the technique of official state visits abroad in behalf of his foreign policy and of Islamic and Arab causes. Diplomatic connections were maintained with some forty-five foreign countries; the country continued to abstain, however, from relations with any

Communist state, and no known Communist was permitted to reside in the country.

Relationships continued to be close with the United States and the West, especially in reference to the oil-based economy, despite dissatisfaction with the United States on the Arab-Israeli issue. Relations with Great Britain, broken between November 1956 and January 1963 because of the Suez crisis of 1956 and the separate problem of claims to the Buraimi Oasis, were generally good in 1970. The question of the Buraimi Oasis, located about ninety-five miles east of the capital of the Persian Gulf sheikhdom of Abu Dhabi, and other Saudi Arabia-Abu Dhabi boundary questions were still unresolved. King Faisal continued to maintain his claim, and the announced intention to withdraw British forces and commitments from the gulf region by the end of 1971 heightened Saudi Arabian interest in the area. The government was not opposed to the proposed federation of the nine princely sheikhdoms of the gulf coast. Little progress had been made by late 1970 in negotiations between these states to form this federation, however.

Relationships with other Arab and Muslim states in the Middle East during the 1965–70 period continued to reflect the differences between those states classed as conservative or moderate, including Saudi Arabia, and those controlled by revolutionary-socialist regimes, sometimes classed as radical or radical-nationalist. Despite these differences, the basic identification of the country and its government with Arab causes of independence, nationalism, and opposition to Israel was not in question.

Since the establishment of the state after World War I by King Saud, father of King Faisal, it has never been in a colonial or protectorate status. The foreign policy of the country, while supporting controlled economic and developmental arrangements, has in general avoided permanent military alliances and has approached the questions of nationalism, political organization, and political alignments in a context of Islamic independence. For example, the Taif Pact of August 30, 1962, with Jordan (and the related Joint Defense Council announced November 4) was a mutual defense and nonaggression agreement between the two conservative Muslim states.

Faisal and his government played a leading role at the Khartoum Conference of Arab leaders in September 1967, and Saudi Arabia, along with Kuwait and Libya, assumed responsibility for major financial aid payments to the United Arab Republic (Egypt) and Jordan. Although Faisal has provided financial and moral support for the continuing Arab opposition to

Israel and insisted that the Israelis must relinquish control of Jerusalem's Islamic shrines, Saudi Arabia has nevertheless avoided direct military involvement in the intermittent Arab-Israeli battles of the 1968–70 period.

During the late 1960s the Persian Gulf area received considerable attention from both Saudi Arabia and Iran, its neighbor on the eastern side of the gulf. As more and more deposits of petroleum were discovered and exploited around the gulf, both Saudi Arabia and Iran sought to protect their interests in the area, with an apparently mutual desire to discourage any increase in influence exerted by other nations in this isolated but wealthy region. Negotiations between the two nations concerning the territorial limits of each nation on the continental shelf in the Gulf were concluded successfully in October 1968, and further discussions on Saudi Arabian and Iranian spheres of interest and defense of the gulf area appeared to be making progress in 1970.

Saudi aid to the royalists in Yemen, on Saudi Arabia's southwestern border, was reported to have been resumed late in 1969, following a renewal of active conflict between Yemeni royalist and republican forces during late November and early December. Additional raids were reported in January 1970, but aid was reportedly brought to an end early in 1970. On July 23, 1970, Saudi Arabia recognized the Republic of Yemen, ending eight years of estrangement since the republican overthrow of the royalist *imamate* in 1962. Diplomatic recognition was withheld, however, from the radical regime of the People's Republic of Southern Yemen. Also, relations were strained with Syria because of ideological differences and because of that country's delay in allowing repairs to sections of the Trans-Arabian pipeline (Tapline) located in Syria.

In 1969 King Faisal, supported by Iran and Jordan, had led the call for the Islamic summit meeting held in Rabat, Morocco, in September 1969. Saudi Arabia and the Islamic World League organization, revived after the Rabat conference, have supported in general, if not always in specifics, the Arab cause of the liberation of Palestine and the Palestinian Arab guerrilla groups, such as Al Fatah. At the Arab summit meeting of December 1969, also in Rabat, King Faisal did not concur with President Gamal Abdul Nasser on questions regarding the degree and management of the financing of the Arab struggle against Israel, but relations were not broken or exacerbated to the extent that had often prevailed before 1967.

The intrusion of radical socialist movements in the area of the Persian Gulf sheikhdoms, the overthrow in July 1970 of the traditional sultan of Muscat and Oman by his son, and reports of growing Chinese Communist influence in the region occasioned increased external security precautions by Saudi Arabia. The government has since 1965 held close-working relationships with King Hussein's government in Jordan. Military support has been made available to Jordan at various times, although no Saudi Arabian forces were actually engaged in the 1967 Arab-Israeli War. King Faisal participated in the meeting of the Arab kings and presidents in Cairo designed to end the September 1970 civil war in Jordan and endorsed the cease-fire agreement of September 27, 1970.

MAIN POLITICAL EVENTS, LATE 1965–1970

On August 9, 1965, at Amman, Jordan, delegations from Saudi Arabia and Jordan signed an agreement cited as the "final determination of the boundaries between their two countries." This agreement, both by maps and narrative description, delimited for the first time the older, undemarcated, and never fully adjudicated boundaries. In this determination and the resulting exchange of territory, Saudi Arabia had a net gain of about 580 square miles— mostly at the southeastern corner of Jordan, thus enabling a better administrative alignment of Saudi Arabia's northern province.

Included in the agreement was the proviso that, if petroleum products were discovered in any of the exchanged areas, the "rights, interests, and profits" were to be shared equally between Saudi Arabia and Jordan. In addition, continued rights to pasturage and water were secured to the tribes of both countries according to prevailing custom, and free passage through the exchanged areas was mutually guaranteed for travel and trade along specified routes. This agreement, the 1965 border delineation with Qatar, and the Continental Shelf Agreement of October 1968 with Iran were the principal boundary determinations in the years from 1965 to 1970. Elsewhere around the largely undelimited eastern and southern rim of the peninsula, the Saudi Arabian claim line of October 1955 presented a basis for future negotiations.

During the spring and summer of 1965 the insurgent royalist faction in the Republic of Yemen initiated new military offensives, gaining some success, in the unsettled situation that had prevailed since the revolutionary overthrow of the old royalist Yemeni *imamate* in 1962. Tensions increased again between Egypt, supporting the republican regime with a substantial troop presence in Yemen, and Saudi Arabia, reportedly supplying material and financial aid to the royalist insurgents. After preliminary discussions in Cairo and Jiddah during July and August, President Nasser and King Faisal met on August 22, 1965, in the Saudi Arabian port city of Jiddah and on August 24 signed what became known as the Jiddah Agreement.

This determination provided for: an immediate cease-fire; the stoppage of Saudi Arabian aid to the royalists; the withdrawal of Egyptian forces from Yemen by September 1966; the establishment of a provisional Yemeni government; the holding of a conference of Yemeni factional representatives under joint Saudi Arabian-Egyptian sponsorship at Harad in November 1965; and a national plebiscite in November 1966. This agreement was welcomed by the United Nations, the United States, the Soviet Union, and certain Arab states but was polemically assailed by Syria.

In accordance with the Jiddah Agreement, twenty-five Yemeni republicans and twenty-five royalists met at Harad on November 23, 1965, to discuss the proposed plebiscite, a system of transitional arrangements, and the form for a provisional government. At the conference itself, Egypt and Saudi Arabia were each represented by two observers. The conference was deadlocked from the start, could reach no agreement on an agenda, and broke up on December 24, 1965, with the intent to resume on February 20, 1966. The conference was not resumed, and tensions again increased between Saudi Arabia and Egypt amid charges of intransigence on both sides.

Fighting broke out again in the central and northern part of Yemen in January 1966, in the wake of the withdrawal of Egyptian forces, and the royalist faction claimed extensive victories. The republican side, however, held that these hostilities were not politically indicative but that certain of the Yemeni tribes had simply reverted to banditry. Nevertheless, in a speech on May 1, 1966, President Nasser took a stern attitude toward Saudi Arabia, threatening air attacks and invasion.

The third in the series of Arab summit conferences begun in January 1964 at Cairo had been held at Casablanca, Morocco, in September 1965 in a climate of general cordiality, but this atmosphere then deteriorated in the aftermath of the breakdown of the Jiddah Agreement. Among other factors contributing to the breakdown were the Egyptian reactions to the proposals, put forward in December 1965 by King Faisal and Mohamad Reza Shah Pahlavi, the Shah of Iran, for an international Islamic conference and to a series of international visits made by King Faisal during 1966.

President Nasser denounced the proposals for an Islamic conference as constituting a pretext for an alliance or a pact of what he called "reactionary" Muslim states. King Faisal, on the contrary, consistently held that his efforts for Islamic unity were not aimed at developing a political pact but at providing a basis for Islamic cooperation and coordination. Addressing pilgrims at Mecca on March 27, 1966, the king stated that he would not be deterred by criticism and that "what we ask is for Muslims to come together and support one another in their every need."

The fourth meeting of the Arab heads of government took place in Cairo from March 14 to 17, 1966. Among other resolutions taken were the following: a determination not to renew diplomatic relations with West Germany (the Federal Republic of Germany), broken in 1965 because of that country's recognition of Israel; a reaffirmation of support for "liberation movements" throughout Africa and Asia; and the scheduling of the next summit meeting for Algiers on September 5, 1966. President Nasser announced on July 22, however, that his government would not take part in the Algiers conference, and the secretariat of the Arab League announced on August 5 that the meeting had been indefinitely postponed.

After this postponement, much high-level diplomatic activity took place within the Muslim and Arab worlds. A number of states indicated varying degrees of support for King Faisal's basic position that no one state, such as Egypt, should dominate the Arab League. Faisal began a tour of five Muslim countries on August 29 and received indications of support in each of the countries for an Islamic conference.

Divisions between Saudi Arabia and Egypt on the Yemeni question were deepened in late 1966. Negotiations for settlement of differences undertaken under the good offices of the ruler of Kuwait had resulted in a new agreement between the Saudi and Egyptian governments on August 17, 1966, but the agreement was never implemented. Serious hostilities in the Yemeni civil war again broke out in September 1966, and the Egyptian government announced its intention not to withdraw any additional Egyptian troops from Yemen. Egyptian aircraft carried out a series of heavy strikes against royalist installations and villages and also struck the southern Saudi Arabian towns of Jizan (Qizan) and Najran on October 14, 1966, January 27, 1967, and again on May 13 and May 14. The Saudi government on February 9 closed both Egyptian banks operating in Saudi Arabia, and on February 10 Egypt sequestered the property holdings in Egypt of King Faisal and 210 other Saudi citizens.

During December 1966 and January 1967 radio transmissions originating in Cairo and said to be representing a "Union of People of the Arabian Peninsula" claimed that a series of terror bomb attacks had been made in Saudi Arabia against residences and persons of the royal family, as well as against United States and British personnel, and would continue. On January 10 the Saudi Ministry of Interior confirmed that a number of arrests had been made of persons accused of sabotage, mostly Yemenis. Trials were held at Riyadh, and on March 17 the ministry announced that seventeen Yemenis had been found guilty and, in accordance with Saudi Arabian law, they were publicly beheaded.

This action provoked some protest in the Arab world. Former King Saud, who had lived in Cairo with President Nasser's permission after King Faisal assumed the crown in November 1964, visited Sana, the capital of Yemen, from April 23 to 25. He presented a personal gift of the equivalent of US$1 million to the Republic of Yemen and made statements indicating that he might have been considering an attempt to regain the throne in Saudi Arabia. The Arab-Israeli crisis of May 1967, however, diverted Arab attention to that priority.

On May 23, 1967, President Nasser announced that Egypt was closing the straits of Tiran at the southern outlet from the Gulf of Aqaba. King Faisal, then on a state visit to England, announced in London on the same day that his country supported the Egyptian position and that he had ordered Saudi Arabian forces to be ready to participate in "the battle against Israeli aggression." He declared that all Arab countries, whatever their differences, were united in their attitude toward Israel. On May 24 the Jordanian government announced permission for both Saudi and Iraqi forces to enter Jordan. Some Saudi units entered southern Jordan the same day; others remained in readiness near the border. None were heavily engaged in the succeeding hostilities.

During the Six-Day War of June 1967, most of the Arab states broke diplomatic relations with the United States and Great Britain on the basis of the often-stated Arab conviction that these Western powers were actively backing the state of Israel and opposed to the Arab cause. On June 6 Egypt closed the Suez Canal; on the same day Saudi Arabia suspended oil shipments to the United States and Britain, but it maintained diplomatic relations with both countries. In Saudi Arabia the Arabian American Oil Company (Aramco) was able to resume operations on June 14, but exports to British and United States destinations were banned.

After the Six-Day War, the foreign ministers of all Arab countries met briefly but inconclusively in Kuwait on June 18 to discuss the oil embargo against the West. On June 30 the Saudi Arabian minister of petroleum and mineral resources urged Arab countries to study seriously the effect of the embargo on their economies. Radio Mecca, on July 7, broadcast an official government statement noting that the Arab world was not the only source of oil and that there was no reason to continue the ban on oil exports to the United States and Great Britain because it was now seen that there was no factual evidence to support Arab allegations during the war that military aircraft of these powers had assisted Israel.

Between August 1 and August 6, 1967, the Arab foreign ministers met in Khartoum, Sudan, and considered a range of topics in preparation for a convocation of Arab heads of state. During this time the Egyptian representative indicated his government's willingness to return to the Jiddah Agreement of 1965 as a means of solving the Yemen question. President Abdulla Sallal of Yemen rejected this proposal, but the Saudi Arabian response was generally favorable. King Faisal stated on August 18 that the essential requirement was that all Egyptian forces should be evacuated from the Arabian peninsula. "On that condition," he said, "we shall stop our aid to the Yemeni royalists." On August 24 the prime minister of the Sudan, acting as mediator, announced that King Faisal and President Nasser had agreed to resume talks in the interest of a settlement.

The Arab foreign ministers again met in Khartoum on August 26 and August 27, 1967, to finalize the agenda for the Arab summit meeting, which began August 29 and continued through September 3. This meeting, known as the Khartoum Conference or Khartoum Summit Conference, set the general line of Arab policy for the next three years.

The Khartoum Conference resulted in four major decisions. It was agreed that the Arab oil-producing countries should resume production. Although not explicitly stated, this was taken to mean an end to the oil embargo against the United States and Great Britain, which in fact followed. Saudi Arabia, Kuwait, and Libya undertook to provide direct financial aid to Egypt and Jordan, in the total annual equivalent of US$378 million. This aid, to counter the adverse economic effects of the 1967 war with Israel on the two recipient countries, was to be paid in quarterly installments, with Egypt receiving annually a total equivalent to US$266 million and Jordan, US$112 million. Of the total, Saudi Arabia's annual contribution was set at the equivalent of US$140 million. In late 1970 these payments were continuing and constituted for the donor states a factor of significant influence in Arab affairs.

The third decision of the Khartoum Conference called for the elimination of all foreign military bases in Arab territory and for necessary actions to consolidate Arab military strength to face any possible aggression. The conference also reaffirmed the Arab principle of nonrecognition of, and nonnegotiation with, Israel either collectively or individually.

Later reports showed that at the Khartoum Conference on August 31, 1967, King Faisal and President Nasser had agreed to seek a peaceful solution in the Yemen civil war, that all Egyptian forces should be withdrawn, that Saudi Arabian aid to the royalist faction should cease, and that a tripartite committee composed of the foreign ministers of the Sudan, Iraq, and Morocco should attempt to devise a new government to include representatives of all the major factions in the Yemeni dispute.

The tripartite committee was duly formed, conducted preliminary hearings in Lebanon, and proceeded to Yemen on October 3. President Sallal, however, refused to receive them. He rejected the Khartoum Agreement, as he had consistently rejected the earlier Jiddah Agreement, on the general grounds that it had not been developed with Yemeni participation, and he alleged that Saudi Arabia was continuing to provide aid to the royalists. After visiting King Faisal, the members of the committee then dispersed to their places of origin. The Egyptian troop evacuation, begun on September 26, was completed on December 9, 1967.

Meanwhile, serious divisions had arisen in the Yemeni republican structure, and, while abroad, President Sallal was deposed in a bloodless military coup on November 5 and replaced by a republican council. This council accepted those parts of the Khartoum Agreement that did not deal directly with internal Yemeni affairs. A renewed royalist offensive in November was unsuccessful, and the tripartite committee endeavored in December, again unsuccessfully, to bring about a peace council, amid countercharges of continued Saudi aid to the royalists and impending Soviet aid to the republicans, as the new regime attempted to organize its administration.

Another royalist offensive in October 1968 again failed, and the failure greatly intensified the existing divisions among its leaders. By January 1969 press reports indicated that the new Yemeni republican regime was attempting to attain some degree of reconciliation with royalists and that its governmental form was inclining to moderate policies rather than radical socialism. At the same time, observers suggested that Saudi Arabia was preparing to normalize relations with Yemen, since Yemenis bearing republican passports were being admitted to Saudi

Arabia, and Yemeni republican charges of Saudi aid to the royalists ceased.

Saudi Arabia's relations with the non-Arabic but Muslim monarchy of Iran, its biggest neighbor on the Persian Gulf littoral, have improved steadily since 1965. An important development was the conclusion between the two countries, on October 24, 1968, of the Continental Shelf Agreement regarding seabed rights and certain claims in the Persian Gulf. Under this agreement, executed at Tehran, Saudi Arabian sovereignty over the island of Al Arabiya and Iranian sovereignty over the island of Farsi in the gulf were recognized, along with a twelve-mile belt of territorial waters around each. Elsewhere in the gulf, interests were to be separated by a straight line generally down the center of the gulf.

The Continental Shelf Agreement formed a substantial basis for the continued improvement of relations between the two oil-rich monarchical states, supported by a common sense of cooperation within the Islamic context. In addition, in December 1968, Great Britain reiterated its intent to withdraw from commitments in the Persian Gulf region by the end of 1971, thus intensifying the interest of both Saudi Arabia and Iran in the security and stability of that area. No formal alliance was made, but the two governments undertook to consult with each other on matters of mutual economic and security interests.

Former King Saud died on February 23, 1969, in Athens, Greece. This event did not, however, result in any significant political development.

On August 21, 1969, fire broke out in the Al Aqsa Mosque in the Old City of Jerusalem. The ancient shrine, part of the Dome of the Rock mosque area and including relics from the time of Saladin and earlier, is generally held in Islamic veneration only below the sites at Mecca and Medina in Saudi Arabia. King Hussein of Jordan immediately proposed that an Arab summit meeting be convened, and the foreign ministers of the fourteen Arab states met in Cairo on August 25. Through his representative, King Faisal presented a proposal that the convocation be an Islamic summit meeting. This proposal was endorsed by King Hasan of Morocco as well as the Shah of Iran. It was accepted by King Hussein and was adopted despite the opposition of President Nasser. It was agreed that the conference should be organized by Saudi Arabia and Morocco and convened by the latter country.

Accordingly, the Islamic Summit Conference, with King Hasan presiding, was convened and opened at Rabat, Morocco, on September 22, 1969, thus realizing an objective that King Faisal had sought since 1965. Representatives of twenty-five of the thirty-six invited countries were present on opening day. The conference ended on September 25, having adopted a resolution on the status of Jerusalem and the Middle Eastern situation generally.

The resolution called upon all nations, and in particular "the great powers," to "intensify their efforts on the collective plane as well as on the individual plane to ensure the prompt withdrawal of Israeli military forces from all the territories they have occupied as a result of the June 1967 war, on the principle that acquisition of territory by military conquest is inadmissible." In addition, the resolution reaffirmed full support of the Palestinian people and a continuing commitment to peace "within the framework of honor and justice."

On November 10, 1969, the foreign and defense ministers of the Arab League (less Tunisia), meeting in Cairo, determined to recommend to their governments that an Arab summit meeting be held in Rabat during the next month to discuss measures for continuing the Arab struggle against Israel. King Faisal met briefly with President Nasser in Cairo on December 18 en route to Rabat, but no statement was issued. The meeting was held in the Moroccan capital from December 21 to 23, 1969, with Prime Minister Jaafar al Namari of the Sudan presiding. Early in the proceedings, the heads of state of the Republic of Yemen and the People's Republic of Southern Yemen jointly endeavored to introduce the Yemen question into the agenda. In June republican forces had captured the northern Yemeni town of Sadah, and fighting had broken out again in October. The royalist efforts were increasingly indecisive and unsuccessful; Yemen had renewed its charges of Saudi Arabian aid to the royalists, and Southern Yemen claimed that Saudi Arabian patrols had encroached upon its territory.

At the summit meeting King Faisal declined to inject the Yemen question into the discussion and, through the efforts of President Nasser and King Hasan, the conference was steered back to the purposes for which it had been called. Broad proposals were then introduced by the Egyptian delegation involving joint mobilization plans against Israel and increased financial contributions. Agreement could not be attained on these or other proposals, since the principal donor states claimed the plan was not sufficiently specific and did not allow them sufficient voice in the control of their resources. Consequently, the conference broke up on December 23, 1969, in some disarray and without issuance of a communiqué.

As an outgrowth of the Islamic Summit Conference of September 1969, the foreign ministers or representatives from twenty-two Islamic states met in Jiddah from March 23 to 28, 1970. This conference established a permanent Islamic secretariat, to be located in Jiddah and to function there as long as Jerusalem should remain occupied by Israel. Annual meetings of foreign ministers were agreed upon, and Malaysia was designated to provide the first secretary general. This office was then to be rotated every two years.

Later reports indicated that an important development at this conference was the initiation of a new series of talks aimed at solution of the Yemen question. The leader of the Yemeni royalists, after a final and unsuccessful effort to rally support in northern Yemen, had withdrawn in February to take up residence in Saudi Arabia, and the royalist effort had become attenuated and decimated. After further development of the talks begun in March, King Faisal's government extended formal recognition to the Republic of Yemen on July 23, 1970.

Also on July 23, 1970, in the neighboring traditional sultanate of Muscat and Oman at Saudi Arabia's southeastern corner, the ruler, Said bin Timur, was overthrown by his son, Qabus bin Said and took refuge in Saudi Arabia. British-educated Qabus stated on August 9, 1970, that the country would henceforth be known simply as the Sultanate of Oman and would emerge from the isolation imposed by his father. He announced a number of reform and development plans as objective goals and specifically expressed gratitude to King Faisal for the greetings and felicitations that he had received from him.

International press reports in 1969 and 1970 pointed to increased Chinese Communist interest in the Middle East and possible support of Arab socialist-nationalist movements in the Persian Gulf area of Oman and in the sheikhdoms along the gulf. These organizations, such as the so-called Popular Front for the Liberation of the Occupied Arabian Gulf, were also sometimes reported as having received assistance from the radical Baath parties in both Syria and Iraq. They were described by experienced observers as having their bases in Southern Yemen and Oman and posed a potential security problem to Saudi Arabia.

In the Arab-Israeli confrontation, air and ground hostilities along the Suez Canal and the Jordanian front stepped up markedly in the first six months of 1970. The proposals advanced on June 25, 1970, by the United States secretary of state, however, were accepted by Egypt, Jordan, and Israel. A ninety-day ceasefire began on August 7, and negotiations through the medium of a United Nations mission were again attempted. Iraq, Syria, and the Palestine guerrilla movements rejected the cease-fire arrangement.

There followed five acts of air piracy, or hijacking, perpetrated by members of the Popular Front for the Liberation of Palestine against aircraft in international transit. Three of these aircraft were detained in Jordan and destroyed by guerrilla forces, although all passengers were released and evacuated by September 29, 1970. Preceded by a series of violent clashes and brief truces, the longstanding jurisdictional and policy conflict in Jordan between the established government of King Hussein and the guerrillas led by Yasir Arafat erupted during this time into the full-scale civil war of September 16–27, 1970. The guerrilla forces failed to overthrow King Hussein or to hold the capital of Amman. The government of Saudi Arabia maintained its policy of support for the government of Jordan, but Saudi regular troops were not introduced into the conflict.

The fighting was formally ended on September 27, 1970, by the signing of a fourteen-point agreement in Cairo between King Hussein and Yasir Arafat. King Faisal had arrived in Cairo on September 23 and participated in the Arab summit talks arranged by President Nasser in the interests of working out a cease-fire. King Faisal assisted in drafting the agreement and, along with nine other Arab heads of state, witnessed its signature. Its provisions included the undertaking that, if either of the principal signatories violated the agreement, that side would be subject to action by the Arab states witnessing the agreement.

King Faisal returned to Saudi Arabia on the morning of September 28. Later that day, after the departure from Cairo of numerous heads of state and delegations, President Nasser died of a heart attack. Prince Fahd Ibn Abd al Aziz al Saud represented King Faisal and Saudi Arabia at the funeral in Cairo on October 1, 1970. In Mecca the constituent assembly of the Islamic World League met from October 3 to 18. It endorsed the Cairo agreement ending the Jordanian civil war and called for continuation of the Palestinian liberation struggle.

On November 8, however, the heads of state of Egypt, Libya, and the Sudan announced in Cairo their intent to form a federation of these three Arab socialist-nationalist countries. In view of the great agricultural resources of the Sudan and the oil wealth of Libya, some observers concluded that one of several probable motives for this development was an effort on the part of Egypt to reduce its dependency on the Saudi Arabian subsidy. In late 1970 the effects upon Saudi Arabian policy of this federation, as well as the change of regime in Syria that occurred on November 13, were not yet clearly established.

In the Persian Gulf area the deputy rulers of the nine sheikhdoms of the proposed Federation of Arab Amirates met on October 24 at Abu Dhabi to prepare the way for a ruler's meeting intended to establish the federation. The deputies were unable to reach agreement, however, and the rulers' meeting was indefinitely postponed. Saudi Arabia favored the basic idea of a federation but was closely interested in these developments from the standpoint of security threats that might arise should subversive radical groups succeed in infiltrating the sheikdoms in the wake of the British withdrawal in late 1971.

ECONOMIC CHANGE

In late 1970 oil production and the revenues generated from the processing and sale of that production continued to be the prime determinant of the country's economic growth. The government announced in mid-1970 that explorations and studies concluded earlier in the year had furnished evidence that the nation's oil reserves were about 147 billion barrels, approximately 30 percent of the world's proven reserves. This was an increase of about 60 percent from the previous estimate of 92 billion barrels.

During the late 1960s oil revenues regularly accounted for nearly 50 percent of the country's gross domestic product (GDP) and over 50 percent of the GNP (see table A). In 1969 and 1970, however, the increases in oil production were of a relatively modest nature. Between 1965 and 1966, for example, there was an 18-percent increase in oil production, from nearly 805 million barrels to about 950 million barrels, whereas from 1968 to 1969 there was only a 5.3-percent increase, from slightly over 1,114 million barrels to nearly 1,174 million barrels.

The lower rate of increase in oil production in 1969 and 1970 was in large part a result of the closing of the Trans-Arabian pipeline (Tapline), by which a significant portion of the oil exports were routed to West European markets. The Tapline, which runs from the oilfields in Saudi Arabia through Jordan and Syria to the port of Sidon in Lebanon, was damaged in Syria in early 1969 and was out of operation for 110 days. It was closed again in May 1970, but in late 1970 the Syrian government announced that it had discussed the matter with the Tapline officials and that the pumping of oil through the line would be resumed early in 1971.

Table A. Gross National Product of Saudi Arabia by Industrial Origin, for Selected Years [1,2]

Sector	November 5, 1964 to October 25, 1965 — Islamic Year 1384/85	October 15, 1966 to October 4, 1967 — Islamic Year 1386/87	September 24, 1968 to September 12, 1969 — Islamic Year 1388/89
Mining and Quarrying:			
Crude petroleum and natural gas	4,508.8	6,052.2	7,360.6
Other mining and quarrying	25.1	35.4	41.7
Agriculture, forestry, and fishing	874.4	862.4	974.4
Manufacturing:			
Petroleum refining	658.3	736.2	967.1
Other manufacturing	191.3	237.0	299.0
Construction	501.7	707.1	834.2
Electricity, gas, water, and sanitary services	128.2	166.9	195.6
Transport, storage, and communications	739.4	976.4	1,172.1
Wholesale and retail trade	718.0	876.3	1,175.9
Banking, insurance, and real estate	59.1	81.9	102.7
Ownership of dwellings	430.0	494.0	601.0
Public administration and defense	853.3	1,079.5	1,195.1
Services:			
Education	261.2	379.8	426.0
Medical and health	103.3	136.0	140.2
Other services	205.4	257.5	324.6
Gross Domestic Product	10,257.5	13,078.6	15,810.2
Minus net factor income payments to the rest of the world	2,200.0	2,961.0	3,492.0
Gross National Product	8,057.5	10,117.6	12,318.2
Minus Depreciation	805.8	1,011.8	1,231.8
National Income	7,251.7	9,105.8	11,086.4

[1] The Islamic (lunar) calendar is eleven days shorter than the Gregorian calendar. Roughly every three years, one month in the Gregorian calendar must be skipped to adjust to the Islamic calendar.

[2] At current factor cost; value in millions of Saudi riyals; SR4.5 equal US$1.

Source: Adapted from Kingdom of Saudi Arabia, Saudi Arabian Monetary Agency, *Annual Report: 1388–89 A.H.*, Jiddah, 1970, p. 97.

During the late 1960s Aramco continued to account for the bulk of the oil production and, hence, of the oil revenues and royalties. In 1969 Aramco accounted for over 93 percent of the production; Arabian Oil (Japan), for nearly 5 percent; and Getty Oil, for almost 2 percent. During 1969 Aramco completed and placed in operation its first offshore plant in the Persian Gulf. This plant, a gas-oil separator, had an initial daily capacity of approximately 200,000 barrels.

Despite the increase in oil production and revenue in the late 1960s, increased demands on foreign exchange resulted in small deficits in the country's balance of payments in 1968 and 1969 (see table B). The deficits were caused by a combination of three factors: oil revenues were less than anticipated; imports, based on anticipated oil revenues to sustain planned economic and social projects, were increased; and cash subsidies to Egypt and Jordan were continued into their third year. In 1969, for example, the foreign exchange earnings were estimated to be the equivalent of US$2.06 billion; about US$152 million were paid to Egypt and Jordan. This constituted over 7 percent of the gross foreign exchange earnings, about 11 percent of net foreign exchange earnings, and about 12 percent of total government expenditures.

In 1967, when the aid to Egypt and Jordan was instituted, and again in 1968, the aid funds came from savings in the budget and from reserve funds accumulated from budget savings of previous years. By 1969, however, those sources had been exhausted, and in 1969 and 1970 the government was forced to make extensive inroads into its foreign exchange reserves and to curtail some of its domestic economic development projects. As a result, the budget estimate for the fiscal year from September 13, 1969, to August 31, 1970, included either modest decreases or a bare maintenance of earlier levels of expenditure by such ministries as communications, agriculture and water, health, and commerce and industry (see table C).

The diversion of funds from development programs to defense and to other Arab countries and the slowdown in the growth of oil exports were reflected in a general slowdown in commercial activity and economic growth. During the early and middle 1960s the GNP had experienced a yearly increase of about 10 percent, but the increase during the fiscal year that ended on September 12, 1969, was less than 9 percent over the previous year, and the estimated growth for the fiscal year that ended on August 31, 1970, was about 7 percent.

Table B. Estimated Balance of Payments of Saudi Arabia, 1966–69 [1,2]

	1966	1967	1968	1969
Current Account:				
Receipts:				
Exports (free on board)	1,543	1,568	1,784	1,845
Oil royalties from companies other than Arabian American Oil Company	44	50	55	54
Pilgrimage	59	63	72	94
Miscellaneous	46	64	80	68
Total Receipts	1,692	1,745	1,991	2,061
Payments:				
Imports (cost, insurance, and freight)	629	647	796 [3]	839 [3]
Nonmonetary gold	32	23	11	16
Investment income payments	606	602	698	725
Government expenditures abroad [4]	81	138 [5]	270 [5]	278 [5]
Travel and personal transportation [4]	58	70	77	85
Tapline expenditures abroad	22	23	24	23
Other services	143	152	160	154
Total Payments	1,571	1,655	2,036	2,120
Current Account Surplus or Deficit	+121	+90	−45	−59
Capital and Financing Account:				
Direct investment liability	−35	−95	+16	+39
Gold, foreign exchange holdings, and investments of Saudi Arabian Monetary Agency	+113	+60	−56	−121
Commercial banks' net foreign position	−15	+49	−12	+10
Errors and omissions	+58	+76	+7	+13
Total Capital and Financing Account	+121	+90	−45	−59

[1] Gregorian calendar year.

[2] In millions of US$.

[3] Provisional.

[4] Not included elsewhere.

[5] Include US$35 million paid to the Arab countries in 1967; US$140 million, in 1968; and US$14 million, in 1969.

Source: Adapted from Kingdom of Saudi Arabia, Saudi Arabian Monetary Agency, *Annual Report: 1387–88 A.H.*, Jiddah, 1969, p. 30; and Kingdom of Saudi Arabia, Saudi Arabian Monetary Agency, *Annual Report: 1388–89 A.H.*, Jiddah, 1970, p. 33.

Table C. Budget Estimates of Saudi Arabia, October 15, 1966 to August 31, 1970 [1]

	October 15, 1966 to October 4, 1967 Islamic Year 1386/87		October 5, 1967 to September 23, 1968 Islamic Year 1387/88		September 24, 1968 to September 12, 1969 Islamic Year 1388/89		September 13, 1969 to August 31, 1970 Islamic Year 1389/90	
	Percent	Amount[2]	Percent	Amount[2]	Percent	Amount[2]	Percent	Amount[2]
Revenues:								
Oil royalties	23.1	1,161	22.8	1,127	21.2	1,177	22.2	1,326
Income tax	56.2	2,826	49.3	2,433	55.4	3,065	59.0	3,522
Customs duties	3.5	175	3.9	192	4.4	243	4.1	242
Others	17.2	863	24.0	1,185	19.0	1,050	14.7	876[3]
Total	100.0	5,025	100.0	4,937	100.0	5,535	100.0	5,966
Expenditures:								
Private Treasury	3.4	173	3.5	173	2.9	173	2.9	173
Royal Cabinet	0.2	8	0.3	15	0.2	13	0.2	14
Council of Ministers	0.4	19	0.3	17	0.3	19	0.3	18
Ministries:								
Defense and Aviation	23.1	1,163	14.6	723	14.5	841	13.9	831
Foreign Affairs	1.1	56	1.1	52	1.1	65	0.9	56
Labor and Social Affairs	1.7	87	1.7	84	1.6	92	1.5	92
Interior	7.4	370	8.2	406	9.1	528	9.2	546
Education	7.9	399	7.8	383	7.7	483	9.4	558
Communications	2.4	119	2.0	98	1.9	111	1.8	106

Agriculture and Water	1.8	88	1.6	80	1.5	89	1.4	82
Finance and National Economy	1.2	62	1.2	58	1.2	71	1.1	68
Petroleum and Mineral Resources	0.3	17	0.3	16	0.3	19	0.3	19
Health	2.7	154	2.5	122	2.7	156	2.6	155
Commerce and Industry	0.3	15	0.3	13	0.3	16	0.2	14
Hajj and Awqaf	0.8	42	0.9	43	0.8	44	0.7	43
Justice (Judiciaries)	0.7	33	0.6	32	0.6	36	0.6	36
Information	0.8	39	0.7	35	0.8	49	0.8	45
Religious Organizations	1.0	48	1.0	48	0.4	24	0.4	24
Civil defense	0.6	31	0.4	20	0.5	30	0.3	20
Emergency expenses	0.9	46	0.6	31	0.7	40	0.7	41
Projects	34.2	1,717	43.5	2,146	43.9	2,570	45.0	2,682
Other expenditures	6.7	339	6.5	322	6.7	396	5.5	328
Cost increase and subsidies due to devaluation of riyal[3]	0.4	20	0.4	20	0.3	20	0.3	15
Total	100.0	5,025	100.0	4,937	100.0	5,885	100.0	5,966
Minus expected saving						350		
						5,535		

[1] The Islamic (lunar) calendar is eleven days shorter than the Gregorian calendar. Roughly every three years, one month in the Gregorian calendar must be skipped to adjust to the Islamic calendar.

[2] In millions of Saudi riyals; SR4.5 equal US$1.

[3] Included in this figure are SR413 million expected to be received from oil during the fiscal year.

Source: Adapted from Kingdom of Saudi Arabia, Saudi Arabian Monetary Agency, *Annual Report: 1388–89 A.H.*, Jiddah, 1970, pp. 78–79.

In late 1970 it was uncertain what impact, if any, the economic slowdown might have on the country's first economic development plan, which was approved in September 1970. According to the plan, which was developed with the assistance of the Stanford Research Institute of California, approximately one-fourth of the estimated equivalent of US$4 billion of total investment should go to the development of human resources—that is, education, health, and social welfare. Even if this investment target were achieved, however, the number of skilled workers in 1976 would be 1.3 million, whereas the plan projects a labor requirement of 1.5 million.

Although the details of the plan were not available in late 1970, it was known to include projects and programs designed to diversify the economy and to lessen the economy's almost total dependence on oil production. This would entail, among other things, an intensification of the efforts to introduce new agricultural methods in an attempt to achieve self-sufficiency in terms of foodstuffs. In 1970 nearly half of the population of about 4.75 million was engaged in agriculture, including the herding of sheep, goats, and camels. Except for an occasional oasis, however, the scarcity of water has precluded anything more than marginal cultivation. Hydrological surveys suggest that there are extensive underground water resources, and the government's agricultural development plans are geared in large part to the tappings and utilization of these resources.

Although no significant increase in agricultural productivity is possible without the exploitation of underground water resources, the government in 1970 was aware that a massive shift to agriculture based on irrigation would require not only a massive financial investment but also a drastic social change. In particular, the nomadic and seminomadic tribes would not only have to be persuaded to forego their traditional life style but also have to be educated and supervised in the intricacies of irrigation agriculture.

The plan also provides for a continuation and intensification of transportation facilities and of small but vital industrial projects. Between 1964 and 1969 the total number of miles of surfaced roads was almost doubled, increasing from about 2,200 miles to over 4,200 miles. In 1970 an additional 1,500 miles were under construction, and nearly 3,000 miles were scheduled for construction in the immediate future.

In 1970 work either was in progress or was scheduled to begin on expansion and modernization of the ports of Jiddah, Dammam, Yanbu, and Jizan. In addition, the government had launched modernization projects at various fishing ports, such as Jubayl on the Persian Gulf, to assist and encourage the fishing industry.

In 1969 the government announced that there were 283 industrial organizations in the country, the most important of which were firms engaged in electricity generation, food processing, cement making, tile making, and soft-drink production. Oil companies, mineral industries, repair shops, and bakeries were not listed as industrial units. According to the government, approximately 10,000 persons were employed by the industrial firms.

Electricity generation and cement production increased markedly during the late 1960s. Between 1965 and 1969 electricity generation more than doubled, to approximately 600 million kilowatts. Cement production increased from about 30,000 tons in 1958 to about 574,000 tons in 1969. By late 1971 annual cement production should nearly meet the consumer demand, which reached 1 million tons in 1969.

A key element in the country's economic development activities has been the General Petroleum and Mineral Organization (Petromin), which was founded by the government in 1962. In addition to acting as the government's agent in many aspects of granting and supervising oil exploration concessions to foreign-owned companies, Petromin and its affiliates often engage in joint-venture industrial operations with foreign firms. Among the projects initiated by Petromin during the late 1960s were: a steel rolling mill that began operations in 1967 with an annual production of 45,000 tons; an oil refinery that was started in 1968 with a capacity of 12,000 barrels per day; and a fertilizer plant that began operations in late 1969 with a daily production capacity of 1,100 tons of urea, 600 tons of ammonia, and from 35 to 50 tons of liquid sulfur.

The government in November 1969 promulgated new labor legislation and issued new social security insurance. The social security legislation provides that the employee contribute 5 percent of his income toward retirement and that the employer contribute a total of 10 percent of the employee's gross wages for old age and survivors' insurance and for disability benefits. This legislation has had an inflationary impact on an economy that in the past had experienced only moderate inflationary pressures. Using 1963 as the base year of 100, the cost of living index for households with an average income of SR300 per month rose from

101.8 in 1965 to 108 in 1970. The government reported, however, that between 1963 and 1969 wages increased by approximately 31 percent, which raises a question as to the reliability and comparability of the indices.

The 1969 labor legislation is a comprehensive regulation that, among other things, provides for training centers, employment offices, and a special commission to hear and resolve labor disputes. The law includes detailed regulations as to safe working conditions, hours of work, overtime pay, vacation and sick leave provisions, and related matters. In late 1970 there was no information as to the extent the legislation was being observed by the employers and enforced by the government.

The Saudi Arabian Monetary Agency (SAMA) continued in 1970 to function as the government's auditor, fiscal control center, and statistical analyst and to perform many of the functions of a central bank. An important role is the supervision and extension of credit to the commercial banks. In 1969 there were ten commercial banks, with fifty-two banking offices. Although only three of the banks were domestic in 1969, they extended about 69 percent of all private-sector credit and held about 64 percent of the country's deposits. Bank deposits increased at a rate of about 10 percent annually during the late 1960s, a rate that was in harmony with the country's economic growth. In 1969 and 1970, however, the commercial loan interest rate was 9.5 percent, an increase over the previous rate of 7.5 percent. This rate was a function of the overall slowing down of the rate of economic expansion in 1969 and 1970 and was expected to be decreased by the mid-1970s.

In addition to supervision of the operations of commercial banks, SAMA in 1965 established the Agricultural Bank to extend short- and medium-term loans to agriculturalists. By early 1970 the bank had made over 13,000 loans, mostly for the purchase of agricultural equipment and livestock.

In 1970 SAMA announced that an industrial bank, to be known as the Industrial Finance Institution, would begin operations sometime in 1971 and that a "bank for people of small means" would be established the following year. The government also intends to create a housing finance corporation as soon as it is financially able to do so.

BIBLIOGRAPHY

Arabian American Oil Company. *Aramco Handbook: Oil and the Middle East*. Dhahran: Arabian American Oil Company, 1968.

Assah, Ahmed. *Miracle of the Desert Kingdom*. London: Johnson, 1969.

Barody, George M. "Sharia: Law of Islam," *Aramco World Magazine*, XVII, No. 6, November-December 1966, 1-7.

Bethman, Erich W. *Basic Facts on Saudi Arabia*. Washington, D. C.: American Friends of the Middle East, 1967.

Binder, Leonard. *The Ideological Revolution in the Middle East*. New York: John Wiley, 1964.

Borthwick, Bruce M. "The Islamic Sermon as a Channel of Political Communication," *Middle East Journal*, XXI, No. 3, Summer 1967, 299-313.

Connor, Walker. "Ethnic Nationalism as a Political Force," *World Affairs*, CXXXIII, No. 2, September 1970, 91-97.

de Gaury, Gerald. *Faisal: King of Saudi Arabia*. New York: Praeger, 1967.

Dejany, Aouney W. "Saudi Arabia Celebrates National Day Today," *Japan Times*, 23 September 1970, 10, 12.

Duguid, Stephen. "A Bibliographical Approach to the Study of Social Change in the Middle East: Abdullah Tariki as a New Man," *International Journal of Middle East Studies*, I, No. 3, July 1970, 195-220.

Furlonge, Geoffrey. "Illusion and Reality In the Middle East," *Journal of the Royal Central Asian Society* (New Series), I, Part 1, June 1970, 147-156.

"Giant Among the Dwarfs," *The Economist*, Supplement, June 6, 1970, xii-xvi.

Gibb, Hamilton A. R. "The Heritage of Islam in the Modern World," *International Journal of Middle East Studies*, Part 1, I, No. 1, January 1970, 3-17.

———. "The Heritage of Islam in the Modern World," *International Journal of Middle East Studies*, Part 2, I, No. 3, July 1970, 221-237.

"Health Report from the Kingdom to the World Health Organization," *Al-Madinah*, 25 June 1970, 8. [Translated by U.S. Department of Commerce, Office of Technical Services, Joint Publications Research Service (Washington). JPRS: 51,246, 1970.]

Holden, David. *Farewell to Arabia.* New York: Walker, 1966.

Hurewitz, Jacob Coleman. *Middle East Politics—The Military Dimension.* New York: Praeger, 1969.

Hurewitz, Jacob Coleman (ed.). *Diplomacy in the Near and Middle East.* 2 vols. Princeton: Van Nostrand, 1965.

International Yearbook of Education. XXVIII, 1966. Geneva: United Nations Educational, Scientific and Cultural Organization. International Bureau of Education, 1967.

International Yearbook of Education. XXIX, 1967. Geneva: United Nations Educational, Scientific and Cultural Organization. International Bureau of Education, 1968.

International Yearbook of Education. XXX, 1968. Geneva: United Nations Educational, Scientific and Cultural Organization. International Bureau of Education, 1969.

International Yearbook of Education. XXXI, 1969. Geneva: United Nations Educational, Scientific and Cultural Organization. International Bureau of Education, 1970.

Kerr, Malcolm H. *The Arab Cold War: 1958–1967.* (2d ed.) New York: Oxford University Press, 1967.

Khouri, Fred J. *The Arab-Israeli Dilemma.* Syracuse: Syracuse University Press, 1968.

Kingdom of Saudi Arabia. Saudi Arabian Monetary Agency. *Annual Report: 1387–88 A.H.* Jiddah: 1969.

———. *Annual Report: 1388–89 A.H.* Jiddah: 1970.

"Kingdom's Television Network Rates High in Human Changes," *Saudi Arabia Today,* VI, No. 1, January 1968, 1–2.

The Middle East and North Africa: 1970–71. (16th ed.) London: Europa Publications, 1970.

Political Handbook and Atlas of the World, 1970. (Eds., Alba Amoia and Richard P. Stebbins.) New York: Simon and Schuster, 1970.

Rahman, Fazlur. "Islamic Modernism: Its Scope, Method and Alternatives," *International Journal of Middle East Studies,* I, No. 4, October 1970, 317–333.

Reich, Bernard. "Crisis in the Middle East, 1967: Implications for U.S. Policy," Washington: Washington Research Analysis Corporation Report RAC–R–39. February 1968.

Rentz, George. "The Wahhabis." Pages 270–284 in A. J. Arberry (ed.), *Religion in the Middle East,* II. Cambridge: Cambridge University Press, 1969.

"Saudi Arabia: Women Begin to Emerge from Traditional Role," *Labor Developments Abroad*, XV, No. 6, June 1970, 20.

Sheean, Vincent. "Birth of a Bureaucracy," *Aramco World Magazine*, XXI, No. 1, January-February 1970, 2-5.

Statistical Yearbook, 1969. New York: United Nations. Statistical Office of the United Nations. Department of Economic and Social Affairs, 1970.

Thomas, Alfred, Jr. *Saudi Arabia: A Study of the Educational System of the Kingdom of Saudi Arabia and Guide to the Academic Placement of Students from the Kingdom of Saudi Arabia in United States Educational Institutions*. Washington: American Association of Collegiate Registrars and Admissions Officers, 1968.

United States. Agency for International Development. Office of Program and Policy Development. Statistics and Reports Division. *AID Economic Data Book: Near East and South Asia*. Washington: AID, 1970.

United States. American Embassy, Jiddah, Saudi Arabia. *Economic Trends: Saudi Arabia: ET 70-123*. Washington: Department of Commerce, 1970.

World Radio-TV Handbook, 1970. (Ed. J. M. Frost.) Hvidovre, Denmark: H. P. J. Meakin, 1970.

Yamani, H. E. Ahmed Zaki. "Islamic Law and Contemporary Issues." (An address at the American University of Beirut on February 7, 1967—available in English reprint from Embassy of Saudi Arabia, Washington, D. C.)

(Various issues of the following periodicals and newspapers were used in preparation of this section: *Aramco World Magazine* [New York], July-August 1968—September-October 1970; *Christian Science Monitor* [Boston], August 3, 1970-December 18, 1970; *The Economist* [London], August 1970-December 1970; *Economic Intelligence Unit Quarterly Economic Review: The Arabian Peninsula and Jordan* [London], January 1967-September 1970; *International Financial News Survey* [Washington], September-December 1970; *Keesing's Contemporary Archives* [London], Vol. XV, 1965-Vol. XVII, 1970; *Middle East Economic Digest* [London], January 1968-December 1970; *New York Times* [New York], August 1, 1970-December 20, 1970.)

COUNTRY SUMMARY

1. COUNTRY: The Kingdom of Saudi Arabia. Established in 1932 by Abd al Aziz Ibn Saud, who formed a kingdom composed of tribes, villages, and towns of the Najd, the defeated kingdom of the Hijaz, and its various dependencies. Capital: Riyadh (Ar Riyad).

2. POPULATION: In 1970 approximately 4.75 million, with a 2 to 2.3 percent rate of population growth. Population estimates varied, however, from 3.4 million to 7.7 million. *Composition.* Ethnically homogeneous, with a few non-Saudi Arabs living in religious cities of Mecca (Makkah) and Medina (Madinah), the commercial center of the country, Jiddah (Juddah), and the oil-producing region of Eastern Province.

3. GEOGRAPHIC DESCRIPTION: Unified plateau occupying four-fifths of the Arabian peninsula; official government estimate of area about 865,000 square miles. *Topography.* The surface is mainly desert, with lava beds in the west-central portion and sand composing most of the remaining areas. Many relatively level areas broken by the rugged mountain chain paralleling the Red Sea coast and the steep slope of the Tuwayq mountains north and south of Riyadh. No permanent rivers or bodies of water. *Wadis* (seasonal riverbeds and springs) provide water for oasis agriculture. *Climate.* Generally desert climate of extreme heat and little rain. In the interior, summer temperature averages 112°F., with high humidity on the coasts of the Persian Gulf and Red Sea; frosts and freezing weather occur in interior regions in winter. Rainfall is erratic, averaging two to four inches annually. The region of the Asir, along the southern coast of the Red Sea, is subjected to climate influences different from the rest of the country, resulting in dry winters and an average of twelve inches of rain in the summer.

4. LANGUAGES: Arabic is spoken by virtually everyone in the country; English is medium of diplomacy and international trade.

5. RELIGION: Islam is practiced by all but a few and has important influence on all aspects of Arabian life. Within the faith, 90 percent adhere to the Sunni branch; the remaining are of the Shia branch.

6. EDUCATION. Government-sponsored public education is free at all levels, with separate schools for boys and girls. Relatively low enrollment on secondary and university levels, with 90 percent of students on elementary level. Literacy estimated at 15 percent in 1970.

7. HEALTH: Inadequate sewerage facilities, scarcity of pure water, chronic food shortage, and diet deficiencies are major health problems. Incidence of contagious disease has dropped sharply owing to government programs of vaccination and inoculation. Government provides free medical care, but lack of an adequate number of trained personnel limits effectiveness of public health services. Morbidity and disease statistics unavailable.

8. GOVERNMENT: Independent monarchy combining religious and political leadership in role of king, whose authority is based on Islamic law. Legislation is by royal decree or ministerial regulation. The king acts as prime minister, foreign minister, and commander-in-chief of the armed forces and police, with an appointed Council of Ministers that advises him.

9. JUSTICE: System of religious courts consisting of courts of petty affairs, high courts of *sharia* law, and Special Appeals Court. Courts presided over by *qadis* (Islamic judges) headed by the chief *qadi*, who is appointed by the king. No jury system, but judges respected for their expeditious and fair administration of justice.

10. ADMINISTRATIVE DIVISIONS: Five provinces, subdivided into districts and subdistricts; administered by governors general, governors, and headmen, respectively. Provincial councils, presided over by provincial governors general, are responsible for specified educational, agricultural, and municipal projects. Municipal affairs controlled by chief administration officers, together with popularly elected municipal councils.

11. ECONOMY: Based primarily on oil production, which provides 83 percent of government's revenue. Estimated gross national product (GNP) in fiscal year 1968/69 was US$2.7 billion. Industry other than oil is small scale and traditional; agriculture is on a subsistence level.

12. EXPORTS: Exports dominated by petroleum and petroleum products, comprising well over 90 percent of total exports. Remaining exports include fish and fish products, dates, and pearls. Western Europe and the United States major market for exports.

13. IMPORTS: Foodstuffs—including grains, sugar, coffee, and dairy products—account for over 30 percent of total imports. Transportation equipment, machinery, appliances, and building materials total nearly 40 percent of all imports. United States, Western Europe, and Japan are major suppliers.

14. INDUSTRY: Development of petroleum industry encouraged by government to include refining and marketing facilities. Mari-

time and traditional handicraft industries are minimal. Some small, modern industrial developments in progress.

15. LABOR: An estimated one-third of population in the labor force. Pastoralists account for almost 75 percent; wage-earning occupations, about 25 percent, including 5 percent employed by oil industries. The remainder accounted for by those who are self-employed in small businesses or service industries. Largest single employer is the government. Arabian American Oil Company (Aramco) leading industrial employer.

16. FINANCE: Saudi Arabian Monetary Agency (SAMA) functions as governmental agent in financial matters under authority of the Council of Ministers. Prosperous economy between 1965 and 1970 owing to sound fiscal administration. *Currency:* Standard unit is Saudi riyal (SR); 1970 rate of exchange listed at SR4.5 equal US$1, or SR1 equals US$0.22.

17. COMMUNICATIONS: *Radio.* Most important channel for public information. National service broadcasts in both Arabic and English by the government-owned and -operated Broadcasting Service of the Kingdom of Saudi Arabia. In 1965, one receiver per ten persons estimated. *Television.* One government and one noncommercial private station transmitting daily. Estimated 60,000 sets. *Telephone.* Major cities linked by automatic telephone system installed under contract with a Swedish firm.

18. RAILROADS: Saudi Government Railroad, built in 1947-51 period, provides 351 miles of passenger and freight services, connecting Dammam on the Persian Gulf and Riyadh. Some 24.5 million passenger-miles and 32.3 million ton-miles of freight were operated in 1969. In 1970 the government was rebuilding Hijaz line connecting Medina with Amman, Jordan, and Damascus, Syria, to be used principally by religious pilgrims.

19. ROADS: Approximately 4,000 miles of paved roads, plus many unimproved roads and camel routes.

20. AIR TRANSPORT: International airports located at Jiddah and Dhahran (Zahran). Government-owned Saudi Arabian Airlines provides service to twenty-five domestic points and fourteen cities in Europe, the Middle East, and Africa.

21. PORTS: Jiddah on the Red Sea is major port, with Dammam and Ras Tanura providing important port services, primarily for oil industries, on Persian Gulf.

22. INTERNATIONAL AGREEMENTS, MEMBERSHIPS, AND TREATIES: Member of United Nations and its specialized agencies; Organization of Petroleum Exporting Countries; and Arab League. Defense agreements with Jordan and Iran.

23. AID PROGRAMS: International Monetary Fund, International Bank for Reconstruction and Development (World Bank), and agencies of the United Nations have provided financial and advisory assistance. Government loans from United States and France, but major sources of technical assistance are private foreign companies, including German, Italian, French, Swedish, and United States firms.

24. THE ARMED FORCES: In 1970 voluntary military personnel in the army, navy, and air force totaled about 35,000; additional 24,000 lightly armed tribal levies, used primarily to maintain internal security.

SAUDI ARABIA

TABLE OF CONTENTS

	Page
FOREWORD	iii
PREFACE TO THE SECOND EDITION	v
SUMMARY OF EVENTS: JANUARY 1966–DECEMBER 1970	vii
Social Changes—Political Developments— Main Political Events, Late 1965–1970— Economic Change—Bibliography	
COUNTRY SUMMARY	xli
PREFACE TO THE FIRST EDITION	xlix

SECTION I. SOCIAL BACKGROUND

	Page
Chapter 1. General Character of the Society	1
2. Geography and Population	9
Political Boundaries—The Land—Climate—Soils—Population—Settlement Patterns	
3. Historical Setting	25
Pre-Islamic Arabia—Rise of Islam—Arabia in Eclipse—Origin of the House of Saud—Nineteenth-Century Arabia—Creation of Saudi Arabia—Saudi Arabia after Abd al-Aziz Ibn Saud	
4. Ethnic Groups and Languages	47
The Arabs—Minority Ethnic Groups—Languages—Government Policies	
5. Social Structure	59
Nomads and Seminomads—Villages—Towns—Social Status and Mobility	
6. Family	69
Structure—Life Cycle—Daily Round of Activities—Trends	
7. Social Values	79
Determinants of Values—Traditional Values—Modern Elements	
8. Artistic and Intellectual Expression	83
Intellectual Expression—Literature—Music, Dance and Drama—Plastic Arts	
9. Education	91
Development of Education—The Public Education System—Private Education—Students Abroad—Literacy Campaign—Teachers and Teacher Training	
10. Religion	105
Islam—Religious Practices—Religion and Government	

Chapter 11 Health and Welfare 119
         Sanitation and Water Supply—Nutrition and Diet—Incidence and Treatment of Disease—Medical Organization—Standard of Living—Traditional Welfare—The Government's Role in Welfare—Aramco and Public Welfare

SECTION II. POLITICAL BACKGROUND

Chapter 12. Constitution and Government 133
         Legal Bases of Government—The Structure of Central Government—Regional and Local Government

      13. Political Dynamics 151
         Political Developments, 1953–64—The Royal Family—The King—New Groups

      14. Foreign Relations 161
         Mechanics of Policymaking—Relations with Foreign Countries—International Organizations

      15. Public Information 177
         Press — Radio — Television — Cinema — Information Directed Abroad—Foreign Information Directed to Saudi Arabia—Informal Public Information Channels

      16. Public Order and Internal Security 189
         Developments under Abd al-Aziz—Modern Security Forces—Administration of Justice—Internal Security

      17. Attitudes and Reactions of the People 201

SECTION III. ECONOMIC BACKGROUND

Chapter 18. Character and Structure of the Economy 207

      19. Agriculture 213
         Land Use—Land Tenure—Organization of Farm Units—Crop Production—Farming Practices—Animal Husbandry—Forestry—Fisheries—Agricultural Credit—Government Role in Agriculture

      20. Industry 241
         Mineral Resources—Power—Traditional Industries—The Oil Industry—Industrial Development—Government and Industry

      21. Labor 257
         Size and Composition—Special Characteristics and Problems—Conditions of Employment—Labor Relations

      22. Domestic Trade 267
         Trade and Marketing—Pilgrim Trade—Transportation and Communications

      23. Foreign Economic Relations 277
         Foreign Trade—Balance of Payments—The Trading Community—Government Regulation of Foreign Trade—Oil and Foreign Economic Relations—Foreign Assistance—Foreign Investment

      24. Monetary and Financial System 297
         Background—Money Supply—Banking and Credit—Fiscal Administration—Budget

Section IV. NATIONAL SECURITY

    Chapter 25. The Armed Forces 321
            Military Background—Mission and Organization—The Military Establishment and the National Economy—Foreign Influence—Quality and Source of Manpower—Training—Pay and Allowances—Arms and Equipment—Leave—Awards and Decorations—Military Justice

BIBLIOGRAPHIES 337

INDEX 363

LIST OF ILLUSTRATIONS

Figure		Page
1	Saudi Arabia	1
2	Topography of Saudi Arabia	10
3	Distribution of Population in Saudi Arabia	20
4	Selected Tribes of Saudi Arabia	49
5	Organization of the Government of Saudi Arabia, 1965	141
6	Main Agricultural Areas of Saudi Arabia	216
7	Concession Area of Arabian American Oil Company, as of 1965	246
8	Transportation Network of Saudi Arabia, 1965	272

LIST OF TABLES

Table		Page
A	Gross National Product of Saudi Arabia by Industrial Origin, for Selected Years	xxix
B	Estimated Balance of Payments of Saudi Arabia, 1966–69	xxxi
C	Budget Estimates of Saudi Arabia, October 15, 1966 to August 31, 1970	xxxii
1	Growth of Public Education in Saudi Arabia, 1952, 1960 and 1964	95
2	The Moslem Calendar for 1385 A.H. (1965–66)	114
3	Council of Ministers of Saudi Arabia, 1965	142
4	Newspapers and Selected Periodicals of Saudi Arabia, as of Mid-1965	179
5	Major Radio Stations in Saudi Arabia, as of 1965	183
6	Estimated Average Annual Income of Saudi Workers, 1964	263
7	Value of Saudi Arabian Imports and Exports, 1960–61 Through 1963–64	279
8	Selected Imports of Saudi Arabia, 1958–59, 1960–61 and 1962–63	280
9	Direction of Saudi Arabian Export Trade, 1959–60 and 1962–63	281

xlvii

LIST OF TABLES—Continued

Table		Page
10	Direction of Saudi Arabian Import Trade, 1959–60 and 1962–63	283
11	Saudi Arabian Balance of Payments, 1961–63	284
12	Money Supply in Saudi Arabia, 1960–64	306
13	Commercial Bank Operations in Saudi Arabia, 1961–64	307
14	Estimated Expenditures in the General Budgets of Saudi Arabia, 1964 and 1965	312
15	Estimated Development Budgets of Saudi Arabia, 1963–65	313
16	Estimated Revenues in the General Budgets of Saudi Arabia, 1964 and 1965	315
17	Defense Budget of Saudi Arabia, 1961–65	327

PREFACE TO THE FIRST EDITION

The Kingdom of Saudi Arabia is new as a political unit, but the society of Arabia on which it is built is ancient. Only in the present generation has it been open to the influences of the modern world of technology, introduced with the exploitation of the country's huge oil resources.

The people and government of Saudi Arabia remained, as of the end of 1965, strongly committed to the values connected with their ancient Arabic and Islamic culture. The trend of change which usually accompanies the introduction of Western technical culture is slow. Some changes were occurring, but the most important and rapid ones in the past 20 years were economic and technological.

It is the purpose of this *Area Handbook for Saudi Arabia* to delineate the basic political, social and economic elements of contemporary Saudi society in order to give the general reader an understanding of the interplay of the complex factors of continuity and change operating in this society. It has been the intent of the authors to describe the Saudi society as objectively as possible and to avoid as fully as possible the kinds of value judgment which color so much reportage on the country.

Data on Saudi Arabia are sparse and open to question. Even such basic facts as the size and population of the country cannot be ascertained with any degree of precision. In some such cases, the authors have selected a figure which appears to comport best with other available data. In others, they have had to be satisfied with giving an idea of magnitude and to indicate the gap in data. Another source of difficulty lies in the inconsistency in transliteration systems used by various sources, often inconsistencies within a single source. An effort has been made to establish a common, simple transliteration system which will allow the general reader to understand the Arabic word and approximate its pronunciation. Esoteric symbols and diacritical marks have been avoided. When standard spellings appear in *Webster's New International Dictionary of the English Language* (unabridged), these have been used. The spelling of place names follows generally the usage of the United States Geological Survey (1:2 million scale) map of the Arabian peninsula, published in 1963.

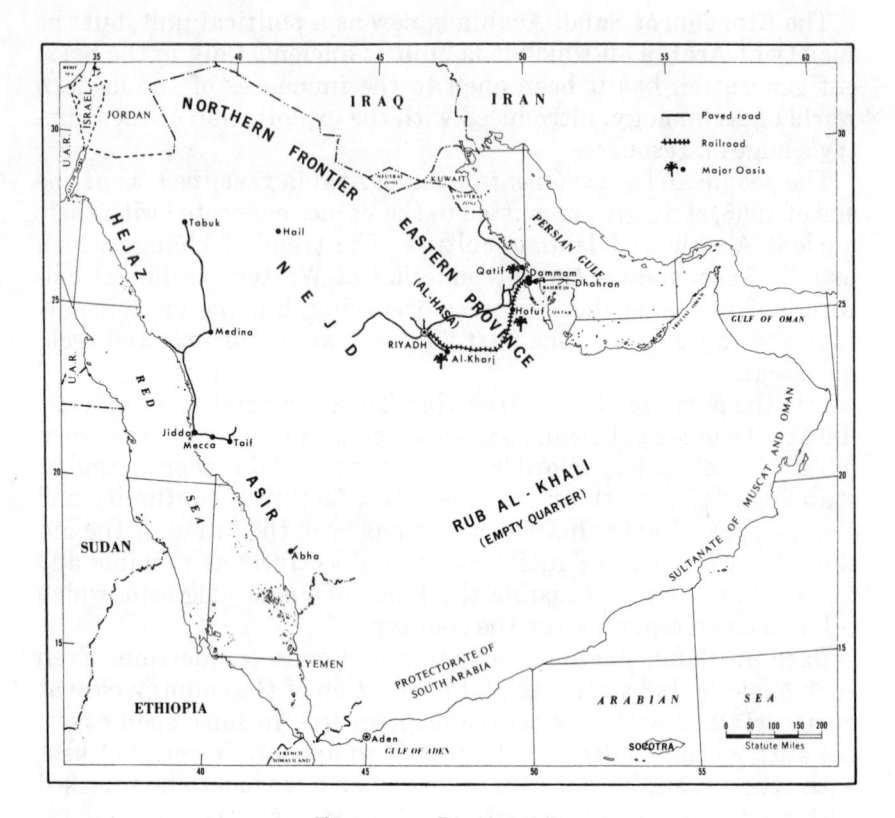

Figure 1. Saudi Arabia.

SECTION I. SOCIAL BACKGROUND

CHAPTER 1

GENERAL CHARACTER OF THE SOCIETY

The kingdom of Saudi Arabia occupies about four-fifths of the Arabian peninsula south of Jordan, Iraq and Kuwait, excluding only the southern coastal fringe. The area of the kingdom—officially estimated at about 870,000 square miles—is not precisely known because few of the borders with the neighboring states of southern Arabia have been fixed (see ch. 2, Geography and Population).

The arid and largely desert peninsula has since ancient times been sparsely peopled by Semitic Arabs, mostly nomadic Bedouin camel herders or seminomadic sheepherders and goatherders. After having taken little part in the dramatic history of the ancient Middle East, which was played mainly in the Fertile Crescent, north of the peninsula, the area suddenly moved onto the center of the world stage in the seventh and eighth centuries A.D. as the homeland of Islam, the religion taught by the Prophet Mohammed (*ca.* A.D. 570–632) and propagated by his conquering armies throughout the Middle East, North Africa and much of southern Asia.

The political center of the rapidly expanding Islamic Empire quickly moved from its birthplace in Mecca, a peninsular city near the Red Sea Coast, to Damascus and Baghdad in the more sophisticated Fertile Crescent. Mecca remained, as it has to the present day, the religious center of Islam, but its political importance rapidly declined, and for most of the 1,300 years from the beginning of Islam to the creation of Saudi Arabia, the peninsula remained isolated from the social and political changes taking place in other parts of the world. The unity it had experienced under Mohammed disintegrated, and its religiomilitary society deteriorated into a congeries of warring tribes and independent towns. Only Mecca and the Red Sea coastal area north of the city—the Hejaz—had any contact with the outside world, Mecca as the goal of Moslem pilgrims from all over the Islamic world and Hejaz as a result of its subjection after the sixteenth century to the Ottoman Empire (see ch. 3, Historical Setting).

The formal establishment of the Kingdom of Saudi Arabia in September 1932 climaxed 30 years of conquest and amalgamation by Abd al-Aziz Ibn Saud, also known as Ibn Saud. The son of an emir (Arab chieftain) who had been forced into exile by a rival tribe, Abd al-Aziz devoted himself from the age of 20 to restoring the earlier political eminence of the Saud family and to uniting the Arabian peninsula under Saudi rule.

Abd al-Aziz based his unification campaign on the puritanic Islamic movement founded in the eighteenth century by Mohammed Ibn Abd al-Wahhab, who had been closely allied with the Saud family, which then controlled the central Arabian oasis region —known as the Nejd. Wahhab had taught strict adherence to the precepts of the Koran (the holy book of Islam). This puritanism and the forceful personality of Abd al-Aziz appealed to the nomadic Bedouin who inhabited the Nejd, and the Saudi leader was quickly able to gain the loyalty of the majority of Bedouin tribes of the Nejd and Al-Hasa (the desert and oasis region along the Persian Gulf now known as Eastern Province).

Abd al-Aziz created a powerful desert army on the basis of a brotherhood—known as the Ikhwan—of fanatical adherents to the Wahhabi puritanism. Thus, he utilized a partnership of religious and military fervor similar to that used by the founders of Islam as the driving force behind his campaign to unify the peninsula. By the mid-1920's, Abd al-Aziz's Ikhwan armies had consolidated Saudi control over all of the Nejd and the great Rub al-Khali desert (the Empty Quarter) south of it, and had conquered the Hejaz, the mountainous farming area of Asir south of the Hejaz, and the Bedouin grazing lands north of the Nejd and bordering on the Fertile Crescent. His northward expansion was halted by British resistance to the Ikhwan campaign against their protected Arab kingdoms of Iraq and Transjordan (present-day Jordan) (see ch. 3, Historical Setting).

The Saudi Arabs, roughly estimated at between $3\frac{1}{2}$ and $5\frac{1}{2}$ million in 1965 and probably closer to the lower figure, share a common ethnic origin—all but a few small minority groups are Arabs—and a common belief in Islam (see ch. 4, Ethnic Groups and Languages). Historically, however, the urban people of the cities of the Hejaz, the settled farmers of Asir, and the nomads and oasis dwellers of the Nejd and Al-Hasa had little consciousness that they shared a common heritage. Until the conquests of Abd al-Aziz, loyalty seldom extended beyond the tribe or· local community, and intertribal warfare was commonplace. Abd al-Aziz succeeded not only in suppressing this warfare and enforcing a respect for law and order within the area, but also in sowing the seeds of a sense of nationhood among the parochial tribes. Although this process was not yet complete in 1965, almost all

Saudi Arabs felt a strong loyalty to the Saud family's regime (see ch. 17, Attitudes and Reactions of the People).

The most important unifying force in Saudi society is Islam. The people are intensely conscious of their Islamic heritage. A large portion of the population makes the pilgrimage to Mecca each year to participate in the religious rituals taught by the Prophet Mohammed. As the state religion, Islam permeates all aspects of the life of all citizens. The king is also imam (leader of the faithful) of Saudi Arabia and protector of the shrines of Islam, that is, particularly the holy cities of Mecca and Medina. Every important government act is justified by its adherence to the *sharia* (Islamic law). The king has repeatedly assured his people that his policies are motivated by a responsibility to preserve and promote Islamic values.

Islam has exercised a more intense and permeating influence over the lives of the inhabitants of Saudi Arabia than anywhere else in the Islamic world because of the association of the area with the birth of the religion and because of its isolation from competitive social influences. Islamic precepts affect all aspects of the lives of its adherents. These include the observance of daily prayers, strict fasting during the Moslem month of Ramadan, abstinence from drink and gambling, making the pilgrimage to Mecca, total reliance on God, and assisting the needy in the name of God. Traditional Bedouin social practices, such as the seclusion of women, the high value on kinship ties and family honor, the severe punishment of theft and adultery, and the relative absence of social differentiation among men, have been sanctioned by Islam and are deeply inculcated in Arab society (see ch. 10, Religion; ch. 7, Social Values).

Because of the isolation of the peninsula from the outside world, the social structure and mode of living of the people changed little over the centuries until the discovery of oil in the peninsula in the 1930's. Economic development impelled by the growth of the oil industry has been extremely rapid, and between 1945 and 1965 most of the population, including the nomads, were introduced to Western technology and material culture. Despite the impact of this exposure on the living conditions of most Arabs, however, social and political change have been slow. The society in 1965 remained heavily imbued with the ancient values, and the development of modern forms of political activity had hardly begun.

Moderation of the strict adherence to traditional Islamic mores has been restricted largely to the still-small groups of urbanized educated young Arabs. Among this group higher values are being placed on greater opportunity for girls to attain status in a society completely dominated by men, ambition to gain material benefits for oneself through work and prudent investment, and reliance on one's own abilities rather than on family connections. They are looking for a loosening of the most severe restrictions imposed by a strict adherence to Islamic precepts, and some have expressed a desire for a greater voice in the political life of the country (see ch. 7, Social Values; ch. 13, Political Dynamics).

The Arabian American Oil Company (Aramco) has been the chief agent through which Western culture has been introduced into Saudi Arabia. Aramco, a consortium formed in 1944 by four major United States oil companies, was created to exploit the great potential of the large area of eastern Arabia granted in 1933 on a concession basis to one of its founding members by King Abd al-Aziz. After 1944, oil production expanded at a dizzying rate as it was realized that Saudi Arabia contained one of the world's largest oil reserves. By 1965 production reached an average of over 2 million barrels a day (see ch. 20, Industry).

Aramco built and fostered the expansion of several cities in the oil fields of Eastern Province and around the oil refinery and terminal near Dammam on the Persian Gulf. The company built for the Saudi Government a railroad connecting Dammam with the capital at Riyadh. It also introduced television into Saudi Arabia through the network it operates for its employees; its programs are viewed by many thousands of Saudi Arabs throughout Eastern Province.

In addition to pumping huge quantities of money into the Arabian economy through its payment of royalties and taxes to the Saudi Government, Aramco has become by far the largest private employer in the country, employing a total of almost 13,000 in 1964, of whom over 10,000 were Saudi Arabs. Through its high wages, training and general education programs and such worker benefit programs as homeownership plans, pensions and advanced health facilities, the company has attracted a stable and skilled labor force which is having an influence on work habits and conditions of employment throughout the Saudi economy. It began an extensive program for its Saudi employees and gradually promoted increasing numbers of them into technical, supervisory and managerial positions (see ch. 21, Labor).

The company has carefully eschewed political activity or any actions which would give the appearance of exerting influence with the government. Its relations with the government have been generally good, inasmuch as it believes that a strong, stable government is essential to the long-term interests of Aramco.

The unprecedented wealth that came from oil revenues after World War II created a serious problem for an unprepared government. The basically agricultural economy was incapable of absorbing the huge injection of capital, and the government—that is, essentially the royal family—had not yet developed a formal system of financial controls. A financial crisis in the late 1950's, resulting from a slowdown in the rate of expansion of oil exports, forced the government to reconsider its fiscal policies. A modern fiscal system, including for the first time the strict adherence to government budgets and financial controls, was established, and the groundwork was laid for the creation of a modern national economy (see ch. 24, Monetary and Financial System).

Since 1962 the government has supported large-scale efforts to broaden the economic base to end the country's almost total dependence on oil and on foreign technical and managerial personnel. It has begun to create a modern economic infrastructure through the promotion of private banks, road and air networks, technical training programs and agricultural projects. This program was still, as of the end of 1965, in the early stages, but economic activity was increasing rapidly and newly trained Saudi technical and managerial personnel were steadily moving into positions formerly held by foreign specialists (see ch. 18, Character and Structure of the Economy).

Despite the rapid growth of cities after World War II, particularly the oil centers of Eastern Province and the capital, Riyadh, in the Nejd, the population is still overwhelmingly rural. About half are still nomadic or seminomadic herders; almost all are seminomadic sheepherders and goatherders who spend much of the year in camps outside the cities or oasis settlements. As of 1965 there were estimated to be only about 200,000 to 300,000 true nomads, the Bedouin camel herders, left in the country. About one-quarter of the population is settled as farmers in the Asir highlands, the only area in the country which receives enough rainfall—about 12 inches per year—to support regular cultivation, or in the oases where dates and some grain are grown on land irrigated from wells (see ch. 19, Agriculture).

Because of the strength of Islam's hold on Arab culture, even the introduction of Western ideas and exposure to Western values have had little effect on the traditional Arab social structure, family life and value system. Although Abd al-Aziz suppressed tribal warfare and established the authority of the Saudi dynasty over the tribes, he did not destroy the traditional tribal structure based on kinship ties. The Saud family—numbering several hundred closely related members and a wide circle of more distant relatives—assumed the role of the dominant tribe. The leader of this Saudi family, the king, is considered sheikh of sheikhs and relates to the majority of the population through their tribal leaders. The tribal structure has been weakened with the gradual settlement of nomads and seminomads into villages and with the growth of towns and cities, which are organized around local territorial units more than around kinship, but kinship is still important in determining an individual's place in society (see ch. 5, Social Structure).

The long-established principle in Arab social structure that the leader seeks the consensus of his followers in making decisions affecting the group and can be replaced if he loses that consensus, still operates throughout Saudi Arab society. Just as the tribal sheikhs hold court (*majlis*) to hear the opinions of senior members of their tribes, the king receives the most important tribal sheikhs and other important local government officials in frequently held *majlis*. The responsibility of the king to the royal family was exemplified on three occasions since the death in 1953 of King Abd al-Aziz—in March 1958 and in March and November 1964—when family councils decided to increase Crown Prince Faisal's role in government at the expense of his brother, King Saud Ibn Abd al-Aziz who had succeeded his father in 1953 (see ch. 13, Political Dynamics).

It is through the royal family, and particularly through the king, that the effort is being made to reconcile the imported Western ideas and the ancient Arab and Islamic culture. King Faisal Ibn Abd al-Aziz al-Faisal al-Saud, a son of the founder of the kingdom and younger brother of former King Saud, has played an important part in the government of the kingdom since its foundation and has been king since November 1964. He is a devout Moslem (believer in Islam) and identifies closely with the Bedouin culture. He is also, however, aware of the needs of a modern society and convinced of the desirability of introducing modern ways into Saudi Arabia.

King Faisal has attempted to modify the more restrictive and ultraconservative attitudes of the *ulema* (body of leading Islamic scholars in the country who are responsible for interpreting the *sharia*) in order to permit the modernization of the society (see ch. 7, Social Values; ch. 10, Religion). He has been instrumental in developing the formal governmental structure of his country, in forming its relations with the rest of the world, and in fostering the development of a modern education system, a modern transportation network, modern channels of public information, and the beginnings of a modern industrial economy. He has sought to settle the Bedouin, to improve the agricultural potential of the country, to emancipate women from their traditional seclusion, to promote the physical well-being of his people, and to permit them greater individual freedom, while at the same time preserving the essential values of Islam and promoting the cause of the religion in Arabia and throughout the world.

The unification of the country under Abd al-Aziz and, particularly, the incorporation into the Saudi empire of the politically more advanced Hejaz cities made the establishment of a formalized central governmental structure imperative. Until after World War II, however, administration of the country remained highly decentralized and little developed. The government of the Hejaz was administered as a viceroyalty under then Crown Prince Faisal. With a council of ministers, a representative consultative assembly and local governments in the various cities, its political structure was more advanced than the rest of the country. Al-Hasa (now Eastern Province) was administered as a semiautonomous emirate governed by the Ibn Jiluwi family, closely related to the Sauds. Direct government from Riyadh, the capital of Saudi Arabia, was restricted to the Nejd and its dependent areas to the north and south, which were governed along traditional Islamic lines. Not until 1953 were the first steps taken to create a national Council of Ministers. Since then, the central government has been steadily strengthened and its administrative control extended to the entire country. As of 1965, however, the process of developing the full panoply of modern governmental institutions, particularly at the local level, was not yet complete (see ch. 12, Constitution and Government).

Political activity on the national level is conducted only by the royal Saud family and a small group of the leading tribal sheikhs and leading members of other important families close to the royal family. Labor unions are prohibited, and public gatherings for other than religious, cultural or sports purposes are officially discouraged (see ch. 13, Political Dynamics).

The government operates the domestic radio networks and in 1965 was establishing a government-owned television network. Newspapers and periodicals are privately owned but are closely scrutinized by the Ministry of Information, which also must approve the membership of the press institutes responsible for each publication. Aramco has been extremely careful to avoid any political expression in its television programing or anything which might offend the government (see ch. 15, Public Information).

There were no signs at the end of 1965 that the extreme unevenness in the effect of foreign influences which the country was experiencing was causing any instability. The strong hold of Islamic values on the population at large and the evident interest of the Saudi regime to improve the living conditions of its people minimized the pressures for political change such as have occurred in other developing countries of the Middle East. Self-conscious economic classes had not yet developed, and those individuals imbued with Western values as a result of having been educated in the United States or Europe were generally being absorbed into the growing governmental, economic and professional institutions (see ch. 16, Public Order and Internal Security).

Saudi leaders are conscious of the need for Saudi Arabia to participate in world affairs. The government has joined the United Nations and the Arab League and has established diplomatic relations with about 40 states, excluding on principle only Israel and the Communist states because of their antipathy to Islam.

Despite its growing economic strength and its central role in Islam, Saudi Arabia has hesitated to play an active part in the international affairs of the Middle East. Its primary concerns have been to oppose what it considers the illegally constituted state of Israel and to prevent the creation of any coalitions which might threaten its position in the peninsula. In keeping with these policies, it gave modest support to the Arab League in the Palestine War of 1948 and to the government of President Gamal Abdul Nasser through the period of the Suez crisis in 1956. After the creation of the socialist and antimonarchic United Arab Republic, however, relations with Egypt began to deteriorate. The Saudi Government saw a threat to itself in the military support given by the United Arab Republic to the republican government which overthrew the Yemeni monarchy in September 1962. It therefore supplied military support to the royalist forces in the long, indecisive civil war which followed the coup d'etat.

King Faisal gained considerable international prestige in August 1965 when President Nasser, who only a month earlier had threatened to extend the war, traveled to Jidda to reach a cease-fire agreement and prepare for the end of the Yemen civil war and the withdrawal of Egyptian troops. Shortly thereafter, King Faisal, who considers Saudi Arabia's international role to be the promotion of the interests of the Islamic world, began to favor a vaguely-defined solidarity movement between the Islamic states which would group not only the Arab League countries, but such non-Arab states as Iran, Afghanistan, Pakistan and Turkey (see ch. 14, Foreign Relations).

CHAPTER 2

GEOGRAPHY AND POPULATION

The kingdom occupies about four-fifths of the Arabian peninsula. Few of its land boundaries have been determined, and only the short length of the boundary with Yemen from the Red Sea to Najran has been marked on the ground. As a result, the exact size of the country is unknown; estimates vary from about 618,000 to 927,000 square miles, depending on how much of the disputed areas—particularly those of the southern flanks of the country—are included. The official government estimate of the area is about 870,000 square miles (see fig. 1).

In the absence of a census, estimates of the population vary even more widely—between 3 million and 15 million. Saudi Government statisticians placed the figure at about 3.3 million in 1962, but as of the end of 1965 the government continued to use estimates between 6 and 15 million. Less than 1 percent of the total area is suitable for settled agriculture, and population distribution varies greatly among the towns of the eastern and western coastal areas, the densely populated interior oases and the vast, almost empty deserts. The problem of making an accurate population count is complicated by the fact that half of the population lives a nomadic or seminomadic existence and that privacy in matters relating to the family is highly valued among Moslems.

The Arabian peninsula is a unified plateau tipped slightly toward the east, with a major fault line along the Red Sea coast. In the extreme west a line of rugged mountains parallels the Red Sea coast and forms the watershed for the peninsula. East of this range the land is relatively even; the gradual drop toward the Persian Gulf is broken only by the escarpment of the low Tuwaiq mountains, which extend along a west-facing crescent north and south of Riyadh (see fig. 2).

Most of the surface is sand-covered forming the great deserts of the Nafud, the Dahna and the Rub al-Khali (Empty Quarter). Outside these deserts the surface is gravel or, in limited areas in the west-central portion, consists of jumbled beds of lava. The climate of most of the peninsula is debilitatingly hot and dry. In Saudi Arabia only the Asir highlands along the Red Sea receive enough rain to permit a degree of nonirrigated cultivation (see ch. 19, Agriculture).

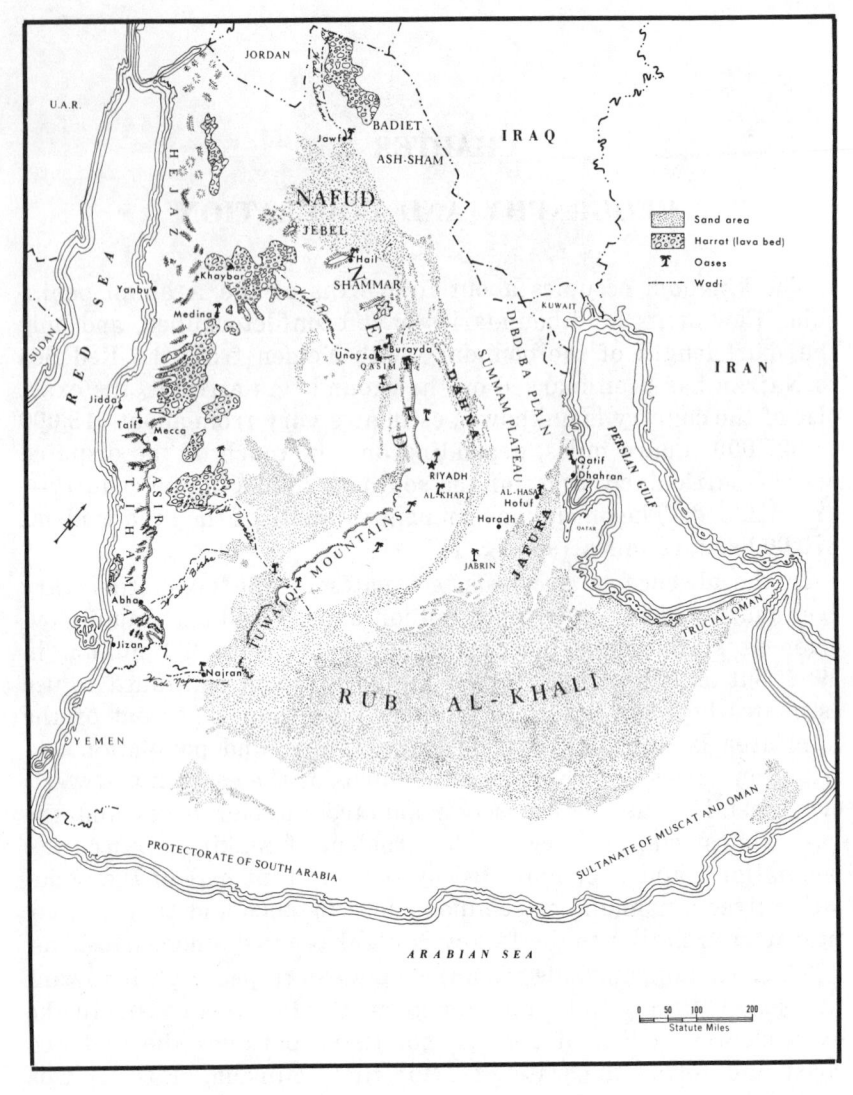

Figure 2. Topography of Saudi Arabia.

POLITICAL BOUNDARIES

Less than half of the country's long borders follow natural features. On the west the Red Sea forms the entire border. The northern half of the eastern border lies along the Persian Gulf. Since 1958, Saudi Arabia has claimed a 12-mile limit in the Red Sea and Persian Gulf. Saudi Arabia has exploited offshore oilfields in an area between Dammam and the Saudi-Kuwait Neutral Zone stretching halfway across the Persian Gulf, about 70 miles offshore. The boundary with Bahrein has been surveyed through the channel separating it from Saudi Arabia. The border with northern Yemen, which follows a mountain ridge for about 200 miles inland from the Red Sea to the region of Najran, has been demarcated since 1934.

As Saudi control spread outward from the center of the peninsula, growth of the kingdom was limited in the north by international treaty and along its southern boundaries by self-imposed limitation. The northern boundaries were established in the 1920's by a series of treaties negotiated between Abd al-Aziz Ibn Saud and British officials representing the interests of Jordan, Iraq and Kuwait (see ch. 3, Historical Setting). These artificial boundaries have never been marked on the ground, and the precise demarcation of the desert frontier remains uncertain. The treaties created two diamond-shaped neutral zones, one on the Iraq border and the other on the border with Kuwait, as a means of avoiding border conflicts. The neutral zone with Kuwait was partitioned in 1964 for the purpose of dividing the oil wealth in the area. The western half of the border with Jordan was agreed to only in mid-1965.

The entire southern frontier region is desert, largely unexplored and uninhabited, and only the borders with northern Yemen and with Qatar—established in 1965—have been determined. In his conquest of the peninsula, Ibn Saud was motivated by the need to crush his enemies rather than by the desire to gain territory for its own sake. Therefore, there was no motivation for expansion into Qatar, Oman, Muscat, the Hadhramaut or Aden, with whose leaders he had no quarrel. On the contrary, Ibn Saud was anxious to avoid arousing the enmity of these neighbors, who were under the protection of Great Britain, during a period in which he was occupied with consolidating his control at home. Ibn Saud specifically declined to annex Yeman after his victory in the Yemeni war of 1934. Since the discovery of oil, however, several of the boundaries have become the subject of dispute. The most serious dispute has concerned the Buraimi Oasis claimed by Saudi Arabia, the Sheikh of Abu Dhabi and the Sheikh of Oman (see ch. 14, Foreign Relations).

THE LAND

The geological structure of the Arabian peninsula was determined by the ancient eastward tilting of the area associated with the creation of the fault known as the Great Rift, which extends from the Mediterranean along both sides of the Red Sea and southward through Ethiopia and the lake country of East Africa, gradually disappearing in the area of Mozambique, Zambia and Rhodesia. On the peninsula the eastern line of the Great Rift fault is visible in the steep and, in places, very high escarpment which parallels the Red Sea between Aqaba and Aden. The eastern slope of this escarpment is relatively gentle, dropping to the exposed shield or extremely ancient landmass laid down before the faulting occurred. A second, lower escarpment, the Tuwaiq mountains, runs roughly north-south through the area of Riyadh. East of this escarpment the shield is covered by layers of sediment increasing in thickness toward the Persian Gulf. Oil is found in the lower strata of these sedimentary layers.

The northern half of the region of the Red Sea escarpment is known as Hejaz, and the more rugged southern half as Asir. In the south a coastal plain, the Tihama, rises gradually from the sea to the mountains. Asir extends southward into the borders of mountainous Yemen. The central plateau, the Nejd, extends eastward to the Tuwaiq escarpment and a short distance beyond. A long, narrow strip of sand desert known as the Dahna separates the Nejd from eastern Arabia, which slopes gradually eastward to the low-lying sandy coast along the Persian Gulf. North of the Nejd a larger sand desert, the Nafud, isolates the heart of the peninsula from the steppes of northern Arabia. South of the Nejd lies the largest sand desert in the world, the Rub al-Khali.

Hejaz and Asir

The western coastal escarpment can be considered as two mountain ranges separated by a gap in the vicinity of Mecca. The northern range in Hejaz seldom exceeds 7,000 feet, and the elevation gradually decreases toward the south to about 2,000 feet around Mecca. The mountain wall is rugged, dropping abruptly to the sea and having few and intermittent coastal plains. The western slopes have been stripped of soil by the erosion of infrequent but turbulent rainfalls. The eastern slopes are less steep and are marked by *wadis* (beds of seasonal rivers) which mark the course of ancient rivers and still lead the rare rains down into the plains. Scattered oases, drawing water from springs and wells in the vicinity of these *wadis*, permit some settled agriculture. Of these the largest and most important is Medina.

South of Mecca, the mountains are higher, exceeding 8,000 feet in a number of places; some peaks reach nearly 10,000 feet. The rugged western face of the escarpment drops to a rather step coastal plain, the Tihama, which averages only about 40 miles in width. Along the Red Sea the Tihama is a salty tidal plain of limited agricultural value, backed by potentially rich alluvial plains. The relatively well-watered and fertile upper slopes of these plains are the most productive region of Saudi Arabia. These slopes and the mountains behind them are extensively terraced to make possible the maximum use of the land. An average of about 12 inches of rainfall per year permits the cultivation of grain, coffee, *qat* (a mildly narcotic plant), fruits and vegetables (see ch. 19, Agriculture). The top of the mountain ridge is covered in places with narrow strips of the only natural forest in the country, mainly of juniper. Luxuriant undergrowth gives these strips—many only a few dozen feet wide—the character of a tropical rain forest.

There is an almost total absence of natural harbors along the Red Sea coast. Only Jidda, with its newly built quays permitting dockside cargo handling, offers possibility for large-scale handling of sea traffic. Minor ports exists at Yanbu and Jizan, but freight must be transferred by lighter from ship to shore (see ch. 22, Domestic Trade).

The eastern slope of the mountain range in Asir is gentle, melding into a plateau region which drops gradually into the Rub al-Khali. Although rainfall is infrequent in this area, a number of fertile *wadis*, of which the most important are the Bisha and the Dawasir, make possible oasis agriculture on a relatively large scale. A number of extensive lava beds (*harrat*) scar the surface of the plateaus east of the mountain ranges in Hejaz and Asir and give evidence of fairly recent volcanic activity. The largest of these is Khaybar, north of Medina.

Nejd

East of Hejaz and Asir lies the great plateau area of the Nejd, the birthplace of the country (see ch. 3, Historical Setting). This region is mainly rocky plateau interspersed by small sandy deserts and isolated mountain clumps. The best known of the mountain groups is the Jebel Shammar, northwest of Riyadh and just south of the Nafud desert. This is the home of the pastoral Shammar tribes which, under the leadership of Mohammed Ibn Rashid, were the most implacable foes of the Sauds in the nineteenth and early twentieth centuries. The capital of the Shammar district is the large oasis of Hail.

In conformity with the peninsula as a whole, the plateau slopes toward the east from an elevation of about 4,500 feet in the west to about 2,500 feet in the east. A number of *wadis* cross the region generally in an eastward direction leading from the Red Sea escarpment toward the Persian Gulf. There is little pattern to these remains of ancient riverbeds; the most important of them are the Rumma, the Surra and the Dawasir. Generally, rainfall in the region averages less than 4 inches per year, and several years may elapse between rains. When rain does occur, it may be torrential and cause the *wadis* to flood, in some cases doing serious damage to settlements and making travel impossible until the water disappears into the gravel and sand base.

The heart of the Nejd is the area of the Tuwaiq escarpment, an arc-shaped ridge whose steep west face rises between 400 and 800 feet above the plateau. Many oases exist in this area, which is one of the most densely populated in the country. The most important of these are Burayda, Unayza, Riyadh, Al-Kharj and Aflaj. An extensive agricultural project in Al-Kharj district covers about 3,000 acres of irrigated land in several oases. Irrigation from wells and pools in the oases permits intensive grain and vegetable agriculture (see ch. 19, Agriculture).

Outside this oasis area, the Nejd is sparsely populated. Desert grasses and scrub which grow briefly after the winter rains form the basis of animal husbandry by nomadic and seminomadic pastoralists. Camel-herding Bedouin nomads range widely from the eastern slopes of the Red Sea escarpment to the northern borders of Saudi Arabia and beyond. Seminomadic sheepherders and goatherders spend the dry part of the year generally in the vicinity of the oases or in the uplands, moving out into the plateau in search of grass only in the late winter and spring.

The Great Deserts

Three great deserts isolate the Nejd from north, east and south as the Red Sea escarpment does from the west. In the north the Nafud—sometimes called the Great Nafud since Nafud simply means desert—covers about 25,000 square miles of sand dunes at an elevation of about 3,000 feet. Longitudinal dunes, scores of miles in length, as much as 300 feet high and separated by valleys as much as 10 miles wide, characterize the Nafud. Iron oxide gives the sand a reddish tint, particularly when the sun is low. Within the area are several watering places, and winter rains bring up short-lived but succulent grasses which permit nomadic herding during the winter and spring.

Stretching for more than 400 miles south from the Nafud in a narrow arc only about 30 miles wide is the Dahna. Like the Nafud, its sand tends to be reddish in color, particularly in the north, where it also shares with the Nafud the longitudinal structure of sand dunes. It also furnishes the Bedouin with winter and spring pasture, although water is scarcer than in the Nafud.

The southern portion of the Dahna curves westward following the arc of the Tuwaiq escarpment. At its southern end it links with the Rub al-Khali, one of the most forbidding and until the 1950's one of the least explored sand deserts in the world. The topography of this huge area, covering over 250,000 square miles, is varied. In the west the elevation is about 2,000 feet, and the sand is fine and soft; in the east the elevation drops to about 600 feet, and much of the surface is covered by relatively stable sand sheets and salt flats. In places, particularly in the east, longitudinal sand dunes prevail; elsewhere, sand mountains as much as 1,000 feet in height form complex patterns. Most of the area is totally waterless and uninhabited except for a few wandering Bedouin tribes (see ch. 4, Ethnic Groups and Languages).

Eastern Arabia

East of the Dahna lies the rocky Summam plateau, about 75 miles wide and dropping elevation from about 1,300 feet in the west to about 800 feet in the east. The area is generally barren and has a highly eroded surface of ancient river gorges and isolated buttes.

Farther east the terrain changes abruptly to the flat lowlands of the Persian Gulf coastal plain. This area, about 100 miles in width, is generally featureless and covered with gravel or sand; in the north is the gravelly Dibdiba plain and in the south the Jafura sand desert, which reaches the gulf in the vicinity of Abqaiq and Dhahran and merges with the Rub al-Khali at its southern end. The coast itself is extremely irregular as sandy plains, marshes and salt flats merge almost imperceptibly with the sea. As a result, the land surface is unstable, with water rising in places almost to the surface, while the sea is shallow and full of shoals and reefs for an extended distance offshore. Only the construction of long moles at Ras Tanura has opened the Saudi Gulf coast to seagoing tankers.

Eastern Arabia is sometimes still called Al-Hasa after the great oasis of that name, one of the most agricultural areas of the country. Al-Hasa, the largest oasis in the country, actually comprises two neighboring oases near the town of Hofuf. They total about 60 square miles in area with over 2 million date palms and about 30,000 acres irrigated and under cultivation. The oases reportedly support a population of about 160,000. Al-Hasa is famous for its hot and cold springs and artesian wells, and for the quality of its dates (see ch. 19, Agriculture).

Northern Arabia

The area north of the Nafud desert is geographically a part of the Syrian desert. It is an upland plateau with a surface of dark-colored rock and gravel and scored by numerous *wadis,* most trending northeastward toward Iraq. This area, known as Badiet ash-Sham, is covered with grass and scrub steppe vegetation, and is extensively used for pasture by nomadic and seminomadic herders. The most significant feature of the area is the Wadi

Sirhan, a large basin as much as 1,000 feet below the surrounding plateau, which is the remnant of an ancient inland sea. For thousands of years some of the most heavily traveled caravan routes between the Mediterranean and the central and southern peninsula have passed through the Wadi Sirhan. The most important oases in the area are Jawf and Sakaka, just north of the Nafud.

CLIMATE

Except in Asir, the country has a desert climate, characterized by extreme heat and paucity of rain. Summer maximum temperatures in the Nejd and the great deserts average about 112°F., and temperatures in excess of 120°F. are not uncommon. In much of eastern Arabia mean maximum summer temperatures are only slightly lower. The air cools rapidly after the sun sets; even in the summer, nights are cool. Winter temperatures drop below freezing in central and northern Arabia, and frosts are fairly common. Snow and ice have been recorded, particularly at the higher elevations in Hejaz and Asir.

The low relative humidity in the interior mitigates somewhat the effects of the high temperature, but along both the Persian Gulf and Red Sea coasts excessively high humidity, often reaching 100 percent for extended periods, adds significantly to the discomfort. Fogs are common, and summer nights are hot and airless.

Generally, the prevailing winds are from the nothern quadrant, although strong southerly winds sometimes come up with great suddenness, presaging rain and, in the Persian Gulf, severe storms known as *kauf*. A strong northwesterly wind, the *shamal*, typically blows for most of the summer months, particularly in eastern Arabia, and frequently whips up violent sandstorms.

Rainfall is infrequent and erratic, averaging 4 inches or less per year everywhere except Asir. It frequently occurs in one or two sudden torrential cloudbursts which flood the *wadis* and then rapidly disappear into the soil. The average also varies widely from year to year; several years may pass in some areas between rains, and at times the total annual rainfall more than doubles the average. Except in Asir, the rainy season—also subject to wide variation—is usually between October and March. In Asir the southwest Indian Ocean monsoon prevails during the summer, and during the winter the area is subject to the northerly winds common throughout the peninsula. Within this general pattern there is great variability in local winds.

The climate of Asir is subject to different influences from the rest of the country. The Tihama and the western slopes of the Asir mountains feel the effect of the Indian Ocean monsoons. During the summer months the southwest monsoon drops an average of about 12 inches of rain on the area, whereas the winter months are dry.

The country has no permanent rivers or bodies of water. The *wadis* contain water only after the rare rains, and then for only a short period, but water which seeps through the porous surface is trapped above impervious rock layers underground. It is known that huge reservoirs of good water underlie much of the peninsula. Particularly in eastern Arabia and in the oasis of the Tuwaiq escarpment region, artesian wells and springs are common. In Al-Kharj and Al-Hasa are a number of large, deep pools which are constantly replenished by artesian springs. These springs and wells permit extensive irrigation in the oases of these areas. In the Nejd and the great deserts watering places are more widely scattered, and water must be hoisted or pumped to the surface. In Hejaz and Asir springs and wells are abundant in the mountainous areas.

The Saudi Government and the Arabian American Oil Company (Aramco) have made separate and joint efforts to exploit the underground water resources. One of the most spectacular projects was that which produced the water for the successful agricultural experimental station near Haradh, southeast of Riyadh (see ch. 19, Agriculture). Aramco has also built a number of pumping stations and reservoirs along its Trans-Arabian Pipeline (Tapline), which the government has used in its efforts to encourage the Bedouin to settle. In recent years, however, the government has expressed concern over the possibility that the underground reservoir may be overused and in 1965 was undertaking a number of water conservation studies.

SOILS

Much of the soil is fertile when irrigated. Improper irrigation has, however, exacerbated the problem of salination, which presents a grave threat to land use, particularly in eastern Arabia. It results primarily from leaching of the soil and from the deposit of salts, lime and potassium on the surface by the percolative effect produced by extreme surface heat. Saline soils, known as desert marls, permit limited agricultural production with salt-resistant crops, such as date palms, when the surface is not crusted in surface saltpans. These marls are most prominent in Hejaz and in eastern Arabia. In extreme cases no vegetation can grow on the crusty saltpans or limestone pans.

Sand-covered areas are suitable for agriculture if sufficiently watered. One of the most serious limiting factors in their use is the susceptibility of dunes to shifting according to the wind. This mobility, often reaching 40 feet a year, has made the dunes a grave threat to oases, particularly to those in Al-Hasa. The government has undertaken countermeasures, such as planting over 6,000,000 tamarisk and eucalyptus trees against the dunes, erecting sand fences and spraying the windward side of the dunes with asphalt to stabilize them.

A heavy sand-gravel soil is found mainly in Nejd, but also in Al-Hasa. Not suitable for cultivation, it produces a luxuriant, but ephemeral vegetation following desert rains which is excellent for grazing.

Loam soils, which have good agricultural potential when properly irrigated, are found predominantly in the Nejd highlands. These soils are clayey and basically not cultivable, but when mixed with sand, they are highly productive.

The best soils are the alluvial soils of the *wadi* banks. Rich and fertile sandy-loam soils, they are intensively cultivated, mainly for cereals.

POPULATION

In 1965, as a national census had never been taken, demographic information was scanty and questionable. Population estimates ranged from 3 million to 15 million. The Saudi Government has used various estimates between 6 million and 15 million. Authoritative foreign sources, including the International Bank for Reconstruction and Development (IBRD), accept 5 million to 5½ million as a reasonable estimate.

In 1962–63 the Department of General Statistics of the Ministry of Finance and National Economy undertook a comprehensive survey of the population of five cities: Jidda, Mecca, Medina, Taif and Riyadh. As a result of this survey and later investigations, government statisticians estimated the population at about 3.3 million, but the government had not accepted this figure as of late 1965.

STRUCTURE

More than half of the population is under 20 years old. The birth rate is believed to be well above the world average, but it is largely counterbalanced by a high death rate, thought to be among the highest in the Middle East. Infant mortality in Asir and among the nomads has been estimated at between 60 to 70 percent, and a high death rate of women in childbirth is reported. It is believed that the ratio of women to men drops sharply after age 17. Population growth rates though undeterminable, may well exceed 2 percent per year.

The population is relatively homogeneous ethnically (see ch. 4, Ethnic Groups and Languages). Non-Saudi Arabs are concentrated in the holy cities of Mecca and Medina and in Jidda, generally having settled there after pilgrimages. It was estimated in 1963 that between 15 and 20 percent of the population of Mecca, Medina and Taif, 23 percent of Riyadh's population and 35 percent of Jidda's population was non-Saudi in origin. Yemeni refugees entered Asir in large numbers after the September 1962 coup d'etat. The population of the eastern Arabian cities was also largely foreign as a result of the import of non-Saudi technicians, although the need for them is diminishing as Saudi Arabs are being trained.

DISTRIBUTION

Since over half of the country is considered wasteland and since less than 1 percent is suitable for settled agriculture, the estimated average population density of 4 to 6 persons per square mile is misleading. Estimates of population density in some oasis settlements, for example, exceed 2,000 per square mile.

Approximately half the population is believed to be nomadic or seminomadic, and the remainder divided more or less evenly between settled farmers and urban dwellers. This estimate is debatable, however, since it is often difficult to distinguish between seminomads and settled farmers.

The definition of urban areas is also vague, depending primarily on the character of the settlement; that is, whether it is oriented primarily toward agriculture or toward trade or administrative services. The 1962 five-city government survey showed unexpectedly low populations: Riyadh, 169,185; Jidda, 147,859; Mecca, 158,908; Medina, 71,998; Taif, 53,954. Previous estimates of Riyadh's population, for example, had run as high as 300,000. No other urban center is believed to exceed 50,000 in population, although the oasis centers of Hofuf and Qasim may have more than 60,000 inhabitants.

Outside the cities the population is concentrated in three parallel north-south bands across the middle of the peninsula (see fig. 3). The first includes the cities of Hejaz and the settled agricultural areas of Asir and Hejaz oases. The second comprises the belt of oases in the Tuwaiq escarpment area. The third includes the Al-Hasa oases, which have a total population of possibly 160,000, and the oases and towns in the Persian Gulf coastal plain, of which the agricultural center of Qatif, the administrative capital of Dammam, and the Aramco headquarters town of Dhahran are the most important. Since 1950 new settlements of seminomadic herders, attracted by the water-pumping stations, have grown up along the Tapline across northern Arabia.

The cities and these population belts include virtually all the urban residents, and most of the settled farmers and seminomadic herders. The 200,000 to 300,000 Bedouin wander in the otherwise uninhabited desert areas of the Nejd and the great deserts.

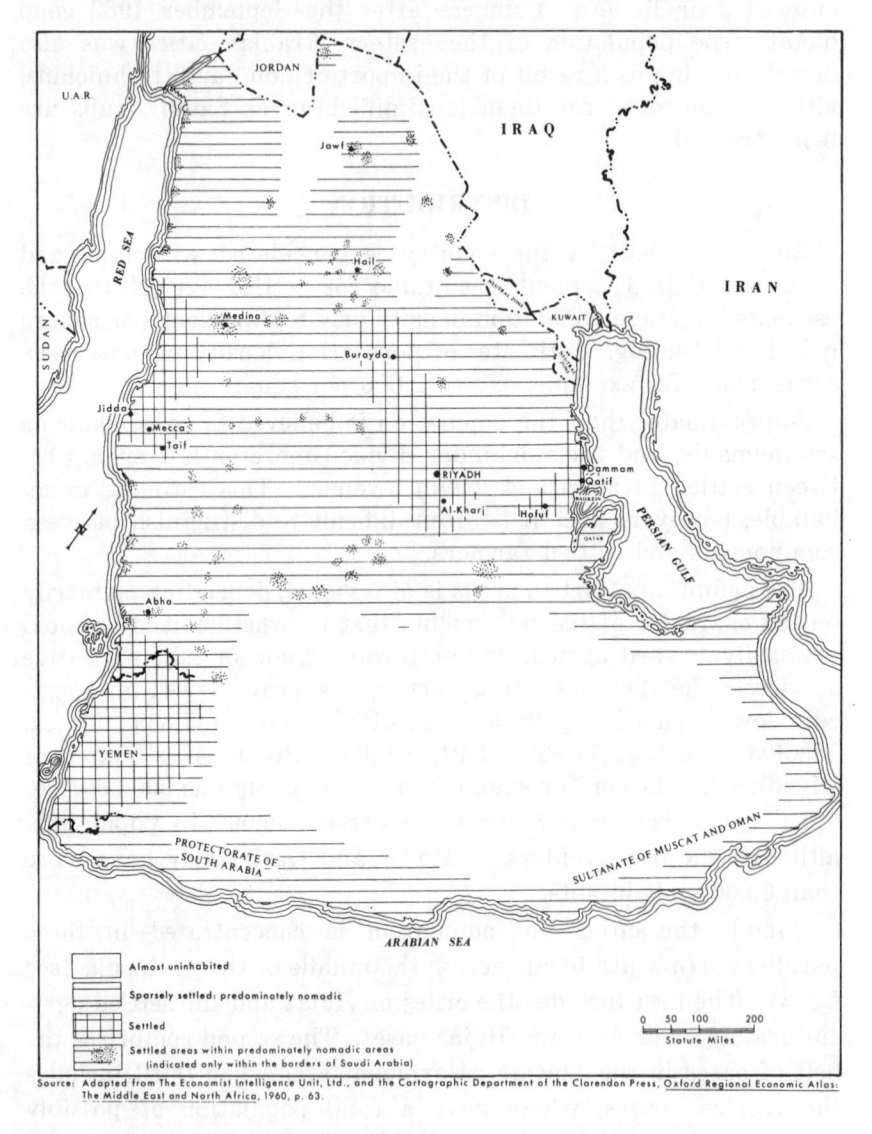

Figure 3. Distribution of Population in Saudi Arabia.

Population Movement

With the development of the oil industry and the wealth that it introduced, new urban centers have sprung up, particularly in eastern Arabia, and the modernization of the older cities has attracted increasing numbers of migrants from the outlying areas. Dhahran, Abqaiq and the port of Ras Tanura were oil-boom towns populated largely by non-Saudi Aramco employees and their families. Under the influence of Aramco activities the small fishing village of Dammam grew into a rapidly expanding industrial city which since 1953 has been the capital of Eastern Province and by 1965 had a population of about 45,000. Al-Khobar, a few miles east of Dhahran, is an entirely new city of modern buildings, boulevards and parks. In 1965 it numbered about 40,000 inhabitants. Qatif, an older town centered in a large date oasis, has grown to about 10,000 people, and its surrounding area has become an important cultivated agricultural area.

Elsewhere in the country urban growth has also been progressing rapidly since the end of World War II. It is impossible to estimate the rate of growth of Riyadh (which before World War II had about 30,000 inhabitants) or the Hejaz cities, but the presence of distressed areas and tent communities on the outskirts of each of them testifies to a large-scale immigration by farmers and seminomads. These people have been attracted by such facilities as electricity, urban water supplies, medical services, education and radio and by the job opportunities in the cities. As economic growth and the pace of urban life continue to increase, the migration of seminomads and farmers into the cities can be expected to accelerate.

The government has been trying to encourage the settlement of nomads and seminomads, not only into the cities but also into agricultural settlements. Such projects as the Tapline settlements and the Haradh agricultural community have attracted large numbers of pastoralists (see ch. 19, Agriculture).

SETTLEMENT PATTERNS

Towns, although varying in appearance from one part of the country to another, display certain common characteristics. Almost every town, at least originally, was well fortified with massive mud or stone walls. In some towns the fortifications were the outer walls of adjoining houses. Towers with battlements reinforced the walls at intervals. With the improvement in public security since the establishment of Saudi Arabia, many of the walls have been allowed to deteriorate, and newer villages and towns are built without walls. Urbanization has forced towns to expand beyond their original walls and to absorb the surburbs which originally comprised the tent camping grounds of the nomads.

The number of mosques depends upon the age of the town and the number of quarters it contains. A characteristic of every town is the central *suk* (bazaar), which is the central market and gathering place for the inhabitants. In the desert towns of Nejd they are frequently the temporary camping grounds for visiting Bedouin. Narrow meandering lanes, along which are found little shops grouped according to the type of article sold, radiate out from the *suk*. In addition, there often are markets for the sale of livestock.

Since the advent of new wealth and modernization, the old cities have begun to change rapidly. Riyadh, Jidda, Mecca, Medina and other cities have expanded far beyond their old city walls. Riyadh is a rapidly expanding capital city with new palaces, government buildings and a growing Bedouin encampment on its outskirts. In several of the newer cities, particularly in the Eastern Province, the areas around the old town are laid out on a modern pattern with broad avenues and parks. Jidda, a busy seaport with modern suburbs, modern buildings and many small industries, has in recent years doubled its size several times. Outside the old walls of Mecca and Medina, new suburbs where the wealthy elite and middle class live have been built.

Villages ordinarily consist of tightly packed clusters of buildings surrounded by the orchards and fields or of a more dispersed arrangement of family houses, each with its own orchard, and the village clusters as a whole perhaps enclosed by a mud wall. In either case the lands for growing cereal crops, which require less water than do trees and garden vegetables, are located outside the village clusters, with the pasturelands at their outer edge.

In mountainous and hilly regions the inhabitants could take advantage of the natural defenses offered by the terrain in choosing a village site; villagers living on the open plain often constructed strong walls around their villages and gardens. In many of the villages of Nejd the mud-brick houses were built adjoining each other so that the outer walls could be used for defense. The gardens were also fortified, and square, defensive towers stood at intervals along the walls. Because of their vulnerability to the raids of nomads, isolated farmsteads were rare. With the establishment of internal security by the Saudi Government, the defensibility of new village sites ceased to be of primary importance.

Villages range in size from hamlets of a few households to settlements of several thousand people. An oasis with a year-round supply of water usually contains one or more villages, both large and small, usually located on the outskirts of the oasis.

The sites of the majority of the older Saudi Arabian villages were originally chosen mainly according to the availability of water. Most of the villages of the interior plateau are tight clusters situated at the edge of oases or strung out along the rim of *wadis,* which are usually irrigated by dug wells. The villages of the more fertile mountain region of the southwest coast are generally clustered around shallow wells or near pools created by dams constructed across the intermittently flowing streams. In some areas where the land or the water supply cannot support many people, a small walled hamlet of as few as two houses is common.

Most of the old villages show little planning, but the new villages being built by the government are laid out in more orderly fashion. The larger and older villages share a number of common features. Each generally has a *suk* where periodic markets are held and which also serve as a gathering place for special occasions. At oases, where a number of small hamlets may be in close proximity, generally one *suk* will be found in the largest and oldest hamlet. Close to the *suk* may be a village mosque, which is generally a simple rectangular building of one or two stories. The *kuttab* (Moslem elementary school), where it still exists, is held in one of the rooms of the mosque (see ch. 9, Education). Depending on its size, a village has one or more coffeehouses.

CHAPTER 3

HISTORICAL SETTING

Saudi Arabia, named after the ruling Saud family, was created as a result of the conquest, between 1902 and 1926, by Abd al-Aziz Ibn Saud of the tribes of the Nejd, Al-Hasa (now Eastern Province) and Asir, and the defeat of the Hashemite king of the Hejaz. It become a united kingdom in 1932. Until the 1930's Arabia had been virtually closed to foreign influences, but as a result of the discovery of oil during this period and of the relatively progressive policies of the Saudi kings, the country has since witnessed an extraordinarily rapid modernization.

PRE-ISLAMIC ARABIA

For at least 3,000 years the Arabian peninsula has been inhabited by Semitic-speaking peoples. Some scholars consider Arabia the original home of the Semites and assert that the Islamic conquests of the seventh century A.D. were only part of a series of eruptions which resulted in the spread of the Semitic peoples beyond their original limits. These speculations have not been proved, but it is clear that Arabia was early inhabited by nomadic Semitic tribes who developed ways of life suitable for desert living which are only now being modified.

From earliest known times a sharp distinction existed between the way of life of the nomads of the interior deserts and that of the more settled peoples of the periphery of the peninsula (see ch. 5, Social Structure). The earliest known large-scale political units were the South Arabian kingdoms of the Minaeans and the Sabaeans, which arose in the mountains of Yemen more than seven centuries before the Christian era. The few historical records left by these kingdoms shed little light on their dates, but it appears that they were contemporaries for much of their history —some historians believe that the Minaeans rose to power somewhat before the Sabaeans, possibly as early as 1200 B.C.—and both were supplanted by the new kingdom of the Himyarites in the second century B.C.

At their height the Minaeans and Sabaeans each controlled much of South Arabia, which became under them an important trade center and an area of great prosperity based on an advanced agriculture. The Sabaeans established colonies in what is today the Hejaz of northwestern Saudi Arabia, but otherwise these early kingdoms had little effect on the peninsula north of Yemen and the Hadhramaut. Particularly in the early centuries of the Christian era, the ties of this area were closer with Abyssinia (present-day Ethiopia), which overran the Himyarite kingdom, and with Persia than with the interior.

Other petty kingdoms grew up on the northern fringes of Arabia. The earliest of these was that of the Nabataeans, whose capital city of Petra, in present-day Jordan, was an important trade center during the Hellenistic and early Roman periods (about 350 B.C. to about A.D. 100).

In the fifth and sixth centuries A.D., Arabia was under a number of diverse external influences. In the northwest the Ghassanids, who claimed descent from one of the South Arabian tribes, were under Byzantine influence; in the northeast the Lakhmids of the kingdom of Hira were under the protection of the Sassanid Persians. In the south the remains of the Himyarite kingdom were controlled first by the Christian Abyssinians and later by the Persians. During this period leaders of the Kinda tribe of central Arabia made the first attempt to unite the interior of the peninsula. For a brief period they gained power also over Hira, but were quickly suppressed by the more powerful northern Arabian kingdoms.

After the decline of South Arabia, in the fourth century A.D., small city-states rose at the intersection of major trade routes, particularly along the west and east coasts. One such town, Mecca, originated about A.D. 400 as an aggregation of tribal groups, notably the Quraysh, camped about an artesian well. As the town developed as a trading center, the townspeople began to shed some of the customs of their nomadic heritage. The tribal-kinship basis of the social order was modified in favor of one based on the relative wealth of the various tribal groups. The Quraysh, in seeking to further Mecca's importance as a commercial center, included idols of neighboring tribes in the Kaaba, the local religious center (see ch. 10, Religion). In addition, the Kaaba sanctuary area was expanded to include the entire city, thus ensuring Mecca's stability and development as a pilgrimage and trading center.

RISE OF ISLAM

Into this cosmopolitan city-state, Mohammed was born about A.D. 570, a member of the Quraysh tribe, the protectors of the Kaaba. He was left an orphan at an early age and reportedly managed the caravans of a rich widow, whom he married and by whom he had several daughters. Troubled by the social inequities and heterodox religious practices of his fellow Meccans, he retired to religious study. According to tradition, at about the age of 40 he was called by God to preach a stern monotheistic and egalitarian religion based in part on the teachings of Judaism and Christianity. Ridiculed and persecuted by the leaders of Mecca, including many of his own tribesmen, who feared that his teachings would end the economic prosperity of the city by eliminating the profitable pilgrimages to the Kaaba, Mohammed and his small band of followers were forced in 622 to flee from Mecca to Medina.

In Medina, Mohammed quickly gained a following for his new religion, which he called Islam, from the Arabic meaning "submission to the will of God." After 8 years of conflict the Meccans also accepted Islam, and Mohammed and his followers were permitted to worship in the Kaaba, where according to local legend, people had worshiped since the time of Abraham and Ishmael. Mecca became the religious center of Islam; the Kaaba became Islam's holiest shrine; and the flight (*hegira*) to Medina marked the beginning of the Islamic calendar.

The universality of Islam joined the isolated tribes of the peninsula through a spiritual bond and a common interest. By the time of Mohammed's death in A.D. 632, most of the peninsula had been won to Islam through diplomacy or military conquest. Islam was a theocratic force; Mohammed was accepted not only as religious leader but also as the supreme temporal leader of the Islamic community. After Mohammed's death this theocratic organization was continued through the caliphs (successors to the Prophet).

Mohammed died without male heirs. The leaders of the Islamic community in Medina selected as first caliph his father-in-law, Abu Bakr, whom Mohammed had chosen to act as imam (religious leader) during his last illness. During the caliphate of Abu Bakr the Arab armies under the banner of Islam began their campaign of conquest and conversion outside the peninsula. Within 20 years of Mohammed's death the Islamic armies, swelled by new converts, had decisively defeated the Byzantine and Persian armies and gained control over a vast territory from Tripoli in North Africa to the eastern limits of Persia.

Within 25 years of Mohammed's death four caliphs succeeded to the leadership of the rapidly expanding Islam. All were elected by the leaders of the Islamic community in Medina. After Abu Bakr's death in 634, Omar, elected second caliph, pressed the military expansion and began organizing religious and civil affairs. He instructed that the revelations of God to Mohammed be preserved in writing in the Koran (the holy book of Islam). In the interest of making Arabia purely Moslem he expelled a large number of Christians and Jews who had settled in the peninsula. He established the civil administration with its capital in Medina and created a powerful military organization.

The reign of Othman, who succeeded Omar in 644, revealed the internal stresses created by the rapid expansion and the lack of firmly established organizational principles. Whereas the first two caliphs belonged to the Hashemite family of the Quraysh tribe, the family to which Mohammed belonged, Othman was a leader of the more powerful rival Umayyad family of the same tribe. By favoring members of his family in the appointments of governorships to the outlying Islamic provinces and other important offices, Othman aroused strong jealousies which led ultimately to his murder in 656.

When Ali, the husband of Mohammed's daughter Fatima, was elected as the fourth caliph in 656, the incipient split in the leadership of Islam came into the open. Muawiya, the governor of Syria and a kinsman of Othman, rebelled against Ali, accusing him of implication in Othman's assassination. Ali lost control of the caliphate in 657 when he forfeited probable victory in battle in favor of arbitration with Muawiya. For the next 4 years, Islam was torn by bitterly opposed factions. Ali was assassinated in 661, and Muawiya had himself proclaimed caliph, thus establishing the Umayyad dynasty which was to rule Islam for almost 100 years. When Muawiya named his son Yazid as his successor, the caliphate ceased to be an elective office, and the Islamic leaders of Medina lost the source of their political power.

Ali's death provoked the most decisive event in Islam since its founding—the split into Shiite (from *shiat*, meaning "party") and Sunni (from *sunna*, meaning "custom" and connoting "orthodox practice") sects (see ch. 10, Religion). The Shiites believed that Mohammed intended Ali to be his successor and that the caliphate was to be hereditary in the line of descent from Ali's children by Fatima, hence directly descendent from Mohammed. Sunni doctrine held that Muawiya restored a legitimacy of succession which was lost after Othman's assassination.

ARABIA IN ECLIPSE

The caliphate of Ali was the last to be centered in the Arabian peninsula. After 656, when Ali left Arabia in a vain attempt to crush the forces opposed to his succession, the center of Islamic power moved from Medina northward to Syria and Mesopotamia. Muawiya established Damascus as the capital of the Umayyad caliphate.

The wealth of the fertile basins of Mesopotamia, Syria and Egypt attracted the Arab Bedouin (nomads). The early raiders remained in the north to create settled Arabian empires, draining the peninsula of its vigor, leadership and youth. From the time of Ali, Islamic dynamism brought to mind not Medina, but Damascus, Baghdad, Cordova and Constantinople. Centralized political structure disappeared under the pressure of tribal rivalries.

The peninsula was not significantly affected by the defeat in 750 of the Umayyad dynasty by the supporters of the rival Abbasid faction. The Abbasid caliphate established its capital in Baghdad, from where it ruled Islam until the middle of the thirteenth century, although with decreasing effectiveness after the beginning of the tenth century.

As the Abbasid dynasty grew progressively weaker toward the end of the ninth century, dissident Shiite movements began to develop in the peninsula. Of these, the most important was that of the Carmathians, which originated in Yemen about 880. By the beginning of the tenth century the Carmathians had gained control of much of Al-Hasa along the Persian Gulf and were strong enough to defy the authority of the Abbasid caliph. Under the leadership of Abu Said and Abu Tahir they expanded through military conquest until by 928 they had united much of the disorganized peninsula and occupied Mecca. They removed the sacred black stone from the Kaaba and for 20 years kept it in their capital in Al-Hasa (see ch. 10, Religion).

For a time the Carmathians allied themselves with the Shiite rulers of North Africa, the Fatimids, against the Sunni Abbasids. In the latter half of the tenth century, however, they shifted their allegiance to the Abbasids in resistance to the Fatimid expansion into Egypt and Syria. In attempting to seize Egypt and Syria from the Fatimids, the Carmathians expended themselves in battle and intrigue and soon were forced to retreat into Al-Hasa, where the sect disappeared by the end of the tenth century. Arabia returned to the isolation and tribal parochialism which had characterized it since the middle of the seventh century.

After the Carmathian collapse the only semblance of political order in the peninsula was in the Hejaz, where the Meccan sherifate (from sherif, meaning "descendant of Mohammed" and hence having noble connotations) was established in 966. Although nominally subject to Fatimid Egypt or Abbasid Baghdad rule from the tenth to the early sixteenth century, the Meccan sherifate was autonomous the greater part of the time, ruled by the local sherifian aristocracy. After the beginning of the thirteenth century, leadership in Mecca became hereditary in the Hashemite family of the Quraysh tribe. The wealth and influence derived from the Meccan pilgrimage trade enabled the sherifate to extend its political control over Medina and Taif.

When the Ottoman Turks conquered Egypt in 1517, they were recognized as rulers of the Hejaz. Ottoman presence effected the most significant foreign influence on Arabia in the peninsula's history. A relative calm was brought to the peninsula which enabled Mecca, despite subordination to Constantinople (the capital of the Ottoman Empire), to extend its rule over the Bedouin tribes south to Asir and east through much of Nejd (see ch. 2, Geography and Population). The Ottomans, moving south along the Persian Gulf, also established themselves along the Al-Hasa coast in 1555, although their control there was nominal.

Mecca's growing importance both as a religious center and as the key to Nejd, Asir and Yemen led the Ottoman rulers to install a Grand Mufti (leading religious and legal official) in 1539 to oversee their interests and to limit Meccan expansion. Antagonism between the Meccans and the Ottomans increased markedly in the following centuries.

As the Ottomans became engaged in wars with Austria, Russia and Persia during the seventeenth century, their power to patrol the Red Sea and regulate conditions in the Hejaz was considerably weakened, and Arabia was left to fend for itself. The interests of the Hejaz merchants and traders gradually turned both south and east. Trade and communication were expanded to the Nejd and, from there, east to Al-Hasa on the Persian Gulf.

ORIGIN OF THE HOUSE OF SAUD

The development of the country from the middle of the eighteenth century is intimately connected with the religious movement of Mohammed Ibn Abd al-Wahhab (1703–92). Wahhab, born at Ayaina in Nejd, where his father was the religious judge (*qadi*), showed an early interest in religion. Shocked by the deviations from Koranic teachings that he observed at Mecca, he started preaching a puritanical form of Islam aimed at returning to the strict teachings of the Koran. He considered the worship of saints to be polytheistic and he frowned upon smoking and ostentation. Expelled from Ayaina in 1742, Mohammed Ibn Abd al-Wahhab found refuge with the ruler of the town of **Dariya**, Emir Mohammed Ibn Saud, the founder of the present ruling dynasty, who embraced Mohammed Ibn Abd al-Wahhab's doctrines.

The mobilization of religious fervor on a political base attracted a large Bedouin following, fanatic in support of the Wahhabi religious movement. By marshaling Bedouin support, Mohammed Ibn Saud was able to capture Riyadh in 1764. By the time of his death a year later, he had established his supremacy throughout Nejd by a web of conquests, marriages and alliances, a pattern emulated by later Saudi rulers. Mohammed Ibn Saud's conquests were continued by his son, Abd al-Aziz, who retained Mohammed al-Wahhab as his religious and political adviser and began the expansion of the House of Saud beyond the Nejdi core to the peripheries of the peninsula.

The early Saudi rulers introduced a new factor—territorial organization—to their conquests. They built moated forts, garrisoned by mercenaries, outside the towns they captured. In the larger towns a *qadi* and a *mufti* (religious leader) were installed; in the smaller towns, only a *qadi*. District governers were appointed to collect taxes and recruit soldiers. Rule was centralized, and all important decisions were personally made by the emir.

Saud, who succeeded his father, Abd al-Aziz, as emir in 1803, launched his Bedouin army through Asir and Yemen, and by 1806, Saudi forces had captured Mecca, Medina and Hejaz. Quickly, they occupied most of the peninsula and parts of Iraq and invaded Syria.

The Ottomans, aware that their empire was threatened by Saudi expansion, called upon the Ottoman viceroy of Egypt, Mohammed Ali, to crush the Saudi-Wahhabi empire. An Egyptian army under Mohammed Ali's son Tusun captured Mecca in 1812 and, shortly thereafter, occupied the rest of Hejaz. Saud's death in May 1814 left his son and successor Abdullah to carry on the war against the Ottomans.

Ibrahim Pasha, another son of Mohammed Ali, continued the Egyptian-Ottoman offensive, capturing and razing the Saudi capital, Dariya. In 1818, Abdullah was deported to Constantinople and beheaded. The first Saudi-Wahhabi empire, which at its height extended in a broad band from the Persian Gulf to the Red Sea and from Yemen to the gates of Damascus, was left an insignificant emirate in Nejd under Egyptian suzerainty.

NINETEENTH-CENTURY ARABIA

The history of what is today Saudi Arabia was one of intrigue and bloodshed during the century following the collapse of the first Saudi-Wahhabi empire. It was complicated by the very different influences which determined the history of Hejaz and Nejd during the period.

Hejaz

Mohammed Ali retained control over the Hejaz from 1812 until his death in 1849. Through the French officers who accompanied his forces into the Hejaz, Europeans became interested in the peninsula, a land hitherto closed to non-Moslems. British and French consulates were established in Jidda, and the British moved to establish predominant influence over the ports and coastal areas of southern Arabia to support their interests in India.

During the last 18 years of his life, Mohammed Ali rebelled against his Ottoman overlords and attempted to assert direct authority over Hejaz, Nejd, Asir and Yemen. This attempt brought him into conflict with the British, who were allies of the Ottoman Sultan and feared Mohammed Ali's expansion into their sphere of influence. As Mohammed Ali pushed south into Yemen, the British countered by occupying Aden and signing protectorate treaties with the sheikhs of South Arabia. Gradually during the next 50 years, Great Britain gained a predominant influence along the southern Arabian coast and the Persian Gulf coast through protectorate treaties with the Sultan of Oman, the Sheikhs of Qatar, Bahrein and Trucial Oman and, at the end of the century, the Sheikh of Kuwait. In this way the limits of future Saudi expansion to the southern and eastern coasts of the peninsula were set.

After Mohammed Ali's death in 1849, the harsh reimposition of Ottoman rule resulted in growing discontent among the Hejazi townspeople, who had achieved a degree of autonomy under Mohammed Ali. An Ottoman edict regulating social conditions within the peninsula precipitated a series of riots in Mecca which culminated in a xenophobic uprising in June 1858 at Jidda and resulted in the death of two European consuls. As the situation proved beyond the control of the Ottomans, the British ordered a naval force to bombard Jidda and sent Marines to ensure public safety until Ottoman authority could be locally reestablished.

During the remainder of the nineteenth century, Ottoman control of the Hejaz was relatively firm. Mecca remained under the authority of the Hashemite Sherif of Mecca, who owed allegiance to the Ottoman Sultan. Ottoman control was strengthened after 1904 by the construction of a railroad linking Medina with Damascus and the main centers of the Ottoman Empire.

The Nejd

For most of the nineteenth century the Nejd was an arena for violent personal rivalries within and among the powerful tribal families of which the Sauds were only one. The Ottomans did not keep powerful military forces in the area, but sought to consolidate their grasp by fostering these rivalries and particularly by supporting the opponents of the Sauds.

In 1824, 6 years after Abdullah's death, Turki (a cousin of Saud, Abdullah's father), assumed the Nejdi emirate; established himself in Riyadh, a few miles south of Dariya; and consolidated his power over the Nejd area around Riyadh, while acknowledging, however, the nominal suzerainty of Mohammed Ali. When his son Faisal refused to continue to pay tribute to Mohammed Ali, the Egyptian leader sent a force into the Nejd in 1838 to depose Faisal, who was forced to surrender and was exiled to Cairo. The Egyptians were soon withdrawn from the Nejd to support Mohammed Ali's revolt against his Ottoman overlords, and in 1843, when Faisal escaped from captivity and returned to Nejd, the Saudi leaders quickly rallied to him and reasserted their authority over the bulk of the peninsula. Oman, Yemen and the Hejaz remained, however, outside their sphere of influence, refusing to accept again the Wahhabi puritanism.

Quarrels and intrigues, omnipresent though submerged during Faisal's reign, swept to the surface after his death in 1865, and the long civil war caused by the struggles between two of his sons led to the disintegration of the Saudi state. The Al-Kharj and Qasim oases, to the south and north of Riyadh, respectively, became independent entities.

By the late 1880's, Mohammed Ibn Rashid, a Wahhabi tribal sheikh of the Shammar tribes centered in Hail, began to develop a powerful political base which gradually incorporated the greater part of the Nejdi sheikhdoms. In 1891, Ibn Rashid signed a pact with the Ottomans, who had occupied Al-Hasa in 1871, and formed a coalition with the powerful Harb Bedouin against the remnants of the Saudi emirate. Later in 1891 the Rashids seized Unayza and Burayda, hitherto Saudi tributaries, and captured Riyadh. Abd ar-Rahman, Faisal's third son, who had in 1889 assumed leadership of the besieged remnants of the Saudi emirate, fled to exile in Kuwait with his 10-year-old son, Abd al-Aziz Ibn Saud, who was destined to be the founder of modern Saudi Arabia.

CREATION OF SAUDI ARABIA

Reconquest of the Nejd

From exile, Abd ar-Rahman continued a small-scale desert war against the Rashids. In 1901, when Abd al-Aziz Ibn Rashid, nephew and successor of Mohammed Ibn Rashid, threatened Kuwait, Abd al-Aziz Ibn Saud was permitted by the Sheikh of

Kuwait to mount and expedition against Riyadh. With a band of about 50 armed men he stole into the city on January 15, 1902, and by surprise overpowered a much larger force under Ibn Rashid's governor. Hailed as a hero by the citizens of the city, Abd al-Aziz reestablished a Saudi foothold in the Nejd.

Neighboring Bedouin tribes, impressed with Abd al-Aziz's valor and success and never fully under Rashidi control, rallied to his banner. He called on his father, Abd ar-Rahman, to return from exile in Kuwait to legitimize the Saudi position and consolidate popular support. Abd ar-Rahman abdicated his title as emir in favor of Abd al-Aziz (also known as Ibn Saud) but retained the position of imam (religious leader) of the Wahhabis. From this period, Abd al-Aziz came increasingly to be called Ibn Saud and the two names have since been used interchangeably.

Through a series of military operations from 1902 to 1904, Abd al-Aziz expanded his rule throughout the Nejd. His strategy of uniting tribes through marriage alliances and his skill in taking advantage of the opportunism of some tribal leaders were so successful that by early 1904 Rashidi control was limited to their home area of the Jebel Shammar in northern Nejd.

Ibn Rashid made a desperate plea to his Ottoman protectors for reinforcements. In May 1904 eight Ottoman battalions, supported by two artillery units, joined in Ibn Rashid's forces, but after an indecisive campaign during the summer, they were routed by Abd al-Aziz's mobile desert fighters.

Abd al-Aziz's victory helped win the loyalty of hitherto neutral sheikhs, and his diplomatic capacity was demonstrated when he convinced the Ottomans not to send reinforcements. In return for Ottoman recognition of Saudi rule in the Nejd, he accepted, in 1904, both nominal Ottoman suzerainty and the maintenance of Ottoman garrisons at Unayza, Burayda and Qasim. He kept up guerrilla warfare against the Ottoman occupation forces, however, and by late 1905 forced the remaining Ottoman troops to withdraw from the Nejd. This victory was followed by the overwhelming defeat of Rashidi forces near Burayda. Abd al-Aziz Ibn Rashid was killed in April 1906, and the long struggle for control of the Nejd was won.

Saudi interest then shifted toward Al-Hasa and the Persian Gulf. Abd al-Aziz requested the Kuwaiti sheikh, Mubarak, who had been instrumental in his early success at Riyadh, to intercede in obtaining British support, or at least acquiescence, in Abd al-Aziz's capture of Al-Hasa from the Ottomans. Encouraged by evidence of British neutrality and by Ottoman preoccupation with revolts in Europe, he launched an attack on Ottoman Al-Hasa, which was quickly successful, and by the summer of 1913, Abd al-Aziz Ibn Saud was sovereign of the Nejd and Al-Hasa.

The Ikhwan Movement

As was the case with his predecessors in their attempts to unify Arabia, Abd al-Aziz found that any attempt to establish a stable, large-scale political organization in the conquered territories was impeded by the difficulty of creating loyalties beyond those of the local units, whether it was tribe or village. He sought a remedy in religion by regularly sending Wahhabi missionaries to the tribes and encouraging settlements of Bedouin in agricultural communities founded on and governed by Wahhabi precepts. The pilot project, established in 1912 at Artawiya, an oasis in northern Nejd, proved successful in settling 10,000 Mutayr nomads into a community. Within a few years, such settlements numbered over 60 and sheltered some 40,000 nomads.

The ultrapuritanic Wahhabi movement became known as the Ikhwan (brethren) movement and was aimed at uniting all true believers, regardless of tribal affiliation, behind a larger loyalty to the movement as a whole. By 1916 the Ikhwan movement in Nejd had spread to such an extent that Abd al-Aziz was compelled to assume direct control of it or face its threat to his rule. Abd al-Aziz ordered all Bedouin tribes to join the Ikhwan and pay *zakat* (alms tax) to him as imam (see ch. 24, Monetary and Financial System). He also required the tribal sheikhs to attend the school of Islamic law and religion at the Riyadh mosque. When the sheikh of an Ikhwan tribe completed his religious instruction, he was often given a house in Riyadh and invited to remain in attendance of Emir Abd al-Aziz; the sheikhs were thus usually kept under close supervision to ensure their manageability.

Wahhabi Bedouin were taught to believe that they alone were true Moslems; they were called on to aid one another in case of need and to abandon the practice of blood feuds within the brotherhood. Abd al-Aziz abolished tribal raiding and created from the Ikhwan a highly trained, loyal armed force. The Ikhwan could be mobilized within 96 hours, with 25,000 men under arms, but not more than 5,000 were ordinarily called upon to take part in action. Abd al-Aziz's creation of the powerful Ikhwan enabled enforcement of both his rule and the tenets of Wahhabism on even the most reluctant tribes.

Arabia and World War I

Before World War I the British controlled most of the southern and Persian Gulf coasts of the peninsula through their treaties with various local sheikhs, while the Ottoman Empire held the

Hejaz and Asir along the Red Sea and occupied the Middle East north of the Nejd. Saud Ibn Rashid, who in 1908 had succeeded his father Abd al-Aziz Ibn Rashid in commanding the Rashidi enemies of the Sauds in the Jebel Shammar, was allied with the Ottomans, who were in turn allies of the Germans and thus enemies of the British. The Hashemite leader Husein, whom the Ottomans had made Sherif of Mecca in 1908 in the hope of strengthening their hold over the Hejaz, was showing unexpected independence and moving to spread his own influence through agreement with the tribes of the Hejaz and Asir. To Abd al-Aziz Ibn Saud, then in substantial control of the Nejd and Al-Hasa, Husein was becoming a greater threat than the Rashids.

In the early months of World War I the British sought the support of both Husein and Abd al-Aziz against the Ottomans. They sent Captain W. H. I. Shakespear, British political agent in Kuwait, to meet the Saudi leader and convince him to move against Saudi Ibn Rashid. The Rashids precipitated the action by invading the Saudi areas; Abd al-Aziz joined the battle in Qasim in January 1915, but the outcome was undecisive. Shakespear was killed in the fighting, and the British lost interest in a Saudi alliance.

In December 1915, however, a British representative, Sir Percy Cox, concluded a treaty of friendship with Abd al-Aziz, guaranteeing his independence but assuming control over his relations with foreign powers. The following year, a second treaty was signed recognizing Abd al-Aziz's title of Emir of the Nejd and Al-Hasa and granting him a monthly subsidy of £5,000 in return for an understanding that he would renew the fight against Ibn Rashid. This he did in 1918, when he led an expedition that extended Saudi control to the outskirts of Hail, the Rashidi capital.

The focal point of the Arab war against the Ottomans shifted after 1915 to the Hejaz, whose other British representatives of the Cairo-based Arab Bureau of the British Foreign Office reached an agreement with Sherif Husein. In June 1916, Husein revolted against the Ottomans, forcing them out of the Hejaz and defeating their army at Aqaba. It was with these forces that Colonel T. E. Lawrence achieved world renown.

Relations between Husein and Abd al-Aziz worsened steadily during the war. The Saudi leader of the Nejd resented Husein's assumption of the title "King of the Arab countries" and his efforts to gain support of Nejdi tribes. In late 1917 the British sent a mission headed by H. St. John Philby to convince Abd al-Aziz not to take action against Husein but instead to redirect his military effort toward Ibn Rashid. Abd al-Aziz made systematic attempts to wean minor sheikhs away from allegiance to

Husein through Wahhabi proselytism. In 1917 the sheikh of the strategically located Khurma oasis on the eastern approaches to Mecca accepted Wahhabi tenets and transferred his allegiance from Husein to Abd al-Aziz. In May 1919, Husein, confident of British support, sent his son at the head of a 14,000 man army to recapture the oasis, but the army was decimated in a night battle at Turaba, about halfway between Khurma and Taif, by a fanatical force of Ikhwan desert warriors.

Abd al-Aziz declined to follow up his advantage against Husein at that time, satisfying himself with consolidating his position against the frontiers of the Hejaz and expanding in other directions. In 1920 he moved against Asir, which was conquered by an Ikhwan army under the command of Abd al-Aziz's son, Faisal Ibd Abd al-Aziz al-Faisal al-Saud, the present king of Saudi Arabia.

Formation of Saudi Arabia

The San Remo Conference of 1920, convened by the British and French to settle the postwar Middle East situation, altered the political balance of the Arabian peninsula by making Husein's sons, Abdullah and Faisal, kings of Transjordan (present-day Jordan) and Iraq, respectively. As the Hashemites began negotiations with Abd al-Aziz's enemy, the Rashids, Abd al-Aziz's fear of a Hashemite rise from the north and west appeared to be approaching reality.

To counter this threat, he sent Ikhwan raiding parties against Hail, the Rashidi capital, despite an appeal by Husein to the British to hold back the Saudis. The British, made cautious by the Saudi show of strength at Turaba, refused to intervene in what they considered a quarrel between two rulers of the inner desert. In late 1921 the Ikhwan captured Hail. Abd al-Aziz married Saud Ibn Rashid's widow (Ibn Rashid had been killed the previous year by one of his cousins), adopted his children and brought the surviving male members of the Rashid family to Riyadh as honored guests.

Emboldened by success, the Ikhwan disregarded Abd al-Aziz's orders not to cross into Transjordanian territory, and raiders penetrated into Transjordan, where they seized the key caravan oasis of Jawf and destroyed Turayf, leaving half the population dead in their wake. The British, bound to the defense of King Abdullah of Transjordan and fearing a Saudi expansion to the Mediterranean littoral, counterattacked with aerial support and decimated the Ikhwan forces. The survivors were said to have been put to the sword by Abd al-Aziz for violating his command to remain within Saudi territory.

Abd al-Aziz Ibn Saud met with the British Resident Minister of Iraq, Sir Percy Cox, at Uqair, late in 1922 to negotiate a general relaxation of tensions between the two countries. Acceding to British demands for a fixed frontier between Nejd, Iraq and Kuwait, vital to British interests in view of newly discovered oil deposits, Abd al-Aziz agreed to respect the frontier line proposed by Sir Percy. The agreed-upon borders featured two neutral zones with shared rights to avoid conflicting claims, one between Iraq and the Nejd and the other between Kuwait and Al-Hasa (see ch. 2, Geography and Population). No fortifications were ever to be built on either side of the frontier. This agreement effectively limited Saudi ambitions in the rich area of the Fertile Crescent north of the Nejd and caused Abd al-Aziz to shift his attention again to the Hejaz.

In the Hejaz, Husein's position steadily weakened. Disillusioned by Great Britain's failure to abide by wartime agreements guaranteeing the independence of Arab states, he quarreled with the British. Maladministration of the holy cities, poor health conditions and exorbitant taxes alienated Moslems both within and beyond the peninsula. In an effort to restore his prestige he laid claim to the ancient title of caliph in March 1924, a few days after the Turkish National Assembly under Mustapha Kemal Ataturk voted the abolition of the title.

This step isolated Husein from Arab opinion and caused the British to lose patience with him, whereupon Abd al-Aziz moved against the Hejaz. In September 1924 the Ikhwan army occupied Taif, on the road to Mecca, forcing the retreat of a Hashemite army under Husein's son Ali. Ikhwan forces pillaged the town and massacred several hundred of its inhabitants before they were brought under control by Abd al-Aziz's representatives. News of the event resounded throughout the Hejaz, spreading fear of the Ikhwan.

Popular pressure forced Husein's abdication in favor of his son Ali in October 1924. Husein fled to Transjordan, then to Cyprus where he died. Ali abandoned Mecca to the advancing Ikhwan armies, and Abd al-Aziz, dressed as a pilgrim, entered the city in mid-October. Ali retreated to Jidda, which was put under siege by the Saudi forces. The British refused Ali's requests for assistance, and the dwindling Hashemite armies were unable to prevent Saudi occupation of most of the remainder of the Hejaz, which they opened to pilgrimage in 1925. Medina and Jidda surrendered in December 1925, and Ali fled to Iraq. The conquest of the Hejaz was completed. Abd al-Aziz was crowned King of the Hejaz in Mecca in January 1926.

Abd al-Aziz sought to legitimize his conquest of Mecca by convoking a pan-Islamic conference in 1926 to regulate the affairs of Mecca as the holy city of Islam. His capacity for maintaining order and his introduction of the rigorous Wahhabi interpretation of Islamic, or *sharia* law did much to improve conditions for the pilgrims. Abd al-Aziz remained in the area for nearly 2 years as ruler before turning over administration of the province to his son Faisal as viceroy. The civil administration of the Hejaz under Faisal was the first example of institutionalized government in the realm (see ch. 12, Constitution and Government).

In January 1927, Abd al-Aziz united his conquered territories under a single title when he was crowned, in Riyadh, King of the Hejaz and Nejd and Its Dependencies. In May the British Government recognized the new kingdom's independence by the Treaty of Jidda, which renounced the protectorate provisions of the 1915 treaty between Abd al-Aziz and Sir Percy Cox.

The 2 years Abd al-Aziz had spent in the Hejaz took their toll, however, on the unity he had imposed on the tribes from his Nejd base. His ban on raiding and his penchant for modernization drew the ire of the tradition-minded tribal leaders. When it was revealed that Abd al-Aziz had recognized the Hashemite kingdoms of Iraq and Jordan and that Great Britain had violated the 1922 Uqair treaty by erecting forts along the Iraqi-Saudi frontier, many tribal leaders rebelled against the King's authority.

Toward the end of 1927 several tribal leaders—particularly those of the Mutayr tribe—took matters into their own hands and raided into Iraq to attack those building the frontier forts. The British Air Force retaliated by bombing the tribal camps in the Nejd, and an undeclared war ensued. Abd al-Aziz moved to restore his control over his rebellious tribes while unsuccessfully demanding that the British dismantle the frontier forts.

The rebellion reached its climax in early 1929 when Sheikh Dawish, leader of the Mutayr tribe and Abd al-Aziz's chief desert strategist, joined forces with Sheikh Hithlain of the Ajman tribe. Dawish attempted to form a political unit comparable to that of Abd al-Aziz and began to collect taxes from villages and caravans under his control. The tribes continued sporadic raids into Iraq and Kuwait.

Abd al-Aziz defeated the rebels in pitched battle in March 1929, but when he left the Nejd for several months to make a pilgrimage to Mecca and handle administrative problems in the Hejaz, the tribes regrouped under Dawish and pressed their rebellion. Abd al-Aziz returned to Nejd and took the field himself during the last half of 1929. With a fleet of motor vehicles he had purchased from the British, he pressed the attack against the rebels and by January 1930 had decisively defeated them. Those who fled into Iraq were returned to Abd al-Aziz for punishment. This rebellion marked the end of Abd al-Aziz's use of the Ikhwan as a military-religious force. Several of the Ikhwan settlements had been destroyed in the course of the fighting, and gradually the remainder were abandoned. Ikhwan veterans were pensioned or transferred to the regular army which Abd al-Aziz was creating along more modern lines.

In September 1932, Abd al-Aziz proclaimed that his reunited realm was to be called the Kingdom of Saudi Arabia. The kingdom was a union of tribes, villages and towns joined by loyalty to the Saudi family. Aware of the need to cement ties with tribal sheikhs, Abd al-Aziz utilized tribal subsidies and marriage to daughters of tribal leaders.

In 1926, Yemen began to challenge the new kingdom's authority in Asir, particularly its claim to the region of the Najran oasis. A crisis was reached in 1934 when the Emir of Asir sought to withdraw from the kingdom in order to unite with Yemen, which was then strongly supported by Fascist Italy.

Abd al-Aziz's army invaded Yemen, and the British, fearing possible Italian designs on Suez, sent the warship *Enterprise* to protect the Saudi Arabs. The Treaty of Taif, signed in 1934, annexed the Najran area to Saudi Arabia and guaranteed Yemeni independence while ensuring that Yemen's foreign policy would thereafter be in agreement with that of Saudi Arabia and that Wahhabi preachers would have unrestricted entry (see ch. 14, Foreign Relations).

The most far-reaching event in the modern history of the country was the discovery of oil in the 1930's. King Abd al-Aziz agreed in 1933 to grant a wide-ranging concession to Standard Oil of California (renamed in 1944 the Arabian American Oil Company—Aramco) for oil prospecting and exploitation. The first well began producing in 1938, and when large-scale production started after World War II, large amounts of foreign exchange began to flow to the government (see ch. 20, Industry; ch. 24. Monetary and Financial System).

World War II and After

Although Abd al-Aziz was favorably disposed toward the Allied cause, his associates discouraged him from participating in the war. The wartime stoppage of pilgrimage traffic and suspension of oil production caused economic hardship. In response to the King's requests, stopgap economic aid was provided by the United States by including the country in the Lend-Lease Program and by allocating to it a portion of United States wartime loans to Great Britain. Abd al-Aziz acceded to United States requests to be permitted to build and lease an airfield at Dhahran in return for United States military equipment and advisers. Concern about future developments led President Roosevelt to meet Abd al-Aziz off the Hejaz coast in February 1945. Discuscussions between the two leaders centered on the United Nations, oil developments and the Palestinian question, on which the United States President promised to take no stand without first consulting with the Arab states. Saudi Arabia accepted the principles of the United Nations and declared war on Germany in March 1945.

The end of World War II brought to fruition Arab nationalist hopes with the emergence of Syria, Lebanon, Iraq and Jordan as independent states. Saudi Arabia, Egypt and Yemen joined them in creating the Arab League in 1945 as a vehicle for coordinating mutual interests. Saudi Arabia, following its traditional pattern of isolationism, played a limited role in Arab League affairs. While opposed to the creation of a Jewish state in the Arab-Islamic Middle East, Abd al-Aziz's primary interest was in developing his country into a modern nation. Therefore, Saudi military participation in the 1946-48 Palestine war was minimal. Other Arab League decisions, such as the Palestine boycott, were more fully implemented (see ch. 14, Foreign Relations).

With the expansion of oil production after the war, the government undertook rapid economic and social development. The introduction of modern oil technology and the influence of a relatively large foreign colony made impossible the continuation of isolation. Several of the princes of the Saudi family were educated in Europe and the United States and returned home with new concepts which contrasted sharply with the traditional Saudi ways.

Particularly since 1953, the government has been undergoing intensive modernization. Its activities as well as those of the oil company have begun to change Saudi society. Aramco built for the government account a large deepwater port at Dammam on the Persian Gulf and a 360-mile railroad connecting the port with Riyadh. Hospitals and schools were built. In the Hejaz, facilities for Moslems making the annual hadj (pilgrimage) to Mecca were improved, particularly in the areas of sanitation and personal security. As a result, the number of pilgrims increased rapidly from year to year. Modern buildings, roads, lighting and other utilities were built in Jidda, Mecca, Riyadh, Dhahran and other urban centers.

Modern fiscal policies were introduced between 1958 and 1960 to restore and maintain economic stability which had been threatened by the sudden and initially somewhat fluctuating oil income. A program to broaden the industrial base of the country was initiated in the early 1960's, and government programs to settle the Bedouin, to increase education and literacy, to improve standards of living and to introduce modern conveniences have begun to change the face of the country (see ch. 11, Health and Welfare). All these projects were based initially on oil wealth.

As Abd al-Aziz became gradually weakened by advanced age, he recognized the need for a more fully developed political administration. Accordingly, a Council of Ministers was established in October 1953. He named his eldest living son, Saud Ibn Abd al-Aziz (al-Faisal al-Saud), heir to the throne and commander in chief of the armed forces and appointed his second son, Faisal, foreign minister and governor of Hejaz. The following month, on November 9, Abd al-Aziz Ibn Saud died of heart failure. An unprecedented display of mourning throughout the country attested to the widespread popularity of the founder of Saudi Arabia.

SAUDI ARABIA AFTER ABD AL-AZIZ IBN SAUD

When King Saud ascended the throne, he promised in his initial speech from the throne, to continue the foreign policy of his father, based on cooperation with the United Nations and the Arab League, and to pursue domestic policies aimed at promoting the economic, social, health and educational welfare of his people.

As Saudi Arabia became increasingly open to outside influences and modernization, problems became more complex. The relatively large numbers of skilled laborers, technicians and teachers brought in from Egypt, Syria, Palestine and other Moslem countries introduced Saudi workers to new ideas. Evidence of labor unrest was shown in a strike of Aramco workers in 1953 and reinforced by a new work stoppage in 1956, and, as a result, the government and Aramco increased their activities aimed at improving the social and economic position of industrial workers. At the same time, however, the government prohibited work stoppages or the organization of labor unions (see ch. 21, Labor).

During the early years of his reign, King Saud created new ministries of commerce, education, information and agriculture. He appointed Crown Prince Faisal prime minister as well as foreign minister, but retained for himself control of all domestic and foreign policy. He increased expenditures for schools, roads, communications, urban development and facilities for the pilgrimage. A small but growing number of students were sent abroad to universities—mainly to Egypt, Western Europe or the United States.

As absolute monarch, King Saud used the rapidly increasing oil revenues for his official obligations, for financing the small governmental structure, for his personal requirements and the expenses of the large royal household and for maintaining charitable and religious institutions, making gifts to the tribes, and living up to the Arab tradition of almost boundless generosity and hospitality. Oil revenues were rapidly depleted, and the government's financial position steadily worsened. This situation became critical between 1955 and 1958, when oil revenues leveled off after a rapid postwar climb. By the beginning of 1958, Saudi Arabia's financial position was precarious as the continuing high level of expenditures outran receipts. The exchange value of the riyal dropped rapidly; capital fled the country as confidence in the economy lagged; the cost of living increased under inflationary pressures, and Saudi Arabia's standing abroad was seriously affected (see ch. 24, Monetary and Financial System).

In foreign relations King Saud, during the first several years of his reign, followed a neutralist course similar to that of Egypt's President Gamal Abdul Nasser. He strengthened ties between Saudi Arabia and Egypt through commercial and technical assistance agreements, culminating in October 1955 with a friendship and mutual defense pact. He cooperated with Nasser in promoting Arab nationalism by demanding the liberation of Palestine and Algeria and joined him in financing an effort to keep Jordan out of the British-negotiated Baghdad Pact. During 1956 he postponed renewing the United States lease to the Dhahran airbase. In the peninsula, King Saud was embroiled after 1951 in a dispute with Great Britain over possession of the Buraimi Oasis in the undefined border area between Saudi Arabia and British-protected Oman. This dispute dragged on for more than 10 years (see ch. 14, Foreign Relations).

When Great Britain, France and Israel invaded Egypt in November 1956, King Saud honored his mutual defense pact with Egypt to the extent of a money grant amounting to about $10 million, breaking diplomatic relations with Great Britain and France and banning oil shipments to the two countries. He did not, however, give direct military support to Egypt. He renewed oil shipments to France and Great Britain in March 1957 and renewed diplomatic relations with them in 1962 and 1963, respectively.

Beginning in early 1957, King Saud abandoned his neutralist foreign policy. While on a protracted visit to the United States for medical care, he conferred with President Eisenhower; supported the Eisenhower Doctrine, which pledged United States support to any Middle Eastern country menaced by communism; agreed to the 5-year renewal of the United States lease to the Dhahran airbase; and undertook a rapprochement with his traditional enemies, the Hashemite kings of Iraq and Jordan. Relations with Egypt steadily worsened during this period, reaching a low point in February 1958.

Shortly after Syria joined Egypt in the United Arab Republic, which King Saud opposed, a high official of the Syrian police publicly accused King Saud of involvement in an alleged plot against President Nasser. The princes of the Saud family, who already had been dubious about both the financial and foreign policies and activities of King Saud, now expressed themselves as being fearful about the consequences to the stability of King Saud's regime. They forced him in March to relinqish full power over the country's domestic and foreign policies to Crown Prince Faisal, who had been largely powerless during the previous 5 years.

Faisal immediately subjected government finances to strict accountability and reduced the amounts available to the royal family. His program quickly restored the country to financial health (see ch. 24, Monetary and Financial System). In May he issued a new statute, further institutionalizing the government by granting to the Council of Ministers increased executive powers (see ch. 12, Constitution and Government). In foreign affairs he assumed a neutral position between the United Arab Republic and the Arab Federation, which had been created by the Hasemite kings of Iraq and Jordan as a counterweight to the United Arab Republic. He made some effort to normalize relations with President Nasser, however, by supporting him in his moves to bar Israeli ships from the Suez Canal.

By mid-1960 differences between King Saud and Crown Prince Faisal became apparent over several policy matters, including the budget. The end result was that Prince Faisal submitted his resignation and that of his Council of Ministers in December.

King Saud assumed the prime ministership in December 1960 and named Prince Talal, a younger half-brother of the King and Prince Faisal, minister of finance and economy. The new government announced its intention to set up a partially elected national council to draft a constitution, but the proposal was not carried out. The government also announced its decision not to renew the United States' lease to the Dhahran airfield, which was scheduled to end in April 1962.

By September 1961 King Saud appeared ready for a reconciliation with Faisal and removed several ministers, including Talal, from the council. In March 1962, Faisal was named deputy prime minister and foreign minister. He acted for King Saud while the latter was in the United States for medical treatment during an extended period in 1962. Talal went into voluntary exile and agitated for reforms in the Saudi Government.

The September 1962 coup d'etat in Yemen and the establishment of a Yemeni republican government supported by the United Arab Republic created a new crisis in Saudi Arabia, which supported the overthrown royalist government. King Saud appointed Faisal prime minister in October; Faisal named Prince Khalid Ibn Abd al-Aziz as deputy prime minister and formed a government of his own supporters, including four princes of the House of Saud. He assumed the position of commander in chief of the army and retained the foreign ministry. The following month he announced a wide-ranging reform program which included the abolition of slavery, the reorganization of local government and justice and proposals for new legislation regarding education, social security and labor.

During late 1962 and much of 1963 the government was preoccupied, however, with the Yemeni crisis, which threatened by November 1962 to break into a full-scale war between Saudi Arabia and the United Arab Republic. Egyptian planes bombed Saudi villages on the Yemeni border, and the Saudi Government gave military assistance to the Yemeni royalists. Riyadh broke diplomatic relations with Cairo in November. The United States recognized the Yemeni republican government, but indicated support of Saudi Arabia against possible interference in its internal affairs by the United Arab Republic (see ch. 14, Foreign Relations). An agreement between the United Arab Republic and Saudi Arabia to end the Yemeni civil war was reached in April 1963, but was quickly abrogated by both sides. Despite the continuing Yemeni war, diplomatic relations between Saudi Arabia and the United Arab Republic were restored. Prince Talal and several of his supporters returned in February 1964 and renewed their allegiance to King Saud and the Faisal government.

In late March 1964, Faisal had the King accept a decision by the royal family and the *ulema* (body of Islamic religious leaders) which reduced King Saud's powers. The Royal Guard was removed from his personal command and placed under the Ministry of Defense and Aviation; the royal court was abolished; the

King's income was cut in half and that of the royal family reduced sharply. From March 28, 1964, Faisal was in control of the government.

Faisal continued to press his modernization program, improving education, developing communications facilities, introducing television, broadening industrialization and planning dramatic improvements in agriculture. He moved slowly, however, in the area of broadening political participation, continuing to rely on the support of the tribes and the established power relationships among the important families which controlled the government (see ch. 13, Political Dynamics).

On November 2, 1964, the *ulema* issued a *fetwa* (legal decision) deposing Saud and pledging allegiance to Faisal Ibn Abd al-Aziz as king. The following day the Council of Ministers, under Prince Khalid, confirmed the deposition decree. During the next several days the army, the governments of the several provinces and tribal sheikhs from all over the country pledged allegiance to Faisal. King Faisal retained the position of prime minister, officially combining the two posts in a decree of November 18 (see ch. 12, Constitution and Government).

CHAPTER 4

ETHNIC GROUPS AND LANGUAGES

The people of Saudi Arabia, who call themselves Arabs, form a relatively homogeneous group, sharing similar physical features, a common language, the religion of Islam, culture and values, and a belief in ultimate relationship through descent from one or two early ancestors. They are proud of their descent from the original inhabitants of the Arabian peninsula and of being the propagators of the Arabic language and of Islam. The sterotype which they admire and emulate, even though it is inconsistent with many modern trends, is that of the Bedouin Arab nomad. This stereotype is also the one believed by Westerners to typify the Arabs.

The population is virtually all Moslem and speaks Arabic, the Semitic language of the peninsular inhabitants, the one in which the holy books of Islam are recorded. Relative physical homogeneity has resulted from the historic lack of large-scale immigration into the area; such differences as are observable have resulted from small-scale immigration on the coasts and borders, from importation of slaves from Africa and from the geographic isolation of certain groups.

Several foreign minority groups are distinguished by the people as outsiders. These include professionals, merchants and entrepreneurs attracted by economic opportunities in the country; Moslems from non-Arab countries who came originally for the purpose of pilgrimage; and Western commercial and diplomatic colonies. Foreigners are concentrated in the cities of Hejaz and the oil-producing region of Eastern Province. Some foreigners, particularly pilgrims who remained in the country after their visit to the holy cities, have become assimilated to the majority of Arabic-speaking Moslems.

There are no Jews in the country today. Those of the Hejaz cities were forced out of the area in the seventh century. In Asir they remained fairly numerous until 200 years ago when they departed under pressure from the Wahhabi puritan movement under Mohammed Ibn Saud. The last Jews emigrated en masse after the Palestine war of 1946-48.

THE ARABS

According to ancient traditions, the Arabs originally were descended from two stocks, a northern and a southern. The southerners, supposedly descended from Himyar, son of Qahtan, are generally agreed to be the true Arabs, whereas the northerners, supposedly descended from Abraham, the prophet, through his son Ishmael and his descendant Adnan, are called the assimilated Arabs. Rivalry between members of the two groups was significant in early Islamic times but is of little consequence today except on the southern fringes of the country where different tribes do not become allies unless they are from the same group. The southerners have maintained a reputation as pure and as the originators of the first kingdoms of the Arabian peninsula, but the northerners acquired prestige through one of their tribes, the Quraysh, the rulers of Mecca and the tribe into which the Prophet Mohammed was born.

Most Arabs still claim to be descended from one or the other of these two stocks, both of which occur in all parts of the country. Nomadic and village inhabitants are likely to claim nobility and to be able to trace their genealogy back from four to eight generations in support of their claim; town dwellers are less likely to be able to substantiate their claim. Mere membership in a group or family which makes a claim is sufficient; it is almost impossible to trace the links from the early tribes to those of the present. Some nomadic groups are considered to be ignoble, or even non-Arab, although they share the language, religion and values of the Arabs. Usually distinguished by their occupational specialties, such groups are the Shararat sheepherders and the Sulaba tinkers; the Sulaba are also physically distinguishable. Sometimes a special name, such as Bani Khadir, is given to Arabs or Arabized immigrants whose specific origins cannot be traced (see fig. 4).

In physical type the people are Mediterranean, of medium stature, with olive to brown skin color, and eyes light to dark brown. Their hair is dark brown to black. Their heads are typically long, and body hair is moderate.

Certain differences between groups have been vaguely described by casual observers, but only a few have been measured with scientific precision, and variation within the general type is more noticeable than group homogeneity. It is generally believed that most northern Arabs are distinguishable at sight from most southern Arabs and that there is a Bedouin physical type differing in some respects from that of the townsman. Men of old urban families of Hejaz are reported to be of medium to tall stature,

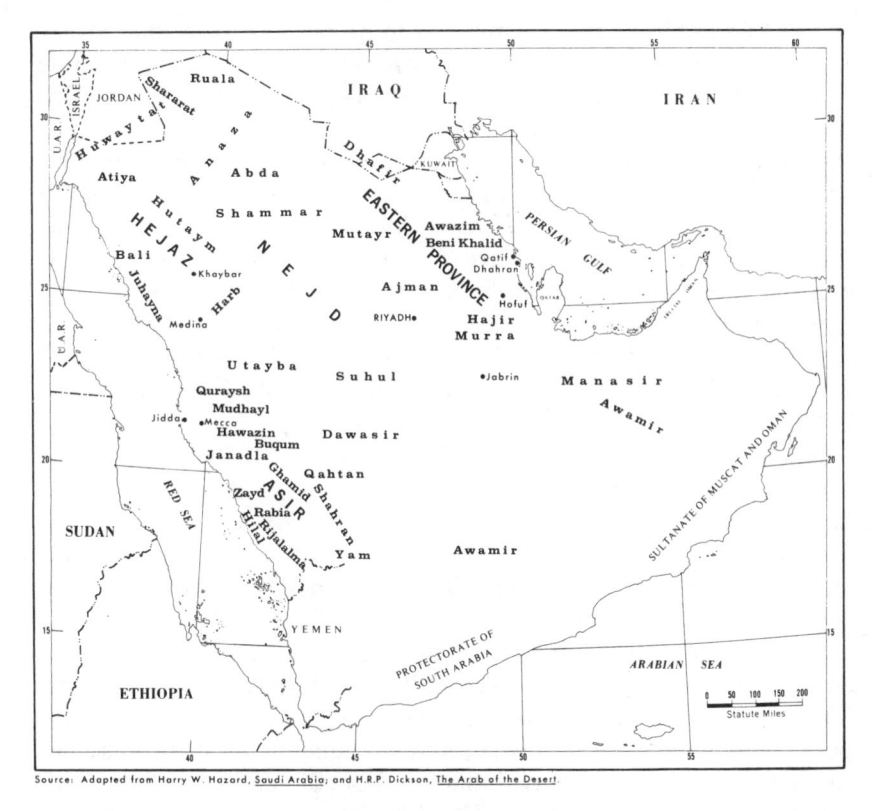

Figure 4. Selected Tribes of Saudi Arabia.

broad shouldered, heavily muscled, broad in the face, and with abundant black or dark-brown hair. Men of Asir are generally darker and shorter than others.

On the perimeters of the country contact with other peoples has occasionally resulted in darker skin color, rounded heads and slighter body frames, with varying facial features. Negroid characteristics are most noticeable on the coast of Asir; Indian and Malayan traits, in the east.

Arabs distinguish among themselves on the basis of the differences seen between the nomadic way of life in the desert and the sedentary way of life of settlements. Since there has been a steady trend toward settlement on the part of nomads, who pass through seminomadic stages, there may be no more than 200,000 to 300,000 wholly nomadic Bedouin, most of whom are in about 100 tribal groups. Yet feelings about the Bedouin—either that they are poor, dirty, ignorant, ill-fed and pitiable, or that they are to be envied their simplicity, independence, nobility and strength—are so strong that a dichotomy is seen between Bedouin and non-Bedouin.

The Bedouin consider themselves to be the purest of the Arabs. They are proud of their heritage and their way of life as it is celebrated in poetry and legends; they regard the *hadari* (settled Arabs) as inferior, the practice of agriculture or crafts as beneath their dignity and a settled life as too confining. They raise camels or sheep and goats and live in tents in the desert where the availability of water and pasture determines their cycle of migrations. Their material possessions are few and portable. They are organized into bands of related families, which migrate and camp together in all seasons, and lineages formed of related bands, which camp together in wetter seasons when the search for pasturage need not take them so far afield (see ch. 5, Social Structure).

Much of the Bedouin ethos is based on the conditions of their life before unification of the kingdom by King Abd al-Aziz Ibn Saud, when they lived by breeding animals, on fees for conducting caravans or tolls levied on caravans and travelers, on raids on each other and settled people, on payments made by weaker tribes or on settlements for protection. They learned to value bravery, hospitality, solidarity among kin and against a common enemy, and independence (see ch. 7, Social Values). In the past 50 years camel transport has been largely replaced by truck transport, raids have been outlawed, and the amount of stock has been too much for the forage available on desertlands, which have suffered from long droughts. The livelihood of the Bedouin has become dependent on breeding stock for sale and on supplemental income from wages. There has been a steady movement of individuals and groups toward a more sedentary life in towns and centers of the oil industry and a stronger tendency for some groups to acquire agricultural land.

Typically, the *hadari,* although many of them boast of Bedouin descent, consider themselves superior to the Bedouin. Some still identify themselves with a tribe from which they were originally descended, or with the one which predominated in the oasis or village in which their forebears settled. Cultivation, trade and craftsmanship are their occupations in agricultural areas or oases, whereas other service and commercial occupations are practiced in the major urban centers. The *hadari* are becoming further differentiated from the Bedouin because they can benefit from educational, agricultural, commercial and health services more readily than the nomads.

The sense of community as members of Dar al-Islam (House of Islam) is far more significant than the differences of observance in the country. The two halves of Islam's great schism are represented, however, the Sunni orthodoxy by over 90 percent of the population and the Shia branch by a few hundred thousand (see ch. 10, Religion).

The Shiites are concentrated in Eastern Province, where they are identifiable within the large community of Arab Moslems. Members of the largest non-Sunni faction in Islam, originally differentiated on the basis of views concerning the relationship between religious leadership and succession to political power, the Shiites follow certain special beliefs and rituals. Unlike Sunni Moslems, they maintain, in addition to mosques *husainiya* (special religious buildings) which are used for assembly halls, lecture halls, schools, places of celebration on anniversaries of leaders of Islam (imams) and general social halls.

The Shiites are almost always settled. They rarely are the exclusive inhabitants of a village or town, but comprise from 10 to 90 percent of the population of individual Eastern Province settlements, where their dwellings tend to be clustered together around one or more *husainiya*. In occupation they are usually farmers, farm laborers and artisans; they were among the first to be successfully employed by the Arabian American Oil Company (Aramco).

Considered to be of lower social status by the Sunni, among whom the largest landholders and political leaders are found, the Shiites marry within their own group, membership in which is usually acquired by birth rather than by conversion. Although there is no official discrimination between Shiite and Sunni Moslems and individuals of the two persuasions work well together in daily occupations, there are social barriers between the two groups, and each group resents administrative decisions which appear to favor the other.

MINORITY ETHNIC GROUPS

The largest minority in the country consists of those Arabic-speaking people who have immigrated from nearby countries, attracted by economic opportunities. They comprise teachers, merchants, professionals, contractors and businessmen, as well as unskilled manual laborers. They differ somewhat from Saudi Arabs in dialect, dress and social customs, and tend to congregate in their own groups. An enumeration of the residents and establishments of the five largest cities of the country sponsored by the Ministry of Finance and National Economy in 1962-63 indicated that the foreign population of those cities comprised from 15 to 35 percent of the total number of residents and about 30 percent of the owners and employees of businesses and service establishments. The professionals and entrepreneurs are generally better educated and more Westernized in their culture than the Saudi Arabs.

For about 2 months each year, during the period of pilgrimage, the population is swelled by over 250,000 Moslems, many of whom are non-Arabic speaking. Each year, some pilgrims stay on, either because they are too poor to return directly to their homeland, are attracted by the idea of becoming guides for their countrymen or otherwise exploiting the needs of pilgrims, or are hoping to spend their last days near the holy cities of Islam. Most of the descendants of past pilgrims live in Mecca, where they are grouped in national communities and retain their languages at least enough to communicate with arriving pilgrims from their homelands. Annual contact with their compatriots contributes to their continued sense of cultural identity as Iranians, Indians, Pakistanis or Indonesians.

Immigrants from certain countries concentrate in certain professions: for example, the Javanese as policemen, Yemeni, Sudanese and Somalis in low-prestige jobs, Egyptians as teachers and civil servants, and Palestinians as artisans and shopkeepers. In the oil industry Pakistanis, Indians and Palestinians form the largest proportion of foreign workers outside of those from the United States.

Some communities of relatively recent Negro immigrants from the Somali Republic, Sudan and other countries have maintained their house type, language and other cultural features; these communities are most common on the Red Sea coast. Agricultural communities of Negroes are found in Hejaz and Asir and at the oases of Khaybar, north of Medina, and Yabrin, southeast of Riyadh; at these oases, where the climate is malarial, Negroes are able to resist disease better than the Arabs. The Aryan and Sabiya groups of Asir are Negro. Other communities show mixtures of Arabs and Negroes; in these the Negroes are thoroughly Arabized in their language and way of life.

Members of the Western diplomatic colony at Jidda and of the commercial colony at Dhahran rarely remain in the country more than a few years. They live in communities which duplicate as much as possible the patterns of housing, education, recreation and material welfare in their home countries. Their isolation, except for professional or diplomatic contacts with Saudi Arabs, is complete.

LANGUAGES

Arabic is the language of virtually all the citizens of the country and most of the semipermanent foreign minorities. Knowledge of foreign languages is limited to the few Saudi

Arabs who have benefited from secondary and higher education, who have traveled abroad, or who have been associated with foreign military and economic missions of Aramco, and to agents for pilgrims and traders. English is the most widespread European language and the medium of diplomacy and international trade. English and French are taught as foreign languages in secondary schools (see ch. 9, Education).

The Arabic language is loved and considered beautiful by its speakers. It is for them a distinct pleasure to hear the language at the mosque, on the radio, in poetic recitation or in daily speech. The more elaborate and classical in form, the lovelier it is.

Arabic belongs to the Semitic group of languages; it is related to the ancient languages of the Bible, of Syria, Mesopotamia and Ethiopia and to modern Hebrew and Amharic. Semitic languages characteristically have three-lettered consonantal roots whose meanings are varied by the addition of vowels between the consonants and of prefixes and suffixes. For example, in Arabic, *mlk* is a root having to do with "ownership"; from it are derived *malak* (to own), *istamlak* (to master) or (get a good grip on), *mulk* (property), *malik* (king), *malakiyy* (royal), *mulkiyya* (ownership), *mamluuk* (owned), and *malaak* (angel). Arabic is written in a cursive script from right to left. The consonants are always written; vowel signs and other diacritical marks are frequently added as aids to pronunciation.

Arabic is usually considered to have three forms: classical Arabic, the language of the Koran and of traditionally educated Arabs; modern literary Arabic with its modern vocabulary accretions; and colloquial or spoken Arabic. Only the first two forms are written, and although vowels and diacritical aids occur more frequently in written modern Arabic, the grammar is little changed from classical Arabic.

Classical Arabic is learned by young Arabs who learn the text of and study the Koran in traditional schools attached to the mosques of villages or in elementary school. Its study is pursued intensively by those who continue into studies of such traditional Islamic subjects as law, theology, grammar and rhetoric (see ch. 9, Education). Classical Arabic is revered as the language in which the Prophet Mohammed expressed revelations from God. Conservative Arabs believe that the Koran, in which these revelations were recorded, is desecrated by translation. In the first centuries after the death of Mohammed the language was studied and its grammatical elements carefully defined. Poets, lawyers and theologians used this refined form of Arabic. Relatively little changed in the course of thirteen centuries, classical Arabic is used by scholars all over the Arabic-speaking world and sets the ideal standard for speech and writing.

Modern literary Arabic is used in the press, for radio and television broadcasts, and for writing about modern subjects. In it the vocabulary of classical Arabic has been expanded by borrowings from other languages and construction upon Arabic roots. The word "film," for example, is used in its original form in the singular but is given an Arabic plural form, *aflam*. Modern Arabic is not pronounced in a uniform manner but varies according to local colloquial pronunciations and to the amount of classical Arabic known to the speaker.

The various dialects of colloquial Arabic differ from classical Arabic notably in vocabulary, in the lack of certain grammatical features, and in the lack of written form. They differ from each other primarily in pronunciation, in the use of different vowels on the consonantal roots and in the use of borrowed words of various origins, but oral communication between people from different parts of the country is usually possible. Differences are generally greater between the dialects of Bedouin nomads and settled people than between the town dialects of different regions of the country.

The spoken dialects of the Arabian peninsula are believed, by their speakers and by others, to be closest to the classical language which found its supreme expression in the Koran. The dialect spoken by the Bedouin is reputedly the most nearly pure; they are very proud of their position as ancient inhabitants and inheritors of the vehicle of the sacred book.

In daily conversation all Saudi Arabs speak their local dialects. Educated people use a varying number of terms and words from classical Arabic and modern terms from literary Arabic—the higher the degree of education, the greater their use; the more classical the usage, the more it is understood by other educated persons. On formal occasions the educated speaker attempts to use formal expressions of address and to employ classical grammar and vocabulary, although the result is frequently basically a learned and archaized form of the individual's own dialect. Only a few Koranic scholars and literary persons can speak good classical Arabic, but the ability to speak any approximation of it is a source of prestige.

Those who cannot write hire professional scribes for their correspondence and petitions to government officials. The scribes, usually not well educated, attempt to write classical Arabic or to record colloquial Arabic phonetically.

GOVERNMENT POLICIES

Officially there is no discrimination among groups of citizens in the realm of public administration or in access to education, health services or housing. All Moslem Arabs are considered to be brothers and to be equal before the government as before God. The Shiite minority of Eastern Province, however, sometimes feels that it has been administratively discriminated against. Except in one or more towns in the Qatif oasis area, all administrators are part of the Sunni majority.

Moslem noncitizens have access to health, labor bureau and other services but are subject to deportation by the government if it feels that they are taking jobs needed by citizens or are in conflict with a citizen or with the law of the land. Non-Moslems are always somewhat beyond the pale as nonbelievers in Islam; Christians are officially tolerated, but the presence of Jews is strictly forbidden.

In civil and legal matters involving Saudi citizens, citizens and foreigners alike are subject to the religious and civil laws of the country. Foreigners frequently leave the country rather than face prosecution by an Islamic court.

Since the development of the oil industry and the beginning of modernization the country has been more hospitable to foreigners than in the past. Until the late 1930's Moslem foreigners were welcomed as pilgrims—and the continued residence of some was permitted, especially if they catered to the needs of their countrymen in the pilgrimage season—but few non-Moslems were permitted to remain in the country. Regulation of the mobility and business activities of Christians has been greatly relaxed during the past generation. Non-Moslems are not permitted to visit the holy city of Mecca.

The government has recognized the need for skilled labor, teachers and technical and professional advisers until such time as Saudi Arabs can be trained for the positions now filled by foreigners. It has accepted the recommendations of the Arab League requiring preferential hiring of nationals of the League countries after the skills of the local nationals have been exhausted. Lebanese, Syrians, Sudanese and Jordanians are the most readily acceptable representatives of these countries. Egyptians comprised a sizable proportion of foreign workers in 1962 when diplomatic relations with Egypt were broken and most of them left the country. The oil industry is cooperating with the government in the training of Saudi Arabians for responsible and skilled positions. It reduced the proportion of foreign personnel in its operations from 34 percent in 1948 to 20 percent in 1964 (see ch. 21, Labor).

Naturalized citizens are in a better position in case of labor or civil disputes than foreigners, who are liable to deportation. Pilgrims have always been permitted to work as migrant laborers in the vicinity of the holy cities of Mecca and Medina for several months about the time of pilgrimage each year, but they are not generally encouraged to remain in the country. If a pilgrim wishes to stay for a year or more, he must acquire a sponsor and a residence permit. Once a permit is granted, it can be renewed from year to year, and after 5 years the pilgrim can petition the king for permission to be naturalized.

The largest proportion of naturalized citizens recently has consisted of Palestinian Arabs, who started coming into the country in relatively large numbers after 1947. Beginning in 1955, Palestinians were considered a threat to local citizens in the labor market and their employment was discouraged, but in 1962 they were declared fully equal with Saudi Arabs with rights to work and to immediate naturalization.

Bedouin nomads are a matter of concern to the government, as their traditional means of livelihood has been seriously circumscribed in the last 50 years by the ban on raiding and the replacement of camels by mechanized transport. Two major policies of Abd al-Aziz Ibn Saud toward the Bedouin have been continued—payment of annual grants-in-aid and encouragement of settlement (see ch. 3, Historical Setting). Although the economic contribution of the Bedouin, who produce meat and animal products through animal husbandry in the desert, is recognized, measures for the improvement of the conditions of their livelihood in the desert are not yet an important part of government programs. Moreover, the difficulties involved in enforcing pasture management or measures to prevent overgrazing by the nomads is recognized (see ch. 19, Agriculture).

Grants-in-aid to Bedouin tribes were initiated in part to ensure their loyalty but also in recognition of the economic and social changes which were affecting the Bedouin and tending to increase their impoverishment. The grants appear as an item in the annual budget. They are disbursed to Bedouin sheikhs at specified distribution points in the winter, when the nomadic groups are congregated in largest numbers.

Settlement of Bedouin through the Ikhwan movement sponsored by Abd al-Aziz Ibn Saud at the beginning of the century had several purposes: concentration of tribal groups to ensure better control over their loyalty, proselytism of the puritan Wahhabi form of observance of Islam subscribed to by Abd al-Aziz and introduction of the economic benefits of sedentary agriculture. Encouragement of settlement through the digging of wells, grants of agricultural equipment and land where it is available or can be reclaimed, and education in methods of dry farming continue to be government policy (see ch. 19, Agriculture). In the distribution of agricultural land leases, priority is given as far as possible to the tribes which previously used the land for grazing.

Purposeful settlement of the Bedouin has not been altogether successful, and they are more likely to become sedentary on an individual voluntary basis than under government fiat. New developments encouraged by the government had indirectly effected a tendency to become sedentary. Bedouin attracted to the new wells along the Trans-Arabian Pipeline, the so-called Tapline, have formed permanent towns; the oil industry has attracted Bedouin employees who become accustomed to the cash, material goods, housing and services available to them in towns; and to some the availability of housing has become important. Whereas it used to require a few generations for a nomad family to become completely settled, individuals are changing their ways with greater rapidity.

CHAPTER 5

SOCIAL STRUCTURE

The society, strongly influenced by the Islamic teaching that all Moslems are brothers in the religious community, shows remarkably little differentiation by social rank. High individual status depends on family affiliation, good financial resources, higher education or an important position in government service, but there is no discrimination in social relations between individuals of differing status.

Outside of the longstanding trading centers of Hejaz with their commercial interests and political centralization, social status did not depend heavily upon economic success or political position until after the consolidation of the kingdom by Abd al-Aziz Ibn Saud (see ch. 3, Historical Setting). Until the vigorous post-World War II exploitation of oil, with its concomitant introduction of modern technology, need for skilled labor and infusion of money into the economy, there was little scope for the development of significant economic differences. In the agricultural areas, the lives of village headmen and tribal leaders were not much differentiated from those of their fellowmen. In the cities there were ruling families, a few rich merchants and a few learned scholars, but no generalized division into classes.

Slavery was a social institution of the country until recently. Slaves were not treated as a separate caste or excluded from personal relations with anyone in the society. Rather they were in a position of trusted servants, either in the field, as agricultural workers or overseers, or in the house, as domestic servants and family retainers. Frequently slaves were given positions of great responsibility or were brought into the family through adoption or marriage. They lived in the family compound, took meals with the family, and shared the fortunes of the family. Individual freed slaves have risen to prominent positions in the country; others have remained with their family patrons as retainers or have become trained for skilled positions in modern enterprises.

The government first attempted to forbid slavery and the importation of persons for the purpose of slavery in 1936. In late 1962 the complete suppression of slavery was proclaimed, all slaves were declared freed, and the government undertook to compensate former slave-owners. The official policy is that all former slaves are to be treated as equals with other citizens.

The society is notable for its lack of organization for recreational, social, economic or political purposes. The government forbids organization of associations or clubs for other than cultural or athletic purposes, and large nonreligious public gatherings are limited largely to soccer games.

Kinship ties and recognition of mutual obligations within the kin group have always been the most important elements in social organization. Every member of a kin unit, whether born or adopted into it, shares in its status and the mutual sense of identification felt by members, and affiliation with a kin group of high or low status has been one of the most important determinants of social position.

The patrilineal extended family is the basic functioning social and economic unit (see ch. 6, Family). Larger kin units—lineages and tribes—are also major determinants of social relations. Lineages consist of several extended families related by descent from a common male ancestor four or five generations earlier. Each is generally only as large as the number of male descendants from a remembered ancestor of a few generations back, with their dependents. Tribes, the most inclusive kin units, are composed of related lineages tracing descent from a common legendary or historic ancestor; they constitute relatively independent sociopolitical units. Some are large, having thousands of members, and others are small, consisting of only a few lineages. In most tribes the claim of common descent can no longer be substantiated, but in a few important ones the genealogies are carefully preserved.

In the period since World War II, new opportunities for social mobility have appeared. The impact of industrialization, combined with continuing changes resulting from the unification and pacification of the kingdom, has been tremendous in the social as well as in the economic sphere. The autonomy of pastoral and agricultural kin groups has lessened, and that of individuals has increased, as they have opportunities to earn cash wages, acquire material possessions, and become independent of family economic activities. A new group of entrepreneurs, small contractors, lower government employees and professionals has appeared. The high prestige group is still dominated by established families, but it now includes individual concessionaires for large foreign companies, and government officials as well. Membership in this group can still be acquired through marriage, but it is increasingly accessible through education, economic enterprise and good social or governmental connections.

NOMADS AND SEMINOMADS

In desert regions kinship is the primary organizing principle. Each unit usually herds the animals owned by its constituent extended families in a certain territory or performs its service in a certain region.

The most cohesive unit within any large kin group is the lineage, consisting of a few extended families whose actual relationship is known and whose common interests are important. The lineage is the unit within which most economic and social problems are worked out. Among the camelherding nomads, it is usually the unit which moves together during the winter wandering season and settles with related lineages near sources of water in the dry summer season. Among the sheepherding seminomads the lineage is usually the unit whose dwellings are bunched together and whose sheep are herded together.

The lineage is led by a sheikh who makes decisions with the consensus of the adult male family heads of the group. The sheikh is usually chosen from a particular family in which the right to provide leadership is inherited.

Combinations of related lineages in tribes are common among the nomadic Bedouin and seminomadic herders, who together constitute about 50 percent of the population. Historically the function of tribes as political units defending the territory roamed by its constituent lineages was most significant for camelherding nomads, but membership in a given tribe was unstable. The trend was for tribes to grow, then to break up into segments, and later perhaps to grow again with accretions. Combinations of kin groups under the leadership of a strong lineage were frequent. Weaker dependent tribes went through a process of becoming clients, of achieving a symbolic blood relationship, and finally of becoming absorbed into the stronger tribe. As a result, in groups larger than the lineage, most kinship relations are fictitious rather than actual.

Some lineages which had once been nomadic but have become permanently settled have maintained ties with a tribe of which they were once a part, but others eventually became more identified with the village in which they settled. Since a large amount of prestige is accorded to those who belong to tribes reputedly descended from either of two ancient putative Bedouin ancestors, Qahtan and Adnan, members of some tribes, such as the Tamin, which have long abandoned the nomadic way of life for settlement in villages and towns, are proud to maintain their tribal affiliation.

Leadership in the tribe is vested in a sheikh who is usually the headman of the leading lineage of the group. His possession of authority implies good heredity and respected personal qualities more than personal power or superiority. Loyalty to him on the part of members of the group is expressed through prominent headmen and is directed as much to his lineage in respect of its status as to him as the incumbent sheikh.

The sheikh regulates disputes within the tribe, makes decisions on affairs of mutual interest to its members, and represents the tribe in its relations with outsiders and with the government, from which his group seeks subsidies and services. He holds regular open council (*majlis*) for the hearing of complaints and conduct of tribal business. The informal consensus of the sheikhs of lineages in his tribe is important for his decisions (see ch. 12, Constitution and Government).

The relative strength of a tribe or tribal confederation, and its ability to maintain size and cohesiveness, depended traditionally on its ability to defend itself and its weaker dependents, on its ability to claim loyalty from a large group of related kin, on the size of its herds, and on its reputation in terms of actual prowess or leadership. Since the unification of the country it has become more important for the tribes, through their leaders, to maintain good relations with the central government. Loyalty to a sheikh, still nominally based on kinship, frequently depends on his recognition by the ruling family and his ability to obtain territorial concessions or new wells and other public services.

VILLAGES

In the village, organization is based on the local territorial unit as well as on kinship. Each village tends to be a separate unit, dependent upon agriculture. It has vital ties to the nomads who sell animal products to the villagers in exchange for staple foods and manufactured items, and to the towns upon which it is dependent administratively and commercially. The loyalty of the villager is strongly identified with the village unit, as it is with his family and lineage which are settled there. His knowledge of the outside world is frequently limited to a few nearby settlements. The young man who has left the village for the region of the oil industry or for one of the big towns almost always returns to his home village to get married and maintains ties with his family.

Kin relations are important, and whole villages or whole sections of villages consist of families who consider themselves related through a common male ancestor. The life and social position of the individual herder or villager is determined by his membership in a particular extended family and by its position within a larger kin group. Relations with other kin groups and with the government are usually carried out by the headman of the group.

Some villages are inhabited exclusively by the members of a single kin group. This is most characteristic of the upland villages of seminomads who are still pastoral for a large part of the year or of small oasis villages originally settled by part of a single tribe in whose traditional territory the source of water was found or developed.

Other villages are characterized by the coexistence of more than one kin group. The community forms an entity of virtue of common residence and common economic pursuits. In the past the need for defense against nomadic raiders was a strong tie between villagers. Many long-settled agricultural villages are examples of this type of residential community. Newer settlements of more than one kin group include Ikhwan (religious brotherhood) communities created by Abd al-Aziz Ibn Saud to settle nomads and ensure their loyalty, new settlements made possible by the digging of wells along the oil pipeline at the northern frontier, settlements of industrial workers in the oil region, and agricultural development projects.

Lineages form residential units within a village, their members living in dwellings placed close together, frequently owning agricultural land near their dwellings in common, and sometimes giving their name to one section of the village. If there are differences in religious practices, as between Sunni Moslems and Shiite Moslems in the villages of Eastern Province, or in occupation, as in desert villages where some lineages specialize in artisanry, separateness between lineages is stronger than if the activities of all the inhabitants are more similar (see ch. 10, Religion). Whereas there may be some feeling of superiority or inferiority between lineages, rivalries are usually friendly.

Leadership in the villages rests with a headman chosen usually from a particular leading family. Like the sheikh of the nomads, the village headman holds *majlis* which all adult men may attend; he makes decisions based on the advice of the headman of the village families and that of the *qadi* (religious judge) if the village is large enough to have one. At the *majlis* the headman assigns community functions, such as mosque maintenance, street cleaning and so forth.

In smaller oasis villages all inhabitants are wage laborers; in most, agriculture is the primary activity. Craft or trading specialties are limited, and few work at these occupations exclusively. The village headman and imam (religious leader) are occupied in the same economic activities as their fellow villagers. Agricultural tasks are carried out together by family groups. Guild or trade associations do not exist.

In villages consisting of a single kin group, the elders and the headman occupy their positions as respected leaders within the kin group and have the support of all its members. In villages consisting of several kin groups, the authority of the headman stems from his position as head of his own kin group, from the hereditary reputation of his group, and from his personal qualities.

The position of the headman is confirmed in larger villages through his appointment as emir by the government. The headman of each village is part of an administrative hierarchy in which he is responsible to the emir of the next highest administrative unit (see ch. 12, Constitution and Government).

In addition to the headman, larger villages may have other influential persons. The *qadi* is versed in *sharia* (Islamic law), and his advice is sought by the headman as well as by other family heads in cases where interpretation of *sharia* is pertinent. The imam is the leader of religious services at the mosque and frequently is the teacher at the religious school. Other influential people are teachers in government schools and government representatives involved in public works.

There are few institutions in the village common to all the inhabitants. Public wells serve a village or one of its quarters. Sometimes a plot of land outside the village is used for religious celebrations. In the center of the village are the mosque, the school, if a government school has already been built under the expanding educational program, the *suk* (marketplace), and sometimes a street or two of small shops. Sometimes a small village has a cafe, or a larger village, several neighborhood cafes, at which the men spend their leisure time, but most visiting and coffee drinking takes place with fellow men of the lineage in the house.

TOWNS

In towns, where social organization is based also on occupational and commercial relationships, the family is still fundamental. Larger kin groups and the maintenance of relations within them are important only when a group is politically or economically powerful or has a longstanding affiliation with a well-known tribe. The most outstanding such kin group—that of the royal family, which is part of the Anaza tribe—is wealthy, and it holds eminent political power.

The towns historically have been the economic, manufacturing, trading, commercial, religious, educational and cultural centers. In them is a small group of prominent families with high status and a large group of workers differentiated mainly by occupation

—unskilled laborers, porters, small artisans and shopkeepers. Since World War II, differences between the two groups have increased, particularly as regards exposure to Westernization, and a middle group of merchants, teachers, master craftmen and government employees has grown.

The town centers of large oasis regions, such as Unayza, Burayda and Hofuf, include in the upper stratum the traditional leading families from which government appointments are made, the religious judges and scholars, a few merchants and a few landowners whose gardens are tended by tenants and hired laborers. In the older cities of the Hejaz this stratum includes more religious scholars and the more or less hereditary elite of established families and wealthy merchants. In Riyadh, the administrative capital, where good connections with the royal family are important, the upper stratum includes high government officials and a relatively large number of tribal sheikhs maintaining their ties with the government. The newly developed industrial towns have a large proportion of successful contractors and Westernized industrialists.

Towns, like the rest of the society, generally lack clubs or gathering places. The two main centers of activity and social intercourse are the site of the administrative buildings and the *suk* with its attendant streets of shops, grouped more or less according to speciality. Social gatherings are limited to informal visits in houses or attendance at cafes. Musical performances, public showings of cinema, and public readings are infrequent, although after 1962 they began to occur more often (see ch. 15, Public Information). The model industrial area on the outskirts of Jidda, which was projected in 1964-65, was to include a mosque, schools, playgrounds, a marketplace, a public library, and police and fire posts, but not community centers or club buildings. However, in the fall of 1964, the Ministry of Labor and Social Affairs announced its intention to establish youth centers in 10 cities, each of which would include an auditorium and recreational facilities as well as a reading room. One women's club was reported to have been formed in Riyadh and to be participating in welfare activities. In 1965 apparently the only sporting associations were soccer teams which completed within the country and against foreign teams. Other sports included horseracing, yachting and trapshooting.

SOCIAL STATUS AND MOBILITY

The social status of the individual is traditionally determined by his membership in a certain lineage, the members of which share high or low status as a group. The lineages acquired their position historically. Most of them were composed of camelherding nomads whose mobility and independence and ability to live in the desert enabled them to dominate in certain regions. Considering themselves to be descendants of the original Arabs, camelherders and their distant cousins who are no longer nomadic claim to be the noble Arabs. Other lineages acquired high status through association with Mohammed, the Prophet of Islam, or through scholarly knowledge of the traditions of Islam. Descendants of the former are called shorfa (sing., sherif), and prominent descendants of the latter who still maintain a scholarly interest in religious traditions and law constitute the *ulema* (see ch. 10, Religion). Still others owed their high status to commercial success or the possession of political power.

The strength of the traditional concept of nobility as applied to camelherders and the respect or fear that settled people felt toward the nomads resulted in the general ascription of lower status to those whose lives were based on different economic activities or who had become dependent upon the camelherders for their physical safety (see ch. 7, Social Values). Thus, sheepherders had less status because of their relative lack of mobility and ability to defend themselves; cultivators had less status because they worked on the land; and those whose occupations were traditionally disdained, especially tinkers and smiths, had lowest status.

Since social status was inherited, occupations, opportunities for marriage arrangements and for social mobility were limited by membership in a kin group and the status traditionally assigned to it. Since World War II, however, these limits have become more flexible. Much importance is still attached to descent and traditional family position, which in the towns is also usually identified with wealth, political power, and religious education and in the rest of the country with ownership of land or livestock, but there are now several other paths of social mobility. Among these are economic success, governmental service, marriage alliances, and education and training.

The earlier, rather static and closed society has been opened by the receipt of large revenues from oil and closer contact with the Western approach to industrialization and with modern cultures abroad. New skills and occupations, which were unknown before the exploitation of oil, provide opportunities for individuals to move out of the social position they were born into. The increased role of the government, in the form of subsidies, development projects and social services, and its need for personnel have permitted many to acquire money, material possessions and education, which are appurtenances of status. A small number of women of wealth and high status have acquired a taste for sophisticated Western-style clothing and beauty parlor hair fashions and have begun to play a role of leadership in social service.

The nomadic and seminomadic sheikhs whose prestige was formerly dependent upon the loyalty of their tribes and recognition by other tribes are now benefiting from the profits of invested governmental subsidies and appointments to official positions. Some have acquired what they would formerly have scorned—agricultural lands, especially in reclaimed projects, or city properties (see ch. 7, Social Values). Others have been able, because of their prestige as tribal leaders, to make advantageous marriages for themselves or their sons and daughters.

Through education, technical training, commercial success or appointment to a position in the government, a significant portion of the population, particularly in the cities, moved to middle-level social positions as shopkeepers, skilled workers, traders, office workers and professionals. The acquisition of wealth in one of these positions sometimes led in turn to even higher social status.

Education, particularly in the traditional form of learning of the Koran and scholarly interpretations thereof and of Islamic law, has always been desired and respected. In the modern period, secular education and technical training are taking their place as factors imparting prestige in themselves and contributing to the achievement of wealth and position. Illiterate villagers and seminomads are demanding education for their children, and technical training institutions are enrolled to capacity. Higher education, particularly abroad, is highly desired by those who can afford it. The educated young men who are becoming the elite of government service have a basic desire to help their country change in the direction of modernization within its traditional Islamic framework.

The oil industry has provided opportunities for acquiring money and training. Some workers attain skilled or supervisory positions in the industry; others earn enough money to invest it in business or in land. Those who have been most willing to move to take jobs in the oil industry have been nomads and seminomads, whose ties to the land are less strong than those of villagers (see ch. 21, Labor). Villagers, particularly from Nejd and Eastern Provinces have followed the nomads, however, and all have sought the visual benefits of wage earning—cash in the pocket, permanent housing and other material goods. Whereas cultivation and other work with the hands have always been denigrated by the nomad, who refuses to take laboring jobs, he is willing to work with machines and frequently acquires prestige-making skills faster than others.

In most agricultural regions, economic circumstances are such that there is a significant difference between those who own enough agricultural land to make a living and those who must become tenants or sharecroppers because their own properties are too small. The latter tend to get further and further into debt to the successful landowners whose well-being and prestige are relatively great. It is better to own a small plot than to own no land at all, however. Men who leave their villages to take paid jobs usually return often enough to ensure the continuation of their landownership. Others, who have had the means to become property owners in their villages only after some time at industrial jobs, are using their prestige as owners to compete for social position with the established families or to acquire position through marriage to a girl of prominent family.

CHAPTER 6

FAMILY

All social relations are at least indirectly tied to family considerations, and the family is the source of each individual's social identity. In practice, family obligations take precedence over all others. Both economic and political life are organized in terms of the family or extensions of it. Among nomads and village cultivators alike, the family is largely a self-sustaining economic unit; in the towns the typical business enterprise is the family concern consisting of fathers, sons and brothers, or uncles and nephews.

In the political sphere the fundamental unit is the extended family and beyond this the lineage. Relations between the people and the central government are carried out through the leaders of kin groups, and the heads of important families strongly influence the government. Family ties play a significant role both in business and government, and disregard of them is generally regarded as reprehensible.

Family matters are regulated according to *sharia* (Islamic law) as set forth in the Koran and the Hadith (recorded sayings and actions of Mohammed) and interpreted by *qadis* (Islamic judges). The law is concerned with such things as filiation of all children in the family of the father, the limitation of the number of simultaneous wives to a maximum of four, the right of a father or guardian to arrange marriage for a daughter, the rights of women to own and inherit private property and to obtain support from their husbands, and the rights of multiple wives to equal treatment from their husband. Other aspects of the family life, such as the veiling and seclusion of women and the strength of mutual obligations within the patrilineal family, are matters of general custom.

STRUCTURE

Composition

Families and kin groups are organized around related males, and descent is traced in the paternal line. The normal family unit is the extended family; several related extended families form lineages. Lineages related through common descent from a certain male ancestor form kin groups known by several different terms in Arabic but usually referred to in English as tribes. The most cohesive tribes are found among the nomadic Bedouin, related groups of whom migrate within specified territories, and among influential settled Arab families, within which it is particularly advantageous to maintain close ties. The members of a kin group are expected to give aid and assistance to their paternal kinsmen and, in turn, may call upon them in time of need. A patriarchal relationship is typical, with the father or head of a lineage making major decisions.

Marriages are arranged within the kin group and are preferably between the children of brothers or other male relatives, and newlyweds as a rule reside in the home of the husband's father or live close by. Most marriages are monogamous, but some men have two or more wives. Wives are considered part of their husband's family, as long as they are married, but ties to their own paternal kin are maintained.

The family household usually includes an extended family, three generations being represented—a man and his wife or wives, their unmarried sons and daughters, and the married sons with their wives and children. Upon the death of the grandfather, the head of the family, one of the sons becomes the new head, and the other sons usually form new family households. It is common for mothers to have a child every year or so, and, although infant mortality is high, families characteristically have many children. Where a husband has established his own family residence, it is common for one or more of his relatives, parents or siblings, to reside with him.

Authority and Responsibility

The Saudi Arab husband is expected to exercise his authority in all family decisions involving outside activities and obligations. Nominally, he makes decisions regarding the family invitations to relatives or friends for a celebration, the education of the children and marriage arrangements. Frequently the husband considers a question or action before it has been discussed by the rest of the family and he simply informs the group of his decision. Other times the decision is made after consultation within the family or pressure from the women. In actions affecting his parental family the husband should and ordinarily does follow the course decided upon by his father.

The well-being of a man's kin takes precedence over that of his wife's family. Activities within the home, however, are under the authority of the wife. She directs the servants, children, daughters-in-law and, to some extent, the men themselves in the maintenance of the household routine. This is her privilege and responsibility.

Relations between husband and wife, or wives, are ideally characterized by respect and consideration. Although a wife should accept her subservient relationship to her husband, she nevertheless has the right to expect kindness from him. Companionship between husbands and wives is relatively limited; their respective relations with close relatives and friends of the same sex are usually extensive and intimate.

Should the husband have more than one wife, it is expected that he keep each in separate quarters. Sometimes a second wife is brought into the household of the first wife, but her presence is regarded as an unethical infringement upon the rights of the first wife unless she has given her approval. So long as a husband observes the Koranic prescription that if he takes more than one wife he should treat them equally and so long as he does not flaunt his preferences among the women, the wives apparently get along reasonably well together.

For all practical purposes, women's activities are confined to the home. If they go out in public, they usually are veiled and chaperoned by a servant or a male member of the family. In public and sometimes in private, when male strangers are present, the woman wears a face covering of black cloth in addition to a black cloak which covers her from the top of her head to her ankles.

Guardianship over the children is legally exercised by the father or his male relatives, although children of divorced parents may be actually cared for by their mother for the first few years. Responsibility for the support of wives and minor children falls upon the father or, in his incapacity, upon his relatives; in this case it is expected that any property which has accrued to minors through gifts, inheritance or endowments will be used for their support. The mother is in no way financially obligated to assist the father in his responsibility for her support and that of their children even if she is wealthy.

Inheritance

An estate is generally divided among those eligible to inherit as defined by the Hanbali version of Islamic law, although other interpretations following the alternative legal systems are permitted (see ch. 10, Religion). Special bequests can be made if they do not exceed one-third of the value of an estate after debts are paid. Ordinarily, from the remainder of the estate, sons receive twice as large a share as daughters. If there are no children in the family, the wife inherits one-fourth of her husband's estate; otherwise she receives one-eighth. A husband, however, receives either one-half or one-fourth of his deceased wife's estate, depending upon whether or not there are children. Daughters have legally recognized inheritance rights, but frequently these are ignored or circumvented by male relatives.

LIFE CYCLE

Childhood

Within the first year of marriage it is expected that a child will be born, and a large number of children is desired. Although marriage itself confirms the maturity of the individuals involved, only upon the birth of a son are the parents regarded fully as adults. Symbolic recognition of this event is signified by a change in the names by which the parents are known. Among friends and relatives, parents henceforth are ordinarily addressed as the father or the mother of so-and-so (the name of the first son). The birth of a child is celebrated by visits from relatives and friends, who are served food by the parents—meat if the parents can afford to sacrifice a lamb.

Children are regarded as bringing a blessing to the home, and a common felicitation is "may you have many children." Special value is placed on sons; it is said that their achievements will add to the reputation of the family, whereas daughters will "build someone else's house."

A son is usually given a name a few days or a week after his birth. Before the announcement of the child's name he is usually known by the name Mohammed. Sometimes the paternal grandfather is given the privilege of naming his grandson.

Children are cared for by their mother and older sisters until they reach the age where they can dress, feed and generally look after themselves. Boys are thought to achieve this level of maturity about 2 years before girls, at about the age of 7. From the time they are able, children begin to help with the work of the household, and little girls are expected to care for their younger brothers and sisters. Until the age of about 7 or 8, there is relatively little difference in the activities of the two sexes, but thereafter boys are more in the company of their fathers, and girls are progressively restricted to the home and to the company of females.

Boys are usually circumcised between the ages of 3 and 7. Several boys may be circumcised at the same time and at a common ceremony. The event is generally treated as a social function, but it has overtones of a religious nature. A boy is expected not to cry during the operation to show onlookers he is able to act like a man.

Mothers tend to be partial toward their sons, but fathers are likely to treat sons and daughters about equally. Each parent, however, generally has a favorite among the children, often the eldest son. Fathers are apt to be indulgent with their children during the early years but more rigorous after they have reached the age of 7 or 8. Mothers are most considerate and friendly toward their daughters in the years just before the girl's marriage, which will take her away from the parental home. Punishment is meted out by either parent as the need for it arises. Use of physical chastisement in teaching respect and good manners during the preadolescent years is common, but, after children reach maturity, they are treated the same as adults, who are shamed into proper behavior.

Marriage

Marriage is regarded as a civil contract. It is arranged by parents on behalf of the young people, and the prospective husband makes a bridal payment to the father of the girl. It is formalized before a *qadi*, a marriage registrar or another respected member of the community in the presence of a witness for each family.

Ideally, the bride and groom should be first cousins related in the paternal line, and occasionally they actually are, but marriages between more distant relatives are more common. Most unions are monogamous, although a man may legally have as many as four wives. Bachelors and spinsters are practically nonexistent, and widows, widowers and divorcees almost inevitably remarry.

Marriage customs vary somewhat in different parts of the country. In the towns and villages they are usually arranged by parents or relatives without the bride and groom seeing each other until the day of the wedding. The bridal payment is usually made in cash. A *qadi* officiates at the making of the contract, or an official recorder acknowledges the intended union. Divorce is less frequent than among the Bedouin; polygamy, on the other hand, is more common.

Among the Bedouin, women are less restricted in their social contacts and are usually not veiled. It is not uncommon for a young couple to have met and talked before the making of the marriage contract. The bridal payment is frequently in kind rather than in cash. The tribal sheikh presides over the contract ceremony, or this function may be performed by a respected man of the clan.

It is considered desirable that girls marry before their sixteenth birthday, and boys usually marry between the ages of 16 and 18. However, a recent tendency on the part of fathers to demand high bridal payments for their daughters is causing the age of marriage to rise, as increased time is required to raise the money.

When the ideal marriage between the children of two brothers is possible, it is not uncommon for the young people to have been betrothed by their parents since birth. A man has the preemptory right to his father's brother's daughter, which he either exercises or explicitly renounces. His right expires upon his taking another girl as a bride. When a marriage between the children of brothers has not been arranged, the parents generally seek a partner for their child among more remote relatives or the children of friends.

Physical beauty and a pleasant disposition are sought in a bride, but the most important consideration is that of relative family prestige. Proper social status and satisfactory material circumstances are regarded as essential foundations for a successful marriage, and the general attitude is that affection should grow out of marriage, not precede it.

Marriage arrangements are usually between families of similar social and economic status, but it is always desirable to find a marriage partner with higher status than one's own child. This status can stem from a better family background, more wealth or better education. After marriage it accrues immediately to the spouse and thereafter to the children of the union. More than one family or clan has increased its status through advantageous marriages.

It is important that the bride be a virgin before marriage and a faithful wife afterward. Adultery on the part of a wife was traditionally punishable by death and is still a cause for disgrace and possibly for divorce. Dishonor is brought to both her husband and her own paternal kin by her misbehavior.

On occasion a young man who has become acquainted with a girl takes matters in his own hands and approaches her parents directly, but more often the suitor's plea is brought to the girl's father by a representative. In the case of widowed or divorced women it is acceptable for a man to negotiate his own marriage and to approach the woman directly.

Ideally, the bride and groom are not supposed to meet one another until after the terms of the marriage contract have been settled. Sometimes a girl's acceptance of the prospective bridegroom is formally ascertained in advance, but it would be considered improper for her to show interest in her prospective marriage partner.

The bridal payment is usually made, according to the contract, to the bride's father before the marriage is consummated. The money is used for the purchase of clothing for the bride, articles for her prospective home, livestock, jewelry and other property as an investment for her future security. In poorer families a substantial portion of the payment is used by the girl's father to defray the expenses of the wedding celebration. The father sometimes retains the money for his own use or to help secure a bride for one of his sons.

The marriage celebration frequently occurs in two stages, one at the residence of the girl's family and one at the bridegroom's home, where the couple will live. The occasion is one of mingled sadness and excitement for the girl's family. She is leaving them to join another family, but in taking her place as a member of the community she is bringing honor on her own family. In urban areas it is traditional for the bride to be seated on a special chair, often elevated, so that her bridal clothes, jewelry and beauty may be observed and applauded by all present. Music, dancing and singing, as well as the serving of sweets or even a full banquet, are part of the celebration at the bride's home. Friends and relatives of the bridegroom usually come to escort the bride to her new home, where there is more feasting.

Divorce

Although marriages are ordinarily entered into with the idea that they will last for the lifetime of the partners, it is not expected that they should be preserved under all circumstances, and there is no disgrace involved in divorce. Many adults have two or three marriages in their lifetime. The most common causes of divorce are incompatibility, barrenness and lack of support.

Although a man has the unqualified right to divorce his wife at any time, interfamily considerations are likely to act as a deterrent, and sometimes the solution to the barrenness of a wife or incompatibility is to take an additional wife. A man can divorce his wife by simple repudiation without stating a cause. A formal divorce can be obtained from a *qadi* for specific causes.

Women are considerably more restricted with respect to initiative in divorce than are men; and they are frequently deterred by pressures from their own families, to whom they would return after divorce. Nevertheless, women do secure divorces for cause through the office of a *qadi*. Mistreatment, lack of support or failure to maintain conjugal relations for a significant period of time are sufficient causes. The taking of a second wife by the husband without his first wife's permission is sometimes specified in the marriage contract as cause for divorce. A man who does not desire divorce demands the return of his bridal payment by his former wife's father. A divorced woman is required to wait at least 3 months before remarriage; if she is found to be pregnant, the baby is claimed by her divorced husband's family.

Death

Fear and grief over the impending death of an ailing member of the family are great, but after death has occurred people reconcile themselves to it as an act of God not to be questioned by man. References to the topic of death are avoided when possible, for to speak of it might invoke evil spirits and bring unintentional harm to an intimate friend or relative. The most telling and emotionally laden of Arab curses are those which contain the wish that the individual or someone dear to him will die.

After a death in the family men come to pay their respects to the bereaved. Women relatives and friends demonstrate their grief with tears and wailing.

Concern over the death of a child passes relatively quickly. The death of a woman is taken hard, especially if she is young, and her children are still small. Most tragic and disturbing is the death of a husband. The wife and mother of the deceased man may keep up a demonstration of bereavement for 40 days or longer.

The death of a husband usually breaks up the household, unless there is an adult son who is capable of supporting the family. Ordinarily, the older children are taken into the house of the husband's father or that of his eldest brother. Young children stay with their mother, who may return to her parents or stay in her father-in-law's house.

A widow is expected to wait for a period of 4 months and 10 days after the death of her husband, or, if she is pregnant, until after the birth of the child, before she marries again. It is considered commendable to marry a widow, and marriage to the widow of a deceased brother ensures that the family is kept together and the children are brought up among their paternal kin. Widowers may marry any time after the death of a wife.

DAILY ROUND OF ACTIVITIES

In the typical household the day begins with the first call to prayer just before dawn. After a light breakfast the day's activities begin—household work and meal preparation for the women, and work outside the house for the men and for the boys, who usually help their fathers.

The largest meal of the day is ordinarily taken in the early afternoon in the urban areas, but among the nomads it is served in the evening. Unlike villagers and townsmen, Bedouin men usually do not return home at midday. Dinner is a family affair unless there are guests who are not close relatives; in such cases the men are served apart from the women and children. In the cities it is considered impolite for an outsider to visit just before the midday meal unless he has been specifically invited for dinner. If he should happen to be there, however, he must not leave without partaking of food. After dinner it is the practice, especially for men, to take a siesta, which in the heat of the summer may last several hours.

Women who have leisure spend time visiting friends and neighbors. The *istiqbal* (fixed visiting day) is observed in the cities by women of high status, each of whom has her regular reception day—usually one a month—when she is at home to receive other female visitors. Irrespective of how they spend the afternoon, women are expected to be home when their husbands return.

In the towns, during the latter part of the afternoon, men gather with their friends at cafes to drink coffee or tea and to discuss current affairs. Early evening is also a visiting period for men, both settled and nomadic. Younger men in the cities often entertain each other with light supper in their homes and spend the evening listening to the radio or talking. Ordinarily, women do not leave the house after dark except for occasional motion picture parties in the homes of the more wealthy and for relatively infrequent visits with their husbands to the homes of relatives and intimate mutual friends.

The daily round of activities is varied somewhat on Fridays, when the men attend noonday services in the mosque and listen to the weekly sermon. Holidays are marked by religious observances and family visits. During the month of Ramadan it is customary for everyone to get up late in the day and, during the daylight hours, to work as little and rest as much as possible. Breaking the daily fast of Ramadan with their evening meal is a happy occasion that is frequently shared with family friends (see ch. 10, Religion).

TRENDS

The economic changes of the past few decades have caused innovations which will have implications for the family system in the future. Really fundamental change is not likely to be rapid, but already some women and girls are attending school and getting out of the house more frequently.

With more money to spend, Saudi Arabs have been able to travel and study in other Middle Eastern countries—particularly the United Arab Republic, Syria and Lebanon—and in the United States and Europe. These travelers have come into contact with ways of life sometimes differing greatly from their own, which they wish to imitate.

A trend among wealthy and educated men to marry relatively sophisticated and educated women from one of the more modernized Arab countries or from Turkey may have an impact on family life. There are probably not more than 100 or 200 such marriages a year, but they have an effect on a very influential group in Saudi society, in leading to greater expectations in companionship between husband and wife, free social intercourse in mixed gatherings and education for children. For a young man who is to be educated through secondary school or university, marriage is deferred past the usual age, and after his education his career depends as much upon his own contributions as on the decisions and influence of his family. The importance of family ties and obligations does not change, however.

The government recognizes that changes in the status of women are occurring and finds it desirable that women be able not only to understand the world outside the home but to participate in it. Since 1960, when the first government-sponsored girls' schools were established, the number of educational institutions for girls and women has increased tremendously (see ch. 9, Education). Female teachers, nurses and health assistants are at work in the community; women's sewing, knitting and embroidery are exhibited; women's voices are heard on the radio; and a woman's page appears regularly in newspapers. The Ministry of Labor and Social Affairs is opening women's social clubs in the leading cities to teach household arts and channel the activities of girls and women into service activities.

Participation of women outside the household is confined to members of wealthy families, and the number of educated women is still so small that their families can command very large bridal payments. In the mid-1960's the majority of city, village and nomadic women had not been significantly affected by changes.

CHAPTER 7

SOCIAL VALUES

Underlying most social practices is a fairly well-integrated system of social values. Conformity to these values was great in the past, since the individual had few alternative ways of meeting problems, and effective social sanctions were brought to bear against those who departed from behavioral norms. As a result of the repression of intertribal raiding, increases in wealth, changes in the inventory of material things, and the limited but significant impact of Western cultural elements, many of the traditional social practices have changed, and their underlying values have been somewhat challenged. The core of traditional values has not yet been shaken, however, and they continue to define the basic meanings and goals of life, for the inherited ways have been kept strong by geographic isolation and religious fervor.

DETERMINANTS OF VALUES

In the traditional scheme of life certain institutions stand out as primary reference points in the definition of the desirable ends and appropriate means of social existence. These are Islam, the family, and the Bedouin way of life. Related to all three is a strong regard for tradition itself as the regulator of individual and group actions.

Islam has been a major determinant of social values (see ch. 10, Religion). Ritual prayer, fasting during the month of Ramadan, and the giving of alms to the poor are publicly enforced obligations on all able members of the community. The precepts and proscriptions of the holy Koran and the related traditions continue to be the basic texts for the reflection of scholars, the conclusions of jurists, and the choices of action by individuals. Classical Arabic, the language in which the Koran is written, is valued as the most beautiful and perfect language in the world.

Moslems believe that, on the final day of judgment, God will decide the fate of each man to go to heaven or to hell. Therefore, piety and adherence to the Islamic concept of proper social relations are important because they bear directly upon one's position in the afterworld. Good deeds such as the forgiving of someone who has wronged you or the giving of alms may improve one's status in paradise.

The Arab is known by the family to which he belongs (see ch. 6, Family). However great his personal talents, a man without a family to back him is not likely to count for much in the community. Large families are desirable. The individual's loyalty and duty to his family are greater than any other social obligation. Family members watch over and protect each other's interests. A brother continues to concern himself with his sister's affairs even after she is married. The closeness of brothers is proverbial. Younger people are expected to take care of their elders, and this obligation is idealized as a pleasant one.

Family obligations are extended in diluted form to lineage and tribe, whose members extend loyalty and mutual assistance to one another. They are expected to lend money or food and clothing, to support each other's plans of action, to promote conciliation in cases of friction, to come to the rescue in case of need, to patronize each other's shops or services, and to charge less to one another than to outsiders.

Honor is largely a family matter. It is constructed on the fortunes and the reputation for courage, probity, and generosity of the male members of the family and tribe. Dishonor is a function of the failures and misdeeds of family members, men and women. Premarital chastity and marital fidelity of women are vital to the honor of their family.

The family is structurally oriented around its male members, and in many ways the traditional society is "a man's world." Men are looked upon as the aggressive and responsible actors in the society who give direction and enforce order. A male child is much valued in the family, and a wife's failure to produce a son is sufficient reason for a husband to divorce her or to take a second wife. To the sons is passed the honor of the family, and upon them rests the responsibility for maintaining it. In legal affairs it takes the testimony of two women to equal that of one man.

Although the large majority of the society are no longer nomads, the way of life of the Bedouin and the qualities which enabled them to dominate their desert habitat and their settled neighbors, as idealized in pre-Islamic and early Islamic literature, have been constantly valued (see ch. 4, Ethnic Groups and Languages). Identification with the Bedouin stereotype by each of the Saudi kings has been one of the great sources of strength of the dynasty. Though townsmen, the kings have made every effort to epitomize the nomadic leader. To many townspeople the term "bedouin" has long been an expression of contempt, referring to poverty of possessions and the harsh circumstances of life in the desert; yet at the same time, in apparent contradiction, they claim Bedouin origin.

TRADITIONAL VALUES

Traditional orientation toward Islam, the family, and the Bedouin ideal has resulted in the support of certain values which have determined the course of action of the majority of individuals in the society. The most virtuous are those who make the right choices in accordance with these values.

The good life is equated with piety, the following of the precepts of Islam, observance of religious obligations and provision as well as possible for oneself and one's family within the fate decreed by God. Value is placed upon acceptance of the hazards of existence and the decrees of God which determine them, although man is expected to do what he can, within the limitations of his environment, to reach his goals.

The wealthy man is expected to redistribute his gains through aid to the family, alms, and other activities for the good of the community. Hospitality and charity are duties toward relatives and strangers alike.

In relations between individuals high value is placed upon politeness, courtesy, and respect. Cordiality, warmth, and friendship are recognized social virtues, and it is considered important not only to maintain one's own reputation and honor and that of one's family but to support that of one's friends.

Priority is given to the interests and solidarity of the kin group as against those of the individual or of those outside the group. Favoritism toward family members is prevalent in the economic sphere, and maintenance of the honor and reputation of the family is an important shared responsibility. As a result, there is little interest in associations not based on kinship relations. Moreover, the social virtues are tempered by the value the individual places upon the interests of his own group. Hostility toward and deliberate exclusion of the outsider are not uncommon.

Privacy is highly respected not only by not intruding within the walls of the houses of others but also by not showing excessive interest in their affairs and by not making a display of one's own feelings in public. Women belong to the private world of the family; they are expected to withdraw from the presence of men not related to them and, in cities and towns, to veil themselves when outside the house.

If there is an ideal man, it is one with the valued qualities of the Bedouin, among which are personal bravery, physical prowess and sexual virility, boldness in opposition to outsiders, generosity within the kin group and among friends, hospitality and loyalty to Islam. The ideal woman is loyal to Islam, domestic in her activities, retiring before male strangers, and committed to the honor of her husband's family. Neither men nor women value recreation or leisure time as such. Their pleasures, such as those of the senses or those involved in social intercourse or in hearing and speaking the Arabic language, are usually part of daily life.

MODERN ELEMENTS

The traditionally valued ideals cannot be lived up to by all, but those who experience a special conflict in values are members of the few small groups whose lives have brought them into contact with new values. They include government employees, merchants who have adopted Western methods, members of the modern armed forces, industrial workers, and the new generation of young people who have pursued secular studies at home and abroad (see ch. 9, Education). These people see value in organization for particular ends, in efficiency of operation, in economy of effort. They are beginning to judge others by their performance and abilities in the modern economic sphere as much as by their family background or reputation for hospitality. They also begin to value the material rewards gained in compensation for their skills. Above all, they recognize that technical training or education in the secular field —religious education has always been valued—is the key to success and modernity, and they are eager to learn.

In certain areas new values are not entirely compatible with the old; for instance, individual instead of collective responsibility; hand skills with traditional contempt for certain manual occupations; efficient use of time with a lack of value on ordered time; secular education with exclusive reliance upon religious texts. However, although changes in the economy and in the position of the country relative to the rest of the world have been dramatic and some young moderns feel themselves to be in conflict with the values of their elders, most adjustments of values are gradual, and accommodations have been possible. The mechanical skills learned by Bedouin nomads, for example, are so new that they cannot be equated with activities which were formerly contemptible. The modernizers have had some success in persuading the conservative religious judges that innovations will, in the long run, contribute to the strengthening of the nation and the Islamic community. The roles of basic Islamic precepts and basic mutal obligations among family members have not as yet been fundamentally challenged by change.

CHAPTER 8

ARTISTIC AND INTELLECTUAL EXPRESSION

In the early centuries of Islam, the folk literature and domestic arts of the Arabs were enriched by contact with rich cultures such as those of the Byzantine Empire and Persia. Outside the Arabian peninsula a creative synthesis, nourished by the acquisition of conquered riches and of leisure time by the Islamic rulers, resulted in one of the greatest flowerings of human expression in world history. The artistic and intellectual achievements of that golden age of Islam did not, however, take permanent root in the peninsula, which remained important only as the location of the holy cities of Islam.

Until the country was opened to the influence of other Middle Eastern countries and the West, artistic and intellectual life were limited. Conditions and resources which might support artistic expression were absent. Most of the people led nomadic or semi-nomadic lives which could not accommodate nonportable art forms. The local form of Islam did not encourage artistic expression or stimulate intellectual development. Isolation from outside influences was also a discouraging factor.

Since the end of World War II, however, changes have been brought about, particularly in the arts, by the phenomenal increase in the wealth possessed and dispensed by a small elite and the emergence of a middle-income group composed of merchants and Arabian American Oil Company (Aramco) employees. Conservative prejudice against ostentation, luxury and art forms have broken down under the leadership of the royal family and wealthy groups. Towns have grown, and alongside old-style buildings, new ones, notable for an emphasis on new design and materials, fine and colorful decoration, and modern, Western-style furnishings, have been built. The craftsmen, architects and artists are generally foreigners, however, and the production of local craftsmen and artisans is declining in competition with foreign goods. In Eastern Province local builders and architects are learning new techniques, skills and design through training by Aramco. Musical performances in public and on the radio are becoming more common, and television and live theater have been introduced (see ch. 15, Public Information).

INTELLECTUAL EXPRESSION

Intellectual expression has been confined almost exclusively to the elaboration of religious dogma, the study and exegesis of the Koran and the Hadith (recorded sayings and actions of Mohammed) and grammar (see ch. 10, Religion). The most significant Arab intellectual contributions to the world, especially during the golden age of Islamic civilization, were made outside the peninsula.

Until recently, there was little understanding of the foreign thought strongly influencing other parts of the Middle East and little interest in fields other than religious dogma. The nomads and villagers had no knowledge of the outside world of thought, since they had only occasional contacts with foreign merchants or Arab sailors. Since 1953, however, radio is reaching an increasing number of Saudi Arabs (see ch. 15, Public Information). Students in fields other than theology and rhetoric—most of them educated abroad—are increasing in number, and generous scholarships are given to them by the government and by Aramco.

Interest in the Arab historic and literary heritage is growing, however. Archaeologists are uncovering traces of early civilizations throughout the peninsula; these discoveries include ancient settlements, tombs, inscriptions and fragments of pottery. Archaeological sites have been uncovered by Aramco explorations and drilling teams, and the government has indicated its intention to establish a museum to preserve the country's historical treasures.

LITERATURE

As elsewhere in the Arab world, poetry and formal prose and speech have long been esteemed as the highest of the arts. The skillful use of language is valued in itself. Moreover, the capacity to make the most effective use of the highly stylized forms of speech preferred by Arabs is a major social asset. Language style becomes as effective as logic. Each element of a literary product is regarded as an individual experience; a line in a poem need have no obvious relation to the whole, and sometimes even the words themselves seem to lose all but aesthetic significance. Within the limits of conventionally approved subject matter, appreciation of sheer rhetorical eloquence transcends any concern for internal coherence and unity.

Until after World War II, literary output was traditional in style and formal in manner. New literary forms and styles in the Arabic language, often imitating the Western models which have developed in other Middle Eastern countries, have begun to appear, and new themes more closely related to the modern scene are being introduced. Young writers have found a vehicle for literary expression in the press, which devotes space to poetry and essays; and literary-political clubs are appearing in the large towns.

Among the first works in written Arabic, and by far the greatest, is the Koran. According to Islamic doctrine, it was originally the word of God as revealed to Mohammed, and was written down by his followers after the Prophet's death. The authoritative version was established in A.D. 651. It is generally believed by Moslems that the divinely inspired style in which the Koran is composed cannot be surpassed. It has had a profound influence on all subsequent Arabian literature and has served as a model. Its language became the universal written language of the Arabs and the source of highest authority for grammarians and lexicographers. Koranic passages and formal, traditional poems describing the life of the Prophet are read at family celebrations by trained reciters and at gatherings during religious holidays, and are heard on the radio. The ability to recite the whole Koran or large sections of it from memory is greatly admired.

The classical or heroic age of Arabian literature was roughly between A.D. 525 and 622, the Jahiliyya (Days of Ignorance) before the coming of the Prophet. The models and forms established by the poets of that period have remained dominant in formal poetry. Political leaders were patrons of the poets who molded and expressed public opinion. The poet was regarded as the possessor of supernatural and oracular knowledge and magical power similar to that of a jinni. He was the repository of tribal history and a guide and spokesman for his tribe. Often a warrior as well, he strove to express in his work the ideal manly attributes of gallantry, bravery, loyalty, independence and generosity. The few fragments of poetry remaining from the period come close to being an Arabian national epic. The *Muallaqat* ("those which are given prizes or posted") anthology, dating from the early period, consists of *qasida* which are sung at the annual fair held at Ukaz, near Mecca.

Three forms of early literary expression have been preserved: the *saj*, unmetered verse or rhymed prose, which earned a sacred repute because of its use in the Koran; the *rajaz*, a simple meter evolved from the *saj*; and the *qasida*, a poem designed for singing or chanting, similar in structure and use to an ode. The *qasida* became the typical poetic form. Written in elaborate meter and style, it was governed by standardized rules; a single rhyme and meter were used. The *qasida* usually opened with a lyrical passage, continued with the description of a place, journey or event, and ended with praise of a patron or a message of ambitions or enmities. Each verse, rather than the whole poem, formed an organic whole, thus it was easy and appropriate to extract and quote single verses and passages. Descriptive passages were rich in detail, and simile was frequently used.

Poems shorter than the *qasida* referred mainly to war and revenge. Their major themes involved satirical treatment of the enemy, praise of the poet's tribe, and laments for the dead, for which women poets were particularly renowned.

During the centuries since Mohammed's death, the supremacy of the conventional *qasida* was firmly established, and the task of writing it down was carried on. The form has resisted change and has continued as the dominant form in formal written poetry, despite the obvious disadvantages of applying a poetic form adapted to tribal pursuits to the preoccupations of a developing urban life. A new form developed at Mecca, however; it was the love lyric, a modification of the first section of the *qasida*.

The strength of the poetic tradition is indicated by the fact that, despite Mohammed's reported distrust of soothsaying poets and the products of Jahiliyya, pre-Islamic poetry was not ignored; it was recorded in collections of the works of particular poets and in anthologies, the most famous of which are the *Muallaqat*, the *al-Hamasah*, and the *Mufaddaliyat*. These collections remain the major sources of the poetry of the Arabian classical age.

A *qasida* in the classical language may still be composed, but other subjects—foreign and modern—which are not relevant to the life of the early tribesmen, have been added. A group of minor poets has appeared among the wealthier elite; this group emulates and experiments with imported styles.

Unlike today's poetry, modern prose writing has few roots in the past. Nearly every author of Arabic prose before the twentieth century employed the traditional pattern of *saj*. Prose literature in the forms known to the West was, strictly speaking, nonexistent, and there was no drama or playwriting. The novel has been attempted, but most prose is in the form of essays and other writing for the press.

Although the illiterate nomad or villager has little access to the literary output of the towns, folk literature comprises proverbs and stories. Professional storytellers, whose activity reaches a peak during Ramadan, the month of fasting, are very popular everywhere. They preserve and transmit a wealth of pious, earthy or heroic oral literature that has been passed on for many generations.

Representative selections of the folk poetry of the desert and rural population have been preserved in writing and occasionally published abroad. Recited in either modified classical or colloquial Arabic, rhymed in loose meter, this poetry covers a wide variety of topics related to the daily life and values of the Bedouin and villager, genealogies and tribal histories. Much of it is humorous; some, bitterly satirical. The popular poets of tribe, village and town maintain their historic role in the formation and reflection of public opinion and the making or marring of public and private reputations.

MUSIC, DANCE AND DRAMA

The religious restriction on public performance of music, dance or drama was strictly enforced by the Public Morality Committees established by Abd al-Aziz Ibn Saud. Although these committees and the *ulema* (body of Islamic scholars) of the major cities still protest public performances which violate their puritan religious values, King Faisal has not only permitted but encouraged music, television and the theater (see ch. 10, Religion).

Music has always been very much a part of the everyday life of the Arabs, although the orthodox interpretation of Islam does not approve of it. In pre-Islamic times songs of war, love, religion and the caravan were common. In the early Islamic years under the Umayyads, Mecca and Medina were renowned as centers of musical accomplishment.

Both vocal and instrumental musical expression has continued on the informal or folk level. It forms part of the poetic tradition and in its traditional form resembles the ballad more closely than it does any other Western form. In the southwest it shows the influence of African music. Instrumental music, accompanied by a drum, has stylized meters, or rhythmic beats, which vary according to the mood and form of the music.

The professional reciter of poetry often recites to his own musical accompaniment and performs wedding poems in praise of a bride and groom. Work poems are sung by grain winnowers, date pitters, camel riders, seamen, stevedores and laborers in the oil industry, who sing individually or in groups, unaccompanied or accompanied by instruments, such as the lute, the zither, the drum and tambourine, or the one-stringed fiddle.

The music is commonly improvised by the performer, who learns by ear and plays according to an informal tradition rather than a clear-cut theory of composition. The life of a song is marked by changes introduced by succeeding generations of musicians. The ability to improvise and embellish a melody, moreover, still constitutes one of the standards by which a performer is judged. The folksong generally possesses short, easy-to-remember rhythmic phrases rather than long, complex scale constructions.

Dance is also closely associated with folk music. It is primarily a group activity and, unlike music and poetry, does not permit displays of individual virtuosity. The few professional female dancers, often coming from the Sulaba group of tinkers, tend to be thought of as vagabonds and frequently are prostitutes (see ch. 4, Ethnic Groups and Languages). Social dancing in the Western sense is not publicly accepted and, if it takes place at all, is confined to the privacy of the home. Group dancing occurs mainly on such festive occasions as weddings, circumcisions and religious holidays. With few exceptions, such as the Bedouin sword dance, men and women do not dance in the same group. Women, however, frequently dance among themselves.

There is no theatrical tradition, with the possible exception of the Shiite passion play commemorating the death of Husein, son of Ali and grandson of Mohammed, performance of which is confined to the small Shiite minority. The theater was introduced in the country in the late 1950's through the Ministry of Education to stimulate social activities among schoolboys. Major secondary schools are furnished with halls suitable for dramatic performances, and plays are performed for the public.

Films are shown privately at evening parties by wealthy Saudi Arabs, by Aramco for its foreign employees and by foreign embassies and legations. Training films are used by Aramco and in the armed forces. Programs on the Saudi Arabian television network, which was initiated on a trial basis in July 1965, are not intended strictly for entertainment; the films are largely educational and informative (see ch. 15, Public Information).

PLASTIC ARTS

The plastic arts are characterized by abstract and intricate designs in floral and geometrical motifs used in an ornate calligraphy, mosaic work and painted decoration. Sculpture is wholly absent. Painting has never flourished, although there have been a few efforts in pictorical painting by Western-educated Saudi Arabs; and drawing is part of the new modern secondary school curriculum, but is restricted to representation of natural objects, such as landscapes and still lifes. In the villages and tribes the graphic and plastic arts are confined to a few handicrafts.

Examples of the decorative arts, such as enameling, tilemaking, stonecutting, glazing, woodcarving, metalworking, calligraphy and bookbinding, are found in the homes of wealthy patrons more frequently than on public buildings. Wooden doors and shutters are also painted in geometrical designs in brilliant colors of red, blue, green, yellow, pink and black, and interior walls are cut by master masons, while the plaster is still wet, into bands of geometrical and floral decorations.

The portrayal of man or any other living creature is forbidden by Islamic law, and the importation of articles bearing the likeness of living things is forbidden by decree. Mohammed is quoted as having said that an artist who makes a caricature of the true work of God will be doomed on the final day of reckoning. The designs which are used are formalized versions of Arabic script and geometric designs or arabesques.

Crafts

Crafts are largely undeveloped. Among the best items are wooden sandals with leather bindings decorated in blue and silver inlay, brass and copper coffeepots and jewelry. Metalworking artisans have suffered from competition with imported manufactured goods, and many have been forced gradually into metal repair work. Some rugs are made from domestic goat's hair or camel's hair, but most are imported from Iran and India. The textile indstry has been patronized by the royal family and other wealthy families. There has been some concentration of the industry into larger organizations. Pottery manufacture has also declined considerably in competition with imports. A variety of wooden articles are made in Al-Hasa. Carpenters, however, usually specialize in construction and limit their artistic production to the decoration of doors, windows and gates. Pottery manufacture is limited to localities possessing sufficient clay. Jidda, which concentrates on the production of large, porous jugs used to cool water, Medina and Asir are the most important pottery centers. Baskets and mats are made everywhere for local consumption, and leatherwork is done in some villages. Nomadic tribesmen do leatherwork and weave rough cloth for their tents and camel bags and to sell in the towns for rug manufacture.

Craftwork is concentrated in Eastern Province, where most craftsmen are Shiites, and in the cities of the Hejaz. The long outer jackets or cloaks (*bisht*) worn by the men are manufactured in Eastern Province. The cloth, usually woven of yarn purchased from Bedouin women or imported from the north, is made in small workshops. The final products, from cheap cloaks to very expensive examples embroidered in gold, are cut and embroidered by tailors. A variety of wooden articles, brassware, copperware and jewelry are also made in the east. The jewelers of cities and towns, who have not suffered appreciably from the competition of imports, make silver and gold bracelets, bangles, necklaces and nose ornaments, as well as the gold and silver jeweled dagger scabbards used by members of the king's bodyguard.

Architecture

Architectural styles in what is today Saudi Arabia were not affected by the Persian and Hellenistic influences evident in ancient sites in Yemen, at Petra or at Palmyra. They remained simple and functional, accommodating a heretofore unchanging way of life. The roofs are generally flat, sometimes with crenelations on the walls surrounding them. Windows are small and usually face inward toward a courtyard.

The buildings are of local materials, usually brown or white in color. The materials used vary from sun-dried mud bricks, limestone and rock to carved coral blocks, which are found on the coast of the Red Sea. The newer palaces and government buildings are built of reinforced concrete.

Single- and two-story buildings are most common in smaller towns and villages, but the old quarters of cities have multistoried buildings crowded close together, with balconies which overhang the streets. In the hot climate of Jidda there are more windows facing outward to catch the breeze. The houses of well-off families constructed during the Ottoman regime at Taif and Jidda often have large, cool rooms with high ceilings.

Changes in architecture have followed increased prosperity, a rising demand for new palaces and other buildings, the ability to afford finer materials and talented craftsmen and the introduction of foreign styles. In Jidda and Riyadh, not only have whole sections of the towns been torn down and replaced by elaborate new buildings, but suburban buildings influenced by European styles have multiplied. Government buildings, airports and new homes for the wealthy are often the products of foreign architects and designers, who use modern technology and ideas.

The Great Mosque at Mecca and the Prophet's Mosque at Medina, the showplaces of the holy cities of Islam, have recently been rebuilt and expanded. These two great mosques are notable for their minarets and arcades, which are not usually found in peninsular mosques, and for their elaborate decoration with carving and tilework.

CHAPTER 9

EDUCATION

A modern educational system has been developed since 1926, when the first government-sponsored schools with an expanded curriculum were added to the traditional system of religious schools. The need of the country for trained administrators and the desire of leading families that their sons also benefit from modern education had also led to the establishment of small private schools in the commercial and administrative centers of the country.
education heightened, it became apparent that governmental educational facilities must be increased. Since the creation of the Ministry of Education in 1954, government-sponsored public education has become more important than private secular or traditional religious education and has expanded rapidly, both in the numbers of students to whom it is available and in the curriculum which is offered. In 1965, however, over 90 percent of the students were still at the elementary level.

The goal of the government's educational policy is to provide a basic minimum of education for the largest possible number of students and to encourage those who desire higher education to obtain it within the country or abroad. Education is to be available eventually for all—girls as well as boys. Tuition and meals in all government schools are free. Liberal maintenance grants are made to both students and their parents to ensure that attendance at school by the children will not be a hardship on the family and that equal educational opportunities are available for all. Liberal scholarships are granted to those who study abroad.

The government recognizes the importance of a curriculum of secular subjects, but it is also trying to preserve elements of traditional Islamic education. Subjects with religious orientation are still emphasized, particularly at the elementary level; religious secondary and higher education programs are operated parallel to the modern program, and separate school systems for boys and girls are maintained in accordance with the traditional segregation of the sexes outside the home.

In 1965 the rapid expansion of education begun in the previous decade was continuing. New public schools were being opened on the average of one every 3 days. Girls were beginning to receive secondary education in government-operated schools and were being given permission for the first time to go abroad for higher education. Both male and female teachers were being trained to replace the Egyptian and other non-Saudi teachers who still made up a large majority of the teaching staff at all levels. Modern techniques, including the use of closed-circuit television, were being introduced in a few of the more advanced schools, most of them in Eastern Province, where the Arabian American Oil Company (Aramco) was giving substantial assistance to the government's educational program. The scarcity of adequate school textbooks, long a problem hindering education, was being solved, as modern textbooks written for particular courses and produced in the country were being introduced into the school system. The first government-operated kindergarten was scheduled for opening in Jidda in 1966.

The universities and government schools for boys are administered by the Ministry of Education. Since their inception in 1960, however, schools for girls have been under the control of the Grand Mufti, who is the leader of the *ulema* (body of Islamic scholars) and chief judge of the country. This division of responsibilities was established in response to the demands of religious conservatives who do not favor the exposure of girls to contact with the man's world outside the home and with secular subjects in school.

The curriculum for girls emphasizes religious and domestic subjects. Boys, after a substantial amount of religious orientation at the elementary level, receive more instruction in the humanities, languages, sciences and vocational training.

The government planned to devote about 13 percent of its budget to education in 1966. Of this expenditure of SR515 million (SR4.50 equal US$1), 25 percent was to go for the construction of new schools and institutes and the expansion of existing establishments.

DEVELOPMENT OF EDUCATION

Before 1926 formal education was conducted entirely according to Islamic tradition, and beyond the elementary level it was available to only a small segment of the male population. Attendance at *kuttabs* (Islamic elementary schools) in the village or neighborhood was most common. The local imam (religious leader) was the teacher; the subject matter was sacred writings; and the learning method was rote memorization. The period of *kuttab* attendance usually began when a boy was about 6 years old and ended when he had memorized the Koran, at the age of 10 or 12.

In 1926 the Directorate General of Education was formed by King Abd al-Aziz Ibn Saud with Egyptian assistance and advice. The Directorate attempted to emulate the Egyptian system, which was of French origin. A 6-year elementary cycle, followed by a 5-year secondary cycle was introduced. It was hoped that training in this system would help to meet the country's needs for trained administrators.

Before Aramco's discovery of oil in 1938 there was neither a large-scale demand for public education nor the financial means to provide it. The exploitation of the oil, however, led to a need for modern educational facilities to meet the administrative and technical requirements of both Aramco and the government.

Even after the introduction of oil wealth and the opening of the country to Western influences, educational facilities developed slowly. By 1953 there were 326 elementary schools with an enrollment of almost 44,000 and 3 secondary schools with about 500 students.

The educational system was completely reorganized in 1954, when the Ministry of Education was formed. In 1958, Saudi Arabia and other members of the Arab League agreed upon a uniform educational system (see ch. 14, Foreign Relations). As a result the program was changed to include a 6-year elementary cycle, a 3-year intermediate cycle, a 3-year secondary cycle and a higher education program consisting of from 4 to 5 years, depending on the school. In 1960 public education was first made available for girls.

As modern educational facilities have developed, the importance of *kuttabs* has decreased. When a modern government-operated school is available, the boys are most often sent there in preference to the *kuttab*, where both the curriculum and the training of the teacher are more limited. In Asir, in isolated Nejd villages and in other places where new schools have not yet been established, boys still attend *kuttabs*.

THE PUBLIC EDUCATION SYSTEM

The three bodies in the Council of Ministers responsible for education are the Ministry of Education, which administers boys' education at all levels; the Office of the Grand Mufti, which oversees girls' education at all levels; and the Supreme Educational Council, an interministerial body which establishes and implements educational policy and supervises the educational budget. The Supreme Council is composed of the Minister of Education, the Grand Mufti and several other Cabinet ministers. In 1965 it was headed by Prince Fahd Ibn Abd al-Aziz, a brother of King Faisal Ibn Abd al-Aziz al-Faisal al-Saud.

The minister of education, appointed by the king, supervises the education of male students and oversees all schooling within the country. Under him are two deputy ministers, one concerned with the administration of education, the other with cultural affairs. At a lower level the office of the director general of education supervises teaching procedures at all levels and handles the administrative aspects of the social welfare and health of students, examinations, libraries and scholarships. The minister of education also acts as chairman of the Supreme Council for the Promotion of Arts, Sciences and Fine Arts, which selects and writes textbooks to be used in schools and translates certain educational material. Other members of the Council include authors, noted scholars, publishers and researchers.

In 1960 the Directorate General of Girls' Schools was created under the Grand Mufti to grant girls access to public education for the first time. The Grand Mufti determines the moral and physical conditions under which girls receive their education and sets the standard of education in their schools. Standards are established in consultation with the Ministry of Education. The Directorate General also administers examinations in girls' schools at all levels.

The country is divided into 16 educational districts, each with a director responsible for the fulfillment of the Ministry of Education's directives in his region. The districts, however, are allowed leeway in determining course electives and selecting textbooks to supplement the basic syllabus, which is uniform in government-operated schools. The Ministry periodically sends inspectors to public and private schools to ensure adherence to its regulations.

Elementary Level

Education at the elementary level is the focal point of the government's drive to expand the nation's educational base. It is also a major tool for fostering integration into the society of isolated segments of the traditionally oriented population. Since 1952 attendance at boys' elementary schools has increased over fourfold, and in 1964 there were over 174,000 boys enrolled (see table 1).

Elementary education consists of a 6-year program which students generally enter at the age of 6 or 7. The curriculum remains traditionally oriented and emphasizes classical Arabic and Islamic religion. History, geography, mathematics and, in some cases, English are also taught. Sports are an integral feature of boys' education.

Modern teaching methods are being adopted in place of the rote method of learning and students are encouraged to participate

Table 1. Growth of Public Education in Saudi Arabia, 1952, 1960 and 1964

Educational Level	1952 Schools	1952 Teachers	1952 Students	1960 Schools	1960 Teachers	1960 Students	1964 Schools	1964 Teachers	1964 Students
BOYS									
Elementary	306	1,472	39,920	712	4,940	104,203	1,072	9,049	174,514
Intermediate and secondary	10	133	1,351	54	617	7,301	78	1,002	113,444 [2]3,472
Religious intermediate and secondary	3	42	335	3	24	567	20	210	3,515
Vocational intermediate and secondary	1	3	37	17	202	1,964	17	n.a.	2,442
Secondary teacher training	1	6	35	3[3]	3[1]0	3[1]41	n.a.	—do—	n.a.
GIRLS									
Elementary				14	125	5,180	133	1,263	40,566
Intermediate and secondary				1	1	24	7	25	576
Teacher training				1	3	20	13	34	713

[1] Intermediate.
[2] Secondary.
[3] Figures for 1962. There were, in addition, 31 elementary teacher training schools with 387 teachers and 5,575 students.
n.a.—not available.

Source: Adapted from Saudi Arabia, Ministry of Information, *Education in Saudi Arabia*, 1963; ibid., *Education for Girls*, 1963; and Saudi Arabia, Ministry of Education, *A Brief Report on the Ministry of Education for the Year 1964–1965*, 1965.

in class discussions. Both imported and locally published books are used as textbooks and most classrooms are equipped with blackboards. Classes are large, with a teacher-pupil ratio averaging 1 to 48. Uniform examinations are administered by the Ministry of Education at the end of the elementary cycle. On graduation, usually at the age of 12 or 13, students receive an elementary certificate (diploma).

Intermediate and Secondary Level

Postelementary education is of two types—in government-operated schools or in Islamic schools operated under the Grand Mufti. In both types it is divided into intermediate and secondary cycles of 3 years each. The intermediate cycle was instituted in 1958 after it became apparent that there was a need for a transitional period between the elementary level and the more rapidly modernizing postelementary cycle. Arabic is the language of instruction in all schools, but foreign languages are introduced as part of the curriculum. The most commonly taught foreign language is English.

Religious

Islamic schooling at the higher level, designed for those who aspire to become *ulema* or *qadis* (Islamic judges), emphasizes *sharia* (Islamic law). Islamic culture, religion and social studies are studied in the intermediate cycle; in the secondary cycle emphasis is placed on the study of classical Arabic grammar and rhetoric, *sharia*, customary law and theology.

In 1964 there were approximately 20 intermediate and secondary religious schools in major towns of the country. The most notable of these were the Dar at-Tawid school at Taif and the Institute of Islamic Jurisprudence at Medina. The school at Taif had 714 students enrolled in 1964, but the number of students at other Islamic schools was not reported.

Modern

Admittance to the modern intermediate cycle is limited to the better qualified students and is determined by competitive examinations. Instruction in this cycle includes traditional and modern courses. Emphasis on spoken and written Arabic and Islamic religious training is still strong, but introductory courses in history, literature, mathematics and science are also offered. In 1964 there were 13,444 students attending intermediate boys' schools.

The secondary cycle serves as preparation for the university. It is the least accessible of the public education cycles. Admission is dependent on both an intermediate school diploma and a scholastic record averaging over 70 percent. In 1964 there were only 3,472 boys enrolled.

On entering the secondary level, a student is expected to choose either arts or sciences as his field of specialization. Students in the sciences program are required to concentrate on English, physics, chemistry and biology, and they must also take courses in religion and history. The arts program entails the study of two foreign languages (usually English and French), history, literature, Arabic, geography and Islamic religion and jurisprudence. Successful completion of the secondary level with passing grades of 50 percent qualifies the student for a general secondary certificate of education.

Vocational

Vocational training—technical, commercial and agricultural—is relatively new and exists only in the larger commercial communities. Nevertheless, since the opening of the first trade school in 1949, it has been rapidly becoming an important part of the country's development planning.

Vocational schools are also organized in two cycles of 3 years each, intermediate and secondary. Intermediate cycle graduates usually obtain jobs as skilled laborers, whereas secondary school graduates are able to work as foremen or assume other managerial positions. The dropout rate is high, especially from agricultural schools. Students frequently leave after attending school only long enough to acquire minimal skills.

The Riyadh Vocational School, founded in 1960, is the government's model technical school. Academic courses are supplemented with on-the-job training in all of the trades, including engineering, architecture and electronics. Trained instructors have been provided by Aramco as well as by the United States and European countries. As many courses taught by non-Arabs are offered in English, an adequate knowledge of the language is a prerequisite to admission. Other technical schools are located at Mecca, Jidda, Dammam, Burayda, Al-Hasa, Qasim and Medina. Total enrollment was 2,442 in 1964.

Prospective employers, taking into consideration the personnel requirements of their firms, have joined the Ministry of Education in organizing the commercial schools. These schools are primarily designed to provide trained typists, stenographers, office workers and bank employees. They are, accordingly, located in the country's trade and commercial centers—Mecca, Jidda, Riyadh and Dammam.

Agricultural training schools, first opened in 1960, operated until 1965 in all major agricultural regions of the country. Emphasis was placed on practical experience as a supplement to agricultural theory; courses were tailored to suit local conditions, with syllabuses jointly prepared by the Ministries of Education and Agriculture. In 1965 the status of intermediate cycle agricultural schools were reconsidered, and it was decided that they were to be replaced by two secondary cycle schools.

Education for Girls

Before 1960, when public education was first made available for girls, only a few girls were given any education beyond instruction in home economics and religion as taught in the family. There were, however, 42 private girls' schools which together could accommodate about 6,500 students, and a few more girls were educated abroad or by private tutors.

The rapid expansion of girls' public education after 1960 demonstrated the heavy demand for it; the number of applications was often three times the capacity of the schools.

The school environment is strictly supervised by the Directorate General of Girls' Schools. Chaperoned bus transportation is provided to and from school. In a few schools the first 2 or 3 years are coeducational, but after the age of 9 girls must attend segregated classes and wear veils in public.

Most girls' schools include both the elementary and the intermediate cycles, although separate postelementary—intermediate and secondary—schools were being established in 1964 and 1965 to accommodate the increasing number of elementary school graduates. In 1962 the class size averaged between 30 and 40 students. The total number of girls in elementary education in 1964 was reported as about 40,500; over 500 girls were in the later cycles and about 700 in teacher training.

The government asserts that the curriculum in girls' schools is equivalent to that of boys' schools, but that girls' education emphasizes those courses assumed to be suitable for women in their role in Saudi Arabian society. Religion, Arabic and home economics are taught in elementary schools. In the intermediate cycle, these courses are supplemented by social studies and foreign languages.

The first secondary cycle schools were opened in 1965. Little information was available at that time regarding the course of study in these schools.

On graduation from elementary school, girls are encouraged to attend teacher training schools to be trained to replace the foreign women teachers upon whom the country was still almost entirely dependent in 1965. Intermediate and secondary level nursing schools are operated by the Directorate General of Girls' Schools in conjunction with the Ministry of Health.

In 1964 the government gave its initial approval for higher education for girls and permitted two girls to attend colleges in the United States. A few other girls were studying at the American University of Beirut and the American University at Cairo.

Higher Education

Institutions of higher learning are of two sorts—traditionally oriented Islamic colleges and modern, Western-type colleges. The curricula of most are being modified to meet the demands for administrators, teachers and technicians capable of coping with the problems confronting the country.

Admission to institutions of higher learning is dependent on the successful completion of the secondary cycle and the passing of competitive examinations. Knowledge of English is required for those pursuing scientific or technical studies. Tuition is free and boarding and lodging stipends are provided for those who need them. In late 1965 no institution of higher learning was prepared to issue other than a bachelor's degree in arts or sciences, although Riyadh University was taking preparatory steps toward the introduction of graduate level facilities.

The Sharia College of Mecca, founded in 1949 by the Ministry of Education, was established for the training of teachers and government administrators. Shortly afterward a faculty for secular education was added to the faculty for *sharia*. In 1964 the two faculties were given their own quarters and considered as separate institutions, the Sharia College and the College of Education. The curriculum of both colleges is a synthesis of traditional and modern education. The Sharia College offers courses in comparative legal systems and foreign languages in addition to Arabic theology and *sharia*. The College of Education incorporates departments of English, mathematics, social studies and physics. In 1964 there were 190 students in the College of Education and 163 in the Sharia College.

The College of Arabic Language and the Sharia College of Riyadh function under the authority of the Grand Mufti as director general of religious institutions. Courses are traditionally oriented and emphasize *sharia,* classical Arabic and Islamic theology. Admission is dependent on graduation from religious or modern secondary schools, although most students are from religious secondary schools. In 1964 there were 660 students studying at the Sharia College of Riyadh and 315 enrolled at the College of Arabic Language.

The Islamic University of Medina was established in 1961 under the auspices of the Grand Mufti to offer a 4-year program leading to a degree of bachelor of arts in Islamic theology. Modeled after Al-Azhar University in Cairo, its curriculum includes studies of the Koran, Moslem and Arab history, Islamic law and ethics and modern Islamic issues. Students from all other Moslem countries are encouraged to attend the Islamic University and are offered scholarships by the Saudi Arabian Government. The University also operates a 3-year preparatory secondary school.

In mid-1965, King Faisal decreed the establishment of the Supreme Judicial Institute in Riyadh to train qualified judges for the *sharia* courts. The 3-year program was to be opened to graduates of the *sharia* colleges.

Riyadh University, founded in 1957 by the Ministry of Education as King Saud University, represents the country's first attempt at a Western concept of education on the postsecondary level. In 1965 the University comprised four colleges—arts, 392 students; commerce, 476 students; pharmacy, 30 students; and sciences, 192 students. An agricultural college is expected to be opened in 1966, and a college of education in 1967. Arabic is the official language of instruction, although technical courses at the colleges of pharmacy and sciences are taught in English. Part-time enrollment is permitted only in the colleges of arts and commerce. Students registered for a course are required to attend 75 percent of the classes in order to qualify for examinations.

The Riyadh College of Engineering was founded in 1962 by the Ministry of Education in cooperation with the United Nations Educational, Scientific and Cultural Organization (UNESCO) to provide training in automotive, civil, electronic and mechanical engineering and serve as a training school for vocational school teachers. Admission is limited to secondary school graduates with a science major who have passed the College's entrance examination. The term of study is 5 years, including 10-week summer training sessions at factories or government installations, after which students receive a bachelor of science degree. Specialization begins after the second year. In 1964, 125 students were registered; 20 percent were from other Arab countries.

The College of Petroleum at Dhahran, founded in 1964, is operated by the Ministry of Petroleum and Mineral Resources, which determines and supervises its curriculum. The College also receives contributions from the oil companies operating in the country. Entrance is open to nationals and nonnationals. The term of study is 5 years, with summer traineeships usually required during summer recess. A bachelor of science degree is offered upon successful completion of the program.

The faculty of the College of Petroleum is multinational, and members of the board of governors of the college have been chosen from among the world's respected educators and industrialists. United States and British personnel predominate; instruction is in English; and teaching methods are ones developed in the United States.

PRIVATE EDUCATION

Private schools are few in number and are mostly for girls. They operate independently of government schools, although they must abide by minimal standards and qualifications as determined by the Ministry of Education. Despite the decline in importance of private schools after the expansion of the public education system, they continue to contribute significantly to the country's educational system. Both the curricula of private schools and the quality of their education are rigorously supervised by the Ministry of Education under the Private Schools Regulations drawn up by the Council of Ministers. The development and educational policy of private girls' schools are controlled by the Directorate General of Girls' Schools.

The government encourages the growth and maintenance of private schools at all levels through subsidies, especially for private kindergartens and girls' secondary schools. The government subsidizes education in private girls' schools by rebating 30 percent of the tuition charges. This policy is to continue as long as there is a shortage of girls' public schools.

By 1964 students in private boys' schools numbered somewhat over 5,100. Of the approximately 4,500 in private schools for girls, about 590 were in intermediate or secondary schools. The country's first private college, King Abd al-Aziz College, to be located at Jidda, was nearing completion at the end of 1965.

Private schools are operated principally either by Aramco or by individuals on private initiative. Non-Islamic religious schools are prohibited.

Aramco has initiated for its employees the most advanced privately operated system of vocational training in the Arab world. It offers schooling from elementary to university education within the country and abroad. The company has also built schools which it has turned over to the government. Other industrial and commercial companies within the country are following Aramco's example in employee training and are increasingly bearing the responsibility of training their employees; for example, Saudi

Arabian Airlines, operated by Trans World Airlines (TWA), announced that an aviation training school near Jidda would be opened sometime in 1966.

STUDENTS ABROAD

Students have been going abroad for their higher education since the country's unification in 1926. According to government estimates, over 3,000 Saudi Arabs were studying abroad in 1965, either under government scholarships or on private initiative. Of these, 600 were in the United States, 590 in Western Europe, and 1,900 in other countries, mostly in the Arab states.

Students who wish to study abroad must be holders of a general secondary certificate of education and have a scholastic average of over 70 percent. Students planning to pursue technical courses usually are sent to Europe; those planning to follow academic courses, to the United States. Students in the United States are required by the Saudi Arabian Government to spend 1 year before beginning their regular college program in overcoming their linguistic handicap and in becoming socially adjusted to the new environment.

While abroad, students continue to be under close supervision of the Ministry of Education, which operates branch offices in all countries where Saudi Arabian students are studying. The government forbids students to marry non-Arabs as long as they are in school. Saudi Arabs have experienced little difficulty in social and academic adjustment, and over 80 percent complete their college or graduate school education.

LITERACY CAMPAIGN

Estimates of the literacy rate range from 5 to 20 percent of the total population; the lower figure, however, is probably more realistic, as emphasis was placed on education and literacy after 1954. In 1965 the Ministry of Education was engaged in a widespread literacy campaign aimed primarily at townsmen. The function of the program was to develop an educated urban population capable of adapting to the rapid changes the society is experiencing.

The literacy campaign among urban adults was being carried out under the government's Administration of Popular Culture. The student was expected to achieve literacy after 2 years of part-time study. An additional followup period of 2 years was designed to give the student a general academic background and religious studies. Completion of the 4-year program was considered equivalent to completing the 6-year elementary school program and qualified the student for an elementary certificate of education. In 1964 over 35,450 adults were participating in the literacy program; over 13,800 completed a minimum of 2 years of the program between 1960 and 1965.

Additional literacy schools are operated by the Ministry of Defense and Aviation, and by Aramco, which hold compulsory literacy classes for their personnel (see ch. 20, Industry). The Ministry of Education has investigated the possibility of using television for literacy instruction; it televised literacy programs in Riyadh and Jidda on an experimental basis in 1965.

TEACHERS AND TEACHER TRAINING

The shortage of a properly qualified elementary school teaching staff has been a limiting factor in the expansion of public schooling and has necessitated the importation of foreign teachers, mostly from Egypt and other Arab countries. For the 1961–62 school year, 2,000 foreign teachers were recruited.

One of the first acts of the Ministry of Education after 1954 was the establishment of teacher training schools. Most are attended by students prepared for the intermediate level; these teachers will become elementary level teachers. Two are institutes for training secondary school teachers. Summer courses train emergency teachers. Since 1954 the training program has been continually expanded and improved, but few teachers have had more than 2 to 3 years' more schooling than those whom they teach. The government announced in 1965 that, in order to raise educational standards and increase teaching abilities, the elementary level training schools then in existence were being transformed into schools of the secondary cycle. Students who had taken the intermediate cycle teaching training course were being encouraged to attend supplementary 2-year courses. In the same year the Ministry of Education reported that the demand for boys' elementary school teachers had been met. There remains, however, a critical shortage of teachers for postsecondary boys' schools and of women teachers for girls' schools.

Teachers from abroad are recruited mainly from the United Arab Republic, Lebanon and Palestine. In addition, a considerable number of temporary United States and British teachers are employed in colleges and secondary schools, usually on 1-year contracts.

Since the renewal of diplomatic relations with Great Britain in 1963, Saudi Arabia has received British assistance for the development of its educational system. Teacher trainees in large numbers have been invited to Great Britain for higher education. Great Britain also contracted in 1965 to supply a minimum of 155 secondary school teachers on a 4-year basis.

At the end of 1965 the Sharia College of Mecca was the only teacher training institution at the college level offering a formal teaching program. However, provision is made for teacher training at all colleges and institutes of higher learning, and in 1965 the government announced that all graduates of Riyadh University were required to teach intermediate or secondary cycle school on a short-term basis after graduation.

CHAPTER 10

RELIGION

Islam is the religion of all the permanent residents of the country. It is a pervasive influence in the lives of its adherents, the fundamental motivating force in most phases of their culture. All desires and daily acts are colored by recognition of their appropriateness or inappropriateness in the light of Islamic precepts, and verbal expression is invariably interspersed with references or appeals to God.

The primacy of Islam is strengthened because of the country's association with the person and life of the Prophet Mohammed, the presence of the holy cities of Mecca and Medina as the objects of pilgrimage and historic isolation from non-Moslem influences. Here, declaration of oneself as a Moslem is a prerequisite for nationality. The people are profoundly conscious that they are Moslems, although they do not all understand the doctrines or practice the teachings of their religion. Conversion of immigrants to Islam is not infrequent, but conversion in the opposite direction does not occur; Moslems do not repudiate their religion, which is a fundamental part of their lives.

At no time since the beginning of the Moslem calendar in A.D. 622 has any non-Moslem power ruled over any part of the present territory of the Saudi state, nor has any non-Moslem religion had more than a handful of followers residing in that territory. At no time has a non-Moslem been permitted to visit Mecca or Medina, the sites of the holy sanctuaries of Islam, if his true indentity has been known, though a few bold adventurers have achieved this feat in disguise, or died in the attempt.

Non-Moslems are regarded as inherently inferior or foolish. Christians working in the country may attend Christian church services, but these are not to be opened to the public. All the Jews formerly resident in the country emigrated in 1948 or adopted Islam, and Jews subsequently have not been tolerated. Members of other non-Moslem religious minorities, such as Indians or Africans, are soon converted, at least outwardly, to Islam.

Indifference to religion is incomprehensible to Moslems who are particularly intolerant of agnosticism or atheism. A show of disrespect for religion in general and Islam in particular causes a violent reaction. A government decree of November 1961 expressly forbids support of any ideology contrary to the principles of Islam, such as communism or socialism.

ISLAM

Islam ("submission," as to the will of God) was first preached by Mohammed, who was born in Mecca about A.D. 570. According to tradition, he received a call from God at about the age of 40 while engaged in solitary contemplation at the mountain of Hira. As a result, he began to preach in Mecca against idolatry and many prevailing polytheistic practices. For more than a decade Mohammed and his small band of followers were ridiculed and persecuted, and finally in A.D. 622 the pressures of hostility forced him to move to Medina. The beginning of the Islamic calendar dates from the year of this flight (*hegira*).

Eight years after their flight to Medina, the Moslems were able to retake Mecca, and to make its principal shrine, the Kaaba, the center of the Islamic religion. Ultimately, Mohammed and a growing number of followers were able to defeat his enemies, to gain converts among the Arab tribes, and to bring the entire Arabian subcontinent under his control. The first several caliphs (successors to Mohammed as the spiritual and political rulers of Islam) continued the campaign to convert the world to Islam by persuasion or by force. Within a century this "holy war" had brought Islam to a vast area from China to North Africa and Spain. Its center was at Mecca, which became the object of great annual pilgrimages.

Islam is based on belief in one God, a warm transcendent God to whom man must submit, or resign, his fate. Submission to this God joins men into one community, the House of God (Dar al-Islam). Islam gives man a total explanation of his existence and propounds a moral system which is not so much a set of general principles as a series of practical obligations and prohibitions. Members of the Islamic community do not separate the spiritual from the temporal; everything in society is believed to partake of the religious essence, and all elements of the society are part of the collectivity of Islam.

Tenets of Islam

The fundamental article of faith is the testimony (*shahada*): "There is no God but Allah; Mohammed is the Prophet of Allah." The recital of the *shahada* in full and unquestioning belief is all that is required to become a Moslem. It is repeated before all ritual prayers and on many other occasions. Allah is believed to be unitary, omnipotent, compassionate, the creator and judge of mankind. Mohammed is believed to be the last and greatest in a line of prophets which starts with Adam and includes Abraham, Moses and Jesus. The prophets do not share in divinity but are the vehicle through whom God has given to mankind a succession of revelations of divine truth.

Other beliefs pertain to a general resurrection, the final judgment of mankind by God, the eternal life of the soul, and the preordainment of every man's acts during life as well as his ultimate fate. Man's resignation to his fate, however, is tempered by his obligation to behave in a manner which is morally good in preparation for the day of judgment and his final disposition in either heaven or hell.

Some actions which are considered morally good or bad are spelled out in the Koran, the holy book believed to be revealed by God, or in Islamic law (*sharia*). Other actions which do not fall within the scope of definition are considered morally indifferent, therefore "permitted." Among actions which are prohibited are usury, gambling and the consumption of carrion, blood, pork and alcohol. Among those recommended are respect for all human beings as equals in the eyes of God, generosity, and fair treatment of others.

The actions obligatory on faithful Moslems, called the Five Pillars, consist of: repetition of the testimony of faith, prayer, almsgiving, fasting and pilgrimage. A good Moslem prays in a prescribed manner, after ritual ablutions, five times daily; at dawn, midday, midafternoon and sunset, and in the early part of the night.

Islam recognizes economic differences between persons and the needs of individuals and requires the payment of a religious tax for charitable purposes. In the early days a tax of about $2\frac{1}{2}$ percent of one's wealth was paid directly to Mohammed, who made the distribution to orphans, widows and other needy persons, and used some for the support of mosques. The regular giving of alms as a sign of piety and means of salvation continues in Moslem countries. In Saudi Arabia the alms tax (*zakat*) is the only direct tax collected by the government from its citizens (see ch. 24, Monetary and Financial System).

Throughout the ninth month of the Moslem year, Ramadan, fasting is enjoined upon all except the sick, the weak, soldiers on duty and travelers. Days of the fast which are missed are supposed to be made up at a later time. The fast involves abstinence from food, drink, smoking and sexual intercourse every day from daybreak to nightfall. Fasting is regarded as a means to a sense of obedience and humility before God and is also prescribed as expiation for various offenses.

Once in his lifetime each Moslem is expected to make the pilgrimage (hadj) to Mecca and the other places in its environs which are held to be sacred because of their association with the life of Mohammed or earlier prophets. The best time for the hadj is considered to be the twelfth month of the Moslem year. A lesser pilgrimage, consisting of a visit to the Kaaba but neglecting some of the other ritual which takes place during the twelfth month, is acceptable if the greater pilgrimage is not possible.

Historically, jihad—permanent struggle to make the Word of God supreme among men—was an important further obligation upon Moslems. Mohammed urged the feuding Arab tribes of his day to compose their differences and devote their energies to converting the world. After the dramatic conquests and conversions of the first century of Islam, jihad was invoked by political leaders to justify the defense of faithful Moslems against heathens and infidels. Today, in the main, Moslem teaching presents jihad as the duty of the individual to struggle for his own salvation and as the duty of the citizen to work for the good of the community.

Sources, Traditions and Law

In the theocratic order established during Mohammed's lifetime, he was judge, lawgiver and social arbiter. His words, uttered in an inspired state, were regarded as direct communications from God and were compiled to form the Moslem holy book, the Koran. His noninspirational statements and the example of his personal conduct (*sunna*), recorded together as the Hadith, provided the basis for a code of behavior which, with local variations and sectarian differences, was to apply throughout Islam.

The revelations of the Koran are considered to supersede and to correct the earlier revelations given to the Jews in the Torah and to the Christians in the Gospels. The Koran is a mixture of recitations of events in the life of Mohammed, stories based on Jewish and Christian traditions, teachings about God and the need to submit to His will, and orders and rules for the regulation of the Moslem community, many of which represent attempts to ameliorate some of the social injustices of Mohammed's time. Its words are considered sacred, and the body of doctrine and practical obligations set forth therein form the core of Moslem religious life.

The Koran is explained and interpreted by the Hadith. Each Hadith is a separate story, a tradition, reputed to have been handed down by those who had been close to Mohammed. The Hadith include almost all the early history of Islam and many of its moral precepts. Many of them, however, are considered to be spurious by some scholars. Certain schools of law or sects accept Hadith which are unacceptable to others.

The early Islamic commentators and jurists devoted themselves to study of the practical implications of the life of Mohammed and his community, thus systematizing the *sharia*. Further developed by analogy and consensus, the law came to include basic beliefs, religious practice, and regulations pertaining to social situations. As Islam spread to new regions where customs differed, some of the prescriptions of the law were incompatible with local custom, but the principles of reinterpretation and consensus emphasized by the scholars permitted mutual adaptation between Islamic and local codes.

Four major schools of jurisprudence, named for their founders and known as Hanifite, Malekite, Shafiite, and Hanbalite, grew up in the second and third Islamic centuries (ninth and tenth centuries A.D.). These had significantly widespread influences and have persisted to modern times. The differences among them were not fundamental, but stemmed from the degree of emphasis laid on the four recognized sources of law—the Koran, tradition, consensus and analogy. Although some professors of Islamic law emphasize one school or another, the division between schools no longer has importance for individual Moslems. Each school predominates in certain geographic regions of the Islamic world, but each recognizes the orthodoxy and acceptability of interpretations based on the other schools (see ch. 12, Constitution and Government).

Adherents of the Hanbalite school in the Arabian peninsula are widely known as Wahhabi, after the eighteenth century Hanbalite reformer, Mohammed Ibn Abd al-Wahhab, although they call themselves unitarians (*muwahhidin*) (see ch. 3, Historical Setting). They advocate a return to the practice of Islam as it was carried out in the time of Mohammed, shorn of superstitious accretions, mysticism and the recognition of intermediaries between the faithful and God.

Schism

Islam has been marked by numerous sectarian schisms between the orthodox community, known as Sunni (from the Arabic *sunna*, traditions), and movements which it repudiates. The sects do not partake of any of the orthodox schools of law and maintain that doctrines or practices not consistent with their own are heretical. The divisions which have been most pervasive had their origins in political dissensions and divergent theories regarding the office of the caliph, the head of the Moslem community as successor to Mohammed.

The Shiites form the most important schismatic sect in Islam, numbering over 30 million altogether. The Shiite movement began as a political party (*shiat*), partisans of the family of Ali, cousin and son-in-law of Mohammed, whose claim to the caliphate was in question. Shiites asserted that a clear mandate was to be found in the Koran to maintain the caliphate in the house of Ali, in contrast to the Sunni who held that the office was elective from within the Quraysh, the tribe to which Mohammed belonged. The movement developed in Persia, where the idea of a hereditary divine sovereign was prevalent.

Most Shiites believed that a body of secret knowledge was transmitted by Mohammed to Ali and thence to his heirs, but they differed and divided on the question of which descendant should be recognized as imam, or religious leader of the community, because of his possession of this knowledge. Gradually the political issue of the succession to the caliphate took on a doctrinal color as Shiism served as a cloak for the introduction of various local Persian, Babylonian or oriental beliefs into Islam. Shiite ritual places more emphasis on festivals, pageantry and saints than Sunni practice, and less on prayer, pilgrimage and fasting.

Mysticism

Manifestations of mysticism appeared early in the history of Islam, particularly among converts from other religions. The need of many Moslems to feel their religion, to approach God in a mystical and emotional rather than a legalistic and intellectual manner, has led to the development of groups or orders who place their emphasis on direct religious experience. Called Sufis (woolwearers) after early ascetics who wore coarse, undyed woolen robes, mystics have often been condemned by more orthodox believers, but their role in the development and spread of Islam has been significant, and elements of Sufism are to be found in all parts of the Islamic world.

Mysticism has generally found its adherents among either religious scholars, who are impatient with the legalism and intellectualism of the orthodox approach to Islam, or less educated persons who are ignorant of the details of theological interpretation but wish to express their religion. Mystics believe in divine love and the rewards of moral purity, and they seek direct contact with God, often through ascetic trance. Their orders encourage asceticism, recitation of the Koran, prayer and emotional transports. Religious brotherhoods founded by mystics are based on the idea that guides are needed to help the practitioner find his way to virtue and divine truth. Individual Sufi leaders and interpreters have frequently been regarded as saints by their disciples.

Organization

Strictly orthodox Moslems acknowledge no communion of saints and intercessors with God, no ordained priesthood or other sacramental institution. Theoretically every Moslem has equal access to God and His Revelation, and no man, even the Prophet, is better in the eyes of God than any other. However, certain religious offices and classes have developed in practice.

The caliphs were Mohammed's spiritual and temporal successors, who bore responsibility for the religion and right conduct of their subjects. The office of Caliph as supreme head of the Moslem community has been vacant since the demise of the Ottoman Empire, but certain political rulers claim to be the imam of their respective states; for example, the King-cum-Imam of Morocco and the King-cum-Imam of Saudi Arabia.

Every Moslem community has a few religious specialists. The call to prayer is given by a *muezzin*. The Word of God as revealed in the Koran is recited and taught to the faithful by an imam or by village Koranic teachers. Members of the brotherhood lead their followers in worship and in certain prescribed rituals. The *qadi* is the judge in matters of religious law. These specialists are usually occupied only part time with their religious duties.

As Islam developed, scholars and interpreters, known collectively as the *ulema*, gained a place of respect as a class of people who constituted the highest authority on the interpretation of the Koran and the sacred traditions. Historically, the role of the *ulema* as educators and governmental advisers has been important and their prestige great. This has been particularly true in Saudi Arabia, which was created by the combined force of the Wahabbi ulema and Saudi military power. The *ulema*, who do not form a unified body of Islamic scholars, but are grouped around important mosques and educational institutions, continue to play an important role in Saudi government (see ch. 12, Constitution and Government). Since, however, their views are strongly conservative, their authority has been opposed, to an extent at least, by those who are trying to modernize the country.

The mosques are the only religious buildings of Islam. They are cared for by the community and are often the center of community spirit, but they are not consecrated. They are simply halls set aside for congregational prayer and the delivery of the weekly sermon by the imam, and they sometimes serve as the site of the local religious schools.

The religious life of the community is supported by direct contributions in the form of *zakat* or by the income from *waqf* (land endowed to religious or charitable institutions). Funds from these same sources are also used to support orphans, widows and needy persons in the community.

RELIGIOUS PRACTICES

The Saudi Arabs vary in the extent to which they understand the fine points of their religion, and the strictness with which they follow the Islamic precepts of outward behavior. At one extreme are the Bedouin nomads who are very much aware of the role of God in their lives but casual in the observance of the pillars of the faith. At the other are the *ulema*, membership in which is concentrated among the Al ash-Shaykh family, descendants of Mohammed Ibn Abd al-Wahhab, whose approach to the strictly orthodox interpretation of Islam they propound. The *ulema* are learned in theology and law, strict in observance, and intolerant of those who embellish the practice of religion with revelry, shrines and superstitions. Between the Bedouin and the *ulema* are the majority of the people, most of whom pray regularly, give some form of alms, keep the fast of Ramadan, make the pilgrimage, refrain from smoking in public, do not drink alcohol, and are generally proud to be Moslems.

The overwhelming majority of the people are Sunni Moslems. The four major orthodox Sunni schools of religious law are represented in the country, although most people do not know enough about the differences between the schools to know the significance of their family belonging to one rather than the other. The Malekite and Hanifite schools are the nominal schools of small minorities in the Hofuf oasis of Eastern Province. The Shafiite school is found in the Hejaz and Asir in the west. The prevailing interpretation, especially in the Nejd and Eastern Province, is the Wahhabi version of the Hanbalite school which has been closely identified with the power of the House of Saud (see ch. 3, Historical Setting).

The people of the Hejaz and Asir had reason to fear the proselytic and intolerant approach of Wahhabi puritans in the past, when shrines were destroyed, the customary behavior of the people was criticized or punished, and men were shipped into the mosque for congregational prayer on Fridays. Since the end of World War II, however, the Wahhabi have become less extreme in their approach, the Public Morality Committees which they support have become gradually less effective, and the differences between them and other Sunni Moslems have become obscured. Outward behavior is more circumscribed in Riyadh, the seat of Wahhabi power, than in Jidda or Mecca, the cosmopolitan commercial cities which are hosts to pilgrim Moslems of all kinds.

In Eastern Province are about 100,000 members of a branch of Shiites which recognizes 12 imams as successors to Ali (see ch. 4, Ethnic Groups and Languages). A few additional Shiites are scattered about the country. Their religious practice differs from that of the Sunnis mainly in the larger number of celebrations they hold and in their support of religious assembly halls (*husainiyas*) in addition to mosques.

Prayer is a private affair for Moslems, performed by women usually at home and by men singly or in groups according to where they find themselves at the time of prayer. Prayer is performed facing in the direction of the Kaaba in Mecca. Each period of prayer has a prescribed form of worship starting with ritual ablutions and including a number of bows and repetition of verses from the Koran. Optional additional prayer is usually limited to thanksgiving and adoration rather than the asking of favors from God. On Fridays, at midday, congregational prayer, which all men are expected to attend, is led at the mosque by the imam, who may also give a sermon. Businesses are closed at least during the Friday midday prayer and frequently all day Friday. Schools are not held on Fridays.

The severest ritual performance for a Moslem is the fast of Ramadan, especially if this month falls in the time of midsummer heat. Since the Moslem year consists of 12 lunar months and is 11 days shorter than the solar year, Ramadan falls 11 days earlier in the latter each year (see table 2). Young men and girls begin to observe the fast when they reach puberty. The most pious observe the fast austerely, passing the day reading the Koran and praying, and eating sparingly after twilight. Others attempt to carry on their regular daytime activities and eat as well as they can at night, but as the month progresses, stamina decreases and tempers become shorter. Ramadan ends with the sighting of the new moon which is the signal for the Feast of the Breaking of the Fast (*Id al-Fitr*), one of the two great festivals of the year, which lasts several days.

Alms are given not only through the obligatory religious tax paid to the government but voluntarily throughout the year. Traditionally there has been recognition of responsibility of relatives to help members of their kin group and for the rich to help the needy (see ch. 6, Family). At certain times of the year, such as Ramadan, food, clothing and money are given to the needy by those who can do so. The government has recently begun to take more direct responsibility for matters which used to be in the realm of private charity (see ch. 11, Health and Welfare).

Table 2. The Moslem Calendar for 1385 A.H. (1965–66)

Moslem Month	Length (in days)	Beginning Date in Terms of Christian Calendar
Muharram	30	May 2
Safar	29	June 1
Rabi al-Awwal (Rabia I)	30	June 30
Rabi al-Thani (Rabia II)	29	July 30
Jumada al-Ula (Jumada I)	30	August 28
Jumada al-Thaniya (Jumada II)	29	September 27
Rajab	30	October 26
Shaban	29	November 25
Ramadan	30	December 24
Shawwal	29	January 23
Dhu al-Qada	30	February 21
Dhu al-Hijja	29*	March 23
Total days	354	

*Dhu al-Hijja has 30 days in leap year, which occurs 11 times in every cycle of 30 years. A.H. (*anno hegirae*) 1385 was a leap year. A.H. 1386 begins on April 22, 1966.

The pilgrimage to Mecca is regarded as the ideal culmination of religious experience, but it is not required of those who do not have the means to perform it. One who has made the hadj may add the honorific al-Hadj to his name. The trip to Mecca and certain preliminary ceremonies are performed any time after the end of Ramadan, but the climactic ceremonies are on the ninth and tenth days of the twelfth month, Dhu al-Hijja. Since the improvement of communications and facilities in the region of Mecca and the port, Jidda, the number of pilgrims at all times of the year has increased. The time of year and weather conditions cause fluctuations in the number, but from 1960 on, the government has reported from 200,000 to 285,000 foreign pilgrims and just under 500,000 or more Saudi Arabian pilgrims during Dhu al-Hijja.

The pilgrimage is an individual declaration of belief but also an immense congregation of Moslems who have a chance to come together under conditions which level all social inequalities. It begins with the trip to Mecca, which for some is long and arduous. The first of the ritual ceremonies is the entering into a state of purity by putting off conventional garments, shaving the hair of the face, head and body, clipping nails, taking off headgear, and donning sandals and a simple garb (*ihram*) consisting of two pieces of white seamless cloth. From this time until the end of the pilgrimage, the pilgrim does not indulge in grooming, in pleasures of the flesh or in the destruction of living things.

Then the pilgrim makes seven tours of the inner court of the Great Mosque at Mecca, circling the Kaaba, a cube-shaped shrine draped in a specially woven black cloth (*kiswa*). On each tour, the pilgrim kisses or touches the sacred black stone built into the southeast corner of the Kaaba. This stone is believed to have been received by the prophet Ishmael from the angel Gabriel during the rebuilding of the temple at which Adam had worshipped. After this tour they visit Zamzam, the sacred well believed to have been found by Hagar and her son Ishmael after they were abandoned by Abraham, and they traverse the distance between two hills of Mecca, Safa and Marwah, seven times in commemoration of Hagar's desperate search for water.

On the ninth day of the month the pilgrims are on the plain of Arafat, about 12 miles east of Mecca where they stand facing Mecca until sunset, praying. After dark they travel to the village of Mina where there are three stone pillars, representing three devils. On the way they stop for prayers at a sacred spot called Muzdalifa. The ritual of the tenth day includes the casting of stones at the devil pillars, the sacrifice of an animal in commemoration of Abraham's offer to sacrifice his son to God. After the sacrifice, the *Id al-Adhha*, the second great feast of the Moslem year, is held. The period of ritual purity ends with the return to one's habitual clothing, shaving and hair trimming.

A pilgrimage may end with another visit to the Kaaba and a trip to Medina, the site of the tomb of the Prophet, although these acts are not required as part of the pilgrimage.

Some religious elements in the daily lives of the people are based on ancient beliefs of the region which are maintained either in conjunction with Islam or as part of Islamic observance. Many of these are among the things which al-Wahhab considered in the eighteenth century to be corruptions of Islam. They include a belief in magic and the efficacy of amulets, veneration of certain tombs or holy places, belief in omens, and the making of vows in the name of God with the hope of obtaining certain desires. Each locality observes particular customs regarding prohibited foods, good luck rituals, or specially venerated places.

Most people believe in the evil eye and in jinns, although educated people especially in urban areas, are less inclined to be concerned with the supernatural. The evil eye is basically the malignant power of the envious glance of another. It is combatted or forestalled by invocations, charms and amulets, but the best protection is avoidance of exposure to it altogether, by covering the head of or isolating the newborn child, for instance. Jinns abound in the supernatural world, some benevolent, but most malevolent, causing sickness, mental illness and death. They are believed to be everywhere but especially in human waste, dark places, and water. They can be propitiated and warded off by recitation of certain phrases and other ritual performances.

RELIGION AND GOVERNMENT

The secular chief of state, King Faisal, is also imam, or spiritual leader of the faithful. As ruler and imam, he upholds the *sharia*, which is still the official law of the land according to which judgment in temporal as well as spiritual affairs is made. Interpretation of the law is carried out under the guidance of the ulema, who are recognized as the highest authority in legal matters. The most important member of the *ulema* is the Grand Mufti, who is also Chief Judge. In 1965 the Grand Mufti was Mohammed Ibn Ibrahim Al ash-Shaykh, a descendant of the founder of the Wahhabi movement. These scholars have had a strong influence, particularly in the legal and educational spheres, and have been a conservative force, chary of innovations in the interpretation of the Koran and other legal sources (see ch. 12, Constitution and Government).

In any conflict between religious and political considerations of principles, those of religion must in theory take precedence. However, in practice, the law has been subject to reinterpretation according to need, and many adjustments have been made under the three Saudi kings since unification of the country and its opening to industrialization and foreign influences. Theoretical justifications for compromise with *sharia* law in the direction of modernity are found in the views that things not specifically prohibited in the source books, such as airplanes, must not be against the wishes of God, and that the protection of traditional values is more important than the perpetuation of specific prohibitions. Not even the most modern advocate of secular activities, however, makes any basic repudiation of Islam (see ch. 17, Attitudes and Reactions of the People).

In the 30 years after unification of the country the conservative views of the *ulema* in regard to many matters have given way. Innovations have been most notable in the communications sphere, where automobiles, railroads, airplanes, radios and television have been introduced, and in the educational sphere, where the government has placed a greater emphasis on secular education and has opened the first government-operated schools for girls. King Faisal, in the first 2 years of his reign, appeared to stand firmly in favor of further modernization, as long as he felt that Islam was not being fundamentally undermined.

The government continues to subsidize the Public Morality Committees, and the two committee heads who divide regional responsibilities are deputy ministers. These committees act as religious police, attempting to enforce pious behavior on the part of the people. Their puritanical opposition to the public use of musical instruments, the sale of dolls, employment of women, and the display of photographs continues, although there are complaints about their activities in the press and from young people with a modern education.

The tremendous administrative problems involved in providing shelter, food, transportation and medical facilities for the pilgrims are the responsibility of the Ministry of Pilgrimage and Religious Foundations, which budgeted $3.3 million for these purposes in 1965. Its other responsibilities include the building and renovation of mosques, the maintenance of archaeological ruins of religious value and libraries to display religious works and archaeological items, and the development of tourist trade. The Ministry has concentrated its work, however, in the region in which the holy places are located.

Sharia is still the only formally recognized law, and the courts are presided over by religious judges, but royal decrees have begun to supplement it, and the Grievance Board and other secular administrative courts have begun to take jurisdiction over matters which are outside the realm of religious law (see ch. 12, Constitution and Government). It is not unlikely that commercial and civil codes will eventually replace some of the functions of *sharia*, which is inadequate for some new types of dispute.

The pilgrimage to Mecca and other holy places of Islam concentrates for a month or more each year, in the cities of the Hejaz, a population three times the normal size. Before the advent of large revenues from exploitation of oil, pilgrims constituted the main source in income to the government, by their payment of a pilgrimage fee. This fee was abolished in 1952, but foreign pilgrims still pay a quarantine fee of SR60 (SR4.50 equal US$1) and the cities themselves profit from the provision of materials and services to the pilgrims.

CHAPTER 11

HEALTH AND WELFARE

Until the 1950's the government played a relatively minor role in social services. As elsewhere in the Middle East, the primary welfare agency has traditionally been the family or larger lineage group. Those who could not rely on such help were assisted by religious foundations or private almsgiving, an obligation of every Moslem.

Since the 1950's the government has assumed a direct responsibility in the field of social welfare and is participating in public health and welfare programs, particularly in the medical sphere. It is making social security, hospitalization and medical treatment available to townsmen and villagers alike. For the first time disease eradication measures are being effected. Smallpox and cholera, long the scourges of Arabia, have been almost eliminated, and the threat of malaria has been dramatically reduced.

SANITATION AND WATER SUPPLY

Inadequate sewerage facilities have contributed to unsanitary living conditions and, in both rural and urban areas, have been a major cause of disease. Surface drainage is the most common method of sewage disposal; drainage ditches generally carry the sewage to the outskirts of the towns, where it is evaporated by the heat. Waste may filter through drainage channels into the source of the water supply. Nomads, villagers and poorer townspeople generally use open-air latrines, which become breeding spots for diseases. Few houses have cisterns or other waste disposal facilities.

Scarcity of pure water also contributes to the incidence of disease. In villages water is generally available from springs or public wells. In urban areas water is conveyed by surface or underground conduits or by canals from springs and wells to centrally located tanks from which townspeople draw their daily water needs. In many localities the water supply is contaminated by human or animal waste. In 1965 piped water systems existed only in certain sections of Mecca, Riyadh, Jidda, Dhahran, Ras Tanura and Al-Khobar.

The General Administration for Public Health, a department of the Ministry of Health, assisted by the Arabian American Oil

Company (Aramco) and the World Health Organization (WHO), is attempting to improve water supplies and sanitary conditions in town and village communities. Government interest in promoting sanitation has led to laws providing for sanitary handling of food and regulations on conditions for the marketing of food throughout the country. In Eastern Province communities where Aramco installations are located, food inspection is rigorously enforced.

NUTRITION AND DIET

Chronic food shortage is a serious problem, and the diet of most of the population is inadequate by modern, Western standards in vitamins, proteins and total calories. Because of transportation problems, much of the produce grown reaches only local markets, and surplus food often spoils before it can be consumed. Meanwhile, the country must rely on imports for much of its food needs (see ch. 19, Agriculture).

Townsmen generally have a more varied menu than do country dwellers. In the past the towns, dependent on the countryside for food, often faced famine during bad crop years, but imported foods from the United States and Middle Eastern countries are now available in the larger towns and coastal seaports.

The Bedouin (nomads) have a more balanced diet than most settled cultivators, but their total caloric intake is lower. The diet of nomads consists mainly of milk and milk products from goats, sheep or camels, together with dates, rice or, less frequently, wheat. Milk is drunk fresh or curdled into yoghurt or cheese. Coffee and tea are the favorite beverages. Meat is eaten only on special occasions, when an animal is slaughtered or when wild game is available. Locusts are also consumed. Nomads eat fresh fruits and vegetables only when they visit the villages of settled cultivators. Despite his meager diet, the average Bedouin generally has considerable physical endurance. In nomadic families the husband and adult sons are generally better nourished than the women and children, who eat the leftovers after the men have finished their meal. Little food is eaten during the day, and the main meal is in the evening.

Although the diet of the average cultivator is more substantial than that of the nomad, it is more deficient in proteins and fats. The staple food of this group is millet, supplemented by rice, barley and wheat, when they are obtainable. These cereals are cooked into a gruel, and wheat and barley are also made into bread. Fruits, especially dates, and vegetables are eaten regularly; meat, only occasionally.

Although goats and camels are eaten, the main source of meat is sheep. Cattle are not numerous and are used mainly as beasts of burden. The consumption of pork is forbidden to Moslems, and the slaughtering of other animals is governed by Islamic ritual prescriptions. Fish is becoming more available but is not widely eaten.

INCIDENCE AND TREATMENT OF DISEASE

The incidence of disease is related to widespread nutritional deficiencies, crowded living conditions, general lack of pure water supplies, improper sanitation and ignorance regarding personal cleanliness and modern health measures.

Illness was traditionally regarded as a manifestation of God's will or as the work of evil spirits. Divine will was regarded as unchangeable, but evil spirits could be warded off by charms or the remedies of folk practitioners. Before the introduction of modern medicine, people depended upon practitioners whose lore represented a mixture of practical folk remedies and magic. Most bazaars still have peddlers of folk medicines. Many of these remedies have real therapeutic value: for example, senna acts as a purgative; copper sulfate crystals are useful in the treatment of trachoma; and mercury is useful for treating syphilis. Folk practitioners are reputed to be skilled also in setting broken bones with splints and in performing minor operations. The folk tradition manifests itself in the preference for injections rather than pills, as the former give the patients greater confidence that they are combating evil spirits.

Townsmen, in general, are apt to be better informed about the relation of germs to disease and about modern methods of treatment than are the nomads and villagers, and they are less fatalistic about sickness. Their faith in modern medicine is becoming more widespread as medical facilities become available and their efficacy is demonstrated. Health facilities and vaccination programs are most effective in urban areas, although since the early 1960's the government has been concentrating on disease-eradication programs in Asir and among the nomads.

Pneumonia, tuberculosis, trachoma, enteric diseases, malaria and parasitic diseases are the major disease problems. Rickets, venereal diseases, typhus, and typhoid, paratyphoid and relapsing fever are relatively common. Morbidity statistics and data on which to base estimates of the incidence of disease are lacking. Most illnesses and deaths go unreported despite a 1962 law requiring registration of vital statistics. In 1965 the government was still without administrative facilities to record such statistics.

Malaria

Previously endemic in much of the country, malaria is now limited to the valleys of Asir, the Tihama region, the irrigated areas of Eastern Province and the Qatif, Jabrin and Al-Khobar oases, which together include two-thirds of the country's population (see ch. 2, Geography and Population). Malarial conditions force the abandonment of certain areas for part of the year. Active malaria control measures by the government, Aramco and WHO have considerably reduced the incidence of the disease. Nevertheless, 9,300 cases were reported in 1962. Antimalaria measures were in 1965 being concentrated in Asir, where mobile units were using DDT, dieldrin and oil to destroy larvae. Aramco health units, following the same measures, greatly reduced the incidence of malaria in Eastern Province, but have encountered increasing immunity of the mosquitoes to both DDT and dieldrin.

Trachoma

Trachoma, a highly infectious eye disease, is endemic throughout the country. It is estimated that 70 to 90 percent of the population suffer to some degree from the disease, which, however, is easily cured if treatment is begun early. Aramco established a trachoma research center at Dhahran.

Venereal Diseases

Both congenital and contracted syphilis and gonorrhea, once most common in coastal towns and villages, are present throughout the country. Bejel, a disease related to these venereal diseases but not transmitted by sexual contact, has apparently long been endemic in most of the Arabian peninsula. The government has established a Venereal Disease Control Demonstration Center at Mecca and diagnostic laboratories throughout the country.

Enteric Diseases

Amoebic and bacillary dysentery and other intestinal disorders occur throughout the country. The absence of adequate sanitary facilities, the abundance of flies and the use of human excrement as fertilizer contribute to the high incidence of these disorders. Diarrhea and enteritis are extremely widespread among infants and are believed responsible for half of all infant deaths.

Parasitic diseases account for the major debilitating maladies, affecting as much as 50 percent of the population. Bilharziasis, chief among them, spreads primarily through the passing of human wastes into slow-moving channels where snails, which transmit the disease, breed. Roundworms, present in agricultural areas, where their eggs are spread through irrigation canals, infect as much as 15 percent of the population.

Respiratory Diseases

Tuberculosis is widespread and considered to be among the most serious disease problems. Rates of incidence are highest in the cities and towns, where the disease is fostered by unsanitary conditions, insufficient diet and crowded living quarters. The Ministry of Health constructed two hospitals for the isolation and treatment of tubercular patients. WHO contributed to the establishment of a Riyadh tuberculosis control center which in 1965 was the projected nucleus of a series of regional tuberculosis prevention centers. Aramco also provided wards in company hospitals for the treatment of the disease and was offering courses in home care.

Other Diseases

Smallpox, formerly epidemic, occurs only in localized outbreaks. Vaccination for smallpox was carried out on a small scale before 1957, but since then the government has undertaken widespread vaccination programs. All government employees and military personnel are required to be vaccinated. In 1963 alone over 950,000 persons were inoculated.

Relapsing fever, carried by lice and ticks, is encountered throughout the country, and dengue fever occurs in irrigated areas throughout the country. Pneumonia and whooping cough are among the chief causes of death among the nomads, especially during the late winter months.

Health Problems Resulting from Pilgrimage

The annual Moslem pilgrimage to Mecca and Medina aggravates the country's health problems. It is estimated that more than 1 million pilgrims crowd into these cities every year, including between 150,000 and 250,000 from outside the peninsula. Many of the pilgrims walk all or part of the way, and even for the strongest the pilgrimage imposes a severe strain. In the past the mortality rate among pilgrims was extremely high because of their weakened state, the unsanitary and crowded conditions in the holy cities, and their exposure to contagious diseases introduced by pilgrims from all over the world. Epidemics of cholera and smallpox were not uncommon.

The government has vigorously attacked the health problems introduced by the pilgrimage. It entered into an agreement among Islamic states to aid in the maintenance of health standards in the pilgrimage areas. Each of the Islamic countries agreed to send a medical mission to help care for the health of their nationals in order to lessen pressures on the Saudi facilities.

The Saudi Government required that all pilgrims be vaccinated against smallpox and inoculated against cholera and yellow fever before entering the country. It established quarantine stations in Jidda and at several other points of entry along the coast and the northern border. It assumed responsibility for caring for sick pilgrims and built modern facilities in Mecca, Jidda and Medina. For example, the quarantine station and hospital in Jidda, built in 1956, can provide medical care for over 22,000 outpatients and hospital care for 1,800 at one time. Mobile hospital units and six health centers have been built along the pilgrimage route. The government also has built modern slaughterhouses and freezers to improve sanitary conditions during the ritual slaughtering of animals during the pilgrimage, which previously seriously aggravated health problems.

As a result of these measures, the mortality rate and the incidence of contagious diseases among pilgrims have dropped sharply. In 1963 only 20 percent of the cases reported to medical authorities in Mecca and Jidda involved diseases or serious illness; the remaining 80 percent resulted from heat prostration or overexposure to the sun.

MEDICAL ORGANIZATION

Effective public health service providing free medical care began with the 1955 reorganization of the Ministry of Health, which was originally established in 1951. The lack of trained personnel required for long-range disease-eradication programs and an inadequate health education program necessitate an emphasis on curative rather than preventive health measures. In 1962, 90 percent of the Ministry's budget allocations were for curative programs. Total budget allocations to the Ministry of Health for 1965–66 were SR117.4 million (SR4.50 equal US$1), over three times that of 1957.

The functions of the Ministry of Health are conducted through 10 regional health districts, each responsible for its own health and sanitation conditions. Each district has a central hospital, which is also planned to serve as a medical training center, and supporting dispensaries in populous areas. Subordinate local centers and mobile health units are dispersed throughout the country.

Governmental Medical Facilities

In May 1965 the government reported that there were 67 hospitals, government and private, with a combined capacity of

5,550 beds; 157 government dispensaries; and 139 government health centers in the country. The rapid growth in health services is shown by the fact that in mid-1962 there were only 44 hospitals, with a combined capacity of 4,400 beds; 81 dispensaries; and 121 health centers.

A WHO medical team in the country in 1962 and 1963 reported that of the 44 hospitals, 35 were operated by the government; 2, by Aramco; 1, by the Trans-Arabian Pipeline Company (Tapline) ; and 6, by private individuals. The government hospitals consisted of 25 general, 3 maternity, 4 ophthalmological and 1 mental hospital, 1 tuberculosis sanatorium and 1 leprosarium. Most of the government's general hospitals were small, with fewer than 60 beds each, but several, including the Shumeyzi (formerly King Saud) Hospital in Riyadh, contained more than 200 beds each.

The 157 government dispensaries operating in 1965 in over 60 villages and towns provided outpatient treatment and performed emergency operations. Most dispensaries were headed by a doctor assisted by a female nurse-midwife, one or two male nurses and an assistant pharmacist. These dispensaries often treated as many as 150 patients a day and, in urban areas, as many as 500 a day.

The 139 government health centers operating in rural areas in 1965 usually consisted of a one-room clinic in a rented house and were staffed by a male nurse or health assistant, aided by one or two servants, often illiterate. These clinics treated an average of 30 to 50 patients daily on an outpatient basis and generally were able to provide only first-aid treatment and minor medication.

The government operated two tuberculosis sanatoriums in 1965, one in Taif, the other in nearby Hada. The Taif sanatorium, 4,000 feet above sea level, accommodated 1,000 patients. The WHO team noted that facilities were good, although admittance procedure was reported as poor, and many who entered were later found not to have had tuberculosis.

A mental health sanitarium, also located at Taif, was originally designed for 240 patients, but in 1963 it was housing 620 patients. At that time it was staffed by one psychiatrist and one physician. Therapy emphasized physical exercises, group activities and workshop activities. Most patients were from Eastern Province, and two-thirds were male.

Clinics for eye diseases and bilharziasis were operated throughout the country, especially in settled agricultural areas. The government also operated a leprosarium and has invited WHO assistance in curbing the incidence of leprosy and furthering its cure.

School medical services were operated through a cooperative effort by the Ministries of Health and Education. In 1965 there were 19 school health units, each serving 10,000 students and staffed by 53 physicians and assistants.

Private Facilities

Aramco is the principal nongovernment source of medical facilities. In 1965 the oil company maintained two private hospitals with a combined capacity of over 240 beds in Ras Tanura and Dhahran, in addition to smaller clinics dispersed throughout Eastern Province and at Tapline stations. Medical care was available at no cost to Aramco workers and to other Saudi Arabs unable to pay for treatment. Aramco's medical teams provided health education, maternal and child care, vermin control and sanitation inspection and operated research centers for indigenous diseases.

In 1963, of the six other private hospitals, five were in Jidda, and one was in Al-Khobar. They had a total of 126 beds and a staff of 13 doctors and 29 nurses.

Red Crescent Society

In 1962 the government approved the formation of the Red Crescent Society, modeled after the International Red Cross-Red Crescent Associations. The Society served as an auxiliary to medical authorities in time of emergency or disaster and participated in the establishment of medical facilities and in the dissemination of health information. It also trained male and female nurses and offered first-aid courses.

The Society had its head office in Riyadh, with branch offices throughout the country. Policy was formulated by a Board of Directors, which included the deputy ministers of finance and national economy, interior, defense and aviation, and labor and social affairs. Operating funds were allocated in the government budget, and contributions were also received from private individuals and *waqfs* (religious charitable foundations).

Personnel and Training

One of the most serious problems facing the medical authorities in 1965 was the shortage of trained personnel. There were only 510 doctors in the country, of whom more than 400 were on government contract. Most of the doctors were non-Saudi Arabs practicing in urban communities.

The WHO survey team reported in 1963 that of a total medical personnel numbering 1,529 persons, 409 were physicians, dentists and surgeons; 336 were male nurses, and 345 female nurses; 116 were health assistants; 101 were medical technicians; and 99 were registered midwives. The Ministry of Health employed 323 doctors; Aramco and Tapline, 73; and other private hospitals, 13. Private medical practice was permitted for government-employed doctors after their official work hours. Only about 55 of the doctors were Saudi Arabs; 174 were Egyptians. Of the 323 doctors working for the Ministry of Health, 217 were general practitioners and 106 were specialists, including dentists.

Progress was being made, however, in training medical personnel within the country. WHO cooperated with the government in founding the Health Assistant and Sanitarian Institute at Riyadh and the Model Health Project at Dammam for the training of health officers, midwives and male and female nurses. Plans are also being made for a medical college at Riyadh. The government also provided many scholarships for students, male and female, seeking medical training abroad. Aramco provides nurses' training for men and women at the Dhahran Medical Center and at the Ras Tanura Hospital.

In 1965 medical assistants were being trained at the Health Assistant and Sanitarian Institute, which offered a 3-year program for graduates of the intermediate cycle of secondary school (see ch. 9, Education). The first 2 years of study consisted of courses in mathematics, natural sciences and English; the third year was a period of internship as assistant pharmacists, male nurses or laboratory or X-ray technicians. Seventeen assistants were graduated from the Institute in 1963. Tuition is free, and students receive a monthly stipend of SR200.

Midwifery has traditionally been regarded as a function of the older female members of the family rather than as a craft performed by trained personnel. The Ministry of Health is attempting to replace traditional midwives by a professional corps of medically trained midwives.

Slightly more than half the country's total nursing staff are female. Nursing is one of the few occupations open to women, and the government is encouraging girls to enter the profession. Government hospitals, however, continued in 1965 to hire mainly male nurses. Male nurses, usually Saudi Arabs, work in outpatient clinics and operating rooms, whereas female nurses, mostly non-Saudi Arabs, are generally assigned to secluded wards out of direct contact with the public.

STANDARD OF LIVING

The standard of living for the majority of Saudi Arabs is at subsistence level and is still essentially determined by geographic circumstance and traditional culture patterns. The government, anxious to raise living standards, has undertaken programs aimed at improving housing conditions, the quality of water supplies and the standard of health. Foreign and international agencies, such as WHO, the United Nations Educational, Scientific and Cultural Organization (UNESCO) and the United States Government, have provided funds and technicians for these programs.

Most Arabs possess few material goods and attach relatively little importance to them. The highest standards of living are in the oil-rich Eastern Province, followed by the Hejaz; in both areas settlement is generally permanent and income higher than in Asir and the Nejd (see ch. 21, Labor).

Refinements, such as electricity, refrigeration and sanitary facilities, are rare and limited to the most developed areas of the country. Rapid urban growth has created an acute housing shortage in the major towns. As a result, tent communities and shantytowns of new settlers have sprung up around these towns.

In the towns the homes are generally mud-brick buildings of one or two stories, clustered irregularly along winding, narrow streets. The larger, more substantial homes of the wealthy are laid out in a more regular arrangement along wider streets. Many are surrounded by walls which also enclose a small garden and a courtyard.

Considerable variety in the use of construction materials and in house design in villages are found from one region to another. In parts of Asir, where African influence is most apparent, the people use reeds for the construction of beehive huts. In mountainous regions houses are built of both cut and uncut stone. In the desert areas most houses and walls are of bricks made of mud mixed with straw and palm; other available woods are used for beams and doors. The house of the average poor family is a one- or two-storied structure of two rooms, one of which may also house the family livestock.

TRADITIONAL WELFARE

Even before the introduction of Islam, Arab society handled welfare and social security through the ancient extended family system in which the unemployed, the aged and ill, the handicapped and the divorced, widowed and orphaned were usually cared for by more fortunate family members. An individual in need of economic help or protection was expected to turn to his kinsmen, to whom he was bound by a network of mutual obligations.

The emergence of Islam in the seventh century, while not fundamentally altering the traditional pattern, superimposed a concept of broader responsibility of Moslems to the Islamic community. Although Moslems accepted inequalities of talent and wealth as ordained by God, they insisted on the moral obligation of the wealthier members of the community to assist the poor. Almsgiving, which represents the direct application of a religious ideal, was originally conceived of as not gratuitous generosity, but as the duty of the donor and the right of the recipient.

In time, alms (*zakat*) came to be collected by the authorities as an annual tax, and the proceeds of the *zakat* were to be used partly for charitable or religious purposes. Since the government began to receive large revenues from oil, the *zakat* has not been as rigorously collected (see ch. 24, Monetary and Financial System). In fact, many farmers and Bedouin have come to expect aid from the government as their right without recognizing any obligation to pay taxes.

This attitude stems partly from a tradition of royal largesse and concern for the needy and partly from the custom established by King Abd al-Aziz Ibn Saud and perpetuated by his sons, Saud Ibn Abd al-Aziz and Faisal Ibn Abd al-Aziz al-Faisal al-Saud, of giving subsidies to tribal sheikhs to ensure their allegiance and submission to the central authority (see ch. 12, Constitution and Government). Although these subsidies were not viewed as payments for welfare purposes, varying amounts generally reached the followers of the sheikhs, who have always assumed a certain responsibility for the well-being of their people.

Another traditional source of charity is the institution of the *waqf*. The *waqf* typically has taken the form of endowments of land left by the donor in perpetuity to his heirs or to charity (see ch. 19, Agriculture). A bequest in the form of a *waqf* frequently carried the stipulation that the income could not be used for charitable purposes until the donor's line had become extinct. Although the institution of the *waqf* has been a contribution to public welfare, it benefits only a small segment of the population.

THE GOVERNMENT'S ROLE IN WELFARE

Since 1962 the government's role in welfare has evolved into a concerted effort by the Ministry of Labor and Social Affairs to establish an integrated welfare program incorporating welfare institutions and a social security agency. The Ministry administers welfare programs through semiautonomous agencies, the Directorate General for Social Affairs, the Red Crescent Society and the Social Security Administration. Twenty-six branch offices of these agencies are operating in localities with over 20,000 inhabitants. Three regional offices exist in Riyadh, Jidda and Dammam.

Welfare Institutions

The Directorate General for Social Affairs, a department of the Ministry of Labor and Social Affairs, supervises the establishment and maintenance of orphanages, reformatories and homes for the aged and disabled. Two women's community service societies, in Jidda and Riyadh, have been established to foster recreational and cultural projects and train members in home economics.

In 1964 there were 20 orphanages, 17 of which were for boys. They represent the first attempt by the state to provide orphans with food, lodging, pocket money and academic or vocational education. Riyadh, Mecca and Medina have homes for the aged and disabled where recreation, medical care, room and board are provided. In 1964 these institutions cared for over 325 patients.

Reformatories are another aspect of evolving attitudes in Saudi society; youths previously condemned to harsh punishments are being sent to reformatories in Riyadh, Mecca and Medina where they receive social guidance and vocational training. After youths are released, reformatories maintain contact with them in order to assist them in adjusting to society. No information was available in late 1965 on the number of youths involved in this program. In late 1964 the Riyadh reformatory was reported to house 190 boys.

Since 1959 the Ministry of Education's Department of Special Education has been operating schools for the blind, called Nour Institutes. In 1965 the program had been expanded from one to five institutes covering academic and vocational education through the intermediate level. This included a school for blind girls in Riyadh opened in 1964. The total enrollment in that year was 720 students, of which 314 were in elementary schools, 32 in intermediate schools and 374 in vocational training. Most of the 118 instructors were Saudi Arabs. Certificates of education offered are the same as those regularly issued by the Ministry.

Textual material for the schools was provided both by talking books received through cooperation with the British Royal Institute for the Blind and by textbooks in braille manufactured in the country.

A boarding school for deaf and dumb children was opened in Riyadh in 1964. It includes training at the kindergarten and elementary school levels.

Social Security

The social security program, enacted in 1962, is essentially the formalization into a government structure of the traditional pattern of dole dispensed by sheikhs and kings. It is aimed at helping individuals and their families to meet emergencies and to support those who cannot care for themselves. The social security program provides a minimum yearly subsidy of SR360 for a family head plus additional amounts depending on the size of the family. Eligibility is limited to fatherless children, families of prisoners, women without support and disabled persons. Special short-term grants are made to those affected by accidents, fires and natural disasters. Thirteen of the 26 regional offices paid out almost SR7.5 million in 1962-63 to about 51,000 individuals in almost 14,000 families.

The Social Security Administration, financed from money received from *zakat* (about SR2.4 million in 1962) and government subsidies, is organized as a semiautonomous branch of the Ministry of Labor and Social Affairs. It comprises representatives from the Ministry of Finance and National Economy and the Directorate General for Social Affairs and five other members forming the executive body.

Insurance and Retirement Plans

Government retirement programs have been in effect since 1945 under the Regulation for Retirement for Government Workers Law, which covers a broad base of government employees (see ch. 21, Labor). The program as amended in 1958 operates on a voluntary basis with employees contributing 9 percent of their salaries. After 25 years of service they receive an annuity based on the average of the last 3 years of employment. Government expenditure on pensions in 1963 was estimated at SR60 million.

There are no laws requiring private companies to provide insurance or retirement plans for their workers.

ARAMCO AND PUBLIC WELFARE

Aramco has established in the oil towns of Eastern Province a number of welfare facilities which directly or indirectly benefit a wide circle of Saudis in addition to the employees and their families.

The company operates a community development program to assist its Arab employees in forming new communities with mosques, markets and recreation facilities. Schools, hospitals and clinics are available for the general public as well as for Aramco workers and their families. The company also cooperates with the government in medical and pest-control programs. Industrial safety measures are enforced, and a workman's compensation fund provides financial assistance to an employee in case of injury or to his family in case of death (see ch. 21, Labor).

Aramco provides a well-developed insurance-retirement program. Their Saudi Arab employees are encouraged to save 10 percent of their yearly income under a Thrift Plan, and in recompense, Aramco matches employees' savings on retirement, or after 15 years. In 1964, 99 percent of eligible workers were participating in the program with combined total savings of SR29 million. Aramco's Employee Housing Loan Plan made it possible for Saudi employees to purchase their houses, and Saudi contractors were given technical advice and interest-free loans for construction projects. The company offers to pay the remaining 20 percent balance on housing loans once 80 percent is paid by employees. By 1964, 5,400 homes were purchased under the program. The company's city-planning service is not limited to the oil area but is available to any community in Saudi Arabia which requests technical assistance.

In the interests of maintaining high standards of health and efficiency, Aramco provides employees on the job with a substantial and balanced diet. The local markets of the oil towns are inspected by company officials, and employees and their families are given instruction in hygiene and preventive measures to reduce the incidence of disease. Extensive as are Aramco's welfare services, they directly benefit only a small proportion of the Saudi population.

SECTION II. POLITICAL BACKGROUND

CHAPTER 12

CONSTITUTION AND GOVERNMENT

Saudi Arabia is a monarchy which was created early in the twentieth century by Abd al-Aziz Ibn Saud, who conquered and unified most of the Arabian peninsula under the banner of a puritanical Islamic brotherhood. The monarchy is controlled by the Saudi dynasty, a noble, old, central Arabian tribe, and is maintained by the consensus of the members of the royal family, by the *ulema* (plural of alem, an Islamic scholar), by the sheikhs (leaders) of the important tribes, by the army and by the bureaucracy which has emerged to deal with the problems of modern national government.

The authority of the monarchy is based on Islamic law, which unites religious and political leadership in the roles of imam (religious leader) and king, and on the recognition of the king as sheikh of sheikhs among the Bedouin tribes and as successor to the Hashemite kings of the Hejaz. The monarch is confirmed as imam by the *ulema* and as king by the emirs (princes) of the royal family.

Gradually, since the formal establishment of the Kingdom of Saudi Arabia in 1932, the king has developed a central government to assist him in running the country. Since 1953 the Council of Ministers appointed by the king has been responsible for advising him on the formulation of general policy and directing the activities of the ministerial bureaucracies created to execute national policy. Legislation is by royal decree or, on minor matters, by ministerial regulation. Justice is administered according to *sharia* (Islamic law) by a system of religious courts headed by the Chief Qadi (Islamic judge) who as Grand Mufti is also leader of the *ulema* and an important official of the government (see ch. 16, Public Order and Safety).

All power rests ultimately with the king who, as chief of state, head of the government, commander in chief of the armed forces, imam and sheikh of sheikhs, is responsible for protecting the institutions of Islam and the interests of the Islamic community, for defending the state and for furthering the interests of the nation.

The power of the king is circumscribed by the requirement that he adhere to the *sharia*, as well as by his need to maintain a consensus among the royal family, the ulema and the important tribal sheikhs. The importance of this consensus was shown in the 1964 deposition of King Saud and his replacement by Crown Prince Faisal which resulted from Saud's loss of support among the royal family and the ulema. The king must also maintain the loyalty of the armed forces and the bureaucracy, on which he depends for the security and continuation of government affairs. At the end of 1965, King Faisal appeared to be in full command of the loyalty of all these elements (see ch. 13, Political Dynamics).

LEGAL BASES OF GOVERNMENT

Islam is the conservative unifying force around which Saudi Arabia's religious, legal and ideological system has been created. The central institution of Islamic civilization has been, and still is, the *sharia*, which is concerned with all of man's activities, from the most private to the most public. Islamic law is not considered to be created by man, but revealed by God. Because secular Western concepts of law have only recently begun to penetrate the country, the *sharia* legal system remains the sole source of public and private law. As such, it constitutes the formal legal basis of authority for the government.

In classical Islamic theory, there are four sources of *sharia* law: the Koran, the Sunna, *ijma* and *qiyas*. The Koran, which contains certain moral and practical injunctions revealed to Mohammed by God, is supplemented by the Sunna (traditions regarding the examples set by the Prophet Mohammed) and the Hadith (recorded sayings and actions of Mohammed). The validity of various traditions as moral guides was decided in the early centuries of Islam by agreement among religious scholars. Their *ijma* (consensus) constitutes another source of Islamic law. Situations for which there was no precedent could, nevertheless, be dealt with through the applications by *qiyas* (analogy) of the Koran and the Sunna to new problems. This constituted for some Islamic legists a fourth source of *sharia* law.

Four major schools of jurisprudence based on different interpretations of the *sharia* grew up in the second and third Islamic centuries (ninth and tenth centuries of the Christian era). The differences between them were not fundamental but were based on the degree of emphasis laid on the various sources of the *sharia*. These differences persist, though they have little significance in the daily lives of individual Moslems. Each tends to predominate for historical reasons in a given geographic area.

The Hanifite school, founded by Abu Hanifa in Iraq, was adopted by the Ottoman Turks and still predominates in regions where Turkish domination was strong, including Hejaz and parts of Eastern Province in Saudi Arabia. Malek Ibn Anas founded the Malekite school, based on the practice of judges at Medina; it predominates in North and West Africa and upper Egypt. Ash-Shafi, founder of the Shafiite school of law now predominant in lower Egypt and among the nomads of the eastern shores of the Mediterranean and parts of the west coast of the Arabian peninsula, used *qiyas* less than the preceding schools.

The fourth and last school of law was founded at Baghdad by Ibn Hanbal (died A.D. 885). By far the most conservative and rigid school, it rejects all innovation and advocates the use only of the Koran and the Sunna as sources of law, opposing the use of *qiyas*. The Hanbalite school was strong for a time in Iraq and Syria but lost influence after the Ottoman conquest in the fifteenth century. In the eighteenth century it was revived by Mohammed Ibn Abd al-Wahhab in Nejd and became the rallying point of the Sauds in their battles to unify the peninsular Arabs. As the school adhered to by the Wahhabi ulema and by the Sauds, the Hanbalite school still predominates in most of Saudi Arabia, although the other schools are recognized and respected.

It is the duty of the imam—who is also the king—to safeguard the practice of Islam throughout the community and to assure the full adherence to the prescriptions of the *sharia*. The continuing importance of this requirement is shown by the statement made by Crown Prince Faisal in November 1962 when as prime minister he proposed the establishment of a written constitution, the so-called Basic Law:

> In order to achieve a unified system of government based on the principles of the Sharia, a Basic Law will be promulgated, drawn from the Koran, the Traditions of the Prophet and the acts of the orthodox caliphs. It will set forth the fundamental principles of government and the relationship between the governor and the governed. ... The government has adopted and will continue adopting means necessary to spread, strengthen and protect Islam by word and by deed.

As the kingdom began to take form and the central government claimed authority over tribal government, modern precedents and written laws were added to the traditional legal bases of government. Government in the province of the Hejaz in the 1920's provided one such modern precedent.

When Abd al-Aziz Ibn Saud conquered the Hejaz in 1925, he found a more advanced state of government than that of Nejd. This was because of the influence of the Ottoman Empire which had long controlled the Hejaz and of greater exposure to the West through the foreign contacts with Mecca pilgrims (see ch. 3, Historical Setting). To accommodate and preserve the advanced institutions of the Hejaz, Abd al-Aziz issued what has come to be known as the Organic Instructions of Hejaz or the 1926 Constitution of the Hejaz. For the most part, this law described already existing institutions and practices and guaranteed their continuation. After the union of the Hejaz and Nejd into the Kingdom of Saudi Arabia in 1932, the 1926 Constitution of the Hejaz remained as a general statement of government in that province.

The recognition contained in the Constitution of the Hejaz that law created by man could supplement the revealed law of the *sharia* was crucial to the evolution of a modern state. The development of manmade law continued and accelerated, particularly after World War II, but always was subordinated to the *sharia*, with which no law may be in conflict.

The traditional form of patriarchal rule by the king with the consent of a few ministers and advisers was adequate until the administrative and financial complexities brought on after World War II by the sudden flow of oil revenues necessitated a revision. The increased volume of government business, requiring a corresponding increase of administrative personnel and leadership, led to the gradual development of a ministerial system.

The ministerial system was not formally institutionalized, however, until October 1953 when King Abd al-Aziz issued a decree creating the Council of Ministers under the leadership of a prime minister. The decree marked a significant step in the creation of modern institutions of government. For the first time the various ministries were brought together into a single body with competence over the affairs of the entire kingdom, at home and abroad. The Council of Ministers had no executive authority. Ministers appointed by the king were to consider the affairs of the kingdom and recommend decisions to the king, who approved all decisions before they became law. In the mid-1950's, most government ministries were transferred from Jidda to Riyadh, signifying a final move in the consolidation of governmental institutions in the Saudi dynasty's traditional homeland in the Nejd.

The next significant step in the development of the legal bases of government, one providing the legal basis of today's ministerial system, was the revised Statute of the Council of Ministers of

May 1958. The reorganization of the Council of Ministers transformed a purely advisory council into a formal, policymaking body with both executive and legislative powers. The new statute advanced the government another step toward a ministerial system.

At the end of 1965 official statements describing the governmental system, the nature of the central authority and the extent of its powers had not been drawn together into a constitution. The need for such a general statement, however, was felt by various elements of the ruling group close to the king. Several attempts in the direction of a constitution had been made, but none had gone beyond the stage of proposal.

Although pressures in the direction of a constitutional law had probably been felt before, the first public demand for such a law occurred in 1960. Prince Talal Ibn Abd al-Aziz, leading a group of liberal members of the royal family known as the free princes, proposed to Prime Minister Faisal a program of more limited monarchy with a partially elected parliament. The proposal was refused and has not been made again (see ch. 13, Political Dynamics).

In November 1962, however, Prime Minister Faisal announced the preparation of the Basic Law, a 10-point program which promised to "set forth the fundamental principles of government and the relationship between the governor and the governed—to provide for the basic rights of the citizen." A consultative council, developed as a legislative authority, was to be included in the Basic Law, and preliminary steps toward the organization of local government under the authority of the central government were to be taken. At the same time, a ministry of justice and a supreme judiciary council were promised, and the immunity of the judiciary from political pressures was to be guaranteed. The judiciary council, composed of leading members of the ulema, was to consider "problems arising from conflicts between the Koran and traditions and the constantly changing experiences of people in worldly affairs." Thus, the need for accommodation between the *sharia* and modern legal problems was recognized and was to be made the responsibility of outstanding Islamic jurists.

Although many of the social and economic reforms to be part of the proposed Basic Law have been promulgated, no unified constitutional law describing the nature and extent of royal power had been issued by the end of 1965, nor had the judicial organs been established.

THE STRUCTURE OF CENTRAL GOVERNMENT

The King

The central institution of the government is the monarchy. With the transformation of Arabia into a kingdom in 1932 and the entry of the kingdom into the community of nations, Abd al-Aziz Ibn Saud assumed the title of King of Saudi Arabia. As such he added the modern roles of chief of state and commander in chief of the armed forces to his traditional roles of sheikh of sheikhs of the Bedouin tribes and imam of the Islamic community. When he created the Council of Ministers in 1953, he appointed Crown Prince Saud to the new post of prime minister; when Saud became king, the prime ministry was delegated to Crown Prince Faisal. The separation of the positions of head of state and head of government between 1953 and 1964 resulted in rivalry between Saud and Faisal, especially after 1958. As a result, when Faisal became king in 1964, he combined both positions for the first time (see ch. 13, Political Dynamics).

It is to the king that all foreign representatives are accredited, and it is the king who appoints ambassadors and other envoys sent abroad. He names all ministers, other senior government officials and the governors of the provinces, and selects all military officers above the rank of colonel. All legislation is by royal decree. The king is also the highest court of appeal, and he has the power of pardon.

The responsible members of the royal family choose the king from among themselves with the sanction of the ulema. The investiture of the king takes place in a traditional ceremony (*baya*), which is a form of contract between the ruler and the ruled. The king promises to govern in accordance with the laws of Islam and the traditions of the country. The *ulema,* the royal family, the council of ministers, the consultative council and local leaders from all parts of the kingdom express their support of the newly chosen king by personally paying allegiance. Technically, either the king or the people may break the oath. Should a king not rule in accordance with the general precepts of *sharia,* he would violate his mandate and could legally be deposed, although the circumstances would be important determinants.

The power of the king is not defined. It is, however, practically limited by the fact that he must retain a consensus of the royal family and, to an extent at least, of the *ulema* and the tribal chiefs. Abd al-Aziz held the loyalty of these elements as well as of the population at large because of his strong personality and his role as unifier of the country. Saud retained the consensus for a time by maintaining close contacts with the tribes by subsidizing and making marriage relationships with them. In 1964, however, when he proved unable to cope with the problems of a modernizing society, the royal family and the ulema deposed him in favor of his brother Faisal. The requirement that he maintain a consensus has restrained Faisal in his exercise of political power.

Assisting King Faisal as chief of state is the Royal Cabinet, the equivalent of a modern executive staff. Economic, social and political advisers, chosen for their expertise as much as for their closeness to the king, head the four principal divisions of the Royal Cabinet: General Administration, Personnel, Translation and Press, and the Office of Bedouin Affairs. King Faisal has also named a Supreme Council for Administrative Reforms, a Directorate of Royal Protocol, a Central Planning Commission, a General Personnel Bureau and a Consultative Council.

The 24-member Consultative or Advisory Council, which evolved out of the regional consultative council functioning in the Hejaz since the 1920's, is chosen by the king from among prominent citizens, businessmen and professionals. The king presides over the Consultative Council. Its purpose is to assist in an advisory fashion the work of the Council of Ministers, such as by considering proposed legislation before its promulgation. The Consultative Council apparently plays no role of decisive importance, which suggests that its function is more honorific than political. Nevertheless, it has been mentioned as a possible prototype for a future legislative assembly. In November 1964 the Consultative Council convened jointly with the Council of Ministers to confirm and approve the decision of the *ulema* and the members of the royal family which deposed Saud and made Faisal king.

Council of Ministers

Ministries are a recent innovation. Abd al-Aziz ruled the Nejd and Al-Hasa along the traditional Arab lines without formal ministries. When he occupied the Hejaz, however, he found a more complex system of government already established by the Ottomans and the regime of the Hashemites (see ch. 3, Historical Setting). A council of deputies was set up under the then Emir Faisal, who was viceroy, representing his father, Abd al-Aziz. Each deputy was in charge of a specific department or agency of the government of the Hejaz and in effect ruled the Hejaz under the viceroy in cooperation with a consultative assembly which still exists.

As the central government expanded its functions—built railroads and schools, took an interest in agriculture, established a postal and telecommunications service and developed a permanent, organized system of defense—it was found necessary to establish ministries on what was at least an approach to the Western model. The first ministries were the Ministry of Foreign Affairs and the Ministry of Finance, established in 1930 and 1932, respectively. In 1944 the Ministry of Defense (now the Ministry of National Defense and Aviation) evolved out of the Agency for Defense. In 1953-54 the Ministries of Communications, Economy, Education, Agriculture, Commerce and Industry, and Health were formed. The Ministries of Finance and Economy were amalgamated in 1954. The Ministry of Information was created in 1955. In addition, other agencies included the Department of Labor and the Directorates General of Petroleum and Mineral Affairs and of Broadcasting, Press and Publications. The Ministry of Interior was established in 1951 for the whole country, but some of the functions, including the supervision of public security, the coast guard and the municipal government, continued to be exercised in Eastern Province by the provincial government.

Although the ministries are organized formally on Western lines, with divisions and field offices which may be shown on charts or tables of organization, Western principles and practices are modified to suit local conditions. In the functioning of any ministry, as in that of any part of the government on any level, the element of personality is very important. Decisions are made by the minister himself, usually after consultation with some of his subordinates.

In 1953 the Council of Ministers was formed. The organization and functions of the Council were redefined by a royal decree issued on May 12, 1958. In 1965 it was made up of King Faisal as prime minister and minister of foreign affairs, Crown Prince Khalid as deputy prime minister, and 12 ministers appointed by the king. Ministers without portfolio and royal counselors may also be appointed to the Council of Ministers (see fig. 5 and table 3).

The King proposed in November 1962 the creation of a Ministry of Justice to deal with the problem of reconciling the *sharia* and decree laws which had been promulgated over the years to regulate commercial and other activities not covered by the *sharia*. As of the end of 1965 this ministry had not yet been established, although it had appeared in the annual budgets since 1962, presumably to cover expenditures for the *sharia* courts and other judicial bodies (see ch. 16, Public Order and Internal Security; ch. 24, Monetary and Financial System).

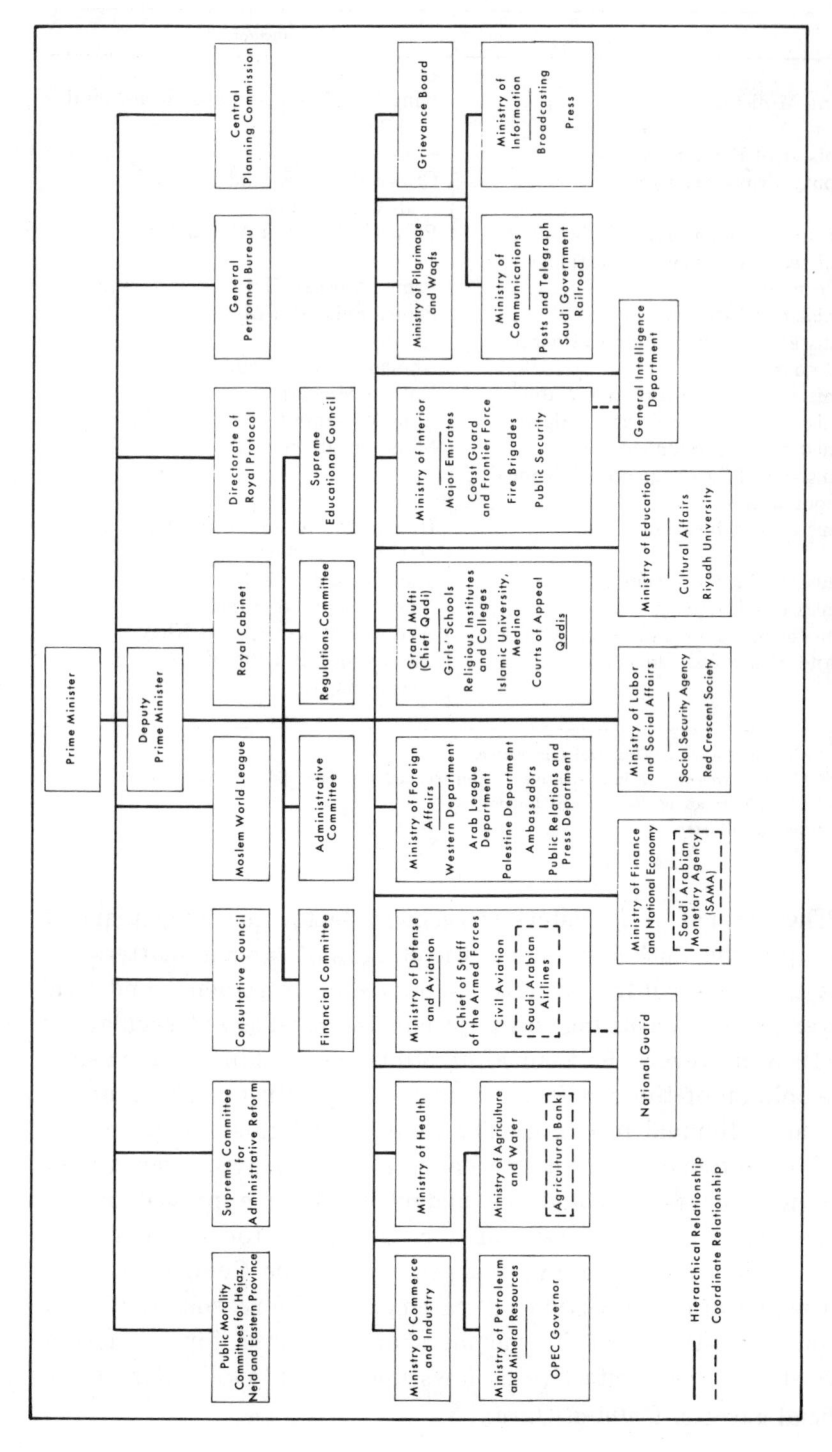

Figure 5. Organization of the Government of Saudi Arabia, 1965.

Table 3. *Council of Ministers of Saudi Arabia, 1965*

Title of Office	Incumbent
Prime Minister	King Faisal Ibn Abd al-Aziz al-Faisal al-Saud
Minister of Foreign Affairs	—do—
Deputy Prime Minister	Crown Prince Khalid Ibn Abd al-Aziz al-Saud
Minister of Defense and Aviation	Prince Sultan Ibn Abd al-Aziz
Minister of Finance and National Economy	Prince Musaad Ibn Abd ar-Rahman[1]
Minister of Interior	Prince Fahd Ibn Abd al-Aziz[2]
Minister of Petroleum and Mineral Resources	Ahmad Zaki Yamani[3]
Minister of Agriculture and Water	Hassan Mishari
Minister of Commerce and Industry	Abid Mohammed Salih Shaykh
Minister of Communications	Mohammed Omar Tawfiq
Minister of Pilgrimage and Religious Foundations	—do—[4]
Minister of Education	Hassan Ibn Abdullah Ibn Hassan Al ash-Shaykh
Minister of Information	Jamil Ibrahim al-Hujaylan
Minister of Health	Yusuf Yaqub al-Hajiri
Minister of Labor and Social Affairs	Abd ar-Rahman Abu al-Khayl
Grand Mufti and Chief Qadi	Mohammed Ibn Ibrahim Al ash-Shaykh

[1] Also Chairman of Financial Committee.
[2] Also Chairman of Administrative Committee and Supreme Educational Council.
[3] Also Chairman of Regulations Committee.
[4] Acting minister.

The Council of Ministers is responsible for the budget and is the supreme authority under the king in financial matters. It has extensive control over the supervision of regional and local government. According to the provincial government regulations of 1963, however, the Council of Ministers is obliged to consider the opinion of the provincial councils in certain matters concerning an individual province. The Council of Ministers has policy-making authority in most internal matters. All laws, international treaties, concessions and the budget must be approved by the king and require the issue of a royal decree for promulgation. Should the king not approve a proposal of the Council, it is returned within 30 days, with a statement of the reasons for its refusal. Two-thirds of its members are required for a quorum. Decisions become effective as laws upon their publication in the official gazette, *Umm al-Qura*.

The Council of Ministers includes a finance committee, an administrative committee, a regulations committee and a supreme educational council. The Grievance Board, created in 1954, may hear any sort of complaint, even of a nongovernmental nature, such as that leveled against a surgeon for operating without the consent of a patient. It is responsible directly to the king, and its functions are a development of the traditional practice of direct accessibility to the king by any citizen with a grievance against the government. Not dissimilar to a modern administrative court, the Grievance Board was devised to deal with those disputes obviously beyond the competence of *sharia*.

The Ulema

The *ulema* is a group of distinguished religious scholars which, in traditional Arab government, was the guardian of the orthodoxy of political acts. Approval or disapproval by the *ulema* was expressed through the issuance of a *fetwa* (legal decision). The transfer of powers from King Saud to Crown Prince Faisal, the deposition of King Saud and the proclamation of Faisal as king in 1964 were first authorized by a *fetwa* signed by 12 of the most prestigious *ulema*. Due to changing social and economic conditions, the real political power of the *ulema* has waned in recent years, although its religious influence is still great. In 1950, when the government attempted to introduce an income tax, the *ulema* was able to exert sufficient pressure to have taxation restricted to foreigners. By the 1960's, however, when the *ulema* protested the use of women's voices on radio programs, the government was able to override its arguments.

Government Personnel

The government is the largest employer in the country. Military forces excluded, a 1960 estimate put the number of civil servants at 30,000. All business connected with government employees is handled through the General Personnel Bureau. According to the general regulations for government employees, which was drafted in the late 1950's but is now under extensive revision, there are nine grades below the ministerial level. Ministers are appointed directly by the king. Grades one to three are poltical appointments based on recommendations from particular ministries. Grades four to nine are nonappointive and based on qualifying examinations. In cases where more posts are open than there are applicants, those with school certificates may waive examination.

Saudi Arabia has suffered from a shortage of trained personnel. In the 1940's and 1950's the government relied heavily, even at the ministerial level, on nationals from other Arab countries, such as Syria and Lebanon, or on Palestinian Arabs. In 1958, however, Saudi Arabian citizenship was made a requirement for membership in the Council of Ministers and, with the increasing number of students returning from abroad, the trend in recent years has been to replace foreign nationals with qualified young Saudi Arabian officials. A parallel trend has been the increasing rise of commoners to high office, displacing certain members of the nobility. In 1965, 4 out of 12 ministers were still princes of the House of Saud.

REGIONAL AND LOCAL GOVERNMENT

Hegemony of the central government over the tribes, especially the nomadic Bedouin tribes, is indirect and in some cases nominal and is exercised through tribal sheikhs chosen by the heads of the most important families and lineages within the tribe. Before the unification of Saudi Arabia the people governed themselves through *majlis* (tribal councils), following their own customary law in some cases where it conflicted with *sharia*, and exercised full autonomy within their area.

With the creation of a central government, Abd al-Aziz created a degree of cohesiveness between the tribes and the government by touring the countryside and holding a royal *majlis* at which the tribal sheikhs could make their positions and desires known to the king, by making marriage contracts with important local families, and by subsidizing regional notables from the royal purse. A similar policy was followed by King Saud, although by the 1950's the sedentarization of the tribes and the increasingly direct application of the authority of the central government over individual citizens made inappropriate the use of such tradational means of government. King Faisal continues to meet on an almost daily basis with Bedouin sheikhs and other notables in his *majlis* in Riyadh, but he does not make extensive visits to the tribal areas. He has also sharply reduced the use of the royal subsidy since 1958 when he separated the government and the royal treasury and made the funds available to the royal family subject to the government budget (see ch. 24, Monetary and Financial System).

Local government remains closer to its traditional form than the national government. Developments in tribal, village, city and provincial politics have, for the most part, been introduced by the central government, but relations between the national and local authorities remain ill defined and intermittent. Although the national leadership has long recognized the limitations of traditional forms of relations with the rural population, the absence of any real pressure for revision tends to perpetuate traditional practices on the level of local government.

Several legal precedents, however, have been established for local government, some of which describe existing structures, whereas others instituted new practices. The 1926 Constitution of the Hejaz put into writing the practices of the region, which were based in large part on principles of Ottoman administration. The growth of towns and the need for some codification of procedure led to the 1938 Municipal Regulations, which neither described an existing situation nor provided a model for subsequent urban administration, but it still stands as a sole statement of government in the larger towns. In 1963 a comprehensive statute finally was drawn up to standardize existing procedures of provincial government and, in some instances, to create new institutions.

Since the consolidation of the kingdom in 1927, relations between the king and provincial leaders have been based for the most part on kinship. The case of Eastern Province is exemplary. Emir Saud Ibn Abdullah Ibn Jiluwi, who is closely related to the royal family, has ruled Eastern Province as a semiautonomous principality since the 1920's.

The central government maintains control over the tribes, villages and municipalities through the territorial emirs. Taxes are collected from the tribes by agents of the emirs. The personal influence of the king as sheikh of sheikhs is still an important element in ensuring the loyalty of the sheikhs and of the tribes.

In the past royal authority was maintained among the tribes by the liberal use of subsidies by the king. Although King Faisal seldom tours the provinces as did his predecessors, traditional tribal leaders frequently come to Riyadh, where the monarch is readily accessible (see ch. 13, Political Dynamics).

Authority in traditional tribal government resides in the *majlis*, which selects the sheikh and confers on important issues. The authority of the tribe extends to all its members and is circumscribed by known geographical boundaries, within which the tribe has exclusive rights to water, pasturage and hunting.

Provincial Regulations of October 1963

Before 1963 regional, administrative appointments, the allocations of local finances, and even the delimitation of provincial boundaries to the extent that they occurred, were not specified in law. They were largely handled by the king. In October 1963 the government decreed a comprehensive statute of provincial regulations. New posts were created, specific duties assigned and old practices prohibited, and the central government was closely linked to the provinces. Boundaries were more adequately distinguished and provincial councils were formally constituted, but no mention was made of municipal councils. By making specific that which had traditionally been carried out by custom, the government took another important step in the direction of establishing a modern state. The extent to which the 1963 provincial regulations had been carried out by late 1965 was not known.

The regulations, consisting of 40 articles, provided for the division of the kingdom into five provinces (*mokata*), which in turn were subdivided into districts (*mantika*) and subdistricts (*raiz markez*). The provinces, as determined by the minister of interior and the Council of Ministers are Nejd (Central), Al-Hasa (Eastern), Hejaz (Western), Asir (Southern) and the Northern Frontier Province. As legal personalities the provinces may own property, control public utilities, and receive and dispense public funds.

A governor general (*hakem*) is the central government's representative in the province. After being nominated by the minister of interior and appointed by royal decree upon the recommendation of the prime minister, a governor general takes an oath of allegiance to his religion, the country and the king.

Provincial governors general administer their provinces according to the general policy of the kingdom. Specifically, the statute of provincial regulations requires the provincial governor general to implement the decisions of the courts, to preserve public order and security, to protect the rights and liberties of individuals within the limits of *sharia,* to oversee and inspect the administration of the districts and subdistricts, to report regularly to the minister of interior, to assist the national government in the collection of revenues, to protect the state's funds and properties, to cooperate with the ministries conducting work in the province and, with the provincial council, to supervise the affairs of the municipalities and to oversee the work of all government employees in the province.

Assisting the governor general is a deputy governor general (*wakil hakem*), who is nominated by the minister of interior and appointed by the prime minister. The tasks of the deputy governor general are to act for the governor general in his absence and to assume the duties of governor of the district in which the provincial capital is situated.

At the district level a district governor, responsible to the provincial governor general, is appointed by the Council of Ministers upon the nomination of the minister of interior. A headman is nominated by the provincial governor general and appointed by the minister of interior to administer the affairs of each subdistrict. The duties of the district governors and the subdistrict heads are similar to the governor general's in all affairs but those relating to the central government.

Provincial governors general, district governors and subdistrict headmen are all prohibited from interfering in any way with the judiciary, from buying, selling or renting any public property within their own province, from requiring any soldier or employee to perform personal services or to serve personal interests, and from utilizing public funds or property for their own use.

Provincial Councils

Almost three-fourths of the 1963 provincial regulations concern the establishment, jurisdiction and general rules of provincial councils. Although the concept of the council has been a central political institution in Arabian history, its formalization into written law is new. Information on the progress of the establishment of the new provincial councils was still difficult to obtain in 1965.

The provincial council, situated in the provincial capital, is presided over by the governor general or, in his absence, by the deputy governor general. A council, the term of which is 2 years, is composed of not more than 30 members. Members are selected from among the inhabitants of the province by a decision of the Council of Ministers upon the nomination of the minister of interior. Representatives of various ministries, the works of which are related to the affairs of the province, are included among the selected members. The presence of members who are also representatives of the central government suggests an attempt at closer central control and coordination of local affairs.

Requirements for membership stipulate that a candidate be 25 years of age, of good moral character, literate, a regular resident and have his income from or be a property owner in the province; in exceptional cases the Council of Ministers reserves the right to waive the requirements of residence, property ownership and literacy. Membership is renewable by reselection at the end of the 2-year term. Except for those members who are representatives of ministries, provincial councilors cannot hold another public office. Any membership requirement which is not lived up to can bring about the cancellation of membership by the minister of interior.

Councilors have the right to submit proposals or put questions to the chairman of the council, who must include such proposals and questions on the agenda of the next meeting. A councilor is restricted from attending meetings at which are discussed matters related to his own interests or interests which he represents; from undertaking himself, or through a third party, any work, contract, tender or purveyance in any business relating to the council; and from contracting with the council any sale or lease. Except for councilors who are also government employees, members are to be paid a salary and travel expenses for official business.

The jurisdiction of the provincial councils is carefully outlined in the 1963 provincial regulations. Although the council is responsible for all that concerns the inhabitants of the province, several categories of responsibility are specified. In municipal affairs the provincial council is to cooperate with and assist in the performance of duties and in the execution of projects. In educational affairs the provincial council is to propose and supervise the establishment of literacy campaigns, vocational training centers and technical schools. In agriculture the provincial councils are to propose the establishment of model farms, exhibits, cooperative societies and subsidiary agricultural industries and to regulate local markets.

Financial responsibilities of the councils include the presentation of an annual budget for approval by the Ministry of Interior (see ch. 24, Monetary and Financial System).

The provincial councils are in charge of the financial affairs of the provinces. It appears that most of the revenue of the provinces come from the central government, although the province is empowered to propose financial revenues, contract loans, accept gifts and receive revenue from utilities. The provincial councils present a comprehensive budget for the approval of the Ministry of Interior.

Except for certain specified matters, the provincial council has no jurisdiction over matters within the jurisdiction of municipal councils. Moreover, it may not discuss military affairs, or national policies, external or internal. Decisions of the provincial council, which are to be made only when the council is in session, may be canceled by the minister of interior should they fall outside the jurisdiction of the council.

Ordinary sessions of the provincial councils are called monthly by the governor general. He may summon an extraordinary meeting and is obliged to do so if it is demanded in writing by half of the councilors. Permanent committees are decided upon and elected from among councilors at the first session of the year.

The provincial council may make proposals or express its wishes (through the governor general and the minister of interior on any matter concerning the general interest of the province) to any minister or the Council of Ministers. Decisions of the councils are made by a simple majority vote of the members present. The vote of the chairman—the governor general—decides a tie vote.

Dissolution of a provincial council may occur by decision of the Council of Ministers, upon recommendation of the minister of interior. Dissolution of all provincial councils is prohibited except in necessary cases decided upon by the Council of Ministers. During the period of dissolution the authority of the council is exercised by the governor general with the participation of members appointed ex officio. A new council must be selected within 3 months of dissolution. Decisions made during the time of dissolution must be submitted to the new council for its information during its first session.

Municipal Government

Government in the larger cities was first regulated under the 1938 Municipal Regulations. Although this law gives little clue to the present-day structure of government in any city, it does provide a basic framework.

A chief administrative officer, appointed by the minister of interior, is in charge of each municipality; the emir presides over an administrative council, which is in charge of drafting the municipal budget. A municipal council, composed of a variable number of members elected for 3 years, meets weekly to recommend action and execute decisions. The municipal council elections are the only instance of elections in the country. A chairman and deputy chairman are elected by secret ballot from among the councilmen. Two-thirds of the councilmen, or the chairman, alone, may call extraordinary sessions of the municipal council.

According to the 1938 Municipal Regulations, municipal councils in Mecca, Medina and Jidda consisted of landlords, members of special crafts and professions, and the notables elected by the king. In every municipality there was an administrative committee composed of the head of the municipality and the directors of its different sections. These committees met at least twice a week to investigate ways and means of carrying out municipal council resolutions.

Village Government

In the village a leader, sometimes called the sheikh, is chosen from the leading lineage of this village. He is expected to show leadership qualities, such as wisdom, learning and maturity, as well as ability to compromise disputes within the village, to maintain good relations with neighboring settlements and tribes and to work effectively with the higher administrative units. In a larger community the leader, known as the emir, owes his position to recognition by the leaders of the prominent families of the town, by the ulema and by the local *qadis*. Succession to the leadership of a village or town is confirmed by the emir of the larger political division.

CHAPTER 13

POLITICAL DYNAMICS

Since the establishment of the kingdom in 1932 political activity in terms of competition for political power has been restricted to the royal family and a small number of religious and tribal leaders closely associated with it. In 1965 even this competition appeared to be at a low level as King Faisal and his supporters seemed to have unquestioned authority. No organized political or other interest groups existed, although pressures for political change were known to have been expressed by individuals or by small groups outside the country.

The competition for power followed the traditional form of individual rivalries among those close to the center of power. Each side sought to acquire legitimacy through the support of the ulema (body of Islamic scholars) and to increase its power by gaining the support of important tribal chiefs, regional governors and elements of the bureaucracy and the armed forces. The scope of competition for the throne has been within the royal family, which numbers several hundred members; fewer than a hundred princes wield political influence, however.

It appeared at the end of 1965 that the overwhelming majority of the people were satisfied to leave national politics to the small ruling group. No significant pressure for broadening popular participation in politics or for permitting the organization of political or other interest groups was known to exist.

The only significant efforts to organize interest groups occurred in 1953 and in 1956, when employees of the Arabian American Oil Company (Aramco), under the influence of Egyptian and other non-Saudi Arab labor organizers, attempted through work stoppages to press their demands for the right to organize labor unions. The government responded by specifically prohibiting the formation of labor organizations, the exercise of collective bargaining or the use of strikes or demonstrations by more than two employees acting in concert. Expression of worker dissatisfaction since that time has been limited to the boycott of the Aramco cafeteria by the large majority of Aramco's workers which began in 1963 and was continuing in 1965. The primary purpose of this boycott appeared to the demonstration of the ability of the workers to organize informally within the limits of the law.

Some Saudi Arabs who studied abroad returned with ambitions to speed the modernization of the country. Some, including an unknown number of members of the royal family, have proclaimed liberal, even socialist, goals. The only organized expression of such a view, however, was that made by the so-called "free princes," under the leadership of Prince Talal Ibn Abd al-Aziz, who in December 1960 acquired positions in the government under King Saud. Nevertheless, they were unable to realize their reformist hopes, and since the return of Faisal to power in 1962, such views have been muted. Instead, Faisal established a policy of gradual modernization aimed at reconciling the demands of the reformers and of the stanch conservatives. His program encompassed significant social and economic improvements and modest legal reforms.

The conservative ulema have challenged certain aspects of King Faisal's modernization program, resisting such innovations as the education of girls, the introduction of television, the employment of women and the moderation of traditional proscriptions against smoking, dancing and the playing of music in public. King Faisal has on several occasions overruled the ulema in pursuing his goals. In all essential areas, however, he has adhered to an orthodox Islamic interpretation of the role of the state and the government in an Islamic society (see ch. 12, Constitution and Government).

POLITICAL DEVELOPMENTS, 1953–64

In the early 1960's the effects of the revolutionary changes in the economic sector of the country were only beginning to be felt in the social order and hardly at all in the political. The amalgamation of traditional and Western technological cultures was slow and uneven. The puritanical Wahhabi Islamic brotherhood tended to exclude foreign influences and to resist what few had entered.

Between the two world wars private American oil interests entered the country, establishing the rudiments of modern organization and widening contacts with Saudi Arabs among the villagers and nomads of Eastern Province. After World War II contacts with American military and diplomatic officials as well as construction supervisors, petroleum technicians and businessmen increased rapidly. In addition, educated and politically sophisticated Arabs from other Middle Eastern countries came, attracted by the need for trained personnel in a rapidly expanding government service. Refugee intellectuals from Palestine worked side by side with civil servants in Riyadh and Jidda; Egyptian teachers spread literacy to village schoolchildren; and military advisers trained desert warriors in modern tactics. From these contacts with the outside, Saudi Arabs learned of men and events in the rapidly changing Arab world around them. Those who came into closest contact with the new influences became translators of new ways to others.

Despite great change in the economic and social sphere, the traditional political system remained almost untouched. Administratively, the government had been streamlined—new ministries were opened and the bureaucracy was vastly expanded—but the narrow base of power was the same. The people who filled the newly created jobs acquired an awareness of different life styles and began to assume new values and new aspirations, but there was no corresponding change from their previously inert role in national politics.

In the mid-1950's, however, a few individuals were beginning to speak of changing the traditional order and were beginning to demand a share in the exercise of national power. Most had been educated abroad and were in occupations which scarcely existed a decade before, but some also came from the royal family itself.

As long as Abd al-Aziz Ibn Saud ruled—that is, from 1902 until his death in 1953—his great prestige gave little room for opposition to his reign. His son, King Saud, however, was forced to deal with the growing political and social awareness of his people without the unquestioned authority of his father. His efforts to preserve paternalistic political patterns and his failure to utilize effectively the rapidly growing oil wealth for the betterment of his people aroused growing resentment. In early 1958 a worsening financial crisis and an international incident, in which King Saud was accused by the Egyptian Goverment of involvement in an attempt to assassinate President Nasser, compelled the royal family to force the King to transfer full executive responsibility to Crown Prince Faisal, who was also Prime Minister. Through this action the rivalry between the two sons of Abd Al-Aziz first became public.

In mid-1960, King Saud began to try to reassert his authority. He toured the provinces to gain support of local tribal leaders, some of whom had suffered from Faisal's austere financial policies. Importers and contractors who depended on government expenditures also felt the weight of Faisal's austerity program.

Within the royal family, Prince Talal, the King's younger brother, led a group of young princes who demanded more rapid modernization of Saudi society. Talal was separated from the possibility of inheriting the throne by more than a dozen others closer in the line of descent. Talal and his supporters in the royal family took up the cause of constitutionalism, which many considered to be only a vehicle in a move to power.

The first signs of discontent with Faisal's regime came in June 1960, when Prince Talal and a small following in the royal family demanded the establishment of an elected body with legislative powers and other constitutional reforms. They proposed a draft constitution and called for a more limited monarchy and a partially elected parliament. As prime minister, Faisal rejected the proposals on the ground that the existing government was adequate and that change was not necessary. Such a position appeared to put him against those who championed the cause of reform and seemed to create the conditions for a temporary alliance between King Saud and Talal.

King Saud's growing impatience at being out of power was reflected in an unusual speech from the throne in November 1960 on the seventh anniversary of his reign. Observers remarked that the vigor and scope of the speech presaged an active bid for a return to power. One month later, Prime Minister Faisal resigned. King Saud immediately announced a new council, naming himself prime minister and giving the key ministerial posts of finance and national economy to Prince Talal and the new Ministry of Petroleum and Mineral Resources to Abdullah Ibn Hammud Tariqi, a strong nationalist.

The political reforms demanded by the liberals soon became the subject of disagreements between the new Council of Ministers and the King. On December 25, Radio Mecca announced that the Council of Ministers had met for the first time and had approved the establishment of a partially elected national council and an order to draft a constitution. Three days later Radio Mecca denied that the Council of Ministers had approved any such resolution. However close the Talal group had come to introducing their proposed constitutional reforms, it soon became clear that King Saud had no intention of implementing them.

Subsequently, Talal increasingly criticized the Saud regime. In Beirut, in the summer of 1961, he again called for the creation of a national assembly to initiate representative government. In September 1961, Talal's dismissal from the Council of Ministers left Tariqi as the only advocate of liberalism remaining in the government.

In 1962, Talal relinquished his royal title and went into exile in Cairo. From Cairo he and three brothers renounced thir Saudi Arabian citizenship, set up a committee for the "liberation" of Saudi Arabia and talked of a Saudi Arab Republic. Talal published a book in which he outlined his ideas for constitutional reform, extolling socialism as a fundamental principle of Islam.

King Saud's chronic illness, however, began to complicate the three-cornered power struggle. When in November 1961 sickness forced him to leave for the United States for medical treatment, in order to leave the affairs of the country in loyal hands, he could turn only to Faisal, to whom he delegated executive responsibility on a temporary basis.

By March 1962 the King's continuing poor health caused him to name Faisal deputy prime minister and acting head of the Council of Ministers. A condition of Faisal's return was the elimination of Tariqi from the Council of Ministers. Thus, barely 15 months after he had resigned from government, Faisal regained effective if not formal executive power.

In October 1962, as a result of threats to the regime brought on by the situation in Yemen, King Saud dismissed his Council of Ministers and made Crown Prince Faisal prime minister once again. During the next year, Faisal took a number of steps to consolidate his position. He replaced King Saud's sons in the Council of Ministers by three of his own brothers—Princes Khalid Ibn Abd al-Aziz al-Saud, Fahd Ibn Abd al-Aziz and Sultan Ibn Abd al-Aziz—and an uncle, Prince Musaad Ibn Abd ar-Rahman, who were loyal to him. He removed most of King Saud's Royal Guard from the palace for duty along the Yemen border, and he outlined a broad political reform program. These acts, which received the approval of Prince Abdullah Ibn Abd ar-Rahman, Faisal's uncle and senior member of the royal family, were facilitated by the King's absence from the country during much of 1962 and 1963. In August 1963 the dissident Prince Talal, plus three brothers and a cousin, requested permission to return to the country; by February 1964, Talal and his followers had returned, admitted they had erred and pledged support of Faisal's program.

On March 22, 1964, King Saud moved to recover his political position by demanding that full executive powers be returned to him. Faisal rejected the demand and mobilized the National Guard. On March 25 the Grand Mufti (leader of the *ulema*) informed King Saud of Faisal's intention to retain power and requested the King to issue a decree of compliance. Refusing, King Saud mobilized the remaining elements of the Royal Guard. Faisal retaliated by ordering the powerful National Guard to surround the palace and by issuing an ultimatum to the Royal Guard to withdraw. The Royal Guard complied and swore allegiance to Faisal.

In view of the chaotic effects the conflict was having on the country, the *ulema* issued on March 29 a legal decision (*fetwa*), endorsed by the royal family, authorizing the transfer of executive powers from King Saud to Faisal, while preserving to Saud the title of king. The *ulema* specifically explained that the decision in Faisal's favor was caused by King Saud's health and his inability to carry out the affairs of state.

Following the decisions of the *ulema* the Council of Ministers in a series of resolutions on March 28-30 withdrew from King Saud's control the Royal Guard as well as his personal guard, transferring these units to the Ministry of Defense and the Ministry of Interior, respectively. The Council of Ministers also abolished King Saud's royal court, reduced by half his yearly allowance to SR183 million (SR4.50 equal US$1) and declared him unfit to conduct the affairs of state. Finally, the Council decreed that all royal powers be transferred to Crown Prince Faisal.

On assuming the powers of the king, Faisal took on the titles of regent, viceroy, crown prince, prime minister and commander in chief of the armed forces. Sixty-eight princes of the royal family signed a proclamation approving the transfer of powers and endorsing Faisal's action.

The events of March 1964—King Saud's loss of support among the members of the ruling family and his replacement in all but title by Faisal—were a repetition of the transfer of powers in 1958. The difference was the brief resistance put up by King Saud and the more emphatic and legal nature of the transfer of powers the second time. Faisal's second takeover put an end to the rivalry which had disturbed the kingdom for the preceding 6 years.

The de jure acknowledgment of Faisal's supremacy came 7 months later, in November 1964, when the royal family deposed Saud from the throne and proclaimed Faisal king. After Faisal promised, in the traditional oath-taking ceremony (*baya*), to govern in accordance with the laws and traditions of the country, the *ulema* (led by the Grand Mufti), the royal family, the Consultative Council, the Council of Ministers and leading personalities from all parts of the kingdom, pledged their allegiance to him. Before leaving the country in January 1965, ex-King Saud belatedly gave his allegiance to the new king. In March, King Faisal named a new crown prince—his half-brother, Prince Khalid.

With the reunion of power and authority in the monarch, the divisions in the royal household were healed. In the first year of his undisputed rule, Faisal decreed two important changes; he united the offices of king and prime minister and gave the king the exclusive power to appoint, dismiss and accept the resignation of ministers. Since the ministers were made responsible directly to King Faisal, the king's powers were as extensive as they had been under the reign of Abd al-Aziz.

THE ROYAL FAMILY

The Saud family has been able to maintain itself in political power despite the far-reaching economic and social changes which have occurred around it. Often referred to as the "House of Saud," it comprises hundreds of relatives—brothers and sons, uncles, nephews, cousins, and their wives and children—offspring of each of the three Saudi kings. However, only the responsible male members closely related to the king are involved in the decisions made in the name of the family. The 68 signatures which appeared on the November 2, 1964 proclamation by the royal family transferring royal powers to Faisal gives an indication of the size of the decision-making group.

The selection and removal of the king is the exclusive domain of the royal family, sanctioned by the *ulema*. The king's designation of an heir to the throne, the crown prince, must also be generally acceptable to the rest of the royal family. As of 1965 the senior member of the family was Prince Abdullah Ibn Abd ar-Rahman, the oldest living brother of former King Abd al-Aziz. A younger brother—about 15 years younger than his nephew King Faisal—is Prince Musaad Ibn Abd ar-Rahman, whom King Faisal named to his government as Minister of Finance and National Economy in 1962.

Several branches can be distinguished within the Saud family. A number are so powerful in their own right that the king must take account of their interests in his policy decisions. The Jiluwi branch, for example, has long held the governorship of Eastern Province and has established a strong position there. Prince Khalid, a half-brother of King Faisal whom the King named Crown Prince and first in line of succession to the throne, is related through his mother to the Jiluwi branch. The seven Sudayri brothers are sons of Abd al-Aziz but of a different mother than Faisal; they are related through their mother to the Sudayri family and have maintained a cohesiveness which has assured them an important voice in the family council. Two of these brothers, Princes Fahd and Sultan, are, respectively, ministers of interior and of defense and aviation in King Faisal's government.

The durability of the political power of the royal family in the face of rapid economic and social changes attests to its ability to maintain the bonds of loyalty among the religious and tribal leaders and the business community, bureaucracy and military. The family has satisfied the chief demands of the traditional leaders for the preservation of Islamic values and many of the aspirations of the emerging leaders of the modern segment of the population for improved living standards and the modernization of living patterns.

THE KING

The king is at the center of all political activity. He incorporates all legislative and executive functions and may on occasion exercise judicial authority. Legally, his power is limited to the precepts of *sharia* (Islamic) law and, practically, by the need to maintain the consensus of the royal family and of important tribal leaders. Political considerations by the royal family, usually sanctioned on religiolegal grounds, can curtail the exercise of a king's power, even to the point of his deposition, but no group or individual outside the royal family can make equivalent restrictions on his power.

Because the powers of the king are nowhere defined, the nature of royal power has varied with the ability and personal style of the ruler and the circumstance of the times. King Abd al-Aziz ruled almost singlehandedly, close to the ideal of absolute monarchy. His son King Saud attempted to handle modern problems in a complex period of history in the traditionalist, paternalistic fashion of his father.

The record of King Faisal, a half-brother of former King Saud, reveals him to be capable of effectively carrying out the delicate tasks of ruling a country emerging from traditional society. He has shown an awareness of the need to adapt Islamic law to enable it to handle the problems introduced by modern industry and contacts with the outside world and an interest in expanding government services to satisfy the growing demands of his people for improved living standards and welfare. He is, however, essentially a gradualist, limiting the rate of change to that which the traditional Islamic order can accommodate.

King Faisal has been able to deal effectively with the representatives of both the traditional and modern forces. When dealing with Western diplomats or businessmen, he is sophisticated, and expert in representing the interests of his country in international negotiations. He can with equal ease associate with the Bedouin sheikhs from remote villages or desert camps who regularly visit him, exchanging stories of nomadic life and enter knowingly into their discussions of tribal movements and local news. He continues to dress in the Bedouin manner on all occasions.

King Faisal is modest, even austere in his habits. In his investiture speech, he emphasized that he considered himself one of the people, a brother and a servant to them. He asked not to be called "your majesty" or "holder of the throne" because those terms were to be reserved for God.

King Faisal's domestic policies since his return to the prime ministership in October 1962 reflect his concern with accommodating the opposing forces of tradition and modernity. In November 1962 he announced a 10-point program promising modest political and legal advances and extensive social and economic reforms. This included a basic constitutional law proposal, plans for standardized provincial government and the abolition of slavery. One year later, in October 1963, he announced that proposed regulations for local government had been drawn up and would become effective within 9 months (see ch. 12, Constitution and Government). Provincial councils having a representative character were to be created, and relations between central and local government were defined for the first time. At the end of 1965 implementation of the political and legal aspects of the program had been very gradual.

Social reforms, however, had made considerable headway. Education and welfare services had been expanded, and slavery was formally abolished, although some ulema opposed its abolition on the grounds that the Koran approved of slavery.

The king was careful to couch the presentation of all changes in the context of Islamic orthodoxy. It was clear that a primary consideration in the king's decision-making was the willingness of the majority of traditionalist elements to accept or at least not oppose specific changes.

NEW GROUPS

The profound economic transformations at work in the country in the 1940's and 1950's brought about corresponding changes in the social structure. Generated by the phenomenal growth of the oil industry and the consequent expansion of the central government, new occupations emerged, creating new wealth and new aspirations.

To an extent, the appearance of nontraditional occupations corresponded with the rise of new towns. The attraction of town life was based on the emergence of new opportunities for employment —by Aramco, by the government and by the subsidiary industries which each had created. Responding to these urgent needs, many Saudi Arabs acquired the skills necessary to become civil servants, military officers, professional men, teachers, journalists and technicians. A new stratum of society was emerging.

The transformations which had begun in the economic sector and which had in turn brought about corresponding changes in the social structure were only slightly felt in the political realm. Traditional political institutions and traditional patterns of power continued to function effectively in the new setting, despite the rapidity of change in other sectors. Pressures for political change have been of little significance.

A few Saudi Arabs—those in most direct contact with Westernized cultures, particularly young people with modern education—would like to press for more rapid political change, but in 1965 had not been able to gain any discernible public support for their ambitions. Most have been absorbed into the government bureaucracy or into the new industries, and their political drive has been channeled into other outlets.

CHAPTER 14

FOREIGN RELATIONS

Since World War II, Saudi Arabia has ended its traditional isolation and established diplomatic relations with more than 40 countries, as well as with the United Nations and a number of other international organizations. In general, the country has not played an active role in international affairs, even in the Arab world, and has been satisfied to maintain good relations with the Western countries on which it relied for assistance in developing its economy. As of the end of 1965 it had no relations with any Communist country, because the atheism of the Communist world was considered incompatible with Islam, nor with Israel, considered an illegal colonization of part of the Arab homeland.

Foreign policy has been determined by a desire to maintain good international relations without entering alliances which might restrict independence of action, a need to maintain the high level of income from the production and sale of oil, a desire to keep out of the Arabian peninsula states whose interests conflict with its own, an implacable opposition to the state of Israel and a desire to conserve the balance of interests in the Arabian peninsula and the Middle East. Accordingly, the government has pursued a policy of close cooperation with oil-buying and oil-producing nations (see ch. 23, Foreign Economic Relations).

The desire to exclude outside powers from the peninsula was exemplified by opposition to the republican regime in Yemen, supported by the United Arab Republic (Egypt). The most important and persistent dispute with Great Britain was over the Buraimi oasis in the undemarcated border area between Saudi Arabia and the British-protected Sultanate of Muscat and Oman and Sheikhdom of Abu Dhabi. This dispute embittered Saudi-British relations throughout the 1950's.

The government has cooperated closely with other Arab countries, backing the decisions of the Arab League in support of the cause of Palestinian refugees and contributing heavily to refugee relief funds. It has, however, refused to commit itself to permanent alignments in the Arab world, remaining uncommitted, for example, between the United Arab Republic (then Egypt and Syria) and the rival Arab Federation (Jordan and Iraq) in 1958.

In 1965, King Faisal Ibn Abd al-Aziz al-Faisal al-Saud appeared to be launching a diplomatic offensive among Islamic states. The Mecca-based Moslem World League, founded a few years before, sponsored in April 1965 a 10-day international conference of Islamic nations. Opinions expressed at the conference revealed a vital interest in freeing Islamic affairs from Arab domination and the possibility of a more cohesive alliance of Moslem states. Saudi Arabia's appeal for closer ties among all Moslems received enthusiastic response from non-Arab Moslems of Africa and Asia as well as from the more tradition-oriented states of the Arab world.

In November, King Faisal, who also held the posts of prime minister and foreign minister, began a long-range campaign to promote Islamic solidarity for the purpose of "strengthening the bonds of brotherhood that unite us." The King denied that this initiative was conceived as an effort to join the more conservative Middle Eastern states, such as Iran, Afghanistan and Pakistan, in an alliance which would offset the more radical Arab states, such as the United Arab Republic, Algeria and Syria. At the end of 1965 the degree of success the King might expect from his efforts to promote Islamic solidarity was undeterminable; Shah Mohammed Reza Pahlevi of Iran publicly supported the idea, however, and suggested that Mecca be the seat of the group.

MECHANICS OF POLICYMAKING

The king has usually had the deciding voice in foreign policy. Since King Faisal is also minister of foreign affairs, the extent of royal control has probably been greater than it was under the two previous kings. The king is assisted by a permanent under secretary and a staff of deputy-level ministers, which includes ambassadors, a deputy minister for Western affairs and a deputy minister for public relations and press. Assistant deputy ministers head the five departments—Protocol, Arab League Affairs, Palestine Affairs, Consular Affairs, and Cables—into which the Ministry of Foreign Affairs is organized. The Ministry of Foreign Affairs and all foreign diplomatic missions are located in Jidda.

Changes in foreign policy have corresponded with the personal style of each of the three monarchs. King Abd al-Aziz Ibn Saud rarely left the country and took only a cautious interest in international affairs, preferring to leave this field to his son Faisal, whom he appointed minister of foreign affairs in 1932. Between 1954 and 1958, a period when the Middle East played a central role in world politics, Abd al-Aziz's successor, King Saud Ibn Abd al-Aziz, involved the country in Arab and international affairs more directly than ever before. In 1958 difficulties in domestic economic affairs as well as in foreign relations affected the transfer of the king's executive powers to his brother, Crown Prince Faisal. For the next 2 years the country concentrated on domestic problems.

In December 1960, King Saud again assumed direct control of the government and named Sheikh Ibrahim al-Suwayyil as minister of foreign affairs. When illness forced King Saud to leave the country in late 1961, he turned over the affairs of state to Prince Faisal, and by March 1962, Faisal reassumed the positions of deputy prime minister and minister of foreign affairs.

When Faisal became king in November 1964, he retained both posts and kept close control over foreign affairs (see ch. 13, Political Dynamics). Foreign policy during Faisal's first year as king was characterized by a disengagement from Arab world politics and a reorientation toward Islamic nations. In August 1965 he came to an agreement with the United Arab Republic aimed at ending the civil war in Yemen, and toward the end of the year he sought to promote a vaguely-defined solidarity movement between Islamic states which some observers regarded as a countervailing force to the predominance of the United Arab Republic in the Arab and Moslem world.

RELATIONS WITH FOREIGN COUNTRIES

The country maintains diplomatic relations with the major oil-producing and oil-buying nations; with all other Arab League states (Algeria, Iraq, Jordan, Kuwait, Lebanon, Libya, Morocco, Sudan, Syria, Tunisia, the United Arab Republic and Yemen), except during intermittent disputes; and with other countries which have a large Moslem population. For the most part, it has such relations only with countries with which it carries out important economic affairs. It has no relations with the Republic of South Africa, whose apartheid policies it vigorously opposes.

The government does not have diplomatic relations with any Communist state, although Moslem pilgrims from Communist-controlled countries are allowed to journey to Mecca. The Soviet Union was one of the first countries to recognize Abd al-Aziz as sovereign of the Nejd and Hejaz in 1926, and his son, Emir Faisal, visited the Soviet Union in 1932, but the Soviet mission at Jidda was closed in 1938. When the Soviet-Egyptian arms agreement was announced in 1955, Prince Faisal made known that a similar offer had been made to Saudi Arabia and was rejected. Saudi Arabia established diplomatic relations with Nationalist China in 1957 and reiterated its refusal to consider opening relations with the Soviet Union or Communist China. In December 1964, however, King Faisal said that he was neutral in regard to the admission of Communist China to the United Nations.

The Arab World

As the homeland of Islam, the country has a special significance to the Arab world and Moslem nations. To make a pilgrimage to the holy city of Mecca is the lifetime goal of millions of Moslems the world over. Relations are closest with the Arab states of the Fertile Crescent and North Africa, where Islamic culture is strongest.

Saudi Arabia's bilateral relations with single Arab states have always been integrated within a total pattern of relations with all Arab states, although since the 1950's, relations with Egypt have dominated all others. In the 1930's, when recognition in the Arab world was sought, the country made several treaties based on "Islamic friendship and Arab brotherhood." One such treaty, the Treaty of Taif, signed with Yemen in 1934, ended a brief border war and resolved to settle any future differences by negotiation.

At the formation of the Arab League in 1945, however, King Abd al-Aziz was hesitant to join. Eager to guard the country's sovereignty, he agreed to sign the charter only with explicit mutual guarantees of each member state to recognize each other's independence and to refrain from attempting to change another state's form of government. His aloofness from Arab policies was evident in relation to the Palestine problem of 1947-48, when he made only a token commitment to the Arab cause, because a stronger stand might have interfered with the American oil concessions.

Relations with the United Arab Republic are most important for Saudi Arabia partly because of its nearness but chiefly because of the predominant influence of that country throughout the Middle East. Since 1926, when Egypt refused to recognize Abd al-Aziz's conquest of the Hejaz, relations between the two countries have alternated between hostility and cordiality. Diplomatic relations were not established until 1936, after the death of King Faud of Egypt.

After World War II the two countries entered a phase of close friendship. King Abd al-Aziz made a state visit to Egypt in 1947, his first official tour outside of the country, and granted King Farouk an annual subsidy of approximately £1 million (about US$4 million). The new Egyptian regime of President Gamal Abdul Nasser was recognized formally after the revolution of 1952 although its ideological orientation was radically different from and in many ways incompatible with Saudi Arabia's.

After the death of King Abd al-Aziz the foreign policies of the two countries took similar courses. In 1954, King Saud followed Egypt's lead in opposing the positions of Great Britain and the United States in the Middle East. He revived the Buraimi Oasis dispute with Great Britain in an attempt to arbitrate a stalemated situation; canceled the United States Point Four economic assistance program because the sums granted to Israel were much larger than those given to his country; and negotiated a new oil-shipping agreement less favorable to Aramco. In October 1955, when Egypt and Saudi Arabia signed a mutual defense pact, the policies of the two countries became even more similar. King Saud became an advocate of neutralism; demanded the liberation of Palestine and Algeria; denounced the Western-sponsored Baghdad Pact, an anti-Communist military-economic alliance among Great Britain, Iran, Iraq, Pakistan and Turkey; and temporarily postponed renewal of the United States lease to the Dhahran airbase, which had been granted in 1946 and renewed for 5 years in 1951. At the time of the Suez crisis in 1956, King Saud contributed about SR40 million (approximately SR4 equaled US$1) to shore up Egyptian financial reserves then frozen in foreign banks and broke relations with Great Britain and France.

In late 1956, however, concern over President Nasser's growing popularity among Saudi Arabs and his friendship with the Soviet Union caused King Saud to reconsider his association with Egypt. Indicative of his changing mood was his reception of King Faisal of Iraq in September 1956. This unusual meeting—the Hashemite kings of Iraq were traditional enemies of the Saudi family—suggested that King Saud was looking for new allies. In February 1957 he went to Washington where he supported the Eisenhower Doctrine—vehemently denounced by Cairo—which pledged United States support to any Middle Eastern state menaced by communism.

While in Washington, King Saud effected a rapprochement with the Hashemite kings of Iraq and Jordan. He met Iraqi Crown Prince Abdul Illah, and an informal Kings' Alliance of Saudi Arabia, Jordan and Iraq came into being. The acceptance of the Eisenhower Doctrine, the renewal of the United States lease of Dhahran airbase and the formation of the Kings' Alliance were incompatible with Egyptian policies, and by the end of 1957 the Cairo-Riyadh axis was virtually defunct.

Saudi-Egyptian relations began to show signs of increased strain after the February 1958 proclamation of the United Arab Republic, comprising Syria and Egypt. While outwardly uncommitted between the United Arab Republic and the rival Arab

Federation of Iraq and Jordan, King Saud feared United Arab Republic domination throughout the Middle East. In March the head of Syrian army intelligence accused King Saud of implication in an assassination plot against President Nasser, and the princes of the Saud family, fearful of the consequences to the stability of the Saudi regime, forced King Saud, 2 weeks later, to turn over full legislative and executive power to his brother, Crown Prince Faisal.

Faisal maintained a neutral attitude toward both the United Arab Republic and the Arab Federation. In August 1958 he and President Nasser, after several days of discussions, issued a joint communique condemning Western aggression in the Middle East, and within a year, King Saud paid an official visit to Egypt.

Toward the end of 1961 renewed signs of deterioration in Saudi-United Arab Republic relations were reflected in mutual recriminations from Radio Cairo and Radio Mecca. Cairo accused Mecca of perpetuating a feudalist regime, whereas Mecca charged that President Nasser was intervening in the affairs of other Arab countries and betraying the Arab cause in Palestine by taking a soft line toward Israel. The Saudi Government refused in May 1962 to receive the traditional Egyptian gift of the *kiswa* (covering cloth) for the Kaaba (holy shrine of Islam) at Mecca. Moreover, its agreement to coordinate foreign, economic, military and cultural policy with Jordan, first announced in the Taif Pact of August 30, 1962, was regarded by some observers as directed against the United Arab Republic, whose "Arab socialism" and close ties with the Soviet Union were disturbing to the two kingdoms.

In September 1962, Saudi-United Arab Republic relations worsened when, after the Yemeni military coup d'etat, the United Arab Republic openly gave military aid to the new republican regime, and Riyadh, under the terms of the 1934 treaty with Yemen, supported the monarchy. In the early weeks of October, United Arab Republic troops entered Yemen by air and sea, and Saudi troops maneuvered near the frontier. On October 5 the Saudi Government permitted the Yemeni royalists to establish a government-in-exile at Jidda. Five days later the newly formed Yemen Arab Republic and the United Arab Republic signed a 5-year military defense pact.

Involvement in the Yemen civil war was widened in November as the Saudi Government created a joint defense council with Jordan as a precaution against threatened attack on its territory by United Arab Republic-supported republican forces. The Jordanian Premier announced that any attack on Saudi Arabia would be regarded as an attack on Jordan.

On November 6, Riyadh broke diplomatic relations with Cairo, citing United Arab Republic air and sea attacks on several Saudi Arabian villages in Asir as the cause. Saudi interests in the United Arab Republic were assumed by Libya, and United Arab Republic interests in Saudi Arabia, by Afghanistan. In late November Saudi Arabian sources asserted that President Nasser's real objective in backing the Yemeni republicans was to establish a base from which he could overthrow the Saudi monarchy and gain control of Saudi Arabian oil facilities.

United Arab Republic bombings of Saudi Arabian towns ceased in mid-November but were resumed at the end of December. As prime minister, Faisal responded in early January 1963 by calling a general mobilization of the armed forces and making a promise of increased aid to Yemeni royalists. Travel restrictions were placed on Saudi Arab nationals, particularly those of Palestinian origin, who were apparently the most susceptible to United Arab Republic propaganda. The number of United Arab Republic nationals in the country as teachers and technicians dropped from 5,000 to several hundred.

Attempts to negotiate the United Arab Republic-Saudi differences began in the spring of 1963 and resulted in a disengagement agreement in April. The two countries were to suspend their military aid to the two warring factions; a demilitarized zone of 12.5 miles on each side of the Saudi-Yemen frontier was to be established; and United Nations observers were to supervise the truce and report any violations in the zone. A 50-man United Nations team, financed equally by the United Arab Republic and Saudi Arabia, arrived in June 1963 and stayed until September 1964, but the war continued. In September Secretary General U Thant reported to the Security Council that no encouraging progress had been made in implementing the disengagement agreement.

A return to normal relations between Riyadh and Cairo began in January 1964, when King Saud went to Cairo for an Arab summit conference to discuss Israel's proposed diversion of the Jordan River. In March an Arab League delegation, headed by Iraqi and Algerian delegates, was successful in bringing about a resumption of Saudi-United Arab Republic diplomatic relations. In a joint communique both sides called for "independence of the Yemen." Also in March, however, Secretary General U Thant announced, in his Fourth Report to the Security Council on the Observation Mission in Yemen, that royalist military activity had resumed and that the United Arab Republic had sent additional forces in January and February. Nevertheless, the two countries exchanged ambassadors in June.

In October 1964, Riyadh and Cairo brought Yemeni royalists and republicans together at a Sudan port town. On November 8 Radio Sana announced a cease-fire to be followed by a reconciliation conference, but fighting erupted again within a month. Saudi Arabia's main policy objective remained the removal of United Arab Republic troops from the Arabian peninsula.

On July 22, 1965, the thirteenth anniversary of the Egyptian revolution, President Nasser stated that he was ready to extend the war "to crush the bases of aggression," if the Saudi Government did not accept a negotiated settlement. In August President Nasser went to Jidda to confer with King Faisal, and the two leaders agreed on a cease-fire, a cessation of Saudi Arabian aid to the royalists and a gradual withdrawal of the 60,000 United Arab Republic troops. Only the first two items were adhered to immediately. In addition, both sides were to make up a peace committee to supervise the military disengagement. Yemeni republicans and royalists, while not partners to the Jidda agreement, were to send representatives to a conference in Haradh, Yemen, in November to decide upon a compromise, interim government before a national plebiscite could be held to determine a permanent form of government.

Accordingly, republicans and royalists met on November 23, 1965, at Haradh to form a coalition government, but talks were stalemated in December, with each side insisting on a form of government unacceptable to the other. Royalists wanted to name the state simply "State of Yemen," whereas republicans wanted to preserve the descriptive term "republic" in the name. At the end of 1965 the cease-fire was still in effect, but no compromise had been reached between the Yemeni factions. Saudi Arabia pointed out that Egyptian troops had still not been evacuated from Yemen and raised the possibility of resuming aid to the royalists.

While relations with other Arab states have in the last decade been deeply affected by the United Arab Republic, Saudi Arabia's bilateral relations with Arab states have not been insignificant.

In the 1950's shifting alliances in the Arab world made expedient a change in the animosity between the Saudi family and the Hashemite dynasties of Iraq and Jordan. The meeting between King Faisal of Iraq and King Saud in Riyadh in September 1956 signaled the beginning of the pro-Hashemite reorientation of Saudi Arabia and suggested a growing suspicion of Egypt for both. In January 1957, Iraqi Crown Prince Abdul Illah and King Saud met while in Washington; later an informal Kings' Alliance was agreed upon; and in May King Saud visited Iraq for the first time, breaking a political boycott of that country by Arab states which opposed the Baghdad Pact. The sovereigns of Saudi Arabia and Iraq also issued a statement condemning communism, imperialism and Zionism, and King Faisal of Iraq visited King Saud again at Riyadh in December 1957.

At the end of 1956, Saudi Arab troops were reportedly in Jordan as a deterrent to the military threat from Israel, and in March 1957, in accordance with a Saudi-Jordanian military agreement, 3,500 Saudi troops were lent to Jordan for deployment at the port of Aqaba, from which the British had withdrawn. During the same period Saudi Arabia, Syria and Egypt agreed to combine resources in an attempt to replace the British subsidy to Jordan. In March 1957, Saudi Arabia had deposited the equivalent of about $14 million in Jordanian banks. In April, during a crackdown on antimonarchist elements in Jordan, Saudi Arab troops were again put at the disposal of King Husein.

Not until 1962 did Saudi Arabia and Jordan find their interests again mutual enough to undertake closer relations. As with the Kings' Alliance of 1957, it was the threat of the United Arab Republic, with its strong aid ties to the Soviet Union and its antimonarchist propaganda, which brought about the alliance of neighbors. A joint Saudi-Jordanian military command, created by the Taif Pact of August 30, 1962, was brought into operation after the United Arab Republic supported the republican coup in Yemen. On November 4, 1962, during the initial United Arab Republic-Saudi Arabian confrontation, the Jordanian premier announced that any attack on Saudi Arabia would be regarded as an attack on Jordan. The next year the two countries appeared to be moving closer together when they signed an economic integration agreement allowing interstate rights of travel, work, residence and investment (see ch. 23, Foreign Economic Relations).

Saudi relations with Kuwait are cordial but not close. When Great Britain conferred independence on the protected sheikhdom of Kuwait in June 1961, the oil-rich state was menaced by an Iraqi claim to its sovereignty. Saudi Arabia supported Kuwaiti independence and sent troops to defend it, which remained until January 1963. In 1964 a Saudi-Kuwaiti agreement partitioned the neutral zone for administrative purposes and maintained their previous agreement on equal sharing of oil resources (see ch. 20, Industry).

The Western World

Contacts with the Western world, particularly with Great Britain and the United States, became widespread after World War II. Before then, Great Britain, preoccupied with controlling the route to India, was the major Western power in the Middle East. In the mid-1940's the United States began to displace Great Britain as the predominant Western influence, chiefly because of the Americans' construction of a major strategic airbase at Dhahran and the expansion of oil exploitation, which was under the exclusive guidance of United States businessmen (see ch. 2, Historical Setting).

Diplomatic relations with France were broken off at the time of the Suez crisis in 1956, and 2 years later Prime Minister Faisal stated that the renewal of relations awaited the settlement of the Algerian war of independence. Saudi Arabia supported the Algerian nationalist movement financially and took an outspoken position against France at the United Nations. Resumption of Saudi Arabian-French relations in September 1962 followed the settlement of the Algerian situation, and in 1963 a cultural-technical accord was signed which set up scholarships for Saudi Arab students at French technical schools. In 1965 an agreement was made with a French oil firm to explore the Red Sea coastal area, and a French company was awarded a contract to construct a 1200-kilowatt radio station at Riyadh (see ch. 15, Public Information).

Relations with West Germany have been principally concerned with private engineering companies engaged in business on the periphery of the large oil companies, but when West Germany recognized Israel in 1965, Saudi Arabia broke diplomatic relations.

Great Britain

Full diplomatic relations with Great Britain date from 1927, when Great Britain recognized the sovereignty of Abd al-Aziz as ruler of Al-Hasa, the Nejd and the Hejaz. In exchange, Saudi Arabia recognized British rights in Bahrein and other parts of the peninsula.

Saudi Arabian-British relations have since been determined by the encircling presence of more than a dozen political entities, vestiges of former empires still under the suzerainty of Great Britain, which dot the rim of the Arabian peninsula. Foreign relations of the Crown Colony of Aden, the various entities of the Protectorate of South Arabia, the Federation of South Arabia, the Sultanate of Muscat and Oman, the seven protected sheikhdoms of Trucial Oman as well as those of Qatar, Bahrein and, until 1961, Kuwait have been conducted in the name of Great Britain. Few of the boundaries of these Saudi Arabian borderlands are precisely known, and the possible presence of oil in such areas as well as separatist rumblings in several sheikhdoms complicated Saudi-British relations throughout the 1950's.

Possession of the potentially oil-rich Buraimi Oasis, for example, on the undemarcated frontier between Saudi Arabia, the sheikhdom of Abu Dhabi, and the Sultanate of Muscat and Oman, brought Saudi Arabia and Great Britain into conflict. When in 1949 it became apparent that the entire coastline of the Persian Gulf was potentially valuable for oil, Saudi Arabia claimed sovereignty over lands which included portions of the British-protected sheikhdom of Abu Dhabi on the Trucial Coast. Boundary negotiations between Great Britain and Saudi Arabia, which took place intermittently after 1949, were broken off in January 1952. In August the Saudi Arabs occupied portions of the Buraimi Oasis, allegedly at the request of Buraimi sheikhs. The Sheikh of Abu Dhabi requested the intervention of Great Britain, which responded by blockading the Saudis in the oasis in September.

Open conflict was avoided by a standstill agreement in October, according to which Saudi and British forces were to remain in position without reinforcement, pending the negotiation of a final settlement. An arbitration agreement was signed on July 30, 1954.

After a preliminary meeting in Nice in January 1955, the arbitration tribunal met at Geneva in September 1955. The British representative resigned and walked out of the tribunal, charging that the Saudi representative had not acted impartially. In October the British Foreign Secretary announced that British-officered Arab troops had ousted Saudi forces from the Buraimi Oasis. Saudi Arabia protested against the British action at the United Nations, maintaining that the Buraimi Oasis was part of its traditional territory and that its inhabitants had long demonstrated this by paying *zakat* (traditional Moslem alms tax) to the Saudi rulers (see ch. 24, Monetary and Financial System).

In November 1956, Saudi Arabia announced that it had broken diplomatic relations with Great Britain because of that country's invasion of Egypt and its violation of the 1954 Buraimi arbitration agreement. Crown Prince Faisal announced in April 1958 that relations could be resumed only if Great Britain would agree to arbitration again or withdraw entirely from the disputed area. In 1960 a United Nations factfinding mission on the Buraimi dispute spent a month in the area, but announced that the original deadlock had not changed.

Saudi Arabia and Great Britain again clashed indirectly over the border area of Oman. British troops, which had moved into Oman shortly after they had retaken Buraimi in 1955, were confronted by a rebellion led by the Imam of Oman in July 1957. The British regained control of Oman in August. Saudi Arabia and other Arabs states have since repeatedly brought the Oman question and the charge of British aggression before the United Nations.

Diplomatic relations with Great Britain, broken for almost 7 years, were resumed in January 1963, although Saudi Arabia was the last Middle Eastern state to do so after the Suez crisis.

In February 1964, Great Britain announced that Saudi Arabia purchased 300 guided antitank missiles, which included a detachment of British military personnel for training. In the spring of 1964 various delegations and ministers traveled between the two countries. The Ministry of Health hired 20 British physicians for Jidda and Riyadh hospitals. At the end of 1965, Saudi Arabia arranged to purchase about £100 million (US$280 million) worth of jet fighter-bombers, radar and other air defense installations from Great Britain, and about $70 million worth of ground-to-air missiles from the United States (see ch. 25, The Armed Forces).

The United States

Saudi Arabian relations with the United States in 1965 continued to be cordial, but were complicated by differing policies toward Israel. Saudi Arabs have been dealing with American individuals since 1933, when King Abd al-Aziz granted Standard Oil of California—renamed the Arabian American Oil Company (Aramco) in 1944—an exclusive, 60-year concession (see ch. 20, Industry). In 1950 a Saudi Arabian-Aramco agreement specified a 50-50 sharing of oil profits, the first of its kind in the Middle East.

Cordiality between the United States and Saudi Arabia has been based on the presence of vast deposits of oil in Saudi Arabia, the possession of advanced technological skills by the American private oil industry, and the mutual benefits resulting from the successful combination of both. Underlying this cordiality has been the constant effort of Aramco to maintain close and mutually beneficial relations with the Saudi Government.

Formal diplomatic relations with the United States Government date from World War II. Although formally neutral, King Abd al-Aziz was the only independent Middle Eastern ruler friendly to the Allies. The financial difficulties felt as a result of wartime restraints on Aramco operations and the reduction of pilgrimage traffic to Mecca had brought the country close to bankruptcy. Financial support was granted in the form of loans made through Aramco, the United States and Great Britain. Bankruptcy was prevented, and by 1943 the country was receiving loans under the United States Lend-Lease Program.

In the same year the first United States diplomatic representation was opened at Jidda. Meanwhile, negotiations were being undertaken for the lease and construction of an airbase at Dhahran on the Persian Gulf. Begun in 1944 and completed in 1946, the Dhahran airfield was a vital link between Cairo and Karachi on the Allied supply route to Japan. As the war progressed, Saudi Arabia was drawn closer to the Allied position. In February 1945, King Abd al-Aziz and President Roosevelt conferred briefly on the United States vessel *Quincy* in Great Bitter Lake, Egypt. In March Saudi Arabia declared war on the Axis powers.

The United State Legation at Jidda was raised to an embassy in 1949, and by 1951, American engineers had helped link Dammam and Riyadh by rail. In 1951, Saudi Arabia was included in the United States Point Four Program of Technical Assistance, and Saudi Arabia extended American usage rights at the Dhahran airfield for a 5-year term in exchange for an expanded military training program and permission to purchase United States arms under the Military Assistance Act.

Relations with the United States and Americans became complicated after the death of King Abd al-Aziz in November 1953. In February 1954 a dispute over the transport of oil broke out when Saudi Arabia awarded an oil transport contract to the Greek shipping magnate, Aristotle Onassis; Aramco claimed the use of its tankers was part of the concession and won its case 4 years later. In August 1954, Saudi Arabia requested the United States to stop its technical aid programs set up under the 1951 Point Four agreement, stating that the US$1.7 million allocated to it was too small in comparison with the amount allocated to Israel.

In October 1955, Premier Faisal announced that his country had rejected an arms offer from the Soviet Union. Instead, it arranged, on August 25, 1955, to purchase 18 United States tanks under the terms of the Dhahran base agreement of 1951 and to continue significant purchases of United States arms.

In June 1956 the Dhahran airbase agreement expired and was extended only on a monthly basis. In February 1957, King Saud, while in Washington, endorsed the Eisenhower Doctrine and agreed to a 5-year renewal of the Strategic Air Command base at

Dhahran in exchange for continued United States arms and aid. The 15,000-man Saudi army was to be doubled and equipped with United States arms, artillery and jet fighter planes, and a training program was to be established for the air force and navy.

The return of King Saud to power in December 1960 marked a temporary revival of the anti-Western mood of the 1954-56 period. In March 1961, Saudi Arabia informed the United States that it would not renew the Dhahran airfield agreement, which would expire within 1 year. King Saud said that the chief cause of the nonrenewal was United States aid to Israel. On April 2, 1962, the United States relinquished its usage rights to the Dhahran airfield and turned over one of the world's largest airports to the Saudi Government. Later that month, Saudi Arabia and the United Arab Republic, acting in concert at the United Nations, brought charges of armed aggression against Great Britain for its position on Oman.

Saudi Arabian-United States friendship was not impaired by the ending of the Dhahran base agreement, however. The continuation of good relations between the two countries was revealed during the Yemen crisis of 1962-65. Crown Prince Faisal conferred with President Kennedy in Washington shortly after the republican coup in Yemen. In October 1962 the President explicitly declared United States support for the integrity of Saudi Arabia in a letter to Faisal.

When United Arab Republic forces bombed the Saudi town of Najran in January 1963, the United States reaffirmed its disapproval, as it did throughout the spring. In May the Department of Defense announced that United States troops were training with Saudi Arab troops, and 2 months later United States Air Force training exercises were carried out openly in Saudi Arabia.

Government scholarships and private company grants have enabled Saudi Arabs to study at American universities. At first students tended to take technical course programs related to the petroleum industry, but increasingly, the almost 200 Saudi students in American universities branched into economics and other social sciences (see ch. 9, Education). The Saudi Arabian Government has also contracted individual United States government agencies and departmental divisions for help on specific projects. The United States Geological Survey was asked to conduct mineral explorations, and the United States Army Engineers Corps was requested to help in the construction of temporary television stations.

INTERNATIONAL ORGANIZATIONS

Saudi Arabia was a founding member of the United Nations at San Francisco in 1945 and belongs to the United Nations Relief and Works Agency for Palestine Refugees (UNRWA) and the following United Nations Specialized Agencies: Food and Agriculture Organization (FAO); International Atomic Energy Agency (IAEA); International Bank for Reconstruction and Development (IBRD); International Civil Aviation Organization (ICAO); International Monetary Fund (IMF); International Telecommunications Union (ITU); United Nations Educational, Scientific and Cultural Organization (UNESCO); Universal Postal Union (UPU); World Health Organization (WHO); World Meterological Organization (WMO).

Its reliance on and continued support of the United Nations was demonstrated during the Yemen war, when in cooperation with the United Arab Republic, it financed most of the United Nations Observation Mission. In general, it votes with the Arab bloc in the General Assembly. It has repeatedly filed complaints with the United Nations Security Council against Israel regarding airspace and other violations and has regularly contributed substantial amounts to the support of Palestinian Arab refugees through UNRWA.

Saudi Arabia was a founding member of the Arab League, created in 1945 to coordinate the mutual interests of its members and originally comprised of Egypt, Iraq, Jordan, Lebanon, Saudi Arabia, Syria and Yemen. It also belongs to the Organization of Petroleum Exporting Countries (OPEC) (see ch. 23, Foreign Economic Relations).

CHAPTER 15

PUBLIC INFORMATION

Formal public information channels are poorly developed, in part because of the low literacy level and in part because of the conservatism of the religious leaders. The progressive policies of King Faisal Ibn Abd al-Aziz al-Faisal al-Saud have led, however, to the rapid growth of government-operated radio and television, to the development of a responsible privately owned press and to the beginning of public showings of commercial films.

As in most countries with a low literacy rate, radio is by far the most widespread and most important channel for public information. It is impossible to determine the number of receivers in the country, but it is widely believed that every Bedouin tribe has at least one transistorized portable radio capable of receiving not only domestic stations, but most other Middle East stations as well. In the villages and towns radios are commonplace. Because electric power is still available only in a few of the largest cities, most radios are battery operated.

Television promises to be a very popular form of public information despite the strong opposition to it by the conservative ulema (body of Islamic scholars) on the ground that it undermines Moslem morality. Extraordinary care has been taken in the selection of filmed materials for broadcasting on television to avoid using any that appear likely to arouse the ire of orthodox Moslems.

Newspaper readership is limited to a few tens of thousands of city dwellers, but these include the most influential people in the country. The government acted in January 1964 to improve the professional quality of newspapers and periodicals, which had formerly been treated largely as private business ventures rather than as responsible channels for public information. As of 1965, six daily newspapers were appearing under the new regulations.

PRESS

The press is of recent origin and little developed. The first newspaper was *Umm al-Qura,* founded in 1924 as a private Mecca weekly, which has become the government's official gazette. The first daily newspaper, *Al-Bilad,* appeared in Jidda in 1953; it had been published as a thrice-weekly newspaper. Between 1953 and

1963 the number of newspapers multiplied from 4 to 19, largely because of government financial support in the form of government advertising, free transportation of newspapers throughout the country and duty-free importation of newsprint and other press facilities.

With the exception of a few special-purpose periodicals published by various government ministries, the press has always been privately owned. Circulation has been uncertain and generally low, and the newspapers have had to depend largely on government advertising for financial support.

As a result, the government has played an important role in guiding the press. It has not resorted to prepublication censorship, but has not hesitated to use its power to suspend newspapers which published materials offensive to it. These would include attacks on the institution of the monarchy, mention of the term "Israel" (Saudi Arabians refer to the area as "Arab Palestine"), any approving references to the Jewish state, praise or condemnation of any foreign state not consonant with Saudi foreign policy and the proscriptions imposed by a strict adherence to the Islamic religious code (see ch. 10, Religion).

The power of suspension was exercised by the Directorate General of Broadcasting, Press and Publications and by the Ministry of Information, which succeeded it in 1961. Although both Prince Faisal in 1960 and King Saud in 1961 announced their intention to lift press censorship, both felt it necessary to continue the close supervision of the press.

A major factor in determining the government's policy was the fact that most Saudi newspapers were operated as the personal vehicles of their editor-publishers. The Ministry of Information complained in November 1964 that "control by one person without sufficient experience limits the use of newspapers for the formation of public opinion." Minister of Information Jamil Ibrahim al-Hujaylar expressed the government's strong dissatisfaction with the low level of Saudi journalism. He stated that most newspapers depended too heavily on government advertising for their revenue—the government placed a total of about SR4 million (SR4.50 equal US$1) per year worth of advertising in the several daily and weekly newspapers—that no newspaper subscribed to any foreign news service, that they depended for foreign news on monitoring Radio Mecca, that no newspaper employed a full-time English-language translator, that none maintained any foreign correspondents and that the owners produced publications that were below an acceptable minimum standard in order to profit personally from the government subsidy.

To improve the professional quality of the newspapers, a new Press Law was decreed by the government in January 1964. Under the new law the government suspended the publication licenses of all privately owned newspapers and restricted new licenses to those newspapers which fulfilled minimum requirements. These requirements included: the establishment by the owners of each newspaper of a 15-man "press institution," made up of members acceptable to the Ministry of Information, to be legally responsible for the newspaper; an initial capital investment of at least SR100,000; and a professional staff including, for a daily newspaper, a full-time editor in chief, four full-time editors, two foreign-language translators, three qualified correspondents resident in three major capitals and one photographer. The required staff for a weekly newspaper was slightly smaller.

By mid-1965 six daily newspapers—in comparison to the four published before the new Press Law went into effect—had begun publishing under the new regulations. At least eight privately published weekly periodicals and several monthly and quarterly periodicals were also believed to be appearing, but it was not known what effect, if any, the new Press Law had on their operation (see table 4).

Table 4. Newspapers and Selected Periodicals of Saudi Arabia, as of Mid-1965

	Place of Publication	Editor	Remarks
DAILIES			
Al-Bilad	Jidda	Sheikh Hamed Mutawi	Liberal; established in 1953 as the first daily in the country.
Al-Jazira	Riyadh	n.a.	Established in July 1964, temporarily as a weekly.
Al-Medina	Jidda	Sheikh Mohammed Alaqi	Established in 1937 as a weekly.
Al-Nadwa	Mecca	Saleh Jamal	Conservative; was suspended for a time in 1963.
Al-Riyadh	Riyadh	Hamed Al-Jasser	Established in May 1965; published by Al-Yamama Press organization.
Al-Ukaz	Taif	Sheikh Mahmoud Arif	Was a weekly until October 1964.
WEEKLIES			
Al-Qasim	Burayda	Abdullah al-Sana	Published since 1959.
Al-Quraysh	Mecca	Ahmed Sibai	—do—

Table 4. Newspapers and elected Periodicals of Saudi Arabia, as of Mid-1965—Continued

	Place of Publication	Editor	Remarks
Al-Raid	Jidda	Abd al-Fatta Abu Madyan	Liberal; established in 1959.
Al-Yamama	Riyadh	Abd al-Aziz Al-Fayyad	Suspended for a time in 1962.
Al-Yom	Dammam	Husein Kazander	Established in February 1965; first Arabic-language periodical in Eastern Province since suppression of *Khaliz al Araby* in 1962.
Commercial Weekly	n.a.	Abd al-Aziz Mumina	Editor previously edited *Usbu*, a liberal weekly suppressed in 1963.
News from Saudi Arabia	Jidda	n.a.	Published since 1961 in English by the Ministry of Information; was called *Saudi Arabia Newsletter* until 1964.
Qafilat al-Zayt	Dhahran	—do—	Arabic-language weekly of Aramco.
Sun and Flare	—do—	—do—	Published in English, mainly for Aramco employees.
Umm al-Qura	Mecca	Abd al-Rahman Shibani	Official government gazette; established in 1924 as a weekly newspaper.
MONTHLIES			
Al-Haj	—do—	Mohammed Said al-Amoudi	Religious; published by Ministry of Pilgrimage and Religious Foundations.
Al-Idhaa	Jidda	n.a.	Published by Ministry of Information for government officials.
Al-Manhal	—do—	Abd al-Qaddos Ansari	Literary.
Qafilat al-Zayt	Dhahran	n.a.	General-interest review published by Aramco.

n.a.—not available.

Source: Adapted from Europa Publications, *The Middle East and North Africa, 1965–1966*, pp. 494, 495; Saudi Arabia, Ministry of Information, *News from Saudi Arabia*, 1964–65, *passim*; and U.S. Government sources.

In addition, the various ministries of the government were publishing special-interest periodicals. These included publications for policemen and government officials by the Ministry of Interior, for students and teachers by the Ministry of Education, for government officials by the Ministry of Information and for farmers and government officials by the Ministry of Agriculture and Water.

The Arabian American Oil Company (Aramco) has maintained an extensive publication program for its employees and the general public. It publishes the English-language weekly *Sun and Flare*, the Arabic-language weekly *Qafilat al-Zayt* and a general-interest Arabic-language monthly review of the same name. These publications have proved popular among the Arabs and are circulated far beyond Aramco circles.

The daily newspapers with the largest circulations are *Al-Bilad* in Jidda and *Al-Nadwa* in Mecca. Both are large format, eight-column and eight-page newspapers. Typically, they carry international news on the front page, with banner headlines and story lead-ins continued on inside pages. Foreign stories and photographs are supplied by the Western news agencies, particularly by Associated Press. Sports, features, editorials, economic news stressing oil developments, human interest stories and a woman's page prepared by women reporters fill the inside pages. Some advertising, including advertisements for imported consumer goods, is included. Layout and the quality of print and photographs are good. News coverage has improved appreciably under the new regulations. Encouraged by the government, several of the newspapers have commented editorially on local problems and criticized local government.

Even if accurate circulation figures were available for newspapers and periodicals, they would have little meaning since a single copy may be read by or to a large number of individuals. It is believed that circulation of most newspapers and periodicals is low and that few exceed 5,000 copies. Estimates in 1964 of circulation of *Al-Bilad* ranged from 9,000 to 20,000; the lower figure was probably the more accurate. Estimates in 1964 of circulation of *Al-Nadwa* ranged from 2,500 to 20,000.

The newspaper and periodical presses depended heavily on Egyptian printers until January 1962, when many of them quit in protest against newspaper criticism of socialism and Egyptian President Gamal Abdul Nasser. The Egyptian printers were gradually replaced by Saudi Arabs. The number of presses is small, and their facilities are limited by Western standards. Book publishing was limited to a single government press, at least until mid-1964.

RADIO

Radio was the first and is still by far the best-developed medium of public information. In the 1920's, King Abd al-Aziz Ibn Saud established a local broadcasting station in Mecca in the face of strong initial disapproval on the part of the puritanical Wahhabi ulema. In answers to their objections, Abd al-Aziz asserted that, since radios were not mentioned in the Koran, it must not be assumed that Allah intended to prohibit their use. He ordered that parts of the Koran be broadcast and was quoted as clinching the argument by asking: "Can anything be bad which transmits the word of God"?

Radio facilities spread slowly until the early 1960's. As late as 1958, only a few low-powered, shortwave transmitters were in operation in the Mecca-Jidda area. Beginning in 1963 the government began an intensive program of transmitter construction to blanket the country with radio broadcasts. By mid-1965 there were two domestic broadcast networks—the Mecca Domestic Service and the Riyadh Domestic Service, audible throughout most of the country, including both coasts and the central Nejd. Mecca Domestic Service broadcast via one 50-kilowatt mediumwave transmitter and four 50-kilowatt and one 100-kilowatt shortwave transmitters as well as several lower-powered shortwave transmitters. Riyadh Domestic Service was using one 50-kilowatt mediumwave transmitter and two 50-kilowatt shortwave transmitters. The government was reported in mid-1964 to be considering installing about ten 1-kilowatt transmitters in smaller cities throughout the kingdom to relay programs from the Mecca Domestic Service. It was not known at the end of 1965 if this plan had been implemented (see table 5).

In mid-1965 the government signed an agreement with a French concern to build a huge transmitter station in Riyadh, to be completed by 1967, comprising two mediumwave transmitters with a total output of 1200 kilowatts to permit Radio Mecca to blanket the entire country both day and night. At about the same time the government also contracted with a Geneva firm to build a 100-kilowatt mediumwave transmitter in Dammam, to be completed in 1966, to relay programs from Riyadh.

The number of receivers has kept pace with the growth in these facilities. It is not possible to make more than the roughest estimates of the number of receivers in the country, but it is believed that they have increased from between 10,000 and 50,000 in 1958 to 250,000 at the end of 1963 and possibly to more than 350,000 at the end of 1965. This would mean one receiver for every 10 inhabitants. Although undoubtedly concentrated in the urban

Table 5. Major Radio Stations in Saudi Arabia, as of 1965

	Frequency	Power (in kilowatts)
Mecca Domestic Service	[1]598	50
	7085	—do—
	9670	100
	11855	50
	11870	—do—
	11950	—do—
Riyadh Domestic Service	[1]647	—do—
	7220	—do—
	9720	—do—
International Service[2]	598	—do—
	7085	—do—
	9670	100
	11855	50
	17840	—do—

[1] Mediumwave transmitters; all others are shortwave.
[2] Transmitters at Jidda; International Service uses several transmitters of Mecca Domestic Service for "Voice of Islam" between 6:55 p.m. and 8:40 p.m.
Source: Adapted from *World Radio TV Handbook, 1965*, p. 185.

areas, receivers are believed to be owned as well by villagers and nomads throughout the country. No data are available on the types of receivers in the country; it is assumed that most are small, battery-operated transistor radios. No estimate is available of the percentage which could receive mediumwave broadcasts, but most probably are shortwave receivers. News-hungry Arabs gather around loudspeakers in town and village coffeehouses, and it has been reported that every seminomadic and nomadic group travels with at least one transistor radio.

Mecca Domestic Service broadcast in 1965 a total of 16¾ hours per day, in two transmissions—from sunrise to about 11:25 a.m. and from about 1:55 p.m. to about 2:10 a.m. Riyadh Domestic Service broadcast in 1965 a total of 15¾ hours per day, also in two transmissions—from sunrise to about 10:45 a.m. and from about 1:30 p.m. to about 1 a.m. These hours are based on Greenwich Mean Time plus 3 hours and are approximate for the summer. Winter broadcasts would begin somewhat later, since broadcasting begins at sunrise, which varies with location and the season. Schedules are also shifted during Ramadan, the Moslem month of fast, as a result of extended nighttime listening habits. Peak listening times are reported to be between 3 p.m. and 4 p.m. and between 7 p.m. and 9 p.m.

Each transmission opens with a reading from the Koran, and religious features are heavily emphasized throughout the day.

Five- and 15-minute news programs are spotted for a total of about 1 to 1½ hours per broadcast day. Other programs include stories, poetry, talks on educational subjects and music. Since 1963 music, which only a few years earlier the conservative religious leaders had been able to prohibit in public, has become increasingly popular. In May 1963, Radio Mecca began to use women announcers on its early morning program and even as disc jockeys. This innovation caused serious protests from the conservative religious leaders, but the majority of the people apparently liked it. Also beginning in 1963, Radio Mecca began to broadcast the soundtracks of Egyptian movies with voices linking the scenes. All programs on the domestic service are broadcast in Arabic.

In addition to these broadcasts on the domestic services, Mecca International Service began in January 1965 to broadcast in English on a single mediumwave transmitter for 3 hours a day—between 8 p.m. and 11 p.m. Although no target was announced for these broadcasts, it is believed that the government was appealing to the foreign community in the western part of the country. Programs include news and Western popular and classical music.

All programing originates with the Broadcasting Directorate within the Ministry of Information, which controls the Saudi Arabian Broadcasting Company. No commercial broadcasting exists in the country.

TELEVISION

Television was introduced into the country by Aramco, which initiated a television service for its employees in 1957. Based in Dhahran, Aramco TV can be heard throughout most of Eastern Province for an average of 4½ hours every evening and operates on the United States standard of 525 lines. Television has proved extraordinarily popular among the Saudi Arabs. There were reported to be about 25,000 sets in use in 1965, and the attraction of television was reported to be having an effect in encouraging the Bedouin to settle.

Aramco TV has emphasized educational programs, devoting about 40 percent of its programs to language instruction in Arabic and English, surveys of Arabic literature, health, agriculture, home economics and basic science. Many hundreds of textbooks have been distributed to Saudi listeners who have written requesting them. Beginning in February 1964, Aramco TV added one morning hour per day in educational telecasts designed for secondary schools in Eastern Province. A half hour per day each is devoted to classes in physics and chemistry; the curriculum is worked out in cooperation with the Ministry of Education. These are taught in Arabic.

Other popular Aramco TV programs have included Westerns and comedy series from American television. Several full-length Arabic films and several American films with Arabic dubbed in are shown each week. Sports and news programs have also proved popular.

In January 1964 the Saudi Government signed an agreement with the National Broadcasting Company International of New York to build a television network in Riyadh and a second one in Jidda. Test transmissions began in July 1965, using temporary stations erected by the United States Army Corps of Engineers for the Ministry of Information. At the end of 1965 the studios and transmitters were completed, and test transmissions were continuing for about 2 hours per day. The minister of information indicated in November 1965 that these tests would continue for some time because "we do not wish to be hasty in doing things, especially in the light of the fact that television from both its technical and social aspects is something new in Saudi Arabia." About 80 percent of the technicians were Saudi Arabs, many of them trained in the United States. The government networks operate on the European 625-line system and thus are incompatible with the Aramco network.

It was anticipated that a regular schedule of about 2 hours per day would be undertaken early in 1966 and would concentrate on educational films and news. During the latter half of 1965 the Directorate General of Television in the Ministry of Information built up a film library, with the help of its American advisers. The selection of suitable materials proved difficult because of the restrictions imposed by the strict adherence to Moslem ethics, which excluded films showing the drinking of wine, "improperly" clad women and any form of intimacy between the sexes. In addition, the Ministry eschews films which contain discussions of religion, praise or criticism of foreign countries, references of any sort to Israel and criticism of monarchic forms of government. Aramco TV has successfully avoided these proscribed materials in its programing.

The antipathy of the conservative religious leaders toward the introduction of television, which has forced the government to proceed cautiously with its program, was exemplified by the attack in September 1965 on the Jidda transmitter station by a group headed by Prince Khalid Ibn Musaad, a nephew of King Faisal. The transmitter was destroyed, but the Prince was killed. The government rebuilt the transmitter and continued with its test transmissions, which are shown on receivers in a number of radio and television store windows in Jidda and Riyadh and which have proved popular with the general public.

Plans were made to build relay stations during 1966 to permit the Jidda programs to be seen in Mecca and Taif. Longer-range plans were being made to build relay stations in Burayda and Al-Kharj and independent television stations in Medina and Qasim which will broadcast programs trucked from the studios in Jidda and Riyadh. Thus, the government was progressing with plans to make television available in most of the major cities throughout the country.

CINEMA

The strong opposition of the conservative religious leaders has slowed the development of public showings of motion pictures. Until the end of 1962 the government banned any display of motion pictures. Since then it has permitted the importation of foreign commercial films for private showings. In early 1965 four outdoor public theaters were reported to be operating in Jidda without official sanction, but also apparently without government hindrance. It is probable that the number of such theaters will gradually increase and that they will prove popular. The government will probably continue to censor all such films to prevent offending Moslem sensibilities.

INFORMATION DIRECTED ABROAD

Since its formation in 1961 the Ministry of Information has conducted a rapidly growing campaign to improve the government's image and increase its influence abroad. It publishes an eight-page weekly newsletter, *News from Saudi Arabia,* outlining major events in the country and emphasizing the efforts of the government to modernize and develop the economy and society. It maintains information services in several countries. The Saudi Arabian Information Service in New York publishes a small monthly bulletin, *Saudi Arabia Today,* specializing in news items and book reviews concerning Saudi Arabia that are of special interest to Americans. A New York public relations firm retained by the government prepares *Saudi Arabia Today,* and in 1965 it produced advertising supplements publicizing Saudi developments for distribution with *The New York Times* and *The New York Herald Tribune.*

The Saudi Arabian Broadcasting Company operates an international service, using mainly the transmitters of the Mecca Domestic Service. It broadcasts 1 hour per day each in Indonesian to the Far East, in Urdu to Pakistan, in Persian to Iran and in Swahili to East Africa. Each of these programs includes news and talks in the foreign language and Islamic religious features, which are broadcast in Arabic. The "Voice of Islam" broadcasts in Arabic to the Middle East for 1¾ hours per day. Its early evening program stresses religious news and features. The purpose of this government-operated foreign broadcasting program is to strengthen the position of Islam in those areas where it has taken root and to stress Saudi Arabia's role as the homeland of Islam.

FOREIGN INFORMATION DIRECTED TO SAUDI ARABIA

Despite the rapid growth of public information facilities, the demand has increased even more rapidly. As a result, foreign books, periodicals and even some films are being imported into the country, and foreign broadcasts are popular. Arabic-language books and periodicals from Cairo, Beirut and Baghdad are particularly popular. American news magazines and *Reader's Digest* also enjoy relatively wide circulation in the cities. All imported publications are subject to close scrutiny by Saudi Government censors before being admitted. Long delays and some deletion of material considered offensive have been commonplace, although restrictions have become less strict since 1963.

Broadcasts from other parts of the Arabian peninsula, Cairo, other Arab stations, Europe and the United States can be heard in most parts of the country. Radio Cairo has long been particularly popular, even during periods of animosity between the two governments. The Saudi Government showed some concern, most notably in 1963, over the reception of such virulently anti-Saudi programs of Radio Cairo as "Enemies of God." In 1965 this program was aimed more against the British position in South Arabia than against the Saudi monarchy, although attacks on the monarchy had not ceased.

An increase in Communist-bloc Arabic-language broadcasts to the Middle East was noted during 1964 and 1965. In 1965 the bloc broadcast a total of slightly more than 190 hours per week. Of this, 104 hours originated in Eastern European countries; about 53½ hours, in the Soviet Union; 14 hours, in China; and a little more than 18½ hours, in Cuba. Cuban broadcasts in Arabic more than trebled during 1964 and 1965. The quality of reception and the size of the audience for these programs in Saudi Arabia are not known. It is doubtful that many of the Communist broadcasts are tailored specially for Saudi audiences.

In mid-1965 the "Voice of America" was broadcasting a total of 35 hours per week in Arabic to the Middle East. Its morning program, between 7 a.m. and 9 a.m., consisted of news, Western music, features and instruction in English. Its evening program, from 9:30 p.m. to 12:30 a.m., included general features and listener request programs. Reception was reported to be generally good.

INFORMAL PUBLIC INFORMATION CHANNELS

The bulk of the population continues to rely largely on informal word-of-mouth communications, which have played an important role throughout Arab history. The urban coffeehouses provide a center where news is read aloud and broadcasts are interpreted and discussed. The nomads obtain news during visits to the villages and towns and transmit it as their caravans move from oasis to oasis.

The news circulated by informal channels is not normally subjected to critical scrutiny or verification. The significance of reports may be exaggerated, and the impact of public opinion may vary widely from place to place. Community leaders usually have an important influence on developing public opinion and on the interpretation of information received through formal channels.

The spread of battery-operated radios and of literacy has increased the influence of formal information channels and reduced the effect of rumor and word-of-mouth communications. Increasingly, even the most remote parts of the country are aware of events in the cities and abroad and are becoming part of a nationwide public opinion.

CHAPTER 16

PUBLIC ORDER AND INTERNAL SECURITY

One of the most notable achievements of King Abd al-Aziz Ibn Saud was the establishment and maintenance of internal security and organized justice in an area which previously had known little of either except on a limited, local level. Before his consolidation of the Saudi state, constant intertribal raiding for livestock and other loot and conflict over grazing areas or water rights characterized the life of the nomadic bulk of the population; crimes against persons and property were rampant and generally went unpunished even in the cities. Settled agriculturists lived in terror of Bedouin raids, and each year hundreds of Moslem pilgrims to the holy cities of Hejaz were attacked and robbed.

King Abd al-Aziz undertook to stamp out banditry and raiding and to reduce the bloodshed arising from blood feuds by bringing the tribes more and more under the authority of his central government. He made travel safe for pilgrims and others throughout his territory, and he harshly repressed crime in the settled areas by the swift enforcement of justice based on rigid adherence to a strict Wahhabi interpretation of Koranic prescriptions (see ch. 10, Religion). At the same time he made the nomads whose judicial practices had traditionally been based on *urf* (tribal customary law), increasingly subject to *sharia* (Islamic law), the basic law of the new state (see ch. 12, Constitution and Government).

King Saud Ibn Abd al-Aziz and King Faisal Ibn Abd al-Aziz al-Faisal al-Saud gradually developed and modernized the organs responsible for public order, but these have remained essentially those devised by King Abd al-Aziz. At the end of 1965 the National Guard and the Ministry of Interior's National Police, Coast Guard and Frontier Police, Fire Brigade and Directorate of Criminal Investigation were the primary organizations charged with maintaining public order and internal security. They were assisted in cases concerning religious law by a special police force attached to the Public Morality Committees administered by the Grand Mufti (the leading Islamic judge in the country) (see ch. 10, Religion).

King Faisal has also undertaken to modify the legal system to take into account the growing number of decree laws and regulations which lie outside *sharia* law and require different judicial treatment. In 1962 he announced plans to create a Ministry of Justice to integrate the modern legal system with *sharia* law and to create a compatible total legal system, but at the end of 1965 the project was still under study.

DEVELOPMENTS UNDER ABD AL-AZIZ

In order to consolidate his power over vast desert areas inhabited by largely autonomous, constantly feuding tribes, Abd al-Aziz early in his rule encouraged the settlement of nomads. A major device in the implementation of this policy was his promotion of Ikhwan (religious brotherhood) colonies, agricultural settlements established under the auspices of Wahhabi missionaries (see ch. 3, Historical Setting). Superimposing a new religious fervor and spirit of comradeship upon traditional tribal loyalties, these settlements provided Abd al-Aziz with a high-spirited, mobile military force. He used this force as a desert militia to reduce intertribal raiding and as an important instrument in his conquest and subjugation of the Hejaz (1924-26). Crime was severely suppressed, the holy places were placed under the protection of Abd al-Aziz's personal guard, and detachments of the Ikhwan patrolled the countryside enforcing compliance with Wahhabi precepts.

From the standpoint of internal security, the Ikhwan experiment was not, however, an enduring success. Tribal loyalties had not been superseded, and, by the late 1920's, Ikhwan leaders had become involved in various tribal rebellions and in attacking settlements bordering Iraq. Abd al-Aziz was forced to crush the movement, and he disbanded it in 1930. Although the Ikhwan ended as a military force, some of the principles embodied in its organization persist in the Saudi Arabian Government's continued efforts to settle the Bedouin population and in some of the traditions of the present-day National Guard, known also as the White Army, which also acts as an internal security force (see ch. 25, The Armed Forces).

Building upon the traditional tribal system of local responsibility for the settling of disputes, King Abd al-Aziz established a flexible administrative system under which tribal sheikhs, subject to their personal acceptance by him, retained considerable authority and responsibility for the conduct of their followers (see ch. 12, Constitution and Government). In return for allegiance to the king and the maintenance of peace and security in all tribal units of their respective areas, the sheikhs were offered official recognition of their authority, a minimum of government interference in their affairs and annual subsidies commensurate with their importance. Under this system, offenses and breaches of the peace were punished by the responsible sheikh, or, in the event of his failure to do so, by a neighboring tribal leader. Only when this local responsibility was neglected were the armed forces brought in to quell the disturbance.

The practice of subsidizing tribal leaders to ensure their loyalty and cooperation has persisted. The system of local control over security matters within the tribes has been perpetuated, and the presence of the armed forces, particularly the National Guard, acts mainly as a deterrent against intertribal warfare or defiance of the central authority.

To a considerable extent, in the settled villages and towns as well as among the nomads, a public security organization exists within the kin group or local community itself, involving a network of social sanctions against crime and of authority for the settlement of disputes. Thus, many crimes are settled informally and are never brought to the attention of government officials.

MODERN SECURITY FORCES

The Ministry of Interior, created in 1951 and one of the earliest bodies to be established by King Abd al-Aziz in his efforts to formalize a modern government, is responsible for the maintenance of law and order and for the internal security of the state. Under the minister of interior, Prince Fahd Ibn Abd al-Aziz, a brother of King Faisal, this responsibility is shared by the general director of public security who controls the uniformed National Police, the director of the Coast Guard and Frontier Police, the director of the Fire Brigade and the general director of Criminal Investigation. The National Guard, a highly mobile and lightly armed military force responsible directly to the king, assists the police in the maintenance of internal order, and the regular army may be called on in case of need (see ch. 25, The Armed Forces).

The members of the National Guard are chosen from among the so-called noble tribes, whereas the police and the army are recruited from among all elements of the population. The National Guard units are usually kept relatively isolated from the general public. It has been noted that when they are called in to deal with any public disorder which the police, or even in some cases, local units of the regular army, have not been able to handle, they have been able to restore peace without resort to excessive force.

Directorate General of Public Security

Based on the 1964 budgeted expenditures for wages and salaries for the Directorate General of Public Security in the Ministry of

Interior, it appeared that the National Police numbered between 15,000 and 20,000. The National Police functions largely in the municipalities and frontier districts. Although the Directorate General of Public Security in the Ministry of Interior nominally has nationwide responsibility for the National Police, in practice the regional emirs have considerable autonomy in matters pertaining to public security. This is particularly true of Eastern Province, where the governing Jiluwi family exercises semi-independent control over the security forces. In addition to supervisory authority over the police of local emirates (basic administrative units in Saudi Arabia), regional emirs have command over their own personal guards, which supplement the regular police as needed. Units of the army regularly patrol port areas and usually assist the National Police and the National Guard in the control of crowds during Ramadan and the pilgrimage season (see ch. 10, Religion).

Like the army, the National Police recruits men mainly from nomadic tribes. Police uniforms are similar to those of soldiers except for a distinctive red beret, but there are no police units that could be regarded as paramilitary in character. As far as is known, police methods are not considered cruel and have not aroused general resentment.

In late 1965 the government acknowledged that its police force was still modest in terms of equipment and training, but stated that it was adopting modern procedures and equipment and establishing modern training methods. It maintained, however, that internal security was as well established as in any country in the world because of "the concept of justice as expounded by Islam and enforced by the government." The government has reduced the public disorder, rioting, assault on pilgrims and intertribal warfare that characterized the area before the establishment of the Saudi Arabian Government.

The government established the Police College in Mecca in about 1960 to train officers. An intermediate school certificate is required for entrance, but the government expected to increase the educational prerequisite to the secondary school certificate in 1966. The police force was also being improved by the introduction of radio communications and mobile police units supplied with motor vehicles. In March 1965 there was a mobile police squad in Riyadh and one in Jidda. Helicopters, radar and television were expected to be added to the police equipment in the near future.

Public Morality Committees

Since King Abd al-Aziz institutionalized them in the 1920's, the government has used the quasi-judicial Public Morality Committees to ensure the strict compliance of the population with the puritanical precepts of Wahhabi Islam (see ch. 10, Religion). Local committees in every town have the power, with local police assistance, to enforce public observance of such religious requirements as the five daily prayers, fasting during Ramadan and the seclusion of women, and the proscriptions against the use of alcohol, the display of human images, public smoking and dancing.

Local Public Morality Committees are subordinate to provincial committees for Hejaz, Nejd and Eastern Province. In 1965 each of these committees was under the control of a member of the Al ash-Shaykh family. An ancestor of the family founded the Wahhabi movement and worked intimately with the Saud family in creating Saudi Arabia (see ch. 3, Historical Setting). The senior living member of the Al ash-Shaykh family, Mohammed Iban Ibrahim Al ash-Shaykh, in 1965 was the Grand Mufti, leader of the ulema (body of Islamic scholars) and Chief Qadi (Islamic judge). Although the Grand Mufti was responsible for the administration of the provincial Public Morality Committees, the king maintained policy control over the committees.

Crown Prince Faisal announced in November 1962 that his government was going to reform the Public Morality Committees, which were resisting some of his efforts to modernize the society in such areas as the gradual emancipation of women and the introduction of radio, television and other forms of entertainment. As of the end of 1965, however, no apparent reduction in the powers of the Committees had been instituted, and the conservatism of religious leaders was still effective in slowing the pace of modernization.

ADMINISTRATION OF JUSTICE

Criminal law and procedure are derived almost entirely from *sharia* law, that is, the Islamic law based on the Koran, and the practices and sayings of the Prophet Mohammed as modified by precedent and as interpreted by the ulema, who function as judicial advisers and religious leaders. The version accepted by the Saudi Arabian Government is that of the conservative Hanbalite school, although followers of other schools are found in the kingdom, particularly in Hejaz (see ch. 10, Religion).

In recent years sacred law has been supplemented from time to time by royal decrees issued to meet such new situations as those arising from industrial accidents. An early example of decree law is the vehicle code, which governs traffic violations. Offenses which in the government's view pose a threat to public order may also fall within the province of decree legislation. Since the end of World War II, tax, corporation and company law, and labor, mining and foreign capital investment regulations have also been codified. Although some integration of decree and *sharia* law is occurring, decree law for the most part is carried out separately from *sharia* court procedures. In keeping with the Arab tradition, by which the local leader acts as a judge, a sheikh or emir is authorized to hear cases of alleged violation of decree law and render judgments within the terms of the decrees.

A case falling under the vehicle code may be tried in a religious court if there is an aggrieved private party. During the course of such a trial, the accused may bring in witnesses and present evidence in his own defense.

Crown Prince Faisal announced in November 1962 that the government intended to establish a judicial council of outstanding members of the judiciary and the ulema to consider problems arising from new situations not covered in *sharia* law. He promised to promulgate legislation guaranteeing the immunity of the judiciary from political interference and to create a ministry of justice to coordinate the legal activities of the government, including the office of the state's public prosecutor. In late 1965 the government announced that it was working on the modification of the legal system and was preparing for the establishment of a ministry of justice.

The Court System and Criminal Procedure

The organization of the religious or *sharia* courts is basically uniform throughout the country, but administrative details vary from province to province. The judicial system in Hejaz consists of three levels of courts under a judicial advisory committee in Mecca. At the lowest level, the courts of petty affairs are like magistrates' courts and deal with minor misdemeanors and small claims. They also hold special sessions for Bedouin affairs. These courts are generally presided over by a *qadi* (Islamic judge) appointed by the headquarters of the Chief Qadi (Grand Mufti) in Riyadh. The next higher courts, the high courts of *sharia* law, located in larger towns, have jurisdiction over all matters beyond the competence of the lowest courts. At the highest level is the Special Appeals Court of the Hejaz. Decisions of the lowest courts may be appealed to the high courts of *sharia* law and then to the Special Appeals Court of the Hejaz. In serious cases, further appeal may be heard by the Judicial Supervisory Committee in

Mecca. This committee cannot alter the verdict, but it may refer the case to the Special Appeals Court for reconsideration. In Eastern Province an appeal from the decision of *qadi* is referred, subject to the approval of the emir, to a council of *qadis* and from there to the Grand Mufti in Riyadh.

In cases involving death or serious injury the accused is usually detained by the police until the time of the trial. The right of habeas corpus is not recognized. Although the regional emir may order the police to accept a bond in the case of minor offenses, the granting of bond lies within the discretion of the local chief of police.

At the trial of minor cases, the *qadi* hears the complaints of the aggrieved party and cross-examines the plaintiff, the defendant and any witnesses they may introduce. The judge assigns great significance to a defendant's sworn testimony under oath. All cases are heard in public by a single judge. The trial by jury is unknown in Islamic law. After determining the guilt or innocence and the right to compensation, the *qadi* attempts to arrive at a fair assessment of reparations acceptable to both parties. In more serious cases the *qadi* may suggest appropriate punishment, but he does not pass sentence. All papers pertaining to such a case are sent to the district or provincial emir, who, with the advice of members of the local ulema, pronounces the sentence.

At the pinnacle of the judicial system is the king, who may act as a final court of appeal and as a source of pardon. King Abd al-Aziz was famed for personally dispensing justice in cases of every description, but he generally refrained from modifying legal interpretations of the ulema without first winning its members over to his view. Kings Saud and Faisal have exercised judiciary power, but to a lesser extent than did Abd al-Aziz.

Gradually, other mechanisms have developed for the solution of problems in this as in other spheres of government. The Grievance Board of the Council of Ministers, for instance, to some extent has assumed the role of final arbiter of justice, at least in cases of decree law. In general, cases falling within the scope of *sharia* law are referred to the appropriate religious authorities rather than reviewed directly by the Grievance Board, but any person who feels himself to be the victim of an injustice and has no recourse in the courts may submit a complaint to the Board.

Theoretically, all residents are equal before the law and are subject to both *sharia* and decree law. All but minor cases involving foreigners are generally referred to the district or regional emir, who tends to give them special consideration.

The handling of cases is usually expeditious, and judges have a reputation for incorruptibility and justice. There is considerable faith—even on the part of foreign observers—in the essential fairness of *sharia* procedures.

Crimes and Punishment

Two categories of crimes are covered by *sharia* law: those which are carefully defined, for which specific penalties are decreed, and those which are implicit in the requirements and prohibitions laid down in *sharia* law, for which penalties may be set at the discretion of the *qadi*. A third group of crimes exists as a result of the various codes and regulations established by royal decree, particularly since the end of World War II. The first two categories of crime are tried by the *sharia* courts; the third by administrators—emirs and other government officials.

In the case of crimes covered by *sharia* law, some of the penalties specified by the law are extremely severe. To what extent these were being carried out in 1965 was not clear. The orthodox legal school officially recognized in the country tends to hold to a strict interpretation of *sharia* law, but the government has discouraged the imposition of severe penalties such as stoning and mutilation. It has stated that crimes which would merit these penalties have become extremely rare as a result of the establishment of a strong central government supporting the orthodox Islamic concept of justice.

The *sharia* law carefully defines homicide and personal injury, fornication and adultery, theft and highway robbery and specifies penalties (*hadd*) for each according to circumstances. Various degrees of culpability for homicide and bodily injury are recognized according to intent, the type of weapon used, and the circumstances under which the crime took place. In Islamic law, homicide is not considered a crime against society in which the state moves against the criminal. *Sharia* law recognizes only the right of the victim or the victim's family to bring charges against the accused for the right to retaliation or to blood-money—that is, a set payment as recompense for the crime.

The right to act in self-defense is recognized as nullifying the commission of a crime. Retaliation permitted to the family of the victim—actually to the next of kin to the victim—includes the killing of the criminal in the case of homicide or exacting the same bodily injury on him as he committed. Retaliation, however, is discouraged in Islamic law; the acceptance of blood-money is considered a preferable penalty. Unintentional homicide is invariably punished by compensation to the victim's family.

In the case of a traffic death or injury the driver at fault is not only subject to the jurisdiction of a *sharia* court as regards the rights of the victim's family to indemnity but also to a penalty (generally imprisonment) under the vehicle code. The lack of distinction in decree legislation between simple and criminal negligence makes imprisonment virtually mandatory for even relatively minor violations.

Fornication and adultery are considered by *sharia* to be crimes against the family and public morality. As such, anyone may bring the accusation before a *qadi*, and the accused persons are severely punished if the crime is proved. In the case of adultery, *sharia* law stipulates that both parties be stoned to death; in the case of fornication, the punishment is 100 lashes administered in public. Islamic law has established rigorous requirements for proof. Four reliable witnesses to the act must swear to the crime. If their accusation does not hold up, they are liable to 80 lashes themselves.

Theft is punished by the cutting off of the right hand of the thief, but, because of the severity of the punishment, a number of qualifications have been introduced to mitigate it. Petty larceny and theft from relatives are excluded, and the theft must take place by stealth from a properly secured place. If the thief repents and makes recompense before the case is brought before a *qadi*, the punishment is reduced, and the victim may merely demand blood-money or he may grant a pardon. Highway robbery is considered a crime against public safety and is more severely punished than theft. If it involves only the taking of loot, the criminal may be punished by having alternate hands and feet cut off and by banishment; if it involves homicide or bodily harm to the victim, the criminal is liable to execution by crucifixion. Repentance reduces the severity of the crime as it does in the case of theft.

Other crimes, for which the penalty is not stipulated in the *sharia* law, include various crimes against religion and public morality, such as drunkenness and gambling or the neglect of requirements on prayer, fasting and other religious duties, and crimes against the rights of individuals, such as the use of false weights and usury. The penalties for these crimes are set by the *qadi*, after considering the case on its merits, and may include public flogging, imprisonment or the imposition of fines. Most commonly, these cases are brought before the *sharia* court by members of the Public Morality Committees.

Prisons in the past were reported to be crowded and unsanitary. In late 1965, however, the Ministry of Interior was making an effort to improve the living conditions in the prisons. It is reported that clinics have been established in the larger prisons to take care of the medical needs of the prisoners and that newspapers and magazines have been provided. Prisoners are reported to have access to programs broadcast by the Saudi Broadcasting Service (see ch. 15, Public Information). The literacy program has been extended to prisoners, for the illiterate and to enable the literate prisoners to continue their education. In an effort to rehabilitate prisoners and to equip them to earn a livelihood after their release, the opportunity to learn a trade is offered in most large prisons.

INTERNAL SECURITY

Subversion in the form of assassination, sabotage and plots has been an important element in the political dynamics of the Arabian peninsula. While the Saudi dynasty was establishing firm control over the tribes of what became Saudi Arabia, it was constantly plagued with subversive attempts against it. After he came to power in 1902, Abd al-Aziz was able to gain the loyalty of the large majority of his people and thus to greatly reduce the possibility of overthrow of the dynasty through subversion (see ch. 3, Historical Setting).

After Abd al-Aziz's death in 1953, and particularly after the overthrow of the monarchy in Yemen in September 1962, subversive activities sponsored from abroad against the Saudi monarchy increased. At the end of 1965, however, the weakness and lack of organization among the dissident elements and the continuing loyalty of the majority to the king precluded the development of a serious threat to the regime.

There was no evidence at the end of 1965 that the Saudi regime was seriously threatened by subversive elements or that there was any popular discontent with which it was unable to cope. From time to time the regime announced the arrest, trial and sentencing of a number of individuals on charges of subversive activity or of membership in secret antiregime organizations. No details were given, but the relatively mild sentences seemed to indicate a lack of serious concern on the part of the government.

In December 1965 the Ministry of Interior announced the arrest of 65 persons on grounds of suspected subversion. The king issued decrees dealing with two groups. One group of 34 persons was tried in a *sharia* court and all were found guilty of "membership in secret deviationist organizations which aim at disturbing the country's security." After each person had submitted in writing a statement of guilt and an appeal for pardon, the king released them, but he permanently dismissed from government employment all among them who were civil servants, and deported all who were foreigners.

The second group consisted of 31 suspected Communists who were arrested and charged with "upholding destructive principles," and being connected with "deviationist organizations which aim at disobeying the legal ruler and at harming the state's security." They were found guilty by a *sharia* court, and 19 were sentenced to prison terms of 5 to 15 years. The remainder were dismissed from government employment and restricted from all future government service, and foreigners were deported.

CHAPTER 17

ATTITUDES AND REACTIONS OF THE PEOPLE

Saudi Arabs, intensely aware of their Islamic heritage, are proud that their land was the birthplace of the Prophet Mohammed and the cradle of Islam. These things are talked about, heard in recitations of poems and learned at the Koranic schools attended by the young (see ch. 8, Artistic and Intellectual Expression; ch. 9, Education).

National consciousness—that is, popular awareness of Saudi Arabia as an independent, unified state—is, on the other hand, relatively little developed. The ethnic homogeneity of the society and the emphasis on Islamic orthodoxy in Abd al-Aziz Ibn Saud's pacification of the tribes in the 1920's obviated the need for an intensive national unification campaign which might have served to create national consciousness among a broad segment of the population.

Most of the population, living in rural areas, knew little of the world beyond the nearest town. Bedouin tribes around the periphery of the country continued to wander across still undemarcated national boundaries in search of pasture. For most of the people awareness of national political life meant simply that they acknowledged the king as their sovereign and identified him as the imam (religious leader) to be mentioned in their prayers.

As a result, national consciousness was in 1965 still limited to the small segment of the population which received some modern education and which was employed by the government or in the modern sector of the economy. With the rapid expansion of education, of means of communication and of the channels of public information, however, awareness of the existence of the state and the ability to differentiate between Saudi Arabs and other Arabs and non-Arabs was growing (see ch. 9, Education; ch. 15, Public Information).

Contacts with other countries, particularly since World War II, have resulted in the beginnings of consciousness of national distinctions between their own and other states. Confrontation with different cultures has been with the British and Americans who introduced the beginnings of Westernization, primarily in the form of modern technology, and with Arab states, particularly the

United Arab Republic (Egypt), which had long been exposed to Western influences and which actively sought to propagate Egyptian influence in Saudi Arabia.

The government has made few efforts to consolidate the growing national consciousness. Its national symbols emphasize the country's association with Islam rather than its individual personality. The national flag is green, the color of Islam, and shows the profession of faith—"There is no God but Allah; Mohammed is the Prophet of Allah"—in white Arabic script and a white sword symbolizing the spread of Islam by conquest. There is also an anthem, but neither it nor the flag seems to evoke a strong popular response. The sole nonreligious national holidays are the anniversary of King Faisal's investiture, on November 2, and the anniversary of the kingdom's unification in 1932, first celebrated on September 23, 1965 (see ch. 10, Religion).

The essentially religious character of the society and particularly the continuing power of the ultraconservative Wahhabi *ulema* (body of Islamic scholars) have inhibited the development of a secular concept of the nation (see ch. 10, Religion). As a result, even among the minority of the population which is conscious of the existence of the Saudi nation, relatively few have developed nationalist sentiments comparable to those existing in most new nations.

Nationalist sentiment was in 1965 more akin to a desire for modernization, and those who called themselves "nationalists" were interested primarily in creating a modern society in which they could take pride on grounds similar to those of the national pride of citizens from other Arab states. Concretely, they desired a wider distribution of wealth by the government, to include more extensive transportation and communication facilities, diversification and expansion of industry and development of agriculture and health services. Most of all, their aspirations were for increases in education, in breadth and depth. Education was recognized as the key to change. The attitude of the modernists was more one of impatience than of strong opposition. In no element of the population was there an approval of any basic departure from Islamic principles.

The degree of modernist attitudes held by individuals was usually determined by the amount of education, by the extent of contact with Western ideas, by residence (whether in urban or rural areas) and by sector of employment (traditional or nontraditional). Occupationally, modernist elements gravitated toward the bureaucracy, although their attitudes tended increasingly to spread among those in or near the management levels in the oil industry, construction business or commerce. The increased availability of liberal scholarships awarded on the basis of merit and the widespread aspiration for education foreshadowed a growing number of individuals with a higher education, who are likely, therefore, to acquire modernist attitudes.

Students returning from several years in foreign universities reportedly go through an often difficult first year of readjustment to the society. Usually absorbed immediately into the bureaucracy, they tend to be dissatisfied because of the lack of opportunity to give effect to their new ideas.

Because of its identity with modernization and secularism, Saudi Arabian nationalism has tended to be confused in the minds of some of its proponents with the broader ideal of Pan-Arab nationalism, a regional, ethnic solidarity which has been identified by some of its proponents with socialism. This transnational sentiment, inhibiting the emergence of a strong Saudi Arab nationalist loyalty, has been complicated by President Gamal Abdul Nasser's leadership of Pan-Arab nationalism and support of Arab socialism. President Nasser has intermittently been friend and enemy of Saudi Arabia. His socialist ideology is considered by many traditionalists to be directly contradictory to the true tenents of Islam. Others consider his "nationalism" as thinly veiled expansionism.

By the 1960's the beginning of a more broadly based popular nationalist attitude toward the state seemed to be emerging. Nearly 3 years of hostilities with the United Arab Republic over the Yemen civil war may have served to spread a more concrete sense of national identity (see ch. 14, Foreign Relations).

Traditionally, loyalty of the local kin group did not extend beyond the tribe, which was led by a sheikh, a member of the leading family of the tribe (see ch. 5, Social Structure). After the various tribes were pacified and subjected to the rule of the Saud family, loyalty was focused, through the tribal sheikhs, on the Saudi king, the "sheikh among sheikhs."

The political authority of the king is still inseparable from his religious authority. Loyalty to him is maintained through the political allegiance of sheikhs, through religion and even by blood-relation. A considerable segment of the population claims to be related to the Saud family by virtue of the many marriages made by King Abd al-Aziz and King Saud Ibn Abd al-Aziz in the first half of the twentieth century.

Most of the people see their country as a network of kin groups held together by personal and religious ties to the head of the ruling dynasty, and most feel that the monarchy is the only suitable form of government. Popular loyalty to the institution of the monarchy, rather than loyalty to a particular king, was demonstrated when the royal family deposed King Saud in 1964 and named Faisal Ibn Abd al-Aziz al-Faisal al-Saud in his place. The family's decision was accepted by the people, and affirmations of support for the new king promptly followed his investiture.

Because the paternalistic form of the state is compatible with Arab and Islamic traditions, it has the loyalty of the large majority of the conservative tribes and villagers. King Faisal cements relations with local leaders by receiving them personally in his *majlis* (council) whenever they have problems to present to him. They respect the King as a strong, moderate, orthodox leader who is aware of their problems and interested in helping to solve them.

Townspeople, particularly the small educated group with a modern outlook, have a more sophisticated view of the king, of his government and of the state generally. Their loyalty is at once more conscious and less intense than that of traditionalist rural elements. They may distinguish between the sacred and secular roles of the king and may differ with the king on some of his policies, but they remain a bulwark of royal support.

Among the proponents in 1965 of a more rapid modernization were a few individuals who appeared to feel that the monarchy was not capable of implementing change at the rapid rate they desired. They seemed to feel that, in order to build a modern, fully developed nation-state, a new basis of allegiance was required, one rooted in a secular concept of law. The overwhelming majority of the population appeared, however, to be satisfied with King Faisal's efforts to use the nation's vast oil wealth to improve the social and economic well-being of his people, and pressures for political change were remarkably absent (see ch. 13, Political Dynamics).

Attitudes toward other countries are determined by the degree of contact with foreigners and education. Because official policy has been one of vehement opposition to the continuation of a Jewish state on what is considered Arab land, popular attitudes toward Israel are marked by severe animosity. No Jews are allowed in the country; complimentary references to Israel may not be made; and even the name Israel itself is not permitted in publications (see ch. 15, Public Information).

Attitudes toward the United Arab Republic are affected by changes in official relations, which were seriously disrupted in 1958 and broken between 1962 and 1964 (see ch. 14, Foreign Relations). Since 1952 no other country has so deeply influenced national policy. Foreign policy was made largely in reaction to the United Arab Republic, and the transfers of power to Faisal in 1958 and 1964 were indirectly precipitated by crises in foreign relations involving the United Arab Republic. Egyptians have been present in the country in large numbers as military advisers, teachers and technicians and have exerted a definite influence.

Attitudes toward Americans, with whom Saudi Arabs have been in contact since the 1930's, primarily through the activities of the Arabian American Oil Company (Aramco) are generally favorable (see ch. 14, Foreign Relations). Military and diplomatic personnel have been in the country since the 1940's, and an American-run airfield was in operation at Dhahran for over 15 years, but the most significant American presence, perhaps the most significant foreign presence of any kind, has been Aramco. Although Saudi Arabs working for Aramco and American employees have been treated equally by their American employers, there is some resentment of the Americans' higher living standard in their foreigners' communities in Eastern Province. In some quarters attitudes toward Americans combine resentment with a desire to emulate.

Non-Arab Moslems, who form large percentages of the population in urban centers, are accepted by Saudi Arabs as fellow Moslems but are regarded as foreigners (see ch. 4, Ethnic Groups and Languages). Saudi Arabians do not as a rule intermarry with them. Their continued residence is discouraged, although the need for foreign skilled workers and professionals is recognized. Cultural, economic and other factors inhibit their complete integration into the society, and the bond of religious sympathy by itself is not strong enough to permit assimilation (see ch. 4, Ethnic Groups and Languages).

SECTION III. ECONOMIC BACKGROUND

CHAPTER 18

CHARACTER AND STRUCTURE OF THE ECONOMY

The economy is dominated by the oil industry, which in 1965 provided over 83 percent of the government's revenue and approximately 95 percent of the country's foreign exchange. Saudi Arabia is the fifth largest producer of oil in the world and possesses the world's second largest proved reserves. Until the discovery of oil in 1938, the stagnating economy, based on subsistence arid-zone agriculture and desert pastoralism, had exhibited little potential for development along modern lines. Beginning in 1944, the large-scale exploitation of oil brought into the country modern technology and large injections of capital which established the basis for previously unimagined economic growth and modernization.

Oil operations were, as of 1965, in the hands of four foreign companies, operating under the terms of concession agreements with the Saudi Government, which owns all subsoil mineral wealth. By far the most important of the foreign oil companies was the Arabian American Oil Company (Aramco), formed in 1944 by four major United States oil companies, including the company which was granted the first concession in 1933 and which first discovered oil.

Operating mainly in Eastern Province, Aramco established in the desert a huge, modern industrial complex and transformed into prosperous communities the existing oasis towns near its oilfields, its refinery at Ras Tanura and its terminal at Dammam. Secondary industries—mostly in construction, services and consumer goods—were established, stimulated by the demands of the company and its employees and by the support and technical advice given by the company to Saudi contracting firms. As the exploitation of oil increased, traditional agricultural pursuits in the area declined in importance. Eastern Province became the economic heart of the country.

As a result of the government's spending of the revenue which it receives in the form of royalties and taxes from the oil companies, the monetized sector of the economy has expanded to areas outside Eastern Province. The resulting increase in consumer demand and in urban development needs has encouraged the establishment of secondary industries in major centers such as Jidda and Riyadh. To support industrial activity, the government has developed elements of a modern economic infrastructure with the expansion of the transportation network, the increase and improvement of health and education facilities, the location and exploitation of water resources, and the establishment of a sound financial system. The country's basic unit of currency, the Saudi riyal (SR), has, since the early 1960's, been extremely stable and is among the strongest currencies in the world.

Commercial activities reflect the increase in general economic activity. Particularly since 1962, imports of both consumer goods and capital goods have increased sharply, but steadily growing oil exports have more than covered them. Trade practices in the major urban areas are gradually acquiring the more sophisticated characteristics of a commercial mechanism geared to a modern economy (see ch. 22, Domestic Trade; ch. 23, Foreign Economic Relations).

In contrast to the rapidly developing industrial and commercial sectors, the traditional agricultural sector has remained relatively static. Production of both crops and livestock is limited by adverse climatic conditions and primitive agricultural practices. The improvement of the sector is especially difficult, expensive and time consuming, as it depends on the discovery and development of water resources and on the introduction of new agricultural techniques to farmers and herders, many of whom are still reluctant to change their methods (see ch. 19, Agriculture).

The country's arid-zone agriculture is based primarily on nomadic pastoralism, since cultivation is possible only on oases and in the area in the southwest corner of the kingdom, which receives adequate rainfall for farming. In 1965 nomadic pastoralism still occupied 50 percent of the country's population. Most pastoralists are seminomads who raise mainly sheep and some goats and who travel smaller distances than do the fewer camel-raising Bedouin. The poor and uncultivable lands used for grazing cover approximately 80 percent of the kingdom's total area and are divided into districts for use by the various nomadic and seminomadic tribes. Since 1925, however, the government has exercised the right of eminent domain over these lands and can legally deny or modify a tribe's usufruct rights to the land.

Sedentary farming, occupying about 25 percent of the population, takes place on less than 1 percent of the total land area. Most of the farms are small and privately owned, with land tenure based on a traditional system governed by Islamic law. Low production compounded with inadequate distribution systems have prevented the farming areas from fully supplying the urban areas' needs for even basic foodstuffs.

As most of the sedentary farmers and the nomadic herders produce mainly for themselves, trade is minimal in the rural areas. The commercial mechanism in these areas, therefore, is simple, based largely on barter, and geared to a low level of demand and the small range of products required to fulfill the basic needs of the subsistence economy.

At the time of the establishment of the oil industry in the late 1930's, the static conditions that characterize the present agricultural sector were prevalent throughout the economy. Thus, when oil revenues suddenly increased after World War II, the economic system was unable to absorb it. The system lacked the financial techniques and institutions to handle an immense income, and there were no programs designed to distribute the oil wealth throughout the economy. The recipients of the oil wealth were restricted largely to the royal family and those traders and entrepreneurs able to profit from the oil-induced boom in the commerce and construction sectors of the economy. Much of the income left the country in the form of Saudi deposits in foreign banks and as payment for imported luxury consumer goods. Only a very small portion was spent for productive domestic investment (see ch. 24, Monetary and Financial System).

In response to a severe financial crisis in 1956-60, the government established a firm basis for a system of monetary and fiscal administration adapted to a modern economy. The crisis, which was brought about by the leveling off of world demand for oil and, therefore, of the increase in oil revenue without a correspondent curtailment of government expenditure, clearly demonstrated the interdependence of internal and external monetary balance and the need for disciplined budgetary policies. Sharp decreases in foreign exchange reserves, rises in domestic prices, and flight of capital due to loss of confidence, ultimately forced the government to take drastic action to check the crisis (see ch. 24, Monetary and Financial System).

With the aid of the International Monetary Fund, the government introduced, in 1958, a strict stabilization program calling principally for strong budgetary controls, strict import and exchange controls and a reform of the exchange system. As the program proved effective, the par value of the riyal was set in 1960 at SR4.50 to $1.00, and the government was able to eliminate all import and exchange controls. To assure monetary stability in the future, the Saudi Arabian Monetary Agency, which had been created in 1952 for the purpose of regulating the value of the currency, was given increased power to enable it to carry out its function (see ch. 24, Monetary and Financial System).

On the basis of the lessons learned from the crisis, the government adopted for the first time a positive policy toward economic development. It had been made fully aware that, in order to reduce the economy's vulnerability to fluctuation in oil revenues in the future, oil revenues currently being received had to be devoted to the diversification and strength of the economy. In November 1962, Prime Minister Faisal stated, "Financial recovery and economic development will be the government's principal concern."

At the invitation of the government, a mission from the International Bank for Reconstruction and Development (IBRD) visited Saudi Arabia during the spring of 1960 to explore the potentialities for economic development. In November it issued a report which became the basis for much of the government's initial development programs. Among its recommendations were: the creation of a central planning body; initial government concentration on a few high-priority projects which would benefit the largest number of people, particularly those which would probably not be undertaken by private concerns; and the conduct of surveys of the country's mineral and underground water resources.

Until 1965 the Supreme Planning Council, established in February 1961, held the technical and financial responsibility for the planning and implementation of projects. It functioned as a ministerial subcommittee, and its members consisted of the ministers concerned with development, presided over by the prime minister. It prepared a development budget, separate from the general budget, allocating among the various projects the funds provided in the general budget for development. After 1963 these funds were supplemented by those from the Economic Development Fund, which was created in that year to hold the revenue the government obtained by virtue of a special agreement with Aramco and Trans-Arabian Pipeline (Tapline) (see ch. 24, Monetary and Financial System).

In January 1965 the planning machinery was reorganized, and a new planning body, called the Central Planning Organization, replaced the Supreme Planning Council. The new organization consisted of 12 economic advisers, headed by a president with ministerial rank who reported directly to the king. It did not handle all aspects of planning, but was assigned only the technical aspects of planning and followup, which it carried out in cooperation with the ministries. The minister of finance and national economy was given the responsibility and duty of budgeting. The allocations for development were no longer spelled out in a separate budget; they formed part of the allocations made to the various ministries in the general budget and were simply earmarked for developmental purposes.

Through its control over most of the national income, the government has the power to influence all sectors of the economy. Despite its control of capital, however, its policy has been one which fosters free enterprise. Its general practice is to hire experts to come to the country to make feasibility studies on the possible investment project. Based on these studies, contracts are then granted to private national or foreign companies on the basis of free competition to carry out the project.

The government's projects have concentrated on the development of infrastructure, with highest priority being given to the extension and modernization of the transportation network, the improvement and increase of health and education facilities and the location and exploitation of water resources for agricultural, industrial and domestic use. Of equal importance are its projects concerning the development of the traditional agricultural sector which are designed to help the farmers and herders achieve a higher standard of living and to decrease the country's dependence on imported agricultural products.

The government's efforts to expand and improve agricultural production include the settlement of desert tribes; the development of water supplies, mainly through flood control and more efficient irrigation systems; the increasing of arable land; and the introduction of modern agricultural techniques. With the aid of foreign experts, it has established several experimental farms, such as Al-Kharj, near Riyadh, which are especially concerned with the development of techniques which can be adapted to the climatic conditions of the country. The government hopes that such farms will serve as an inducement to farmers and herders to use the new techniques and thereby increase their yields of crops and improve their livestock. Moreover, it has established various agricultural centers which provide farmers with technical advice, tools, seeds, fertilizers and animal breeding stations to aid in the improvement of local breeds (see ch. 19, Agriculture).

The development of industry and power generation is left almost entirely to the private sector. The government fosters industrial development not only by improving the infrastructure, but through the issuing of legislation specifically designed to attract national and foreign private interests. Such measures include a program for the "Protection and Encouragement of National Industries" which calls for: exemption from duties on goods necessary for the establishment of a national industrial enterprise; the granting of state land at nominal or no rent for the location of industry; and a certain degree of tariff protection. The same privileges are granted to foreign investors under the Foreign Capital Investment Code, which also grants a 5-year exemption from taxes to those foreign companies in which Saudi participation amounts to at least 25 percent of the total capital (see ch. 20, Industry).

In order to encourage the establishment of major industries based on minerals other than oil, the government, with the technical aid of foreign governments, has conducted surveys of the country's mineral wealth. In 1963 it issued a mining code intended to interest national and foreign companies in further exploration and in the exploitation of minerals.

The development of major industries based on minerals, including oil, will be subject to a certain degree of government participation, as it is being undertaken primarily under the auspices of the General Petroleum and Minerals Organization which was established by royal decree in November 1962. It is a public autonomous organization attached to the Ministry of Petroleum and Mineral Resources, with the specific purpose of fostering the development of petroleum and mineral industries. The most important industries which it has projected for the near future include the country's second oil refinery, a petrochemical complex, and an iron and steel plant, all of which are to be carried out with the assistance of foreign private companies (see ch. 20, Industry).

Providing a firm basis for the country's economic development is the continuously favorable balance of trade. Ample foreign exchange reserves permit a liberal commercial policy, free of exchange controls and general import restrictions. The tariff level is low and structured to permit as free an import trade flow as possible, since the country depends on imported foodstuffs, manufactured articles for consumer use and an increasing number of goods necessary in the implementation of the development program. The development of industry has introduced tariff protection as an element of the commercial policy, but, as of 1965, only a small degree of protection was being given to a few goods, such as gypsum and cement, which can be produced relatively easily by domestic industries (see ch. 23, Foreign Economic Relations).

CHAPTER 19

AGRICULTURE

The almost total lack of agricultural statistics makes virtually impossible any precise estimate of the contribution of agriculture to the national economy. Limited by topographical and climatic conditions, agriculture's contribution seems relatively unimportant in quantitative terms, especially when compared to that of the burgeoning petroleum industry. Nevertheless, possibly as much as 75 percent of the population is engaged in farming and herding.

Outlines of former fields, gardens and irrigation ditches throughout the country and ruins of ancient dams in Taif and Khaybar give evidence of a rather prosperous agriculture in times past. Overuse of ranges, uncontrolled exploitation of trees and shrubs for timber and charcoal, and a general neglect of land conservation and water resources have contributed to the deterioration of much of formerly productive land. In the mid-1960's, the government was making a serious effort to reclaim land for productive agriculture and animal husbandry, mainly by seeking ways of increasing and preserving the water supply, since it is the availability of water which largely determines the areas suitable for agriculture.

Because of the scarcity of available water resources, vast areas of the country are utilized only by nomads who travel long distances with their herds in search of the grass which springs up after the erratic spring rains. Pastoralism, therefore, has been traditionally the most important source of agricultural income and as of 1965 provided a livelihood for approximately 50 percent of the population.

Of these, approximately 200,000 to 300,000 pastoralists are Bedouin, that is, true nomads who wander constantly with herds of camels over hundreds of miles of their desert tribal districts (see ch. 4, Ethnic Groups and Languages). The remainder are seminomads who raise mostly sheep and goats; they remain at permanent watering places near villages in the dry seasons and move out into the remote areas of their tribal districts only after the annual rains. Some live in huts and cultivate crops such as millet, sorghum and watermelons during their sedentary phase.

The decreased importance of the camel as a means of transportation and the government's policies of settling the Bedouin and of increasing crop production are factors which may contribute to the declining importance of nomadic pastoralism. However, the climatic limits on cultivation of crops suggest that nomadic grazing will continue to be an important source of agricultural wealth and the basis of a way of life for a relatively large portion of the population.

Farming takes place on approximately 0.5 million to 0.7 million acres—less than 1 percent of the total land area. Of this area, only 20 percent, in Asir and southern Hejaz, receives enough rainfall to permit cultivation without artificial water sources. The remaining 80 percent is on scattered oases and depends on irrigation by water hoisted and diverted from wells, pits and springs. The most important crops include dates; grains such as wheat, barley, sorghum, millet, maize and rice; alfalfa; and, to an increasing extent, several fruits and vegetables. Coffee is grown in the Asir highlands.

The settled farmers, constituting approximately 25 percent of the population, live in villages and small hamlets in the agricultural regions; they supply most of their own needs and exchange agricultural produce for animal products of the nomads in local markets. Isolation, perishability of marketable foodstuffs and inadequacy of transportation facilities prevent many villages from carrying on regular trade with the larger centers. A substantial amount of foodstuffs must be imported every year to supplement domestic production.

The government has, especially since 1962, increased its attention and allocations to agriculture in an effort to increase agricultural production. It has done this through land reclamation, the introduction of knowledge and technique of modern farming practices to increasing numbers of farmers, the distribution of imported seeds at low cost, and the establishment of production and distribution cooperatives and an agricultural credit bank.

The success of land reclamation and water development projects would permit not only an increase in the production of farm crops for human consumption, but also the possibility of devoting a larger portion of the irrigated lands to the production of fodder crops for livestock. These fodder crops could then be utilized to supplement the inadequate supplies of natural vegetation upon which most of the livestock in the country depend.

LAND USE

Land use is determined largely by the extremely arid conditions prevailing throughout most of the country. Using the government's estimate of 870,000 square miles (556.8 million acres) as the total area of the country, the pattern of land use can be roughly approximated as follows: between 0.5 and 0.8 million acres under cultivation; 230.7 million acres used for grazing, which includes stretches of land which support palatable vegetation only occasionally, following rains; 3.7 million acres of forested land. Presumably, the remaining 321.6 million acres is primarily wasteland. It was reported in 1960 that aerial photographs showed the cultivated area as covering 741,000 acres.

Areas Under Cultivation

Because there are no permanent rivers in Saudi Arabia, the usable water supply depends on rainfall and on exploitable underground water. All cultivation depends on effectively acquiring, preserving and using the scarce water resources. Only 20 percent of the cultivated area, all in the southwest, is rainfed. Eighty percent of the cultivated area must be irrigated with water from wells, pits and springs.

That 20 percent of the cultivated area which is rainfed includes areas in the highlands of Asir and southern Hejaz and the Tihama coastal plain on the Red Sea. Here the climate, which determines the types of crops grown, varies considerably with the elevation. It ranges from the tropical desert climate of the Tihama to the warm temperate climate of the higher elevated terraces in the Asir mountains. The important agricultural concentrations on the coastal plain include the *wadis* (beds of seasonal rivers) of Baysh, Yiba and Jizan. At higher elevations the important agricultural areas are found at Jebel Fayfa, near the towns of Abha and Zahran, at Najran valley plain, and at the *wadis* of Bisha and Turaba (see fig. 6).

A very small amount of semidesertland is cultivated by Bedouin following heavy showers. One member of a lineage usually remains to care for it while the rest wander with the herds.

The remaining 80 percent of the cultivated land which depends on springs and wells for water for irrigation is found on scattered oases. Principal oases are Khaybar, Medina, Mecca, Taif and Wadi Fatima in Hejaz; Hail, Burayda, Unayza, Riyadh, Al-Kharj and Khafs Daghra in Nejd; and Jabrin, Al-Hasa and Qatif in Eastern Province.

Irrigation

Irrigation—perennial in all cultivated areas but the rainfall area—is almost entirely by flooding the fields. The way in which the land is flooded depends on the source of water supply in the various agricultural regions. The distribution devices for flood irrigation are simple and rarely mechanized; they usually consist of pieces of sod or small earth walls used to control the flow of water leading from irrigation ditches onto the cultivated fields.

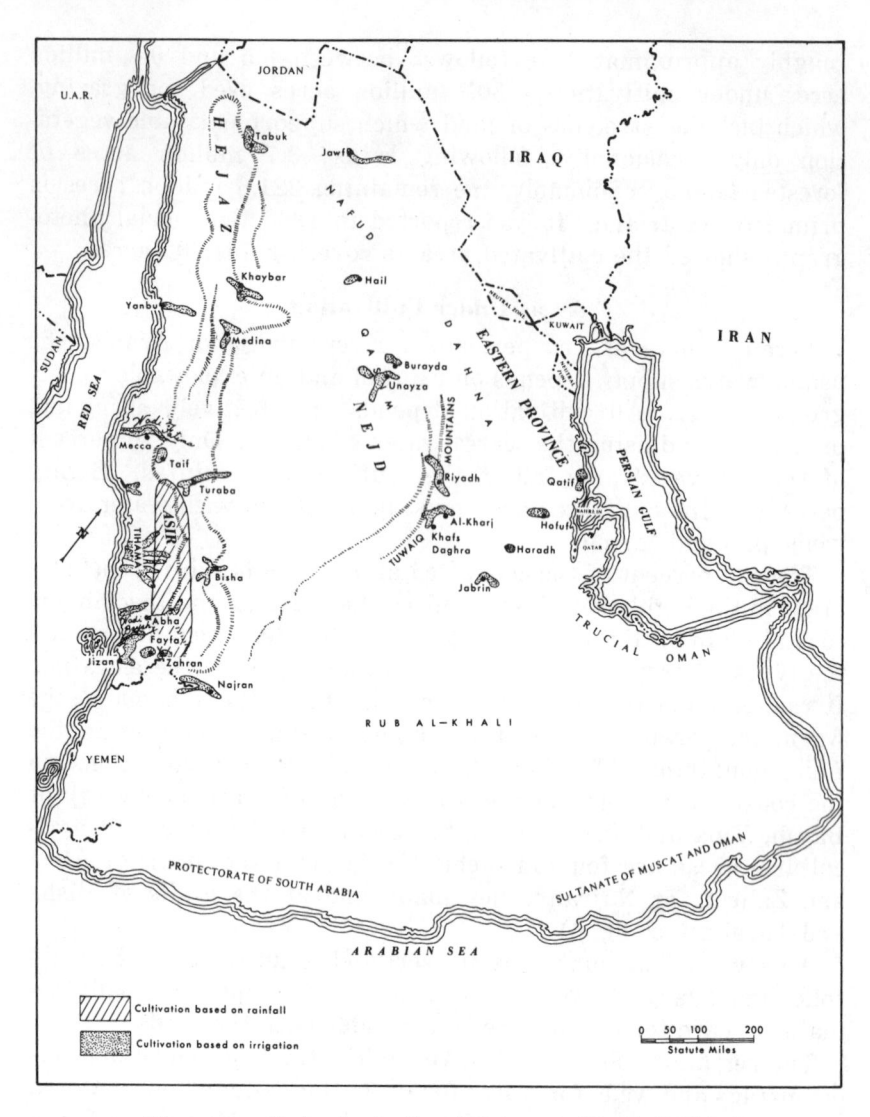

Figure 6. Main Agricultural Areas of Saudi Arabia.

On the Tihama coastal plain, cultivation depends almost entirely on monsoon floods in June through September, although winter rains from December to February permit dryfarming to a limited extent. *Wadis* are dammed partially or completely to divert the floodwaters to the cultivated basins. The basins, which are surrounded by dikes, are soaked one by one, starting with the upper lands.

Dryfarming is practiced to a greater extent on the higher elevations in the Asir mountains, where terrace farming is highly developed. To supplement the meager rainfall the rain falling on uncultivated slopes is collected and diverted to the walled terraces by channels which are often cemented to prevent seepage. The waters are allowed to descend from terrace to terrace. It is generally considered that between 5 and 10 acres of uncultivated land must be used as a catch basin for every acre of land under cultivation.

In Eastern Province, irrigation of the larger fields, which are mainly devoted to dates and rice, is done by diversion of water from artesian springs by gravity through canals to the fields. The fields "drink" at specified times, and then the farmer allows the surplus water to drain into a secondary canal which leads the water to a lower field. The saline content of the water increases as it passes through each field. When it has become too salty to be usable, the remaining water is allowed to evaporate, forming a *sabkha* (salt flat) at the far end of the cultivated area.

To irrigate the smaller fields in Eastern Province, devoted mainly to alfalfa and vegetables, water is lifted from springs and wells by animal power and, less frequently, by mechanized pumps into irrigation ditches running along the sides of the fields or into a reservoir from which it is diverted at will. If only small amounts are needed, the water from the irrigation ditches is lifted by a simple hand-operated lift.

Wells and pits provide the water for the oasis agriculture throughout the country, particularly in the interior and in the Hejaz. Lifting is done by animal power and, to an increasing extent, by centrifugal pumps.

In some areas—namely in the Wadi Yenbo, the areas around Mecca, Medina and Wadi Fatima in Hejaz, in the central highlands of Nejd and a few places in Eastern Province—horizontal wells (*dabbels*), similar to *qanats* in Iran, are used. A well is dug into a water-bearing strata above the level of the land to be irrigated. From this well a slightly inclined tunnel, sometimes several miles in length, allows the water to flow by gravity underground to the irrigation area. The purpose of the *dabbel* is to minimize evaporation of the precious water which would occur from long, surface irrigation ditches. Although there were evidently many *dabbels* in the past, only a few are in use today. They are difficult to construct and extremely expensive to maintain.

With agriculture so dependent on scarce water resources, it is essential that water be efficiently tapped from its sources and carefully preserved. Much water has been wasted because of a lack of knowledge about water requirements for different crops in different environments. Water facilities are generally aimed at immediate water distribution, and there is a lack of modern dams and reservoirs. In several areas, such as Kussebal in Qasim, Khaybar, north of Medina, Jabrin and other areas in Eastern Province, and spots in Al-Kharj, where prolonged flood irrigation is practiced, there is an increased problem of excessive salt content in the soil which is caused by the extremely arid conditions. Intense irrigation combined with inadequate dams, too-shallow ditches and lack of drainage sometimes causes the water table to rise, waterlogging the land. When it reaches the root zone, waterlogging prevents needed aeration and drowns the crop. The intensity of the sun then causes rapid evaporation, and the salts in the water, sucked up through capillary action, are deposited on the surface. In addition, these waterlogged areas are breeding grounds for malaria-bearing anopheles mosquitoes which can render large areas uninhabitable (see ch. 11, Health and Welfare).

Areas Used for Grazing

With the exception of the salt flats and the areas of shifting sand dunes, most of the country supports some form of edible vegetation during certain seasons of the year. The supply of forage is not sufficient, however, to keep all livestock adequately nourished. The major areas used for grazing are found along the *wadi* channels, which provide the most favorable habitats for range forage production throughout the country. Grazing areas are also found on the limestone plateaus located principally in the north-central region, where soil has accumulated in pockets and in areas where the limestone is covered with a layer of sand, and in the western mountains where edible grasses are found under the juniper forests at the higher elevations.

After the spring rains, carpets of short-lived annual grasses grow in the areas of deep sand along the Persian Gulf and in the Great Nafud, Dahna and Rub al-Khali deserts, and in smaller deserts throughout the country. The areas near the villages and the permanent watering places are the most heavily grazed, but practically all pasture areas are constantly threatened with overgrazing.

LAND TENURE

The *sharia* (Islamic) laws governing the inheritance of landed property are complicated, describing the size of shares to be left under varying circumstances to near relatives and, failing these, to distant relatives. The law does not provide for primogeniture. All sons are lawful heirs, and each should receive an equal share; each daughter is entitled to a half share. If applied strictly through suceeding generations, the law leads to extreme fragmentation of the land.

In practice, some landowners hold their land in forms of ownership for which the inheritance law applies only to the usufruct or not at all. It has been estimated that on only 30 percent of the arable land is ownership inheritable. This is primarily in Asir, in the Hejaz mountains, and in some oases in the Nejd and in Eastern Province. On the remaining arable land and all other agricultural land, inheritance applies only to usufruct.

Although the government requires that all land titles be registered, registration is far from complete, making it impossible to present a quantitative description of the various forms of landownership. It is known, however, that most of the land area is in *miri* land, control of which is ultimately vested in the state or the king, but most of which is actually held by tenants or in fief. Land not owned by the state is owned by individuals, extended families, village communities, tribes, or is permanently endowed to religious or charitable institutions (*waqf*).

Miri land includes the pasture districts (*dira*) of the nomadic tribes which constitute about 80 percent of the national territory. Before 1925 they were collectively owned by the various tribes which defended their respective territories by force and were a constant source of friction among the Bedouin. King Abd al-Aziz Ibn Saud abolished traditional tribal rights to these districts in 1925.

The government owns all subsoil rights, and since the *dira* are *miri* land, it holds the right to move the tribes, if necessary, for the exploitation of subsoil mineral resources, such as oil. Otherwise the tribal districts continue in use as before; each tribe has a certain district within which it wanders in search of pastures. For the most part, individual tribes respect the wells, rocks and isolated trees which form the borders of the *dira*. Erratic weather conditions, however, often force tribes to wander over into another's territory which may have received more rain during a particular season.

Ownership of large tracts is generally the result of the government's granting of *miri* land in fief (*ikta*). Many of the original grants were given in payment to military officials. *Ikta* grants were subsequently confined to previously uncultivated desertland.

Although *ikta* grants are a method of increasing significantly the cultivation of semidesert, large accumulations of *ikta* land, mostly in the hands of wealthy merchants, have led to the leasing of this land to sharecroppers at high rates. To discourage this type of exploitation, a royal decree was issued in 1957 requiring potential *ikta* land grantees to obtain the permission of the district emir and the king before acquiring the land and having it registered. Once registered, the land can be freely disposed of through sale, gift, lease or endowment to a religious institution. Thus, although the land remains the legal property of the state, *ikta* tenure is a transition to private property (*mulk*).

Mulk is the only form of full private ownership; the individual owns the land itself and has full rights of disposal. It applies to arable land and is more commonly found in Asir than in any other area of the country. *Mulk* is nonexistent in the extremely arid parts of the interior.

Mushaa land is collectively owned property of extended families who have decided to keep their lands intact rather than partition them to heirs according to Islamic law. The head of the family reports the creation of a *mushaa* to the sheikh of the village or to the emir of the district. In some cases, parcels of land are periodically rotated among the members of the family for cultivation. More often, a son is designated to manage the entire estate. Sometimes the estate is leased out to sharecroppers and is supervised by the head of the family or another designated person. The proceeds are divided according to the law of inheritance, and the individual shares thus get smaller and smaller with each generation. The proportion of *mushaa* land to the total cultivated area is small. It has been roughly estimated at one-sixth and is found most commonly in the Nejd and in Eastern Province.

Village communities, oasis communities and communal pastures belonging to the settled farmers represent a nonfamily type of collective ownership of land. Such village communities, found mostly in Asir, are jointly owned, worked, cultivated and harvested by a group of villagers. The shares of the crop are equally divided among the working adult men and women of the community under the leadership of the sheikh (see ch. 5, Social Structure).

The Jabrin and the Khaybar oasis communities are owned by Bedouin tribes. Because the oases are malaria-infested, the two tribes go to them only to pollinate and harvest dates. During the rest of the year, workers of Negro descent, who apparently have greater endemic immunity to malaria, tend the date groves. The members of the tribes divide the harvest according to the number of adult men, with some allowance made for the size of families.

Some pastures near towns and villages are owned in common by the settled farmers throughout the country. A herdsman is designated and paid by the villagers to supervise the grazing land and to take the sheep and goats out to pasture after the winter rains.

Waqf land is a form of tenure unique to Moslem countries. A Moslem may endow a piece of landed property for the benefit of a religious or charitable institution. The endowment is made by an informal declaration before the court of a town or district. Opinions among Moslems vary as to whether the founder retains the right of possession, but once a piece of land is converted to *waqf* land, it becomes inalienable. In all cases, usufruct rights pass ultimately to the institution, but the founder has the right to decide on the line of beneficiaries of the usufruct on condition that the religious or charitable institution be the ultimate one in that line when all of the founder's descendants or designees have died. This type of *waqf* is known as private *waqf* (*waqf chasusi*). Religious or proper *waqfs* (*waqf hashri*) are those which have been donated directly to the religious institution for its own use. A majority of the *waqf* farm units are of the *hashri* type and are operated on lease by sharecroppers or tenants.

Private *waqfs* are created not only because of religious devotion, but also because of the owner's desire to bypass the Islamic inheritance law. In addition, the founder is protected from indebtedness and from seizure of the land, since *waqf* institutions cannot be confiscated by the government. The Saudi Waqf Authority, which handles the administrative work in connection with the *waqfs,* published in 1959 the following estimates of the number of *waqf* units as a percentage of total number of agricultural units: Asir, 5 percent; Hejaz, 10 percent; Eastern Province and the Nejd, 15 percent.

Tenancy

Although some Moslem legal schools hold that Islam prohibits the taking of rent as a payment, the leasing of land is generally recognized. In fact, tenant farming is more widespread than owner farming. It was estimated in 1956 that approximately 60 percent of all agricultural production units are leased; about 40 percent are owner-managed. Surveys have indicated, however, varying percentages for the different agricultural regions. The percentage of leased farms is highest in Asir and the Hejaz, amounting to approximately 70 to 80 percent.

Land under all forms of tenure—*miri, ikta, mulk, mushaa, waqf* and *tribal*—may be leased through sharecropping agreements, term leases or heritable leases. Lease agreements, usually arrived at through the mechanism of public auction, are written or oral and are strictly observed, whether in written or oral form.

Sharecropping is the prevailing form of tenancy, covering at least 50 percent of the total agricultural area. Estimates by Western observers have been as high as 80 percent. There is no uniform sharecropping system governing the relationship between the landlord and the tenant. Religious law holds that the sharecropping system is permissible only if the landlord provides at least the seeds; it is preferable that he provide the livestock and equipment as well.

In practice, about 70 percent of the sharecropping agreements establish that the owner provide land, water, seed and, in some cases, housing. If the share tenant works all year round and provides draft animals, fertilizers, farm equipment, food and housing, he pays the landowner 50 percent of the grain crops and 75 percent of the dates. If the tenant provides only the labor and comes to the farm only for the threshing and harvesting work, the owner receives 80 percent of the grain crops and 95 percent of the dates. Perhaps no more than 5 percent of the agreements are of this type. About 10 percent of the agreements call for the tenant to provide the seeds, although this is not in conformity with a rigid interpretation of *sharia* law. The tenant then receives a higher share of the proceeds from the grain crops. The shares which go to the landowner vary not only with the amount of his contribution to the production but also with the productivity of the soil and the location of the farm in relation to the markets.

The introduction of machinery in farming units has affected sharecropping arrangements, mostly in the Nejd and Eastern Province, on reclaimed *ikta* land. It has been observed that in general these new sharecropping agreements tend to favor the tenant as compared to the old.

The welfare of the sharecropping tenant ultimately depends on the success of the harvests. During bad years his low share of the proceeds is usually insufficient to feed his family. He is then forced to borrow, usually from the landlord himself, and often gets so deeply in debt that it is virtually impossible for him to get clear; he ultimately becomes completely dependent on the landlord.

The second most common form of lease is the term lease; it usually applies to *miri* land, with a small portion to *mulk* land. The rent, often very high in relation to yields, is determined by the location of the farm in relation to the market, the quality of the soil, the type of irrigation, the number of date palms, the demand for lease farms and the demand for agricultural products. The leases are generally concluded before a justice of the peace (*machgam sharaia*) and are often limited to a term of 5 years, although in Asir they are sometimes for a single year, and government term leases on unreclaimed land are usually for 10 years.

The tenants holding term leases on *miri* land are guided by government-established regulations with which the tenant must comply upon threat of forfeiture of his tenancy. They include the tenants' responsibilities in regard to the maintenance of irrigation works, fruit trees, windbreaks, buildings and the payment of rent to the Ministry of Finance and National Economy once threshing has been completed.

Waqf hashri land leases are controlled by a Waqf Office under the Ministry of Pilgrimage and Religious Foundations in Mecca. Most leases are based on either sharecropping or term tenancy. The rents are collected by the Waqf Office. It has been observed that, in comparison with other leased farms, the rented *waqf* land farms are poorly maintained. The tenants, interested in obtaining benefits as quickly as possible, are reluctant to invest capital on the farm and neglect the permanent crops. There have been discussions about modifying the rules regarding *waqf* land, and in 1957 a new law was introduced in Mecca making it possible to dispose of unusable *waqf* land through sale.

A few *waqf* estates are held under heritable lease agreements. According to these, the tenant pays a sum of money to the Waqf Office when the agreement is made and a fixed annual rent thereafter.

Heritable leases are also held on *miri* land. Under this type of agreement the land does not revert back to the government unless the tenant no longer has heirs or leaves the land uncultivated for a period of 3 years or more.

Government efforts in regard to land tenure problems are directed to the creation of new farmsteads through land reclamation projects. Despite the problems arising from the high proportion of proceeds which sharecroppers and tenants must pay to the landowners, there are apparently no major demands on the part of the populace for land reform. In effect, the success of land reclamation and water development projects, by increasing the amount of arable land, reduces the demand for leased property and thereby reduces the possibility of exploitation of tenants by the landowners.

Water Rights

Most landownership is valueless unless accompanied by the possession of water. Regulations covering the ownership, distribution and use of water are therefore of primary importance. Although the Prophet Mohammed decreed that the entire Moslem community was to have free access to water, and that no Moslem could refuse surplus water to any human being, or allow animals to die of thirst without sinning against Allah, in practice there is no free access to the owned water sources. Community rights seem to apply only to unowned water resources, such as rainwater falling on unowned uncultivated land.

Most water rights can be sold, purchased, rented and inherited independently of land. Thus, those who acquire land in excess of that which they can sufficiently irrigate have the possibility of purchasing or renting additional water rights from those who own more water rights than they need for their plot of land. Only in Asir and on the coastal plain of the Red Sea, where precipitation is relatively plentiful, are water rights bound to the land and not to the individual.

Water regulations among the settled farmers are highly developed and complex, covering the rotation of use of water, the time for and duration of irrigation and the amounts of water which correspond to the water rights. The distribution of water is often supervised and controlled by officials appointed and paid by water owners and users.

Water from wells, pits, springs and *dabbels* is considered "private water," and the rights to it are assigned to individuals. Generally the person or persons who contribute to the construction of the water acquisition equipment own the water and have exclusive rights to use or sell it.

Usually a property owner holds the rights to all the water sources on his land. No permit is necessary for constructing a well on one's own property, but a permit from the district emir is required if the well is to be built on previously uncultivated *ikta* land. Wells which are dug by nomads belong to the tribe as long as it remains in the area. Once it leaves, the well becomes public property and the rule of first come, first served, applies to those who follow.

The rights to water from *dabbels* depend upon the original contribution to the construction of the galleries, to the amount spent on the purchase of such rights, or to inherited rights. The rights are registered with the village administration. Distribution is on a time system on the basis of *wajba* (12 daylight or night hours); the rotation turns being adjustable in order to utilize the water more advantageously. The purchase, sale, lease and distribution of the water are handled by a treasurer (*amin*) with the assistance of a clerk (*katib*) who are appointed and paid by those owning the water rights. Auction sales of surplus water are sometimes conducted; the total amount of money contributed is divided by the number of hours of available water, and each contributor receives an amount of water corresponding to the amount of money he put in. All sales of rights are registered and legalized by a government official.

The water rights for artesian springs which are found in Eastern Province depend on the original owner's contribution to the construction of spring casings, reservoirs and the distribution mechanisms, and on the inheritance or purchase of these rights. They are registered with the village administration, and a "water umpire" supervises the water distribution, which is done on a time basis.

Water rights which are bound to the land, as they are in Asir, are rights to the floodwaters derived from the *wadis* which are dammed to divert the water to the cultivated fields by means of canals (*uqum*). Each *uqum* irrigates a plot of land which carries the water rights. Upper lands are irrigated before the water is let through the lower lands, but if the water is insufficient, the water is let through to the lower lands before the upper ones have been thoroughly soaked.

Primary water rights are limited to the lands which have traditionally held the rights. Lands which have been brought into cultivation since the original water rights were distributed have secondary rights; that is, they are irrigated only if there is surplus water. Some lands have no rights at all and only occasionally receive surplus water. The traditional regulations are so strong that they effectively prevent landowners from increasing their water rights by the construction of new dams even if new *wadis* have been formed.

The contribution toward the upkeep of the *uqum* depends on the size of the land being irrigated. However, the farmer working the lands which have only secondary rights pay half as much as those with land with primary rights. Any problems that arise are settled by the sheikh, assisted by a commission of highly respected individuals (*maruf*) and, if necessary, the district emir.

Rainwater belongs to the owner of the land on which it falls. He cannot, however, refuse this water for the irrigation of land where crops are in danger. Rainwater falling on lands owned by the state can be used by anyone, although the cultivated land nearest the rainwater usually has priority.

ORGANIZATION OF FARM UNITS

Most farm units are small. Their size, limited by the scarcity of water, has also been conditioned by the inheritance practices and Islam's general discouragement of a feudal-type structure in regard to landholding.

In Asir and in Eastern Province farm units are, on the average, smaller than those in the rest of the country; most are between 5 and 12.5 acres. In the Nejd most farm units are between 12.5 and 50 acres. In the Hejaz larger units of between 25 and 75 acres are more common. There are farms of as much as 250 acres and perhaps a few even larger, but the few big landlords usually own several farms rather than one very large one.

Because the plots are small, arrangements are made among the cultivators to permit a more economic and efficient management of the land. Some families hold the entire estate in common (*mushaa*), usually entrusting its management to one of the sons or to a sharecropper, and then share the net proceeds according to the law of inheritance. In Asir villagers who are not members of the same family often agree to plow, sow, irrigate and harvest in common, dividing the proceeds according to the adult working men and women in the village community. Other cultivators plow, sow, irrigate and harvest in a joint effort, but divide the proceeds according to the amount of land contributed.

Agricultural cooperatives have been created in recent years in towns including Taif, Medina and Burayda. They handle functions ranging from planting to storing and marketing of agricultural products, with a view to increasing output and decreasing costs. Since their foundation in 1962 they have been under the control of the Ministry of Labor and Social Affairs; at the end of 1962, seven such cooperatives had been registered, with a combined membership of 1,053 (see ch. 22, Domestic Trade).

Data on the distribution of the type of worker on the farms in the various agricultural regions in the country are not available. In the relatively densely populated areas such as Asir, Hejaz, and the Al-Hasa oasis, family members usually work the farms without hired help. Family members are also used in great numbers in the Nejd, but on the larger units in Qasim and Jebel Shammar laborers are hired on long- or short-term bases. In peak periods the Nejd actually experiences a shortage of agricultural labor because of the competition from the oilfields in Eastern Province.

A survey undertaken in the province of Nejd indicated that more women than men work on the farms. The men frequently take part-time, nonagricultural jobs, such as wholesale merchant, storekeeper in a *suk* (marketplace), mechanic, well builder, village chief, camel caretaker, artisan or laborer with the city government.

Although many farm laborers work on a contractual basis, freed slaves who formerly served families involved in agricultural production generally remained with the families and still work on the farms without formal arrangements. There are also other farmworkers, who, although they were never slaves, work faithfully for a farmer on noncontractual basis; they often own a small date orchard or vegetable plot of their own.

In the Nejd some members of such Bedouin tribes as the Mutayr, Harb and Khalid work as nomadic migrant farm laborers on a short-term basis to earn money.

Foreign migrant laborers are concentrated primarily in the vicinity of the holy cities. They include Yemenites, Palestinians, Sudanese, Somalis, Egyptians, Jordanians, Lebanese, Syrians and

Ethiopians. Most enter as pilgrims and remain beyond the pilgrimage period; some obtain a residence permit and remain for several years, finally becoming Saudi Arabian citizens (see ch. 21, Labor).

CROP PRODUCTION

The small size of farms, the use of traditional agricultural methods by the majority of farmers, and a lack of adequate transportation facilities between producing areas and the markets limit much of the agricultural production to the subsistence level. Most farmers produce mainly to cover their own basic demands; any excess crops are sold or bartered in local markets in return for such items as sugar, textiles and other products not produced on the farms.

Production directed for the market is found on the relatively few enterprises which regularly produce surplus crops or specialized crops which can be easily marketed. These include the large date plantations on the oases of Al-Hasa, Medina, Burayda and Unayza; the vegetable farms in the coastal *wadis* and the oases of Medina and Al-Kharj; and the grape orchards, coffee plantations and *qat* (a mildly narcotic plant) plantations in Asir.

In addition to these pronounced market-oriented production units, here are others in which most crops are grown on a subsistence level, but which regularly produce a surplus of a particular crop which is then marketed. Examples of these marketed crops are bananas in the *wadis* of the Hejaz and in Asir, alfalfa in oases in the Nejd, and dates grown by the nomads in Jabrin and Khaybar oases.

Domestic crop production is insufficient to supply the needs of the population. Despite the government's efforts to increase crop production, many basic foodstuffs still have to be imported to supplement the domestic supply, especially for the towns (see ch. 22, Domestic Trade).

Dates

The date palm grows almost everywhere in the country and constitutes an important subsistence crop for the nomads and oasis dwellers. In addition, it is one of the major sources of wealth in most of the agricultural regions, excepting the mountains of Asir and the Tihama coastal plain. An average of 200,000 tons of dates are harvested from slightly over 8.5 million date palms which cover approximately 88,920 acres, making Saudi Arabia the fourth largest date grower in the world. The best of the more than 70 varieties come from the oases in Medina and Bisha in the west, Al-Kharj in Nejd, and the Qatif and Al-Hasa oases in Eastern Province.

The market-oriented production of dates is restricted to landowners who can afford the large investment in trees, irrigation and soil treatment, and the long period before a tree begins to bear fruit. It has been calculated that the average annual return on date production is only about between SR360 and SR600 (SR4.50 equal US$1) an acre.

Propagation of the date palm is usually by offshoots rather than seed; the palms commence to bear fruit after 8 years and continue to do so for 80 years or more. Their cultivation is in most cases very intense, with many trees planted very close together. Any available area beneath the trees is often utilized by planting alfalfa as a fodder crop. Care of the dates is usually restricted to pollination and irrigation; farm manure is added only occasionally.

The dates are eaten raw, cooked, baked into cakes, or are pressed into a sweet syrup to be used as a sweetening agent. The pits are crushed for fodder; palm wood and fronds are widely used in building houses and making baskets and mats. Although the importance of dates has diminished in the last 15 to 20 years as the Saudi Arabs replace them with rice, meat and other, often imported, foods, they still remain the staple diet of many farmers and of Bedouin, many of whom lived until recently solely on dates and animal products. United States agricultural experts invited by the Saudi Arabian Government are demonstrating to the local date palm growers that thinning out the date palm groves, using fertilizers and using machinery where possible can increase the yield per tree, which now averages only 60 pounds per season.

Grains

Wheat was the country's most important food grain until 1925 when rice was imported at prices which induced a large part of the population to substitute it for wheat. With the restriction of shipping during World War II, the planting of wheat was resumed on small plots throughout the country. It has been estimated that wheat production now covers about 106,000 acres, yielding approximately 37,000 metric tons a year. On the terraced mountain slopes in Asir, where it is the major food crop, yields approximate 900 pounds per acre a year. This yield is smaller than that achieved on the irrigated fields in the Nejd, where wheat is second to dates as a major food.

Barley is generally planted in the same areas as wheat, but covers only about 58,000 acres, with production of about 23,000 metric tons a year. It is generally consumed in the form of bread Some is used as fodder for livestock.

Sorghum and millet are also important grains and are a staple food of many Bedouins and farmers, especially in the Hejaz area. *Durra,* a variety of grain-yielding sorghum, is grown primarily in highland areas of Asir, but also extensively in the Nejd, the Tihama flood plain and southern Hejaz, where it grows large heads and stalks reaching over 17 feet. It is estimated that sorghum production covers 91,000 acres, which produce approximately 37,000 metric tons a year. Millet, known as *dukhan,* is grown in smaller quantities; it is produced on approximately 27,000 acres, yielding about 11,000 metric tons a year.

Corn is grown in parts of Asir and on some of the larger oases in Eastern Province. Its production covers approximately 37,000 acres, yielding about 21,000 metric tons.

Rice has become an important crop in Hofuf in Al-Hasa oasis, where several huge springs provide the necessary water. The rice is sown in field beds and then transplanted to paddies. Most is consumed locally, but increasing amounts are being sent to Riyadh. For the sedentary cultivator it is a staple food, and the Bedouin eat it as a luxury food. The Ministry of Agriculture and Water, in its efforts to increase rice production, has recently obtained technical advice and assistance from Nationalist Chinese experts on rice-growing methods. Projected irrigation schemes in Al-Hasa oasis may enable substantial increases in rice production, which now amounts to approximately 4,000 metric tons a year.

Vegetables and Fruits

Vegetables and fruits are greatly increasing in importance as the population has begun to appreciate their nutritional and economic value. Figures on vegetable production during the last few years are difficult to estimate, but it seems to have been growing constantly. In 1964 vegetable production was estimated to cover 69,000 acres, with an annual total production of approximately 140,000 metric tons; fruit production was estimated to cover over 45,000 acres, with total annual production amounting to 64,000 metric tons.

Vegetables are produced for the market on extremely small plots averaging between 0.6 and 2.5 acres. Because vegetable farming is labor intensive and requires high initial capital investments for such items as pumps and fertilizers, these farms are usually owned by wealthy city-based owners and leased out in small units to tenants. Annual return per acre is estimated at approximately from SR320 to SR640.

Fruits and vegetables are especially abundant in the Hejaz, in Taif, Medina and Wadi Fatima; but considerable amounts are grown in Asir, at the Al-Kharj experimental farm in Nejd, and at other irrigated farms throughout the country. Production of tropical fruits—bananas, papayas—is concentrated on the coastal plains of the Red Sea and the Persian Gulf. The production is usually for local market consumption, and considerable amounts of most fruits and vegetables are still imported. Production would probably increase if cultivation practices were improved. There is in general no systematic planting, and fruit trees often grow too close to one another; lack of pruning often results in the formation of impenetrable thickets.

Coffee is an important product only in Asir, where it is cultivated on the terraced slopes at altitudes between 4,000 and 5,000 feet above sea level. Only about 200 metric tons per year are produced, but it is of an excellent Mocha variety. Coffee plantations are usually worked by hired farm laborers on small farms, usually of no more than 1.25 acres each. The average annual return is approximately from SR2,000 to SR4,000 per acre. Asir coffee is consumed locally, and substantial quantities of coffee must be imported to supply the domestic market outside Asir.

Other Crops

Alfalfa is grown perennially in almost all oases, especially in the areas under the date palms. It is cut by hand and sold green at village markets. It is used as feed for donkeys, camels, poultry and milk animals. Its high price prevents it from being more of a substitute for or a supplement to forage for livestock.

Qat, a green succulent plant grown in Asir at altitudes over 4,000 feet, is also produced as a cash crop. Its broad leaves are chewed for their mild narcotic effect. Small *qat* plantations are usually owned by wealthy landowners who lease them to sharecroppers. The net annual return on *qat* production is estimated to be between SR2,400 and SR4,000 per acre. The Saudi Arabian Government controls the production of *qat* and forbids its transportation to central and north Arabia.

Approximately 1,350 metric tons of sesame are produced yearly on 4,500 acres. Produced mainly for oil, sesame production is most important in the Tihama plain, although it grows in various other areas as well. Other minor crops include lentils, peanuts, almonds, sunflowers, hemp, cotton, sugarbeets, indigo and rattan palms.

FARMING PRACTICES

Farming practices are, in general, ones that have been used for centuries. The ground is usually prepared for cultivation with a *messha,* a cross between a shovel and a pick ax, or with hoes and crowbars or spades. In *wadis* and terraces in Asir and the Hejaz, a wooden drag is used to form the basins and the *wadi barrages* and to level the fields. When a plow is used, it is a metal-tipped wooden plow drawn by a single camel, as in the Nejd, a cow and donkey, or a team of oxen. Some tractors with deep plows have been introduced, but the Saudi farmers evidently prefer field cultivators, since, in an arid climate, the winds and dehydration affect the plowed soil more than they do when it is merely loosened.

Soil erosion by surface water and wind presents a serious problem on cultivated land. Farmers on cultivated terraces practice contour plowing to prevent the erosion; techniques involving the leveling of banks and placing a cover over them or constructing breakwaters in the riverbeds are rarely used. To prevent wind erosion, the farmers build hedges of dead plants or drought-resistant trees, but because continguous plots are owned by various owners, the trees are often not planted close enough together and prove an inefficient wind barrier. The hedges are especially important in the Nejd and in Eastern Province for protection of the land from the drifting sand dunes. Experiments have been made with anchoring the dunes by asphalting their leeward side.

Weeding, which is infrequent, is done with the aid of a short-handled cutlass. Harvesting is done mostly by the women with the use of hand sickles; efforts to introduce the scythe have proved generally unsuccessful. Threshing is mostly by animal-drawn threshing boards. Flood irrigation limits the use of threshing machinery.

With the exception of the alluvial soils in the *wadi* valleys, the soils are seriously deficient in nitrogen and phosphates, but the use of fertilizers is not yet widespread. Intensive fertilizing with manure is carried out in many of the irrigated grain growing fields and in the truck farming areas, but many farmers must still be encouraged to use animal dung as farm manure rather than for fuel. In the arid parts of the mountains in Asir and Hejaz, fertilizing of some plants, such as millet, is actually not advisable; the plants would grow too rapidly during the rainy season and would then wither and die before ripening, because of excessive perspiration and too little moisture. Chemical fertilizers are used only at a few large, private farms and at the experimental farms at Al-Kharj; their use is advisable only for the farms which are near markets, to which surplus products could be easily transported for sale.

Crop rotation is practiced in all agricultural areas. On the irrigated highlands of Asir there is usually a triennial rotation of wheat, sorghum and lentils, or wheat, barley and lentils. Both sets of rotations are planted early in March and harvested in July.

A second growing season applies when the monsoon rains are utilized; the planting is in late May, the harvesting in October. The land remains fallow in the infrequent cases of insufficient rain. In the Tihama coastal plain there is a triennial rotation of sorghum, millet and sesame. On the irrigated land, the crops are planted in late May and are harvested in October. Under dry-farming conditions, they are planted in November and are harvested in July.

Perennially irrigated land is cultivated every year. In Nejd and northern Hejaz a biannual rotation of wheat and barley or barley and, occasionally, legumes is practiced. Planting is in late February or early March; harvesting is in July. The land is left fallow the rest of the year. In truck farming areas such as Wadi Fatima two crops are usually grown each year; in Al-Kharj three crops are grown each year. In the low-lying oases of Al-Hasa and Qatif in Eastern Province, where the availability of water from artesian wells and springs favors agriculture, crops are grown the year round.

ANIMAL HUSBANDRY

Pastoralism is the most important agricultural pursuit in the country. It is a way of life dictated by the arid climate, the scarcity of water, and the meager supply of forage in the deserts. There is little or no information available on the organization and practices of animal husbandry, the number of animals and such matters as the value of animals and losses from disease.

In general, herders measure their wealth in terms of the number of animals they own rather than the quality of the livestock. They therefore slaughter as few as possible and barter or sell them in the market only in order to obtain those necessary items which they cannot provide for themselves. Because feed for the animals is derived almost entirely from natural vegetation, there exists the constant problem of an imbalance between the number of animals and the scanty forage supplies in the country.

The erratic climate permits no fixed pattern of grazing. In 1925 tribal legal claims to particular pasturage districts in the desert were abolished by King Abd al-Aziz in order to maintain peace among the tribes. Since then, the Bedouin and seminomads, who own about 80 percent of the livestock in the country, often disregard traditional tribal limits as they follow the rains. Areas where pasture is found are almost inevitably overgrazed and often prevented from reseeding themselves. Consequently, both quantity and quality of the animals are held down.

The seminomads, who remain at permanent watering places near the villages in the dry seasons, often feed their animals hay which they grow on the semidesert in the rainy season. The settled farmers, who own 20 percent of the livestock, feed them alfalfa, dried or green grass in addition to sending them out to pasture in the grazing lands located near the villages. Barley and clover are occasionally fed to special work or milk animals.

There is no conscious effort to produce high quality animals for the market. Efficient care of livestock in terms of a greater supply of food, disease control and efficient breeding practices is almost unknown except at the government's experimental farms in Al-Kharj, where modern animal husbandry is practiced. Fodder crops grown on irrigated lands are beyond the price which most pastoralists can afford.

Disease control is mostly limited to feeding the sick animal grains or special herb remedies which have been passed down by word of mouth from generation to generation. Bedouin often brand the suspected area of pain. If imminent death is expected, the animal is usually slaughtered and used for food. Planned breeding of animals is almost nonexistent. Very little attention is given the animals during either the mating season or the lambing and kidding season.

Marketing conditions provide no real incentive to take on the risk and expense of fattening animals for the market. Evidently prices for all meat are approximately equal, regardless of quality.

It has been observed that when King Abd al-Aziz took measures to control tribal warfare, the livestock population increased to a level which strained the forage supply. The animals began suffering from malnutrition; a severe drought beginning in 1957 and lasting until 1965 caused the death of the animals in great numbers. It has been estimated that, owing to the prolonged drought, overgrazing of the available areas, and the movement of the younger Bedouin into the cities, the animal population may have decreased approximately 20 percent for the country as a whole. Losses were especially great in the northern part of the country.

A rough idea of the livestock population can be obtained from the estimates prepared by the United Nations Food and Agriculture Organization (FAO) after a 1963 survey of pasture resources in Saudi Arabia: camels, 1,004,000; sheep and goats, 4,158,000; and donkeys, 75,000. In addition, there are cattle, estimated by the Ministry of Agriculture and Water at 270,000 and found mostly in the Tihama plain and at farms at Al-Kharj, horses, numbering between 3,000 and 8,000, and a small, though increasing amount of poultry.

The camel, indispensable to every Bedouin family, still provides the livelihood for approximately 200,000 to 300,000 Bedouin.

The advent of the automobile has decreased the importance of the camel as a means of transportation and has put an end to the formerly large exports of Saudi Arabian camels to Africa, Egypt, Syria and Iraq.

Nevertheless, the camel, which is of the single-humped dromedary type, remains essential to the Bedouin economy in addition to being a source of pride. It is important as a source of meat, milk, hides and as a beast of burden. Despite the government's efforts to settle the nomads, large areas of the country are fit only for camel grazing, and it is likely that many Bedouin will continue to prefer the nomadic way of life, raising camels in the submarginal areas. The availability of water at new wells along the Trans-Arabian Pipeline (Tapline) in Nejd has made it possible for northern Bedouin to increase their camel herds (see ch. 20, Industry).

Sheep and goats also withstand rigorous desert conditions, although to a lesser extent than the camel. Most belong to semi-nomadic herders. Sheep provide the bulk of the meat supply. Sheep's milk is extensively used; either fresh, made into cheese, or curdled into *laban,* a type of yoghurt. The indigenous sheep has a broad, fatty tail, from which a clarified fat is obtained for use in cooking, and grows hair rather than wool, used in making blankets and clothing. Sheepskins are used for a variety of purposes. Goats supplement the milk supply and furnish the black hair from which Bedouin tents and rugs are woven.

Cattle do not thrive in the country, and local breeds tend to be small. Most are the humped Zebu variety found in Asir. At the government's experimental farms at Al-Kharj, Brown Swiss, Jerseys, Guernseys, Holstein, Angus, Shorthorn, and Santa Gertrudes have been imported for dairy use and for beef breeding. The cattle are kept by sedentary cultivators mostly for draft purposes and are usually slaughtered only when they are no longer able to work. Some city dwellers keep a cow and a few goats for their milk supply, feeding them green alfalfa and other fodder grasses purchased on the market.

The donkeys in Saudi Arabia are of the Hassawi and the Baladi types. The Hassawi is generally large, sometimes measuring 10 to 13 hands high and, almost invariably, is pure white. It is more expensive than the Baladi type, which is gray and small. The donkeys are commonly used as beasts of burden in the mountains where camels are unsuitable, for plowing and for hoisting water from wells for irrigation.

Saudi Arabian horses are known throughout the world for their great endurance and beauty. Until the government's curtailment of raiding, they were used by nomadic raiding parties when speed was essential. Increased modern transportation facilities brought about a lessening of interest in the horse except as a luxury item. In recent years racing and riding horses have increased in popularity. Most horses are found at the royal stables at Hofuf and at Al-Yamama near Al-Kharj. Occasionally a few are exported for breeding purposes, but they are no longer of great economic significance.

Estimates of poultry are not available, but practically all farmers have a few chickens. They are left to scavenge for forage, village refuse and manure. Infrequently, they are given a handful of sorghum or millet. At the Al-Kharj experimental farm in Nejd, thousands of chickens have been imported for experimental breeding. A small number of turkeys, ducks and geese are also raised at the farms in the area. Efficiently organized poultry farms are found at Dammam and Al-Khobar in addition to Al-Kharj.

FORESTRY

Statistics provided by the Ministry of Agriculture and Water list 3,749,600 acres as "forest and woodlands." However, most of this land is also used for grazing. It has been estimated that only 24,700 acres are protected from grazing and are currently used exclusively for the production of timber. Official statistics list an additional 4,940,000 acres as potentially suitable for forestry.

The principal varieties of trees include the acacia, juniper, mimosa, jujube, eucalyptus and tamarisk. Most of the forest growth is on the upper slopes of the mountains extending from Asir to southern Hejaz; tamarisk grows wild on the Tuwaiq mountains in central Nejd.

The soil and climate are not favorable for timber; most of the trees are dwarfed and the wood tends to be porous and soft. Juniper, tamarind, and tamarisk trees, however, are commonly used for timber as well as for firewood. Trees such as the eucalyptus and tamarisk are also used as windbreaks and to break up the contours of advancing sand dunes.

Date palms are one of the major sources of timber. The trunks are used for housebuilding, the midribs of the larger leaves for furniture, and the larger fronds are braided into fences which are used to break the advance of sand dunes.

FISHERIES

The seas around the Arabian Peninsula are rich in fish which could serve to increase the country's food supply and provide the basis for a lucrative fishing industry. Among the extraordinarily large variety of species, sardines are abundant in the Red Sea, and sardines, groupers, mackerel, barracuda, tuna and shrimp are found in the Persian Gulf.

Fisheries—including boats, gear and equipment for the fishermen—are little developed. Along the Persian Gulf many fishermen fish inshore and use weirs, thrownets and basket traps. The usual craft for offshore fishing range in size from dhows and dugout canoes to 200- to 300-ton two-masted vessels.

A relatively small demand for fish and other seafood and the inadequate marketing facilities necessary for preservation and transportation have discouraged the expansion of the fishing industry. Moreover, the sudden storms and treacherous shoals of the Red Sea have discouraged the development of fisheries on the west coast. In the Persian Gulf region, the inhabitants have traditionally considered pearling and coral digging as being more profitable than fishing.

The Saudi Arabian Fishing Company was established in 1952 when Prince Mutaab Ibn Abd al-Aziz obtained an exclusive 40-year concession for fishing in the territorial waters of the Red Sea and for processing and exporting the catches. It began fishing operations in 1955 and subsequently erected a freezing plant, cold-storage facilities and an ice factory. Canning factory and fishmeal plant equipment were purchased but not erected. As of October 1963, the company had not really progressed beyond the experimental stage.

Refrigeration facilities established at Jidda and at ports on the Persian Gulf have helped to increase the availability of fish for consumption, but most fish and seafood are still consumed fresh in the area where they are obtained. The total catch in 1953 amounted to about 4,000 metric tons.

AGRICULTURAL CREDIT

In April 1963 the Agricultural Credit Bank was created, with its head offices in Riyadh and a capital of SR30 million. It is authorized to grant credit to individuals, groups, institutions and organizations working in agriculture and to guarantee loans made by other sources. It can issue short-term credit for up to 12 months, medium-term credit for up to 5 years, and long-term credit for between 15 and 20 years, to assist farmers in improvement of soil, irrigation schemes, experiments with livestock and poultry breeding, purchase of agricultural machinery and equipment and to facilitate land reclamation activities. The possibility of receiving the Bank's interest-free loans should permit farmers to avoid the previous necessity of borrowing from moneylenders who charge exhorbitant commissions.

The Agricultural Credit Bank began operations in the summer of 1963; by the end of that summer it had reportedly received 10,000 credit application forms. In April 1965 it was reported that 262 short-term loans, totaling SR1.3 million, had been extended to farmers in 11 areas for the purchase of agricultural equipment such as tractors, pumps and fertilizers.

GOVERNMENT ROLE IN AGRICULTURE

Matters dealing with agriculture are the responsibility of the Ministry of Agriculture and Water, which was established as a separate ministry in December 1953 after 6 years as a directorate under the Ministry of Finance. Its efforts to increase the agricultural production involve a many-sided program dealing with the control of a number of natural hazards, the introduction of new agricultural methods and machinery, the use of fertilizers, range management, agricultural credit, etc. Allocations in the development budget for agricultural projects increased sharply in recent years. Whereas in 1962-63 they amounted to SR34.3 million, or 6.2 percent of the budget, by 1964-65 they had increased to SR149.0 million, constituting 12.4 percent of the development budget (see ch. 24, Monetary and Financial System).

Among the more important projects which have been completed is the establishment of five agricultural centers—in Jizan, Medina, Qasim, Riyadh and Hofuf—to provide farmers with technical advice, mechanical implements, seed and fruit-tree seedings, fertilizers, and education on the prevention and treatment of plant diseases. Each center has a model farm and a plant nursery. Animal breeding stations were established in Medina and Riyadh in the spring of 1957 in order to demonstrate better livestock-raising techniques and to aid in improving the local breeds. Two date-packing plants and a company to process grain have also been established.

Locust Control

A special section of the Ministry was established to cope with the problem of the desert locust. The Arabian deserts are a major breeding area for this scourge of farmers in large parts of Asia and Africa. Locust swarms are capable of flying thousands of miles, descending in clouds upon cultivated areas and pastures to destroy crops and grazing lands. To combat this menace, the government has actively participated in international locust-control measures, starting in 1942 when King Abd al-Aziz invited British antilocust missions to the country. In March 1954 the government signed an antilocust control agreement with FAO. The International Coordinating Center was established at Jidda to coordinate the activities of the various antilocust control missions operating in the country. It studies locust conditions and maintains over 50 vehicles and large supplies of bait and insecticides for use by the locust control teams in the field.

The Ministry of Agriculture has effectively participated in locust control since 1955, setting aside part of the budget for this purpose and organizing Saudi Arabian antilocust teams. It was reported in 1965 that the FAO had supplied a number of radios to facilitate coordination and had helped in establishing a locust research and experimental station at Jidda, providing it with scientific equipment and a library.

The Bedouin's fear that insecticides would kill their livestock, and their belief that locusts were sent by Allah and should not be destroyed wantonly, initially posed a problem for the locust control workers, but it has been largely overcome. As a result of these efforts, measures have been successful in preventing the multiplication of locusts within the country and their entering the kingdom from other countries.

Al-Kharj Project

The Al-Kharj project in the Nejd is an experimental farm set up in 1937 by the government with technical assistance from Iraqi and Egyptian experts. It was put under American supervision from 1945 to 1959 and then was turned over to government-appointed administration. The project consists of approximately 2,175 acres in Wadi Kharj and 2,100 acres in Wadi Khafs Daghra, which are irrigated with water lifted from huge natural pits with modern pumps and distributed by a large network of canals and ditches. Wheat covers a great part of the area, but vegetables, melons, barley, alfalfa and dates are also grown. Valuable experiments have been carried out with new varieties of crops such as potatoes, forage crops, oil seeds and rice. Livestock is efficiently cared for and scientifically bred. A dairy farm supplies approximately 200 gallons of milk a day to Riyadh.

Land Reclamation Projects

In order to increase the amount of arable land, the Ministry of Agriculture and Water has been giving full attention to land reclamation projects, which involve the discovery and prudent utilization of irrigation waters, construction and reconstruction of dams, and drainage of underground water. Among the recently completed projects is the construction of two dams, the $300,000

Akrama dam in the mountains near Taif in 1956 and the Wadi Hanifa dam near Riyadh in 1960.

A third project, the drainage of the Qatif oasis, begun in the late 1950's, was in effect completed in 1964. In this oasis, one of the most important date-growing regions in the country, the ground water level had risen dangerously high, waterlogging large tracts of land and leaving salt crusts on the surface, making much of it unfit for cultivation. The project involved destroying some wells producing salty water and installing control valves on sweet-water wells to prevent the overflow and restore the fertility of the soil. According to the Ministry of Information, 2,000 out of 21,000 acres of cultivated land threatened by flood had been reclaimed through the diversion of streams to the sea as of June 1965.

An important project in Wadi Jizan, on the southern coast of Asir, has been in progress since 1960 with the assistance of the United Nations' Special Fund and FAO. When completed—scheduled for 1966—the dam will store over 12 billion gallons of water and make possible the cultivation of 50,000 acres of currently uninhabited desert land. The project also includes the development of transportation and port facilities. Also in progress in 1965 was the reconstruction of the Abha Dam, long in disuse, in Asir Province.

In April 1964 a comprehensive project to settle nomads was begun in the Haradh Valley, located midway between Hofuf and Riyadh. It is being jointly handled by the Ministry of Agriculture and Water and the Arabian American Oil Company (Aramco) with a view to settling 1,000 nomad families and transforming 10,000 acres of virgin, uninhabited desert into vegetable- and cereal-producing land. The first phase of the project is to see the establishment of a 100-acre research, demonstration and training center. By September 1964, 6,800 feet of concrete-lined ditches had been completed to irrigate the 100-acre center. The availability of water will permit the planting of Sudan grass to tie down the soil, and tree windbreaks will surround each of the 21 fields to be laid out for agricultural research, demonstration and training technicians. The project will include electrification, irrigation and the establishment of a canning factory. In October 1964 the Ministry of Agriculture named the United States Food Machinery Corporation as consultants. Homesteading farmers will initially be given a plot of land, not exceeding 10 acres, which they must satisfactorily farm before receiving full title to the land.

On June 15, 1965, the Ministry of Agriculture and Water signed an agreement whereby an Italian firm, ITALCO, undertook to conduct a study of water and agricultural resources and possibilities in an area covering 220,000 square kilometers in the southern part of the country. The study, which also includes mapping out plans for agricultural research and experimental farms, was to be completed within a 42-month period.

CHAPTER 20

INDUSTRY

Industry is based almost entirely on the exploitation of the country's vast oil reserves. By far the most important oil producer in 1965 was the Arabian American Oil Company (Aramco), formed in 1944 by four major American oil companies to exploit the potential of the concession area granted by the Saudi Government to one of its founding partners in 1933. Oil production, begun on a commercial scale in the late 1930's and in 1965 still in a period of rapid expansion, has affected the Saudi economy in two important ways. It has introduced the Saudi Arabs to Western industrial techniques and created a popular demand for the material conveniences associated with a modern industrial economy, and it has given the government huge revenues with which to modernize the Saudi economy and fulfill these new demands.

The stimulus provided by Aramco and the large injections of capital originating with the oil companies' payments of royalties and taxes to the government has, since the end of World War II, brought about a promising start in modern industrial development in an economy traditionally based on subsistence agriculture and nomadic pastoralism. Secondary industries in construction, consumer goods and services have been established in Eastern Province where the oil industry is concentrated. These are spreading to other major centers in the country in response to the expansion of the monetized sector of the economy, brought about by the government's distribution of its oil wealth throughout the economy.

The government, seeking to broaden the industrial base of its economy and reduce its dependence on the oil industry, is encouraging industrial development. Its methods include the expansion and improvement of the transportation and communication networks, which are linking previously isolated market areas, and the establishment of educational facilities, which are developing the technical and managerial skills needed for a modern economy. In addition, it conducts surveys of the country's natural resources and water supplies.

Despite the fact that most of the capital in the country passes through government hands, the official industry policy fosters private enterprise through the letting of contracts to private businessmen, on the basis of free competition. It is attracting national and foreign interests with legislation which grants them particularly favorable rights and privileges.

The government is participating more directly in some of the major projected industries based on minerals, including oil, through the General Petroleum and Mineral Organization (Petromin), which was created by royal decree in November 1962 as a semiautonomous organization attached to the Ministry of Petroleum and Mineral Resources. In 1965, Petromin was participating in several important projects, among which were a petrochemical complex, an iron and steel plant and the country's second oil refinery.

MINERAL RESOURCES

Oil was by far the most valuable mineral resource being exploited as of 1965. Estimated proved reserves of petroleum at the end of 1964 were 59,172 million barrels, or approximately 18 percent of free world proved reserves, making Saudi Arabia second only to Kuwait in this respect. Associated with the oil are proved reserves of natural gas amounting to over 24,000 billion cubic feet, which can be used for industrial and domestic purposes and which form the basic raw material for a projected petrochemical industry. Continuous exploration for new oil and gas deposits are being conducted.

The government is aware of the disadvantages of excessive dependence on oil as the major source of revenue and has also been active in the search for other minerals which might be developed and become the basis of a major metal and nonmetallic mining industry. The most promising region for mineral deposits is an igneous and metamorphic rock area in western Arabia, referred to as the Arabian Shield. Ancient mining sites in this area give evidence of a once-flourishing gold production and numerous silver and copper mines. Between 1945 and 1954 one of these ancient gold mines was worked by the Saudi Arabian Mining Syndicate, financed by an American company.

Since the early 1960's, the government has made concentrated efforts to locate mineral deposits. A geological map of the whole country, compiled by the United States Geological Survey and Aramco under the joint sponsorship of the Saudi Government and the United States Department of State, was published in 1963 and reconfirmed the possibility of important mineral deposits in western Arabia. In early 1965 the government signed a 2-year agreement with the French-owned Bureau de Recherches Géologiques, Géophysiques et Minières for further mineral exploration to supplement the work being done with the assistance of the United States.

As a result of these efforts, iron, silver, gold, copper, sulfur, phosphates and rare earths have been found in commercial quantities. In addition, a major iron deposit has been discovered near Jidda. It is estimated to contain 1.5 billion tons of ore on the surface alone. It is low grade, however, containing only between 30 and 40 percent iron. Minor iron deposits in the Wadi Fatima area and at Jebel Idsas contain reserves of 50 million tons and 6 million tons, respectively.

Important deposits of nonmetallic minerals, such as barite, fluorite, magnesite, asbestos, talc, high-purity glass sand, gypsum, rock salt, limestone and ceramic clay, have been found. Salt, gypsum and marble were being produced in small quantities in 1965.

POWER

Electric power, produced mainly by diesel generators, is available to residential and commercial users in the major cities, including Mecca, Medina, Jidda, Taif, Dammam, Dhahran, Al-Khobar and Hofuf. Electric service is provided mainly by private power companies, although industrial establishments usually produce their own power. Total generating capacity was 231,815 kilowatts at the end of 1962.

As of June 1965 there existed no code governing the operations of the power companies, and voltage was not unified throughout the country. The power provided by the electric companies was generally insufficient to meet demands, and prices were high.

An important development regarding power was the merger of the Dhahran Electric Supply Company and the Al-Khobar Power Company, effective April 1965, and the replacement of their small diesel plants with two gas-turbine generating plants. This resulted in the availability of reliable power to Qatif and a substantial reduction in power prices. It was anticipated in 1965 that the new plants will eventually be able to supply the requirements of Safwa as well.

TRADITIONAL INDUSTRIES

Before oil began to be exploited, industry was limited to mining, handicrafts and maritime enterprises, notably pearling and fishing. Miscellaneous activities, such as leather tanning, food processing, date packing, and soapmaking were also undertaken on a small scale—generally in households.

The traditional handicraft industries of Saudi Arabia include weaving, dying and embroidery of cloth; mat and basket weaving; pottery making, particularly of large porous water jugs used by pilgrims; working of gold, silver and lesser metals into ornaments or daggers with sheaths studded with semiprecious stones and some wood carving and leatherworking. These products were seldom exported.

The handicraft industries experienced a general decline in the 1950's under the impact of increasing imports of cheap manufactured items. The products which continue to be made by individual craftsmen are generally of low quality and command only a local market. The bulk of handicraft activity is concentrated in the oasis, coastal and oil towns, but some nomads continue to produce tents and household utensils for their own use.

Maritime industries—which include fishing, pearling, the gathering of black coral and sponges, maritime commerce and the related shipbuilding industry—employ about 2 percent of the labor force. Of all the products yielded by the seas in the east and west of the peninsula, pearls have had most significance for the economy. In the past the finest pearls in the world came from the Persian Gulf, and the pearl industry in the area flourished under a steady demand. The effects of the world depression in 1930, however, and the development of the cultured pearl industry in Japan disastrously affected the Persian Gulf pearl industry. Since then some revival of the industry has taken place, owing to a rise of pearl prices and generally prosperous world conditions. Nevertheless, like the country's other maritime activities, pearling has suffered a severe loss of manpower to the oilfields.

THE OIL INDUSTRY

The Concessions

Oil operations in the country are controlled by concessionary agreements between the Saudi Government and foreign oil companies. In 1965 four companies were carrying on operations in Saudi Arabia and in the Neutral Zone shared with Kuwait.

Oil concessions date back to 1923, when a British company secured a concession for oil exploration in Eastern Province. The rights were not exercised, however, and the agreement was canceled 4 years later.

In 1932, King Abd al-Aziz Ibn Saud, aware of the increasing financial needs of his country, was encouraged by the discovery of oil in neighboring Bahrein to grant a second concession for exploration of oil in Saudi Arabia. A 60-year agreement was signed between the government and Standard Oil of California (Socal) in May 1933. The company was given the exclusive right to explore, prospect, drill for, extract, manufacture, transport and export all oil produced. It was not, however, given the exclusive right to market it within Saudi Arabia. The agreement involved an area of 360,000 square miles, the exclusive area covering all of eastern Saudi Arabia, from the Persian Gulf, including territorial waters, to the western edge of the Dahna, and a preferential area covering portions of central and western Nejd. To have exclusive rights over the preferential area, the company had only to meet the offer of any other bidder. The company agreed to build a refinery; supply the government with 200,000 gallons of gasoline and 100,000 gallons of kerosene yearly; and advance loans deductible from future royalties, which were fixed at 4 gold shillings per ton of crude oil (see ch. 24, Monetary and Financial System).

In 1936, Socal sold one half of its concession interest to The Texas Oil Company. The two companies organized the California Texas Oil Company (Caltex) to undertake marketing activities.

Oil in commercial quantities was discovered at Dammam in 1938 after 3 years of drilling operations. A supplementary agreement, also for 60 years, concluded in 1939, enlarged the company's concession area to approximately 440,000 square miles and included rights in the Saudi Arabian half interest in two neutral zones on its borders with Iraq and Kuwait. Both the original agreement and the 1939 agreement were later extended for 6 more years, making 1999 the termination date for the 1933 agreement covering the original concession area, and 2005 the termination date for the 1939 agreement covering the additional area.

In 1944, Caltex was renamed the Arabian American Oil Company (Aramco). In 1948, Aramco sold a 30 percent interest to Standard Oil of New Jersey and a 10 percent interest to Socony Vacuum, making the ownership of the company as follows: Standard Oil of California, 30 percent; The Texas Oil Company, 30 percent; Standard Oil of New Jersey, 30 percent; and Socony Vacuum, 10 percent.

In 1948, Aramco surrendered its preferential rights to the areas west of longitude 46° and its rights in the Kuwait-Saudi Arabia Neutral Zone and obligated itself to a phased program of relinquishing its concession area. By 1963, preferential rights had been relinquished. As of 1965 the total concession area covered 125,000 square miles, including about 14,000 square miles in the Persian Gulf between Dammam and the Saudi-Kuwait Neutral Zone and extending approximately 70 miles into the Gulf. Additional relinquishments of 20,000 square-mile tracts every 5 years, beginning in 1968, will reduce Aramco's exclusive area to 20,000 square miles by 1993 (see fig. 7).

In addition to the agreements affecting the size of the concession area, there have been several agreements involving financial

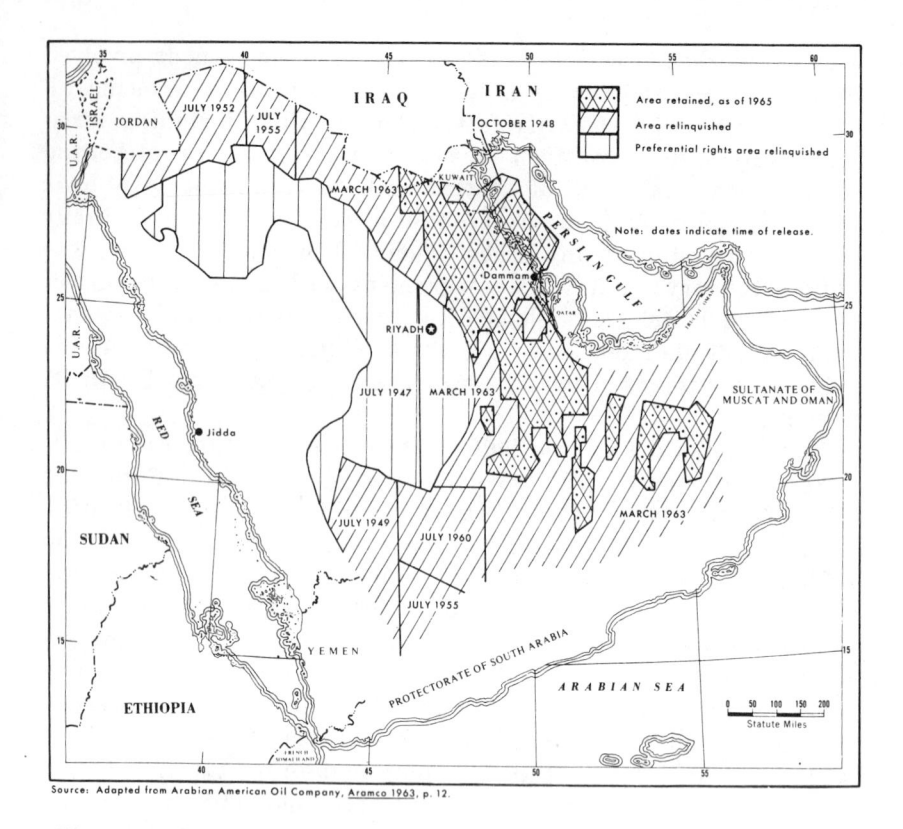

Figure 7. Concession Area of Arabian American Oil Company, as of 1965.

matters. These have resulted in substantial increases in revenue for the government (see ch. 23, Foreign Economic Relations; ch. 24, Monetary and Financial System).

In June 1952 it was agreed that the Saudi Government should be represented in the company's policy deliberations and that the company's headquarters should be located in Saudi Arabia. In keeping with this agreement, Aramco's headquarters were moved to Dhahran, and in 1959 two Saudi government representatives were elected to Aramco's 15-man board of directors.

In 1949 the Getty Oil Company acquired a concession to the Saudi half rights in the 2,000-square-mile Neutral Zone shared with Kuwait and negotiated a working agreement with the American Independent Oil Company, which had obtained a concession from the Sheikh of Kuwait for the Kuwait half. These 60-year concessions also include territorial waters and the islands offshore for a distance of 6 miles.

After a costly succession of dry wells, the two companies struck oil at Wafrah in 1953. Crude oil was first shipped from the area in 1954. Since then, each of the companies has produced oil from specified areas within the field; each has its own pipelines, terminals, tankage and camps. The Getty Oil Company's terminal and refinery are located at Mina Saud in the northeast corner of the Neutral Zone along the Persian Gulf.

In March 1964, Saudi Arabia and Kuwait agreed to partition the Neutral Zone between them for administrative purposes. Existing arrangements are maintained for the equal sharing of natural resources, but any future concession applications are to be considered by a joint Saudi-Kuwaiti Committee which would submit the recommendations to the two governments.

In 1957 the Japanese-owned Arabian Oil Company obtained a concession from Saudi Arabia for the area offshore from the Neutral Zone, to last 44 years, including explorations. Drilling started in 1959, and oil was struck in January 1960 (see ch. 23, Foreign Economic Relations; ch. 24, Monetary and Financial System).

A fourth concession agreement was concluded in January 1965 between Saudi Arabia and the French-owned Société Auxiliare de la Régie Autonome des Pétroles (AUXIRAP) to explore for oil in the Red Sea. AUXIRAP will bear all exploration costs until commercial oil is discovered, whereupon a joint operating company will be established in which Petromin will hold a 40 percent equity but enjoy 50 percent voting rights (see ch. 23, Foreign Economic Relations; ch. 24, Monetary and Financial System).

Operations

Of the four operating oil companies, Aramco is by far the most important one to the Saudi economy. As the sole oil-producing company operating within Saudi Arabia for 32 years, it dominates the national economy, and its establishment and growth have played a key role in the economic progress of the country.

The company's operations began with basic geological surveys and the establishment of basic installations at the first project site at Dammam Dome in Eastern Province. With few indigenous facilities available, Aramco had to import rigging equipment, lumber, hardware, pipes for water, transportation equipment—virtually everything necessary to establish an industrial and residential area.

When the company discovered oil in commercial quantities in the Dammam area in 1938, a small storage and shipping terminal was established at Al-Khobar to enable oil shipment to Bahrein. At the same time work was begun on the installation of crude oil tankage, pumps and moorings for anchorage 3,000 feet offshore at Ras Tanura, which had been selected as the principal terminal site.

Enlargement of the residential and industrial area, drilling and explorations and the establishment of communications continued at a steady pace until World War II, when all unnecessary oil operations had to be curtailed. However, oil shipments of 12,000 to 15,000 barrels a day were maintained during the war. Aramco also assisted the government in its efforts to surmount the difficulties arising from shortages of food by extending technical aid in the study of water resources and agricultural possibilities in the Al-Kharj district in Nejd, supervising the construction of wells and canals and providing transportation facilities.

Moreover, the construction of a refinery at Ras Tanura with a capacity of 50,000 barrels a day and a 12-inch submarine pipeline from Saudi Arabia to Bahrein took place during the war years despite great difficulties in obtaining materials and equipment. The pipeline was completed in March 1945, and the refinery was put in full operation in December 1945. In response to the high world demand for oil after the war, Aramco's production expanded rapidly after 1945, eventually placing Saudi Arabia in the ranks of the world's major oil producing countries.

Pursuing a policy of rapid expansion meant constant exploration and drilling, with the simultaneous construction of facilities for collecting, treating, storing and transporting the oil. The necessary facilities included: gathering and flow lines and pumps to serve them; gas-oil separator plants in every field; stabilization plants for the removal of hydrogen sulfide; pipelines connecting the fields; and pipelines to the refinery and to Bahrein.

Telegraph and telephone communications were improved, and, after 1951, better roads were built with the use of asphalt which the Ras Tanura plant began to produce in that year. By 1952 the refinery at Ras Tanura had been enlarged to give it a capacity of 150,000 barrels of oil a day.

To facilitate the transport of oil to the Mediterranean, a 30-inch pipeline system was laid over a distance of 1,068 miles, connecting the Aramco fields and the Mediterranean port of Sidon, Lebanon. Work on the line, begun in late 1934, was completed in September 1950. The western 753 miles of the pipeline are operated by the Trans-Arabian Pipeline (Tapline) company, which is owned by the same parent companies which own Aramco, in the same proportions. The eastern portion of the pipeline forms part of Aramco's gathering system, and is operated by Aramco itself. The line has four main pumping stations, all in Saudi Arabia, at Qaisuma, Rafha, Badana and Turayf. It cost over $200 million to build, and in 1957-58 the two companies invested over $19 million more to increase its capacity by 25 percent to an average of 470,000 barrels a day.

Crude oil production rose from 21,000 barrels a day in 1944 to over 546,000 barrels a day in 1950; by 1958 it had reached over 1 million barrels a day. In 1964 average daily production was 1,716,000 barrels, and in 1965 it was reported to have exceeded 2 million barrels a day.

Of the 1964 total of 628 million barrels, 160 million were exported via Tapline, 57 million were exported to Bahrein via pipeline, 100 million were refined at Ras Tanura, and 42 million were exported through the Ras Tanura terminal.

Production in 1964 was from approximately 200 wells in the 10 fields: Ghawar, Abqaiq, Dammam, Qatif, Safaniya, Khursaniya, Abu Hadriya, Khurays, Fadhili and Manifa. The Ghawar field, which is the largest in the world, provided 733,500 barrels a day. In late 1964 its production was expanded by 125,000 barrels a day with the completion of a new 67-mile pipeline to the southern Uthmaniya and Haradh areas. Safaniya is the largest offshore field in the world; it contributed 388,500 barrels a day to Aramco's 1964 output, and a $12 million project, started in 1964, was to increase its capacity to 575,000 barrels a day.

In 1964, the average daily throughput at the Ras Tanura refinery was 283,250 barrels. The refinery manufactured 97.8 million barrels of salable products, of which 58.0 percent was fuel oil, 14.2 was diesel oil, 6.0 was jet fuel, 4.1 was liquefied petroleum gas, 3.3 was kerosene, 13.6 was gasoline, 0.4 was aviation gasoline, and 0.4 was asphalt and miscellaneous. Ninety-four percent of total manufactured products was for export.

Although Aramco's most obvious concern has been with the rapid expansion of productive capacity, it has also taken steps to increase the variety of the products refined at Ras Tanura and to improve their quality. To make these improvements, it has installed a catalytic polymerization plant designed to use surplus refinery gases in manufacturing high-quality gasoline blending stock, a catalytic reformer designed to produce 8,700 barrels a day of 92 octane gasoline, a catalytic desulfurization plant to improve the quality of diesel oil, and an alkylation plant to enable the production of aviation gasoline. In 1961 a plant producing refrigerated liquefied petroleum gas was put into operation, and the construction of a new blender with a capacity of 20,000 barrels an hour was completed.

Because of the lack of an adequate market for the natural gas, which is produced with crude oil, most of it was originally flared. Aramco has, however, instituted conservation measures which have resulted in a rather high gas utilization rate. The measures involve reinjection of the gas into the oilfields in order to maintain the underground pressure needed for oil production. Gas injection plants were put into operation at Abqaiq field in 1954 and at Ghawar field in 1959. In 1964 the rate of injection into Abqaiq was 154,921,000 cubic feet daily and at Ghawar, 89,854,000 cubic feet daily. A total of 5,730,450 barrels of liquefied petroleum gas was injected into both fields.

Furthermore, Aramco has encouraged industrialists to use natural gas. Its first industrial use began in November 1961 by the cement plant in Hofuf; subsequently three lime plants near Dhahran have begun utilizing gas as fuel. In 1965, Aramco financially assisted the Dhahran Electric Supply Company in the purchase of two gas-turbine generators. Liquefied petroleum gas is increasingly being used by households throughout the country.

In the continuing search for oil, explorations have been carried on steadily. By 1959 they had covered almost the entire concession area. In 1964 exploration crews using reflective seismographic methods concentrated in eastern and northern Rub al-Khali (Empty Quarter), in the central part of the concession area and in the gravel plain in Dibdiba in the north (see ch. 2, Geography and Population).

A marine seismographic survey was conducted at Abu Safa field discovered in 1963 and scheduled for production late in 1965. Berri, a new field, was discovered in April 1964 northwest of the coastal town of Jubayl.

With regard to the marketing of oil, Aramco's activities are limited largely to the wholesaling of petroleum products through bulk plants located in the major centers of the country. Wholesaling in the western part of the kingdom is carried on by Petromin, which in 1963 was granted countrywide rights of marketing and distribution of petroleum products. In 1964 it purchased Aramco's bulk plant in Jidda, which supplies approximately half of the country's needs.

Shipments of oil are made by rail to points on the government-owned railroad running from Dammam to Riyadh, by tanker to Jidda, and by tank truck to other areas. The retailing of products is handled primarily by private Saudi Arabian dealers, many of whom have received Aramco assistance in planning, construction and operation of 200 service stations in the country. The National Gas Company distributes liquefied petroleum gas throughout Eastern Province and in Riyadh.

With increasing developments in transportation, construction, industry, power generation, transportation, construction and agriculture, and the increased domestic use of gas, the country's demand for gas and petroleum products has been increasing. By 1964, Aramco's sales of petroleum products, natural gas and crude oil within the country reached 6.8 million barrels—equivalent to

10.7 percent of total production for that year. In absolute terms, this represented a 75 percent increase since 1960.

The benefits which Saudi Arabia receives from oil exploitation in the Saudi Arabia-Kuwait Neutral Zone and the offshore area are derived solely from the payments which its concessionaires in those areas—Getty Oil Company and the Japanese-owned Arabian Oil Company—make directly to the government. The petroleum and petroleum products made by these companies are not considered Saudi exports, but their production and sales are of direct concern to the government insofar as they are the basis for the calculation of the government's share of the companies' profits (see ch. 24, Monetary and Financial System).

Production from the concession area, held jointly by the Kuwaiti concessionaire, the American Independent Oil Company, and Saudi Arabia's concessionaire, the Getty Oil Company, totaled 68.8 million barrels in 1964. The oil is divided at the gathering station at Wafra field and then piped to each company's terminal through their independently owned pipelines. Production is primarily from the Wafra field; however, a second field at South Fawaris was discovered in 1962 and brought into production in 1964 with an initial output of 20,000 barrels a day.

Total offshore production by the Arabian Oil Company, which has been producing since 1960, reached 63.6 million barrels in 1964. Its most important field is Khafji field, which lies 40 miles northeast of Aramco's Safaniya field. A promising new field was discovered in 1963 at Hout, approximately 19 miles north of Khafji.

Oil Industry and Local Economy

Because accurate figures on gross national product are unavailable, it is impossible to determine the oil industry's direct contribution to the national economy in statistical terms. Very rough estimates of its contribution—that is, the sum of its payments to the government, the wages and salaries and other benefits of the local employees and that part of wages and salaries of the foreign employees that is spent within Saudi Arabia, and its net investment—range from 50 to 60 percent of gross national product. These figures can be regarded only as an indicator of the magnitude of the oil industry's importance to the national economy.

Of even greater magnitude is the industry's contribution to foreign exchange receipts, which enables the country to maintain its trade relations with foreign countries. Before the establishment of the oil industry, Saudi Arabia, with very few exportable items, depended almost solely on pilgrims' fees and pilgrims' expenditures as a source of foreign exchange. This remains the second most important source, but oil activities by 1948 accounted for 64 percent of total foreign earnings; in 1958 they accounted for 87 percent; in 1963 they had reached 95 percent.

The oil industry's royalty and tax payments to the government provide perhaps the greatest economic impact. This source of revenue constituted 65 percent of the government's first published budget in 1947-48; by 1964-65 oil revenues constituted 83.2 percent of total budget revenues (see ch. 24, Monetary and Financial System). Since the early 1960's public finance has been based largely on the government's awareness that oil is a wasting asset and dependent on foreign market outlets and that, therefore, revenues accruing from it should be devoted in part to economic development in order to diversify the economy and thereby create alternative sources of income.

Aramco has made a considerable, although not easily measurable, contribution to the development of entrepreneurial talents among its employees and contractors and to the expansion of the local market for goods and services. Aramco training has helped to prepare Saudi Arabs for skilled and professional jobs previously held mostly by Americans and other foreigners.

The company's purchases of goods and services from local enterprises have contributed to the stability and growth of the economy. In 1946 it established an Arab Industrial Development Department (AIDD) to systematize its local contracting and purchase program. AIDD arranges contracts with local firms to provide services such as construction work, refinery repair and maintenance, warehouse operations, bus transportation and automobile rental. In order to develop business initiative and competence, AIDD administration of contractors' performance is usually limited to insuring that the job is done to specifications. It provides assistance in the founding and improvement of local firms which provide for the company and the oil towns such goods as steel pipe, motor vehicles, vehicle and equipment spare parts and bottled gas. In 1964, Aramco spent the equivalent of $13 million for services to local concerns and of $24 million for materials and supplies purchased from Saudi businessmen.

INDUSTRIAL DEVELOPMENT

Aramco's presence in the country has resulted in the development of new enterprises to supply the materials and services needed by the oil industry. It has also led to the development of industries which seek to utilize petroleum byproducts in new activities. The construction industry has been the one most directly stimulated by the existence of the oil industry. It has been the most important nonoil industry since World War II.

The first impetus to Saudi enterprise in the field of construction was given by Aramco's requirements for its own operations and the housing of its workers. Such work, together with the servicing of the completed facilities, increasingly has been undertaken by Saudi contractors rather than by Aramco. Saudi contractors have built houses, sewers, roads, hospitals, schools, dining halls, social centers, stores, post offices, mosques, laundries, libraries and cemeteries.

The construction boom spread to areas outside Eastern Province as Saudi initiative responded to the increasing need for government and business building and private homes. Initially, cost of the raw materials needed in construction work had to be imported, but gradually local enterprises began to supply some of the construction materials. In 1960-61 there were reportedly 200 establishments employing 1,600 workers manufacturing construction materials.

Two cement plants, one in Jidda and one in Hofuf, were operating in 1965, each supplying 300 tons a day, or approximately 30 percent of the local demand for cement. The expansion of the Jidda plant and the establishment of a third plant in Riyadh were being carried out to increase the supply of locally produced cement. There were 11 factories producing cement pipe.

The government reported in 1964 that there were 173 factories producing solid and hollow cement bricks; only three of the factories, however, were mechanized. Daily production of the machine-made bricks amounted to 24,000, whereas the output of handmade bricks from the remaining 170 factories was 67,500.

A gypsum factory in Riyadh fabricates about 100 tons daily of wall panels for use in construction. In addition, there are various plants producing tiles, earth bricks and cut marble used in building activities.

Industries catering to the increasing consumer demands include a number of factories producing items such as mattresses, wooden and steel furniture, shoes and leather goods, clothing, paper products and umbrellas. Consumer service industries include at least 3 modern dairies, 2 date-packing plants, 5 bakeries, about 15 soft-drink bottling plants, and a plant producing macaroni. There is 1 salt extraction plant, producing 600,000 tons a year.

Other industries, many of which produce mainly for the oil company and the Aramco community, include 2 oxygen, acetylene and carbon dioxide bottling plants, 7 cold-storage depots, 39 ice-making plants, which produce about 880 tons of ice a day, various bus, truck and taxi transportation firms, several vehicle repair shops, carpentry shops, and 24 printing shops.

The majority of these industries were initially established in Eastern Province under the stimulus of Aramco, but the expansion of the monetized sector has led to the setting up of similar establishments in other major cities in the country. Two important industries recently established were a match factory set up in Riyadh in July 1964, with a capacity estimated at 170 metric tons a year; and a Tide soap factory set up in Jidda in April 1965, which can produce a maximum of 7,500 tons of soap products a year.

Among industries projected for the near future is a paint factory, which is to be established at Dammam by two Saudi businessmen with technical aid from United States firms. Other important projected industries include: a glass factory, grain storage and milling facilities; refrigerator assembly plants; a plant at Riyadh to convert oil from the nearby Khurays field for use in power generation; and a water desalination plant in Jidda, with a daily capacity of 5 million gallons of water.

GOVERNMENT AND INDUSTRY

The government, through its control of capital, plays a vital role in the development process. Its policy, based on the desire to promote free enterprise, consists of providing a favorable environment for private industrial development and the letting of contracts to private businessmen on the basis of free competition. It makes determined efforts to improve economic infrastructure, devoting attention and funds to such matters as education and training, settlement of nomads, transportation, land reclamation and the banking system. Moreover, it has passed legislation specifically designed to promote the development of industry.

To promote local industries, the government began, in 1963, to implement a program for the "Protection and Encouragement of National Industries," established by royal decree. Upon approval by the Ministry of Commerce and Industry, existing and future industrial establishments receive certain privileges. For example, machinery, equipment, primary raw materials and semifinished products necessary for the establishment or expansion of the enterprise are exempted from customs duties, and land is provided by the state at nominal or no rents for the construction of factories and living quarters for employees. To protect local production from competition with similar goods produced abroad, there is a provision providing for limiting the importing of such goods through higher tariffs or quotas. To attract foreign capital, the government has issued progressively more liberal legislation governing foreign investment (see ch. 23, Foreign Economic Relations).

In early 1965 the government announced its intention to participate in the setting up of a model industrial estate in Jidda consisting mostly of small- and medium-sized consumer industries. Similar industrial areas will be established eventually in Riyadh and Dammam.

To promote the establishment of a major mineral industry in the country, the government issued a liberal Mining Code in February 1963 which governs the development of mineral resources, other than oil. It carefully postulates that the government is the exclusive owner of all mineral deposits on the surface, subsurface or in the continental shelf, but at the same time, it provides incentives to encourage national and foreign interests to develop these resources. Development of the resources is to be made through concessionary agreements which guarantee to concession holders such rights as repatriation of both income and capital, optional relinquishment of concessions, and exemption from customs duties on working equipment and the right to reexport it.

Saudi participation in the development of mineral industries is implemented primarily through Petromin, which was created by the government in 1962 as a semiautonomous organization to undertake research on, prospect for, produce, refine, market, sell, transport and distribute petroleum and other minerals and their products. As of 1965 it had initiated action on several projects, including a petrochemical industry, an oil refinery and an iron and steel plant.

Initial steps have been taken in the establishment of a petrochemical complex in Dammam. A contract was awarded in September 1965 for the supervision of the construction and operation of a $20 million ammonia and sulfur plant. In June 1965, Petromin signed an agreement with an Italian petroleum company, Ente Nazionale Idrocarburi (ENI), for the establishment of a polyvinyl chloride plant. In addition, there were in 1964 long negotiations regarding the establishment of a joint Saudi-Japanese industry producing urea, polyvinyl chloride and carbon black; by mid-1965 no agreement had been reached.

The country's second oil refinery was being designed in 1965 and is to have a capacity of 12,000 barrels a day. It will cost approximately $8 million, of which 75 percent is to be financed by Petromin with the balance being open to private participation.

Petromin is participating in a large-scale iron and steel project, the first stage of which—construction of a rolling mill which will utilize imported steel billets—was underway in 1965. It will have an initial annual production capacity of 30,000 tons of reinforced bars and sheets, later to be increased to 45,000 tons a year. The second stage calls for the production of pig iron and various types of steel and awaits the exploitation of medium-grade iron ore located in the area. Petromin is to finance the entire initial cost of the project.

In regard to the rational organization of economic development projects, a central planning body has been in operation since 1961 to coordinate the planning and implementation of all economic development projects. As of November 1965 the country's first 5-year plan was in the final stages of preparation (see ch. 24, Monetary and Financial System).

CHAPTER 21

LABOR

In 1965 the majority of the people continued to engage in agricultural pursuits as pastoralists or cultivators or to earn their living as artisans or traders in the types of handcrafted articles which have been produced in the country for centuries. A significant number, however—perhaps 25 percent of the labor force—were employed as wage workers in the modern sector of the economy, which has developed since the 1930's when the country's oil resources began to be exploited.

The rapid expansion of the industrial sector of the economy has created a serious shortage of trained supervisors, workers skilled in new technologies and educated government workers to cope with the numerous administrative problems that have accompanied the rapid changes. These skills are being developed through various programs initiated by the government, but in 1965 both private industry and the government were significantly dependent on non-Saudi professional, skilled and semiskilled workers.

In recent years the social relations involved in economic activities have been under great pressure for change. Nevertheless, traditional attitudes in employer-employee relations have altered little. The changes that have occurred represent the accommodation of the traditional system at various points to the needs of Western industrial practices. Some accommodations, such as government labor regulations requiring industrial employers in remote places to furnish suitable living quarters for their workmen, are the result of deliberate or conscious effort. Other accommodations have been the result of coincidence and circumstance, such as the plan for the Workmen's Compensation Fund, which was justified because it met the definition of a *waqf* (religious charitable foundation).

Despite the persistence of old orientations, the numerous development projects which have come into being as a consequence of oil operations have introduced some new practices into labor relations. The result has been a certain amount of strain. A notable example is the difficulty accompanying the formalization of labor-management relations. This alien approach has not been conspicuously successful among workers whose expectations have been formed in a paternalistic tradition.

SIZE AND COMPOSITION

The lack of reliable population statistics makes it almost impossible to determine the size or character of the labor force. For the purpose of this chapter, a 1965 population of about 3½ million has been assumed (see ch. 2, Geography and Population).

An estimated 25 to 30 percent of the total population—a little over 1 million persons—is economically active, that is, engaged in work that adds to the family income. Included in the estimated labor force are almost all males over 9 years of age. This does not include women working as unpaid family helpers who do not participate directly in the production of goods for the market. Only a few hundred women—mostly teachers in girls' schools, nurses, midwives and, in a very few cases, clerical workers for the larger business and industrial establishments—are wage workers. Of the remaining women, a few Bedouin women spin wool and weave saddlebags and rugs for sale; in the agricultural communities, some women look after vegetable gardens and raise poultry. The vast majority, however, are engaged in nonincome-producing tasks in the home.

An estimated 75 percent of the economically active—750,000 persons—are self-employed in agriculture or as shopkeepers, artisans or in service industries. No statistical breakdown is available, but it appears probable that an overwhelming majority are engaged in agriculture as herders or cultivators. Those engaged in animal husbandry are primarily located in the Nejd, whereas most of those in crop cultivation are in Asir, southern Hejaz, and in the oases of central Nejd and Eastern Province. Many who are self-employed for most of the year enter the labor market as temporary wage earners during the harvest season or for a year or so to supplement their regular income (see ch. 19, Agriculture).

About 25 percent of the labor force—about 250,000 persons—are primarily engaged in wage-earning occupations. Such workers may be regarded as falling into one of three occupational categories: members of families which for generations have found employment as workers in small craft, trade and service establishments and in agriculture; those who have sought government or other white-collar employment; and those employed in the modern industrial and trade sector.

The government is the largest employer, with about 150,000 employees in 1965. Of these, 90,000 were civilian employees (over half in the civil service and the remainder in noncivil service clerical and other support positions); and about 60,000 were in either the armed forces or police. Government positions, though usually reserved for Saudi Arabs, are open to non-Saudi Arabs because of a temporary shortage of trained Saudi personnel. Government employees have the highest rate of job permanence in the country.

Industrial workers, totaling some 18,000 persons in 1964, are employed primarily in Jidda and Eastern Province towns of Dhahran, Ras Tanura, Al-Khobar and Dammam, where most of the oil and secondary industries are located. The Arabian American Oil Company (Aramco), employing over 10,000 Saudi Arabs in 1964, is the leading industrial employer. In 1961—the latest data for which information is available—1,600 persons were employed in construction companies, and about 3,400 workers were employed in other types of industrial enterprises. By 1965 several thousand additional jobs were believed to have been provided through increasing industrialization.

Although data are not available to permit the categorization of wage earners outside of the government and industry, it is probable that a majority of the estimated 82,000 in this classification in 1965 were agricultural workers. The remainder were scattered among small craft, trade and service enterprises.

SPECIAL CHARACTERISTICS AND PROBLEMS

Because the industrial wage labor force is new, beginning only in the late 1940's with the expansion of the oil industry, few Saudi industrial workers have had more than a minimum of training and experience. The rural Arab finds it difficult to adjust to the pattern of industrial employment with its fixed hours of work, its demand for steady, repetitive activity and its requirement for relatively long-term commitment to the same job. As a result, few Saudi workers have achieved industrial skills, and most skilled workers, technicians and managerial personnel have been brought in from abroad.

In 1965 it was estimated that over 30,000 non-Saudi workers, mainly skilled workers, technicians and professionals, were employed in the country. Of these, about 1,000 were self-employed as shopkeepers, artisans, traders, moneychangers or in services. Most of the remainder were employed for wages in the urban areas of the Hejaz or Eastern Province. About 2,500 were employed by Aramco.

Non-Saudi Moslems performing the pilgrimage may obtain work for 6 months, after which a government-issued residence permit is required. Government policy in 1965, however, was to restrict unskilled non-Saudi Arabs from obtaining work permits and thus competing for job opportunities with Saudi nationals. Those who have stayed more than 6 months and continued to work without a permit are subject to immediate deportation.

Since about 1954 educational and training programs offered by the Ministry of Education and private industrial concerns—particularly Aramco—have created the beginnings of a skilled and semiskilled labor reservoir. Aramco has led the way with an extensive program of both vocational schooling and on-the-job training, which has permitted it to increase dramatically the percentage of Saudi Arabs on its skilled worker, technical and managerial staff.

Of Aramco's 12,880 employees in 1964, 11 percent were Americans, and 9 percent were non-Saudi Arabs. As late as 1952, over 70 percent of the semiskilled and skilled workers, technicians and managerial positions were held by non-Saudi Arabs. As more Saudi Arabs have been availing themselves of education and technical training promoted by Aramco, they are increasingly replacing Americans and non-Saudi Arabs in supervisory positions. In 1949 there were no senior staff Saudi Arabs and only 80 in the intermediate staff; in 1959 there were 44 in the senior staff and 3,017 in the intermediate staff. In 1964, 52 percent of the supervisory and management positions and 78 percent of the first-line supervisors in Aramco were Saudi Arabs.

A high rate of labor turnover has hindered industrial growth and the development of a skilled labor force. In the past, some rural Saudi Arabs came to urban areas seeking employment for limited periods to accumulate enough savings for specific purchases; when they had achieved their objective, they returned to their villages. Others left because they found adjustment to urban conditions and integration into the urban community too difficult. Moreover, qualities which the industrial employer sought in his employees—reliability, punctuality and a willingness to submit to impersonal authority and routine—were alien to the rural Saudi Arab, who was not accustomed to keeping regular hours and who expected his employer to assume a personal, paternalistic attitude.

The new values of the modern industrial and commercial economy are gradually gaining acceptance as more people begin to aspire to material possessions, housing, services and other benefits of the monetary economy. Employers have found that the provision of health services and an adequate diet is more highly valued by workers than are increases in pay and is more effective in building a permanent labor force, since higher pay results only in earlier accumulation of target savings and, hence, faster turnover. Moreover, health services and adequate diet have been reported by employers to result in better output of workers, whose previous work performance was hampered by ill health and chronic malnutrition.

Aramco's experience is indicative of the national trend. Until about 1953, Aramco's labor force was recruited primarily from among Arabs who had little if any experience with wage work. For them, adjustment to modern work conditions represented a new and foreign way of life. As a result, labor turnover was high, and Aramco was forced to recruit skilled and semiskilled workers from outside the country. In 1953, following a major strike by Aramco employees, the company expanded its program of providing schools, health clinics and labor training programs, and granted substantial wage increases. Thereafter, labor turnover ceased to be a significant problem. By 1965 the average length of service for Aramco's Saudi Arab employees approximated 14 years. Three-fourths of these workers have over 10 years' service with the company.

CONDITIONS OF EMPLOYMENT

With the expansion of the oil industry in the early post-World War II period, the Saudi Arabian Government began a process of introducing formal labor regulations and establishing special agencies under the Ministry of Finance to regulate working conditions in the new industrial and commercial sectors of the economy. About 1950 the Ministry of Finance established the Labor Office in Eastern Province to oversee labor conditions and to consider worker complaints. After the labor difficulties in 1953, by royal decree, the Labor Office was removed from the Ministry of Finance and established as an autonomous regulatory body, with expanded responsibilities. Labor offices were established in Jidda and other industrial areas.

In June 1961 the Labor Office was incorporated in the newly created Ministry of Labor and Social Affairs under the Directorate General of Labor Affairs. Regional offices were opened in Jidda, Riyadh and Dammam, and local labor offices were established throughout the country. The labor offices attend to labor disputes on the request of either employer or employee. They also serve as employment offices utilized by the government and increasingly by private employers.

Government Labor Relations

The Labor Code, based on an Egyptian model, was promulgated in October 1947 and has since been amended several times. Its provisions apply to all industrial, commercial or agricultural concerns with 10 or more employees. It provides for a minimum daily wage of SR5 (SR4.50 equal US$1), a minimum working age of 10 years, an 8-hour day, a 6-day work week, 15 days of paid sick leave and 10 days of paid vacation annually, and time-and-a-quarter pay for overtime. Also included are stipulations for termination procedures, including provision for severance pay and disability compensation. The government also requires all workers to possess a work permit issued by local labor offices of the Ministry of Labor and Social Affairs; the permit is held in deposit by the employer during the worker's contract period.

The Ministry of Labor and Social Affairs has the right to inspect any industrial project without notice and to seek information pertaining to employment conditions from employees and employers. Proprietors of industrial projects are required to provide shops from which workmen may buy food, clothing and other commodities at fair prices; to establish clubs, gardens and libraries for workmen and schools for their children; and to do what is necessary to protect the health and well-being of the workmen and their families.

Hiring and Separation

Traditionally, labor has been recruited on a personal basis, with an employer seeking workers from among his family and personal friends; reciprocally, friends, relatives and employees recommend friends seeking employment. Although traditional practices persist in smaller commercial and industrial firms, the government and private companies needing skilled personnel increasingly hire through direct application by workers to company employment offices, local labor offices and in response to newspaper advertisements.

According to the Labor Code, employment contracts may be verbal or written. Contracts concluded for a specific period include a 90-day probation period after which they are mutually binding. If the designated contract period ends without the workman leaving his job, the contract is considered as renewed for an indefinite period.

The Labor Code provides that a contract for an unspecified length of time may be terminated by either party on proper notification, which varies according to the worker's classification. Three days' notice must be given to or by those on a daily wage; a week's notice to or by those paid weekly; and a month's notice to or by those paid monthly.

Employers may cancel a contract and discharge an employee without notification if it is proved that the workman obtained his job through misrepresentation. Other acceptable reasons for discharge of an employee include: proof that a workman intends to cause material loss or other harm to his employer; absence for over 15 days a year or for 7 consecutive days; and performance of a dishonorable act.

Wages and Benefits

Wages in Saudi Arabia are among the highest in the Middle East, primarily because of the extraordinarily high pay scales set by the government, the oil industry and other large-scale firms. In small craft and market businesses, wages are substantially lower (see table 6).

The minimum daily wage of SR5 for unskilled workers provided for in the Labor Code applies only to firms employing 10 or more employees and to the government. Agricultural wages are usually well below those in the commercial, government and industrial sectors; this accounts for the difficulty in recruiting seasonal agricultural workers (see ch. 19, Agriculture).

In 1964, Aramco workers averaged SR10,700 per year, an impressive increase over the 1953 company average of SR3,800; it represents by far the highest wage level in the country.

The second highest income level is that of government employees, with an average yearly income of SR6,500. Most government wages are determined by civil service ratings, established in nine grades plus ministerial supergrades. In 1965 the lowest grade paid a minimum of SR400 per month; ministerial grades started at SR10,000. Minimum monthly wages for noncivil service government employees ranged from SR150 to SR800. Raises, generally given every 2 years, are based on seniority and competence.

Wages outside the government, Aramco and a few other major modern industrial concerns are generally low. It is estimated that among wage earners in the traditional occupations—crafts,

Table 6. Estimated Average Annual Income of Saudi Workers, 1964

	Number (in thousands)	Average Annual Wage (in riyals*)
Government employees		
Civilian	90	6,500
Armed forces	60	6,500
Aramco employees	10	10,700
Other industrial wage earners	8	5,000
Wage earners in crafts, trade and agriculture	82	3,500
Total wage earners	*250*	5,640
Self-employed		
Agriculture	740	1,000
Nonagriculture	10	4,000
Total self-employed	*750*	1,040
Total economically active	*1,000*	2,190

*SR4.50 equal US$1.

service establishments, trade and agriculture—annual wages average SR3,500. Among the self-employed agricultural workers, who make up almost 75 percent of the total labor force, annual earnings probably average SR1,000.

The Labor Code prescribes that medical treatment for workers injured on the job be prompt and paid for by the employer. Illness or incapacity incurred at work entitles workmen to half pay up to 1 month. Accidents occurring at work and reported to local authorities within 30 days of the date of injury entitle the workman to full pay the first week, and to 75 percent of his salary thereafter until the end of the period of temporary disability, up to 1 year.

If it is medically determined that recovery is improbable, the injury shall be considered as permanent and monetary compensation must be made to the injured employee by his employer. Payments are dependent upon the worker's skills and estimated future income.

LABOR RELATIONS

Since 1965 collective bargaining as a method of settling disputes has been illegal. No labor unions or worker associations are permitted by the government; this is to prevent the aggregation of interests which might oppose government policies. All labor grievances are required to be settled on an individual basis between representatives of the workers and those of the owners, with the government assuming a paternalistic role in safeguarding worker interest through the local labor offices.

Settlement of Disputes

The expansion of government and industry and the resultant increase of the wage labor force have altered the traditional basis of labor negotiations. Traditionally, grievances were settled between employer and employee, with the possible intercession of a mutual friend or associate as an intermediate when necessary. Although this procedure still holds true in small establishments, personnel problems of larger firms are increasingly being referred to the local labor offices of the Ministry of Labor and Social Affairs for arbitration when grievances are irreconcilable.

The initial step of a labor office is the selection of an arbitration panel comprising a representative of each of the disputants. If this should prove unsuccessful, the labor office appoints its own arbitrator to the panel. If either party is dissatisfied with the outcome, an appeal may be made to the region's central labor office, the local emir or the *sharia* (Islamic law) court. If the decision remains unacceptable, final appeal may be addressed to the government's Supreme Labor Committee, formed in 1963. Cases taken to this level are usually investigated and evaluated entirely anew and often secure a favorable decision for the employee.

Employers' complaints primarily have concerned carelessness, theft and failure of employees to perform as agreed. Employees' complaints are more varied and include such grievances as insufficient pay, failure to receive due disability compensation, maltreatment and poor working conditions.

Strikes

Foreign companies, particularly Aramco, have been confronted with group complaints, some employees bargaining on behalf of the others. In the latter part of 1953 there was a major strike of Aramco workers, who demanded higher wages, cost of living allowances and union recognition.

The strike reportedly affected 13,000 out of the company's 15,000 workers and paralyzed all Aramco operations. The strike remained unbroken for 3 weeks in spite of the intervention of government troops and the arrest of the strike leaders—mostly Palestinian Arabs.

A compromise agreement was finally achieved under which strike leaders were released and rehired. Aramco granted pay raises of between 12 and 20 percent, agreed to pay transportation and living expenses, and promised promotions for all Saudi Arab employees, schools for employees' children, shorter working hours and the establishment of "communications committees" as vehicles of information exchange between management and employees.

Under the Ministry of Finance, the government expanded the Labor Office at Dhahran to represent workers' interests and to prevent a situation from arising which could lead to another strike. A Royal Commission, established at the time to investigate Aramco's working conditions, reported in favor of the strikers.

Economically motivated labor unrest subsided after the 1953 strike. Rising political interest among educated workers led, however, to a spontaneous demonstration which was staged during the King's visit to Dhahran in June 1956. Government reaction was prompt and severe. Strike leaders were arrested, non-Saudi Arab agitators were deported and the king issued a royal decree prohibiting strikes and work stoppages.

According to the decree, employees of concessionary companies and private firms performing work of public interest are prohibited from leaving their work if their action is a result of the conspiracy of three or more workers. Instigators of work stoppages and demonstrations are subject to imprisonment for not less than 1 year and dismissal from their jobs. More severe penalties are imposed if violence or sabotage accompanies the work stoppage.

Since 1956 there have been only minor labor problems and most were political in origin. In 1962, Egyptian printers in Jidda walked off their jobs in protest against press attacks on the United Arab Republic and its socialist policies. A boycott of the company's cafeterias was instituted by Aramco workers in 1964. The major purpose of this action appeared to be to demonstrate the ability of Aramco workers to coordinate in support of their interests despite the prohibition on worker organization.

CHAPTER 22

DOMESTIC TRADE

The pattern of domestic trade in 1965 was still based on the traditional relationship between the desert nomad, settled farmer and town artisans and merchants. Surpluses of agricultural goods were traded for livestock and animal products; necessities not derived from animals or fields were supplied to the pastoralists and farmers by the townsmen and coastal dwellers in exchange for food and raw materials. Trade has traditionally been restricted in range; production has been geared to local consumption rather than to distant markets, which remained inaccessible because of transportation difficulties.

With the discovery of oil and the enormous increase in revenue came the creation of a large demand for manufactured goods, some previously unknown in the area. Thus, the volume and variety of goods traded have increased significantly as have the number of merchants dealing in imported goods and to a lesser extent those supplying domestically produced goods. The effects of such developments on traditional marketing methods are still largely confined to the larger towns, especially those in Eastern Province.

In isolated rural areas the commercial mechanism remains essentially unchanged and is still geared to a low level of demand and the narrow range of goods required to satisfy the needs of a subsistence economy. It is based on the *suk* (marketplace) where the nomads, the seminomads, the farmers and the merchants from nearby towns meet once a week to exchange their goods. Although the use of money is increasing throughout the country, barter is still a common feature of the trade in these areas.

In the larger towns and cities the *suk* is still the trading center, but it is characterized by an increasing number of permanent shops, and the range of goods sold reflects the changes in demand brought about since the establishment of the oil industry. Most of the goods on display are imported, but domestically produced goods are increasingly entering the trade channels. Although bargaining still prevails as a business method and personal relationships are of great importance, there are a few shops where goods have fixed prices. There is a limited amount of advertising. Most merchants still handle all commercial functions themselves, but the number of middlemen is increasing gradually.

The government has channelled large portions of revenue into the development of modern transportation in order to link the previously isolated market areas. With the rapid growth of towns, increased transportation facilities and steady economic development, the market for agricultural products and manufactured goods continues to expand, increasing the range of tempo of domestic trade.

TRADE AND MARKETING

The great majority of the population carries on trade through the age-old institution of the *suk*. At the rural *suk* the livestock, animal products, produce of the soil, handicrafts, tools, clothing, sugar and a few other necessities are traded among the nomads, seminomads, farmers, artisans and town dwellers.

The village *suk* is normally located in an open market square or between two or three neighboring villages. It is held once a week and is usually named by the day of the week on which it is held—thus, Suk al Ahad (Sunday Market). Each *suk* in the same region occurs on a different day so that they can be attended in succession by the traders. The sellers assemble their goods on the ground in the *suk* and hawk them to potential consumers; auctioneers offer special objects to the highest bidder. Generally, a variety of products are exchanged, although some markets specialize in one commodity, such as livestock.

As the economy develops and more people move into the towns to take jobs in industry and in government, the importance of the village market gradually decreases relative to the markets in the larger towns.

The *suk* in larger towns is a more elaborate version of the rural markets. They are usually located centrally, in narrow streets which are roofed over to protect the market from the sun. The market is organized into sections according to the activities of the merchants or to the categories of goods being sold.

Most trade is carried on through small, permanent owner-operated shops. The articles displayed, most of which are imported, cover a larger range than that found in the rural markets where supplies are geared primarily to a subsistence pattern of living.

Under the impact of the oil industry, the volume and variety of goods sold have increased steadily since World War II, concomitantly with the increase in the demand for and the ability to purchase Western goods, introduced mostly by the Arabian American Oil Company (Aramco). The increased demand for such goods as automobiles, other consumer durables and canned foods led to the rise of independent import houses in Dammam and Al-

Khobar in Eastern Province and in Jidda, which operate alongside the established merchant families in Mecca, Medina, Jidda and Riyadh. Moreover, the number of Saudi Arabian merchants and contractors with businesses dealing in such consumer needs as clothing, food, automobile parts and repairs and in other demands generated by the oil company has been increasing (see ch. 20, Industry).

The majority of merchants, whether dealing in imports or in the few domestically produced goods, handle all commercial functions. Wholesaling and retailing as separate and exclusive functions are rarely encountered apart from a small part of the import business and the marketing of some of the agricultural produce in the towns by commission agents.

Shopowners tend to specialize in the sale of a single product or a certain category of products. Most own and operate only one shop, but frequently the more prosperous ones own a number of shops, operating one themselves and renting the others. The shops are open for about 3 hours in the morning before noonday prayers and in the late afternoon. They close for the night before evening prayers.

A few, but increasing, number of shopowners sell goods at fixed prices. Nevertheless, bargaining, with its emphasis on personal and informal negotiation, persists in the rural areas and in the towns.

Time is of little consideration in arranging a business deal, and the personal exchange between buyer and seller is highly ritualized. Much satisfaction is derived from the bargaining process, which provides an opportunity for those concerned to demonstrate their skill in concluding transactions and to exchange gossip and opinions as well. After a number of proposals and counterproposals, an agreement on a price is reached for which a verbal commitment usually suffices. A clever bargainer gains both social prestige and the gratification of having made a good transaction.

In contrast to the heavy emphasis on personal dealings, very little attention is given to the preparation of goods for the market. Good- and bad-quality produce is generally mixed indiscriminately, and little attempt is made to classify products according to variety and size. Consumers are not conditioned to appreciate the advantage of graded commodities.

Advertising is minimal and is carried on mainly through newspapers, magazines and roadside signs. Radio stations, which are owned by the government, are prohibited from accepting advertising. Foreign companies in the larger trading centers, such as Jidda and Dammam, maintain showrooms and use posters in Arabic for advertising.

Cooperative Movement

A cooperative movement was started in 1962. The cooperative societies being formed are of various types. Multipurpose cooperatives engage in several kinds of social and economic activities including the setting up of fuel stations, power stations, medical units and supply depots handling such items as consumer goods and agricultural equipment, and the purchasing of modern equipment for well digging. Consumer cooperatives specialize mostly in the retail sale of consumer goods to its members; some of the larger ones purchase goods on a massive scale from abroad and from domestic producers and sell them wholesale to smaller consumer cooperatives. Agricultural cooperatives produce, store and market agricultural goods for their members. Production or industrial cooperatives, formed by small producers, aim at cutting production costs and improving the quality of goods.

In November 1962 the government issued the Regulations for Cooperative Societies to control the movement and to integrate it into its program of social development (see ch. 11, Health and Welfare). These required every cooperative society to register with the Ministry of Labor and Social Affairs, from which each would then receive assistance in accounting and administrative procedures for 3 or 4 weeks following its registration.

According to official data, published in early 1964, the number of registered cooperatives of various types totaled 18. In addition, the Ministry of Labor and Social Affairs actively participated in the creation of 10 multipurpose cooperatives and 1 consumer cooperative in 11 of the government's social development centers. Total membership in cooperative societies in 1964 included at least 12,570 persons.

PILGRIM TRADE

Before the exploitation and exportation of oil, the Moslem annual pilgrimage to Mecca provided the government with an extremely important source of revenue. For 13 centuries it was the greatest source of income in the Hejaz, and a great deal of the wealth of Mecca, Medina and Jiddah (the major entry point for foreign pilgrims) has stemmed directly from pilgrim trade.

Business activities in the area are stimulated each year in preparation for and during the hadj (pilgrimage) season. Transportation and health services are provided, the water and food supply is increased and living quarters are prepared. *Mutawifs* (traditional guides) are hired by pilgrims to attend to their physical and spiritual welfare. In 1965 it was estimated that pilgrims spent the equivalent of $60 million for goods and services. Much of the prosperity of the large *suk* in the towns of Hejaz is attributed to the pilgrims, many of whom bring products from their own country to sell.

TRANSPORTATION AND COMMUNICATIONS

Caravan Travel

A number of the ancient caravan routes, over which spices and frankincense were transported in earlier times, are still in use. Parts of some of the old mountain roads, such as the famous Elephant Road and the Coffee Road in Asir, are usable by automobile.

Before the railroad from Hofuf to Riyadh was built in 1951 camel caravans transported goods from the eastern coast to the interior of the country. The caravaneers, mostly professionals drawn from many different tribes, were nomads who were careful to maintain neutrality in their relations with tribesmen whose territory they habitually crossed. Camels are generally used now for transport only in isolated places that are difficult to reach by automobile. Many towns and villages in the high mountains of Asir cannot be reached by motor transport. In the highlands a rough breed of donkey replaces the camel as a carrying animal. Where the roads are better and trucks are available, nomads and cultivators increasingly raise animals for food rather than for use as beasts of burden.

Road Transportation

The government's concern in strengthening the internal economy is shown by its ambitious program of road development, which aims at linking all the main marketing areas in the country. In the 10 years between 1955 and 1965, the total length of paved roads increased from less than 150 miles to approximately 2,000 miles (see fig. 8). An additional 3,000 miles of highway are scheduled for completion by 1970.

If construction is carried on according to plans, a modern highway will, by 1970, unit the kingdom from the Persian Gulf on the east to the Red Sea coast on the west, and from the Jordanian border in the north to Yemen in the south. The transformation of the ancient Dammam-Riyadh-Taif-Mecca-Jidda trans-Arabian route, first ordered by royal decree in 1955, was well advanced by 1965, with a paved stretch connecting Dammam to Riyadh and continuing west to Dawadmi in Nejd.

Paved roads link important cities in the Hejaz, including Jidda, Mecca, Medina and Taif. A paved road extends from Jidda northward along the Red Sea coast to the port of Yanbu; another road

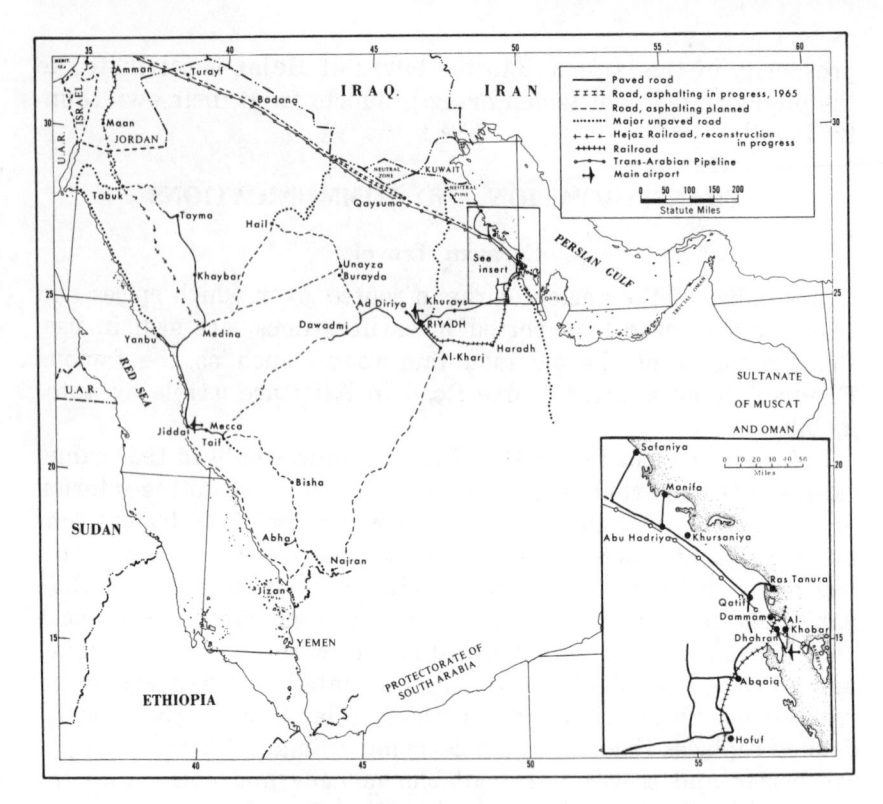

Figure 8. Transportation Network of Saudi Arabia, 1965.

in the interior passes through Khaybar to Tayma and is being extended farther north to Tabuk.

In Nejd modern roads radiate out from Riyadh. One goes east to Khurays, an Aramco oilfield, and thence to Hofuf; another goes north to the Riyadh Airport; and a third goes southeast to Al-Kharj. The road heading west, which will eventually link Riyadh to the cities in Hejaz, in mid-1965 had been paved to Dawadmi, 212 miles from the capital.

In Eastern Province, government-paved roads link Hofuf, Al-Khobar, Dammam, Qatif and Tarut Island. In addition, Aramco has paved roads connecting all of its residential and industrial areas, including Dhahran, Ras Tanura, and its installations a Abqaiq, Ghawar, Safaniya, Khursaniya and Khurays. The Trans Arabian Pipeline Company (Tapline) has undertaken to asphalt the entire 516-mile road along the pipeline which connects its pumping station in Qaysuma to that in Turay. By December 1964, Tapline had surfaced almost 125 miles and expected to complete the road in 1967.

Among the new projects is the construction of roads in the difficult mountainous terrain of Asir; paved roads eventually will

272

connect the rich agricultural areas of Asir directly to towns in Hejaz, Nejd and Eastern Province. Other major roads will connect Medina, Burajda, Hail and Riyadh. In addition to these primary roads, about 3,000 miles of secondary feeder roads to be built in various rural areas are included in the road development program.

The administration of the program is the responsibility of the General Roads Administration of the Ministry of Communications. The design and construction of the new major roads are carried out under contract with foreign consulting engineers or with the aid of United Nations specialists. The roads are built mainly according to United States standards; widths vary usually from 20 to 30 feet and are constructed to support loads of 16 tons. With the exception of 402 miles of the existing roads which are maintained by private contractors, the road network is maintained by the General Roads Administration.

The improvement of the road network has led to large imports of motor vehicles every year. According to statistics published by the General Roads Administration, the value of imports of motor vehicles of various types totaled SR63 million (SR4.50 equal US$1) in 1960–61. Of this, SR26 million was for trucks, which have been replacing camels wherever possible in the transport of goods. In 1963–64 the value of imported cars, buses and trucks was reported to have reached SR198 million.

Railroads

The only railroad in operation is the single-track, standard-gauge railroad owned by the government. It extends for 357 miles, from the eastern port of Dammam through Dhahran, Abqaiq, Hofuf, Haradh and Al-Kharj to Riyadh. Built by Aramco at the request of Abd al-Aziz Ibn Saud, construction started in 1947 and, after many problems of desert engineering had been solved, it was completed in 1951. It cost the equivalent of $52.5 million; no interest was charged, and the government agreed to repay Aramco in yearly installments ending in 1960. In 1963, Aramco turned over management of the railroad to Saudi officials.

Passenger trains run during the day and freight trains during the night. Fifteen freight hauls a week carry oil products, agricultural produce, tools and consumer goods between the eastern coast and the capital. Ocean freighters at the port of Dammam can discharge their cargoes directly into railroad cars for shipment to any point on the line. In 1961 the railroad handled 1.5 million tons of freight and carried 482,500 passengers.

Studies have been made on the possibility of the extension of the railroad to Jidda, by way of Medina, where it would connect with the old Hejaz line which is being rehabilitated and modernized.

The Hejaz railroad was constructed by the Turks in 1904-08 to connect Medina with Amman, Jordan, and with Damascus, Syria. It was used mainly to transport pilgrims to the holy cities. During World War I, it was made inoperative by military action led by Colonel T. E. Lawrence, but was put back into partial service from 1918 to 1924, when it was abandoned.

Plans to rebuild the railroad, first announced in 1953, were put into action in 1964. Syria, Jordan and Saudi Arabia have provided the funds; a British consortium is in charge of construction under the supervision of a West German engineering concern. By January 1965 the entire line had been surveyed and 150 bridges had been built. The actual cost of the restoration of the 500-mile railroad had not been determined, but it was estimated to range from an equivalent of $25 million to $50 million. The modernized line will enable trains to travel at higher speeds than before and will facilitate movement of goods into the area. Nevertheless, its value is mainly sentimental, and its primary function will be the transportation of pilgrims to Hejaz.

Air Transport

Air transportation assumes special importance in a vast country where population centers are separated from one another by hundreds of miles of desert. The country has three first-class airports—in Jidda, Dhahran and Riyadh. The airports at Jidda and Dhahran are regularly served by international airlines which connect Saudi Arabia to the major capitals of the world. The airport at Riyadh is regularly served by the government-owned Saudi Arabian Airlines, which provided, as of mid-1965, internal services to approximately 25 cities and external services to Paris, Milan, Damascus, Beirut, Amman, Baghdad, Kuwait, Bahrein, Teheran, Karachi, Asmara, Khartoum, Port Sudan and Istanbul.

The Dhahran Airport, initially built by the United States Air Force as a base, was handed over to the Saudi Government in April 1962. A first-class terminal building was put into operation at that time.

In 1965 enlargement of the Jidda and Riyadh airports was being carried out, and major improvements were being made at several minor airports including those at Tabuk in Hejaz and Jizan in Asir.

Saudi Arabian Airline was established in 1946 as a government corporation. It began operations in 1947 with all services and maintenance being handled under contract with Trans World Airlines (TWA). In 1963 the airline was reorganized as a state-subsidized corporation with autonomous management under a nine-member board of directors appointed by the Ministry of Defense and Aviation. The board was dissolved in October 1965, and the minister of defense and aviation was temporarily placed in direct control of the airline management "to raise the standards of Saudi air transportation." Although TWA continues to provide technical assistance, Saudi Arabs are being trained as management and operational personnel, with primary emphasis on the development of qualified pilots. Future plans include public ownership of the corporation through the sale of stock, perhaps as early as 1970.

In mid-1965 the airline's fleet consisted of approximately 30 civil transport aircraft, including the Boeing 720-B, Convair 340, Douglas DC-6B and Douglas DC-3. In March 1965 three short- to medium-range DC-9 jet airliners were purchased from the Douglas Aircraft Company in the United States. They were scheduled for delivery in the fall of 1966.

Port Facilities

The three main ports are Jidda, on the Red Sea, and Dammam and Ras Tanura on the Persian Gulf. Jidda, where modern port facilities were developed in 1947, is the major distribution center in western Saudi Arabia, and imports arriving there are sent as far inland as Riyadh. It is also the principal entry point for foreign pilgrims who travel annually to Mecca.

The construction of port facilities at the Dammam harbor, undertaken by Aramco, was completed in 1950. The port was operated by Aramco until 1953 when it was turned over to the government. Fully equipped wharves offer excellent facilities for handling cargo. The importance of the port is enhanced by its proximity to the oil installations and its rail connections to Riyadh. Ras Tanura is used primarily by oil tankers.

Port development projects in the mid-1960's included the expansion of the Jidda port in order to increase its efficiency. Excessive pressure on the port had required the imposition of a 45-percent surcharge on import freight rates; this reduced to 25 percent in August 1965. Improvement of the port involves the construction of eight deepwater berths, two lighthouses, six beacons, transit sheds and other buildings and equipment. To decrease pressure on the port of Jidda during the hadj season, the port at Yanbu was improved in 1965 to enable it to handle the pilgrims going to nearby Medina.

It was reported in 1965 that the old port of Jizan on the Red Sea coast was being improved and enlarged. Projected highways will make the entire southwestern region of the country more accessible and will encourage the development of Jizan as an important shipping center.

Postal, Telephone and Telegraph Systems

Under the Ministry of Communications, the postal and telecommunications systems are also being improved and expanded. Mail must still be carried by mule, donkey or camel to rugged and remote areas; however, airways, railroads and highways have sped up mail deliveries to major centers in the country. In early 1965 there were 35 main mail routes and approximately 300 post offices.

According to a report prepared by the International Bank for Reconstruction and Development (IBRD) in 1960, telecommunications installations existing at that time provided adequate service between major cities, except Jidda and Riyadh, both of which have been growing at a very rapid rate. In 1964 international telegraph service was provided by two radio telegraphic networks. To keep pace with overall development, telephone and telegraph facilities are steadily being increased. The most important recent project in this field was the establishment of an automatic telephone system. Approximately 41,000 new telephone lines will be installed; they will link the major cities of Riyadh, Jidda, Mecca, Medina and Al-Khobar. The project, which was being carried out in 1965 under contract with a Swedish company, was expected to be completed within 5 years.

CHAPTER 23

FOREIGN ECONOMIC RELATIONS

The discovery in the late 1930's of vast oil deposits gave the country an important position in world affairs which it had not previously enjoyed and greatly expanded its contacts with other nations for the purposes of trade, foreign assistance and foreign investment. Before that time, although the economy depended to some extent on imports of basic foodstuffs and manufactured goods, trade was limited by the small purchasing power afforded by the few exports of such items as dates, horses, pearls and charcoal, and by the income derived from Moslem pilgrims traveling annually to the holy cities.

The boom in trade, which started in 1944 with the beginning of large-scale exports of oil, continued until a financial crisis, which began in the mid-1950's, demonstrated the disadvantages of exclusive dependence on oil as a source of foreign exchange and as the major source of government revenue. A sudden leveling off of oil revenue, accompanied by increased deficit spending by the government, resulted in serious balance-of-payments problems. Excessive credit expansion, quickly translated into additional demand for imports, put severe pressure on foreign exchange resources and caused a drastic fall in the exchange rate of the Saudi riyal.

Aggravating the balance-of-payments difficulties were the rising prices under the impact of import controls and the flight of capital due to a loss of confidence in the currency. The crisis was brought to an end only after the successful implementation of a strict stabilization program established in 1958 with the aid of experts from the International Monetary Fund (see ch. 24, Monetary and Financial System).

The success of the stabilization program and a budgetary reform program established in 1960 permitted the removal of virtually all trade restrictions and the establishment of a very liberal tariff structure. Since 1962 imports of consumer goods and luxury items have continued. Of greater importance, however, is the great increase in capital goods imported for the purpose of developing an economy which aims specifically at diversifying the sources of income and reducing the dependence on oil exports.

Large and increasing trade surpluses have provided income which is more than sufficient to finance all imports and to cover high expenditures on invisibles such as the investment income accruing to the foreign oil companies, government expenditures abroad and the large remittances abroad by foreign workers and technicians.

The major market for Saudi exports is Western Europe, although European purchases have been declining in recent years as a result of the opening of oilfields in Libya and Algeria. On the other hand, Japan has sharply increased its purchases of Saudi oil since the early 1950's and by 1965 constituted an important market.

The most important single supplier of goods to the country has always been the United States. Nevertheless, increased oil sales for nondollar currencies has led to increased imports from European countries and from Japan.

Increased contact with foreigners also has been brought about by efforts to overcome the country's lack of personnel trained in technical and managerial skills. Contracts and agreements calling mainly for technical aid have been signed with foreign companies, mainly Western European and American. International organizations, such as the International Monetary Fund, the International Bank for Reconstruction and Development and other United Nations bodies, have provided assistance in the planning of various reforms and in the implementation of development projects. To a small extent, technical assistance is also provided on a government-to-government level.

In 1964 the government issued a liberal foreign investment code in order to attract foreign firms to the kingdom. As a rich underdeveloped country, Saudi Arabia does not need foreign capital as much as do many underdeveloped countries, but its leaders are aware that the economy needs the entrepreneurial and technological experience of the foreign businessmen who are brought to the country by the establishment of foreign firms there.

FOREIGN TRADE

Composition of Trade

Petroleum and petroleum products have for years accounted for over 99 percent of total exports (see table 7). Exports other than oil are negligible; they include small quantities of livestock and animal products, fish and fish products, dates and pearls. Until the closing of the Saudi Arabian Mining Syndicate which operated from 1945 to 1954, the export of gold was second in importance only to oil (see ch. 20, Industry). To a small extent, Saudi merchants reexport machinery and other goods previously purchased abroad, although the practice is officially discouraged.

Table 7. *Value of Saudi Arabian Imports and Exports, 1960–61 Through 1963–64*[1]

Year	Total Imports[2]	Total Exports[2]	Petroleum and Petroleum Products Export Value[2]	Percent of Total Exports
1960–61	1,053.0	3,888.4	3,875.6	99.7
1961–62	1,155.1	4,230.1	4,219.3	99.7
1962–63	1,266.0	4,631.7	4,610.3	99.5
1963–64	1,357.7	5,318.2	5,274.0	99.2

[1] Fiscal years 1960–61 through 1963–64 are roughly approximate to Moslem calendar years 1380–3 A.H. (*anno hegirae*).
[2] In millions of riyals; SR4.50 equal US$1.

Source: Adapted from Saudi Arabia, Ministry of Finance and National Economy, Department of Statistics, *Summary of Foreign Trade Statistics, 1383 A.H.*

It was estimated in 1965 that the value of imports was equal to 30 percent of the national income. The composition of imports is varied (see table 8). Although the traditional essentials—textiles and foodstuffs such as grains, sugar, coffee and dairy products—continue to be basic imports, the composition of imports now indicates the rising level of consumption in the country and the increasing pace of development activity of recent years. The expansion of the monetary sector and rising incomes have led to a stimulation of demand for such goods as motor vehicles, air conditioners, radios, refrigerators and canned foods.

The low level of domestic production of foodstuffs and textiles and the inadequacy of domestic trade channels have meant that the population of the towns always has had to depend on imports to supply their essential needs. Foodstuffs still comprise over 30 percent of total imports every year. However, in addition to basic requirements, food imports now include increasing amounts of meat and of high quality fruits and vegetables, reflecting the increase in incomes among some city dwellers and a substantial change in their food habits. Textiles and clothing usually account for about 10 to 12 percent of total value of imports. They were down to 8.1 percent in 1962–63, but the Saudi Government estimates that they rose again in 1963–64.

The very significant increases in the value of imports of transportation equipment, appliances of various types and machinery point to the ambitious development projects being carried out. The improvement of the Saudi Arabian airline service has led to a substantial increase in imports of aircraft equipment. The total value of imports of transportation equipment, machinery and appliances amounted in 1962–63 to 25.3 percent of total imports. Building materials, such as wood and cement, necessary for the

Table 8. *Selected Imports of Saudi Arabia, 1958–59, 1960–61 and 1962–63*[1]
(amounts in millions of riyals[2])

	1958–59		1960–61		1962–63	
	Amount	Percent	Amount	Percent	Amount	Percent
Foodstuffs	*317*	*32.8*	*344*	*32.7*	*396*	*31.3*
Animals and meat	33		41		53	
Fruits and vegetables	53		51		55	
Wheat and wheat flour	34		40		52	
Rice	53		46		87	
Tea, coffee and cardamum	52		43		41	
Textiles and clothing	*106*	*11.0*	*115*	*10.9*	*103*	*8.1*
Building materials	*89*	*9.2*	*89*	*8.5*	*152*	*12.0*
Wood, timber	17		15		25	
Cement	23		19		23	
Iron bars, sheets, pipe	40		45		69	
Machinery, electrical appliances and transport equipment	*256*	*26.5*	*245*	*23.3*	*320*	*25.3*
Motor vehicles (excluding trucks and tractors)	49		55		} 108	
Trucks and tractors	1		8			
Vehicle parts	38		34		35	
Machinery (excluding agriculture and electrical)	30		17		} 88	
Agricultural machinery	8		11			
Air conditioners and refrigerators	5		8			
Radios and household electrical appliances	8		11		15	
Aircraft equipment	8		5		13	
Chemical products	*57*	*5.9*	*71*	*6.7*	*73*	*5.8*
Medicines and drugs	18		22		23	
Miscellaneous	*140*	*14.5*	*189*	*17.9*	*222*	*17.5*
Total	965	[3]99.9	1,053	100.0	1,266	100.0

[1] Fiscal years 1958–59, 1960–61 and 1962–63 are roughly approximate to Moslem calendar years 1378, 1380 and 1382 A.H. (*anno hegirae*).
[2] SR4.50 equal US$1.
[3] Column does not total 100 because of rounding.
Source: Adapted from Saudi Arabian Monetary Agency, *Annual Report 1381–82 A.H.*, pp. 50, 51; and ibid., *Annual Report 1383–84 A.H.*, pp. 44, 45.

extensive construction activity going on in the country are also important items in the import trade. In 1962–63 their value amounted to 12.0 percent of total imports.

Direction of Trade

The direction of Saudi Arabia's trade is determined by the destination of its oil exports. Although European purchases from

Saudi Arabia have been declining in recent years, as oilfields have opened up in areas geographically more favorable to the European continent, Western Europe continues to be the principal market for Saudi oil exports (see table 9).

Table 9. Direction of Saudi Arabian Export Trade, 1959–60 and 1962–63[1]
(amounts in millions of riyals[2])

	1959–60 Amount	1959–60 Percent	1962–63 Amount	1962–63 Percent
North America	402.6	13.2	434.8	10.1
United States	292.4	9.6	285.4	6.2
Canada	110.2	3.6	149.4	3.5
Western Europe	1,292.7	42.3	1,383.2	32.1
United Kingdom	61.0	2.0	141.4	3.3
France	167.5	5.5	175.7	4.1
Netherlands	178.1	5.8	229.3	5.3
Belgium	89.7	2.9	12.0	0.3
Italy	304.6	10.0	395.3	9.2
Germany	310.0	10.1	107.1	2.5
Spain	107.1	3.5	171.7	4.0
Middle East	517.9	16.9	708.0	16.4
United Arab Republic	52.9	1.7	80.7	1.9
Syria	0.2		0.5	0.01
Lebanon	33.2	1.1	39.7	0.9
Bahrein	408.2	13.4	539.6	12.5
Jordan	7.6	0.2	0.5	0.01
Africa	86.9	2.8	69.4	1.6
Somalia	3.4	0.1	3.5	0.08
Sudan	3.3	0.1	0.5	0.01
Asia	577.4	18.9	1,137.8	26.4
India	163.7	5.4	137.0	3.2
Pakistan	20.0	0.7	19.7	0.5
Japan	334.6	11.0	826.9	19.2
Thailand	2.0	0.1	11.5	0.3
South America	99.1	3.2	389.4	9.0
Oceania	78.9	2.6	191.3	4.4
Total	[3]3,055.5	[4]99.9	[5]4,313.9	100.0

[1] Fiscal years 1959–60 and 1962–63 are roughly approximate to Moslem calendar years 1379 and 1382 A.H. (anno hegirae).

[2] SR4.50 equal US$1.

[3] Excludes exports to United States military services, valued at SR154.4 million; exports of bunker fuel, valued at SR92.9 million; and other exports, valued at 12.2 million.

[4] Percents do not total 100 because of rounding.

[5] Excludes exports to United States military services, valued at SR197.1 million; exports of bunker fuel, valued at SR112.2 million; and other exports, valued at 8.5 million.

Source: Adapted from Saudi Arabian Monetary Agency, *Annual Report 1381–82 A.H.*, pp. 52–55; and *ibid., Annual Report 1383–84 A.H.*, pp. 48–51.

Exports to Asia have increased considerably during the last decade, largely because of the growth in exports to Japan. Exports to South America have also increased. Purchases by Middle Eastern countries have remained relatively stable and account for over 16 percent.

Exports to the United States amounted to only 6.2 percent of the total in 1962–63. The decrease is due primarily to Aramco's policy, initiated in 1953, of selling petroleum and petroleum products for currencies other than dollars in order to maintain the company's competitive position among other Middle Eastern oil products who sell for local currencies.

The largest single source of Saudi imports has been the United States (see table 10). Its preferential position was established initially by Aramco's practice of purchasing equipment and other goods only from American firms.

The increase in Aramco sales for nondollar currencies and Aramco's policy of purchasing as many goods as possible from Saudi firms led to a decrease in imports from the United States. The United States' share of Saudi Arabia's total imports dropped from 72.3 percent in 1952 to 48.9 percent in 1953. Between 1960 and 1965 it hovered at about 20 percent. Foodstuffs, machinery and transportation equipment predominate among imports from the United States.

The closest competitors of the United States in supplying the Saudi market are the Western European countries and Japan, whose positions have improved substantially since the early 1950's. The major single European supplier was the United Kingdom which supplies such goods as tires and tubes, paint, electrical appliances, construction and mining machinery, furniture and detergents. The Netherlands has become the country's major supplier of milk, cream and margarine. Italy supplies mainly domestic electrical equipment and clothing, and Germany supplies cars, trucks, plumbing equipment, medical and pharmaceutical goods, and electrical appliances.

Imports from Japan increased significantly between 1953 and 1963, going from 1.4 percent of total imports to 6.2 percent. They supplement the supply of manufactured goods and have effectively competed with India as a supplier of cheap cotton cloth.

Other countries of the Middle East supply mainly basic foodstuffs and manufactured goods which they in turn had imported from other countries. Lebanon and Syria were the principal suppliers in the area.

Trade with Communist countries is negligible. However, imports from Eastern European countries have increased in recent years, and accounted for 1.6 percent of the total value of imports

Table 10. Direction of Saudi Arabian Import Trade, 1959-60 and 1962-63[1]
(amounts in millions of riyals[2])

	1959-60		1962-63	
	Amount	Percent	Amount	Percent
North America	197.6	21.5	268.2	21.2
United States	187.5	20.4	259.5	20.5
Canada	10.1	1.1	8.7	0.7
Western Europe	262.7	28.6	418.5	33.1
United Kingdom	67.2	7.3	142.2	11.3
France	6.0	0.7	8.9	0.7
Netherlands	47.1	5.1	80.3	6.4
Belgium	26.4	2.9	36.1	2.9
Italy	44.0	4.8	69.6	5.5
Germany	54.6	6.0	58.1	4.6
Spain			0.1	
Eastern Europe	3.2	0.3	20.0	1.6
Middle East	230.6	25.1	245.4	19.4
United Arab Republic	38.7	4.2	24.6	1.9
Syria	38.9	4.2	57.0	4.5
Lebanon	48.0	5.2	68.7	5.4
Bahrein	50.5	5.5	36.9	2.9
Jordan	8.7	0.9	9.7	0.8
Africa	62.0	6.8	86.7	6.9
Somalia	26.0	2.8	37.3	3.0
Sudan	16.9	1.8	22.0	1.7
Asia	152.9	16.7	204.6	16.2
India	21.2	2.3	27.0	2.1
Pakistan	4.5	0.5	27.4	2.2
Japan	55.4	6.0	78.7	6.2
Thailand	47.0	5.1	37.2	2.9
South America			1.0	0.1
Oceania	8.5	0.9	18.8	1.5
Total	917.5	[3]99.9	[4]1,263.2	100.0

[1] Fiscal years 1959-60 and 1962-63 are roughly approximate to Moslem calendar years 1379 and 1382 A.H. (*anno hegirae*).
[2] SR4.50 equal US$1.
[3] Percents do not total 100 because of rounding.
[4] The same source gives total import figure as SR1,266 million in other tables.
Source: Adapted from Saudi Arabian Monetary Agency, *Annual Report 1381-82 A.H.*, pp. 52-55; and *ibid., Annual Report 1383-84 A.H.*, pp. 48-51.

in 1962-63. The goods originating in Communist countries which are found on the market are often reexports from neighboring countries.

BALANCE OF PAYMENTS

Rough estimates of the balance of payments were first published by the Saudi Arabian Monetary Agency (SAMA) in its annual report of 1963. Published SAMA estimates available in 1965 covered only the years 1960 through 1963 (see table 11). Although the estimates are not considered official, and are subject to a substantial margin of error, they provide an indication of Saudi Arabia's transactions with the rest of the world and of the level and composition of the flow of foreign exchange.

Oil exports account for the large and increasing trade surpluses which occur each year. These large trade balances have been

Table 11. Saudi Arabian Balance of Payments, 1961-63[1]
(in millions of dollars)

	1961	1962	1963
GOODS AND SERVICES			
Exports	875	971	1,032
Imports	−247	−294	−311
Trade balance	*628*	*677*	*721*
Net freight and insurance	−24	−28	−29
Net transportation	29	34	34
Net travel	27	11	3
Net income from investment	−369	−410	−450
Government expenditures abroad	−21	−42	−52
Foreign governments' expenditures in Saudi Arabia	8	6	7
Other services	−28	−44	−22
Net services	*−378*	*−473*	*−509*
Net goods and services	*250*	*204*	*212*
TRANSFER PAYMENTS			
Net private	−64	−52	−54
Net government	32	28	38
Net transfer payments	*−32*	*−24*	*−16*
LOANS AND INVESTMENTS			
Net private	−16	−31	138
Net government	−50	−97	−2
Total loans and investments	*−66*	*−128*	*136*
MONETARY MOVEMENTS			
Commercial bank liabilities	−17	9	−11
Commercial bank assets	−8		−22
Saudi Arabian Monetary Agency liabilities			1
Saudi Arabian Monetary Agency assets	−59	−22	−265
Total monetary movements	*−84*	*−13*	*−297*
Net errors and omissions[2]	*−68*	*−39*	*−35*

[1] In contrast to other tables in this chapter, this table is based on the Christian calendar year.

[2] Includes undefined outflows of private capital.

Source: Adapted from International Monetary Fund, *Balance of Payments Yearbook, 1964*. (IMF estimates based on reports by the Saudi Arabian Monetary Agency.)

somewhat offset, however, by net increases in expenditures for services. In 1961 and 1962 these increases were large enough to cause a deterioration in the balance in the account for goods and services.

The largest of these service expenditures is income derived from past investment by foreign companies. The bulk of it consists of interests and dividends paid out to the parent companies of Aramco. A smaller portion is attributable to other resident foreign companies and banks. Saudi Government income from investment is small; it derives from interest accrued on foreign assets held by SAMA.

Another major item which significantly affects the service account is that for government expenditures abroad. In addition to ordinary expenditures by Saudi consular and diplomatic missions abroad, the government has spent significant amounts for defense imports and for contracts with foreign consulting firms, which resulted in a large increase in government expenditures abroad between 1961 and 1963. The receipts accruing from foreign governments' expenditures within Saudi Arabia are small in comparison with the amount that the Saudi Government pays out.

The travel account is primarily determined by pilgrims' expenditures in Saudi Arabia. The receipts from the annual pilgrimages to Mecca and Medina constitute the most important source of foreign exchange after oil (see ch. 10, Religion). The amount of foreign exchange is directly dependent on the number of pilgrims who arrive each year. Although the number decreased from 1961 through 1963, it is reported that since 1963 the number of pilgrims has risen again, and SAMA has estimated that their expenditures in the country increased to a total of approximately $60 million during 1965.

Private transfer payments, in the form of remittances abroad by foreign technicians, workers and employees of foreign-owned companies, constitute a rather large outflow of capital every year. This is offset only partly by net inflow of public transfers, the bulk of which are the payments to the government by the nonresident companies, primarily the Getty Oil Company and the Japanese-owned Arabian Oil Company. Because they operate in the Saudi Arabia-Kuwait Neutral Zone and its waters, the exports of these two companies are not considered Saudi exports, and their royalties and profit payments are entered as transfer payments.

With regard to the capital account, private long-term capital movements reflect mainly transactions by Aramco and a few other major concerns. Through 1962, new investments by the companies were exceeded by amortization of invested capital; in 1963, however, the pattern was reversed, perhaps due to increased confidence in the economy. Moreover, as a result of an agreement signed with Aramco and the Trans-Arabian Pipeline Company (Tapline), the government received a $94 million payment, which was credited to a specially created Economic Development Fund and designated to be spent solely for investment in development projects (see ch. 24, Monetary and Financial System).

The pattern of government capital movements was also reversed in 1963. Through 1962, increasing amounts of funds had flowed out of the country as repayment of the government's external debts accumulated during the severe financial crisis in 1956–60. After 1962, the last year of repayment of this debt, funds flowing out of the country for repayment of loans from foreign countries dropped very sharply. Constantly increasing gold and foreign exchange assets held by SAMA, which holds all government accounts, and by the commercial banks, reflected the recurring balance-of-payments surpluses.

Net errors and omissions, a balancing item in the balance-of-payments accounts, is of special importance, as it is believed to reflect large undefined private capital outflows. The figures suggest that the outflow decreased progressively between 1961 and 1963. It has been estimated that they will continue to drop as confidence in the economy increases and as opportunities for investment open up in the country.

THE TRADING COMMUNITY

The trading community consists primarily of the government, private Saudi merchants and Aramco, which imports directly a large quantity of goods free of duty. Until the discovery of oil, the private trading community centered in Mecca, Medina, Jidda and Riyadh. In Jidda, the major port on the Red Sea, are located the diplomatic representatives and consuls of foreign powers and branches of foreign firms, shipping companies and banks; the port is also the major point of entry for Moslem pilgrims and most other travelers.

In recent years the petroleum industry and the Aramco policy of purchasing supplies locally have stimulated the import business in Al-Khobar and Dammam on the Persian Gulf and encouraged the establishment of branches of traditional Hejaz firms in this area. Many Saudi Arabs, including several once employed by Aramco, have been attracted into commercial activities and comprise a new merchant group, which now supplements the activities of the traditional merchants' groups from the Hejaz and

Riyadh. The existence of this new group contributes to competitive forces which are encouraging the use of new selling methods, including press advertising, trade delegations and showroom displays.

Chambers of commerce have been created in the cities where business is most active, which include Jidda, Mecca, Riyadh and Dammam. They are quasi-official organizations, supervised by the Ministry of Commerce and Industry. Little information concerning the activities of these organizations is available. Apparently they occasionally act as a channel for the exchange of views between government and business on such matters as tariffs, import restrictions and subsidies. Their main function, however, seems to be to receive any complaints in connection with imports which may come from foreign countries and to provide arbitrators for settlement of disputes between local merchants and representatives of commercial insurance companies.

The government does not maintain purchase missions abroad. Instead, it purchases its goods through the local private importers. In view of its positive development policy, it is bound to remain a major consumer of imported goods for a long time.

GOVERNMENT REGULATION OF FOREIGN TRADE

The country's dependence on imported goods essential to the welfare of its people and on oil exports as the major source of revenue led to a very liberal tariff structure and a relative absence of trade restrictions. This pattern was interrupted, however, during the financial crisis of 1956–57, which led to a severe foreign exchange shortage and obligated the government to take remedial measures (see ch. 24, Monetary and Financial System). Royal decrees issued in 1957 banned the importing of luxury goods and regulated the imports of other goods and established exchange controls. For essential licensed goods—food grains, milk, cattle, sheep, vegetable fat, medical supplies, textiles, construction and mechanical equipment, some household appliances and spare parts—foreign exchange was allotted by the government at the official rate of SR3.75 to US$1. Foreign exchange for all other, nonessential goods was obtained at the depreciated market rate.

The steps taken were effective. By the end of 1959 the government debt to the SAMA had been repaid, the value of the Saudi riyal had appreciated and price stability had been restored. All exchange controls and importing licensing were abolished, and since then imports have been almost completely unrestricted and have been financed by an extremely stable exchange rate. The goods which during the crisis had been deemed essential goods continue to be subsidized and are imported duty free.

The tariff structure is based generally on a policy of free trade with some degree of protection to the developing local industry. Most imported goods are dutiable on an ad valorem basis. The duties are mainly in the range of 10 to 20 percent, with a surtax of 10 percent of the customs duty being additionally applied.

In July 1962 several important items for which demand is high were added to the list of goods exempted from the import duties in order to lower prices for the consumer. They included raw cotton, silk, spinning threads, wood, refrigerated transportation equipment and unprocessed leather, all of which had previously been subject to duties ranging from 5 percent to 20 percent. Reductions of up to 50 percent were made on the rates applying to such goods as canned foods, blankets and certain household appliances, including refrigerators, washing machines, sewing machines and fans. On the other hand, tariffs were increased on goods which presented direct competition with goods which can be produced relatively easily domestically, including marble, gypsum, cement and tiles.

Trade restrictions are minimal. Imports which are considered contrary to Islamic religion or to Islamic culture are prohibited. Liquor and pork products are banned entirely, and other goods such as films, musical instruments and records may be imported only by non-Moslems or for educational purposes. Imports of tobacco are subject to a special license and excise tax. The Saudi Government boycotts trade with Israel and with firms dealing with Israel.

OIL AND FOREIGN ECONOMIC RELATIONS

Because of the enormous dependence on oil, the relations between the government and the foreign oil companies, the most important one of which is Aramco, are extremely important. The relationship between the government and Aramco has been conditioned by the vast benefits derived from the company's investment and work in the country and the government's desire to receive as large a share as possible of oil profits and to maintain control over the exploitation of its oil resources.

Relations, in general, have been cordial. From the very beginning of its operations within the country, the company's organization has included a group of specially trained employees whose task is to promote friendly relations with the government and to represent the company when any difficulties involving negotiations occur. The company has sought to integrate as far as is possible its social, as well as industrial, operations with the life of the country through such measures as home-loan programs, promoting industrial progress among the local public and assisting in the improvement of transportation facilities (see ch. 11, Health and Welfare; ch. 20, Industry). The controversies involving matters of finance and policy which have arisen as a result of government demands have for the most part been resolved through negotiations.

The first major controversy arose in 1950 when the government obligated the company to pay income tax (see ch. 24, Monetary and Financial System). Long negotiations resulted in the company's acceptance of an income tax calculated to bring the government's receipts up to one-half of the company's net profits. The half share included the royalty payments in addition to various fees and levies.

As a result of the 50–50 profit-sharing agreement, the first of its kind in the Middle East, the matter of prices became of concern to Saudi officials and the topic of further negotiations. A major controversy involved the granting of discounts to the parent companies; after prolonged talks this question was settled in favor of the government, with Aramco eliminating the discounts.

The nonintegration of the various stages involved in Aramco's operations has been the cause of a longstanding dispute. The government's interest in the integration of these activities stems from its claim that its share of profits should not be limited to those accruing from production but also those derived from refining, transporting and marketing operations. The company has responded that, according to the concessionary arrangements, the government's share is limited to the production phase. It consented, however, in 1956 to submit the proceeds of the Ras Tanura Refinery to the profit-sharing agreement.

A problem concerning the transportation of oil was created in 1954 when the important Greek shipowner, Aristotle Socrates Onassis, announced that he had signed an agreement with the Saudi Government giving his tankers a virtual monopoly in the shipping of Aramco oil. The agreement was later modified to except oil shipped in the tankers of its parent companies operating regularly before 1943. The arrangement was immediately opposed by consuming nations and by Aramco on the grounds that the agreement contradicted concession rights and would hurt the company's marketing arrangements. The issue was taken to arbitration late in 1954; in 1958 the tribunal, at Geneva, charged that the agreement was in fact inconsistent with Aramco's rights, and the project was dropped.

Since 1960 negotiations between the government and Aramco have largely centered around the major issues considered at the conferences of the Organization of Petroleum Exporting Countries (OPEC). This organization was created by Saudi Arabia, Iran, Iraq, Kuwait and Venezuela as a result of a conference held in Baghdad, Iraq, in September 1960. Qatar joined in 1961, and Libya and Indonesia in June 1962. It was created as a means of strengthening the position of these oil exporting nations vis-a-vis the major oil companies whose unilateral actions can so greatly affect the national economies of the exporting countries. It is an instrument for regular consultations among the members in order to unify their petroleum policies and discuss the ways of best safeguarding their interests.

The immediate cause that brought the producing countries together was the reduction in posted prices of crude oil effected by the companies in February 1959 and August 1960. The government revenues in Saudi Arabia, as well as Iran, Iraq, Kuwait and Qatar, are calculated on the basis of such posted prices, which are established by the companies, f.o.b. at the port of export. The deterioration of oil prices is, in effect, the most serious problem which the oil exporting countries face.

The major specific issues which have been discussion topics at the OPEC conferences have been those concerning the restoration of the posted prices to their previous levels; the stabilization of oil prices in general; the elimination of "marketing allowances," which oil companies deduct from their costs at the production stage, but are mainly applicable to operating costs incurred outside the exporting countries; and the treatment of royalties as an expense rather than as a credit against income tax payments.

Negotiations between the government and Aramco have resulted in some progress in the resolution of two of these issues. In August 1963, Aramco agreed to reduce its marketing allowances from about $0.042 a barrel to $0.005 a barrel, retroactively to January 1, 1962; in December 1965 it agreed to eliminate them completely. In January 1965, it agreed to treat royalties as expenses deductible from gross income rather than as a credit against income tax payments as it had done previously. The justification given by the government for its demand that this be done was that the purpose of a royalty is to compensate the government as owner of subsoil resources for the extraction of the oil. Treating it as a credit against income tax payment eliminated the distinction between a royalty and a tax on the net earnings derived from the production of oil; it meant that the government was either receiving no royalty or was not receiving a full 50 percent share of the profits derived from oil production.

No solution has been reached on the question of posted prices. The governments of Saudi Arabia and the other exporting countries have demanded to be consulted on any changes made in the posted prices. A critical situation has been avoided because the companies have not attempted to introduce further price reductions since 1960, despite falling world market prices of oil. In March 1963 an agreement was reached which obligated Aramco, in its calculation of the government's share, to use the posted prices at Sidon, Lebanon, Tapline's Mediterranean terminal, rather than the lower prices at Ras Tanura, for the oil traveling through the pipeline.

In 1965, OPEC was considering the adoption of a regulatory production program in order to control surplus production, which is the key to the price stability problem. The program was still in its theoretical stages and facing the prospect of long discussions among the member states over the allocations of quotas and with the companies themselves over the acceptance of such a program.

Concessionary agreements governing new oil ventures in the country will be conditioned by OPEC's policy decisions as well as Saudi Arabia's experience with Aramco. The government will insure, from the beginning, a larger share of oil profits and a higher degree of Saudi control over oil exploitation. Through the General Petroleum and Mineral Organization (Petromin), which it set up in November 1962, the government will participate to a certain degree in all phases of an integrated oil enterprise, including production, refining, transportation and marketing of crude oil.

In January 1965 a concession implementing the new oil policy was granted to the French-owned Société Auxiliaire de la Régie Autonome des Pétroles (Auxirap) to explore for oil in the Red Sea. It provides for a joint operating company in which Petromin will enjoy 50 percent voting rights, the treatment of royalties as an expense deductible, and an adjustable income tax rate. Petromin will participate in all phases of Auxirap's oil operations (see ch. 24, Monetary and Financial System).

FOREIGN ASSISTANCE

During World War II a desperate financial situation made necessary advances against royalties from the oil company and lend-lease assistance from the United States and Great Britain. In 1946 the country received a $10 million loan from the United States Export-Import Bank.

In 1951, Saudi Arabia signed Technical Cooperation Program (Point Four) and Mutual Assistance Agreements with the United

States. Under the Point Four pact American experts assisted in the establishment of the Saudi Arabian Monetary Agency (see ch. 24, Monetary and Financial System). The investigation of other projects by Point Four technicians was cut off abruptly by the government, and all personnel were ordered to leave the country in 1954 on the grounds that the $1.7 million allocation for Saudi Arabia was too small in comparison with the sums given to Israel.

In 1957, in return for a 5-year extension on the Dhahran airbase, the government received the assistance of the United States in the improvement of Saudi Arabia's civil aviation, air force, army and navy (see ch. 25, The Armed Forces). In 1958 it received a $25 million Foreign Assistance Act grant from the United States.

Between 1960 and 1965, United States assistance was mainly in the field of mineral exploration. Under the joint sponsorship of the Saudi Government and the United States, the United States Geological Survey and Aramco drew up and published, in 1963, a geological map of the entire country. In August 1963 an agreement was signed with the United States Geological Survey calling for further mineral exploration; the Geological Survey supplies the geologists, tools and equipment, and the government pays the salaries and other expenses.

Supplementing the work done by the United States in mineral exploration is that by the French state-owned Bureau de Recherches Géologiques, Géophysiques et Minières, which signed a 2-year agreement with the Saudi Government in early 1965. The government will bear the cost of the operations, but, in addition to exploration operations, the French will train local personnel in mining technology.

Some foreign assistance has been obtained from international organizations to which the country belongs. Experts from the International Monetary Fund, which Saudi Arabia joined in 1957, provided valuable advice on the financial reforms of 1958 to 1960, and on accounting procedures for the balance of payments. The International Bank for Reconstruction and Development, which it joined also in 1957, sent a mission to the country in 1960, the result of which was a report on the economy with suggestions on how to best approach its problems; it became the basis of many of the current economic development projects. The United Nations, of which Saudi Arabia is a founding member, has aided, through its Food and Agriculture Organization, many important agriculture and water development projects, and the United Nations Special Fund in 1965 was assisting in the setting up of an Industrial Research Institute and an Agricultural Research Center.

The planning and implementation of most economic development activities are done not with the aid of experts from foreign government agencies or from international organizations, but with the aid of technicians and consultants of foreign private companies. Aramco, on request from the Saudi Government, has assisted in projects totally unrelated to oil activities. During World War II it installed pumps and irrigation facilities at the government's experimental farm at Al-Kharj and subsequently administered the project for several years (see ch. 19, Agriculture). Another important project carried out by Aramco was the construction of the Dammam port and the railroad which runs from Dammam to Riyadh. In the mid-1960's it was conducting feasibility studies on a number of possible industries, providing advice to Petromin on its major endeavors, making loans to certain deserving industries, aiding in the development of electric power companies in Eastern Province and handling the initial phases of the Haradh land reclamation project (see ch. 20, Industry).

Other foreign companies, active in the country throughout the 1950's, handled primarily large construction work under contract with the government or with Aramco. Since 1962 a growing concern with economic development and with economic diversification has led to the contracting of an increasing number of foreign companies for advice and supervision of many of the most important projects in the fields of culture, communications and industry, as well as in construction.

In the mid-1960's several German and Italian firms were assisting in the construction of modern roads. A Swedish company was under contract to install the country's modern automatic telephone system. French companies were contracted to construct a 1200-kilowatt broadcasting station in Riyadh. American companies were assisting in the establishment of an oil refinery in Jidda, and an ammonia plant in Dammam, and in seismic studies in the area previously considered to be Aramco's preferential area. British companies were handling the construction of a steel rolling mill in Jidda. Water development projects were being carried out with the aid of American, Italian and German firms.

FOREIGN INVESTMENT

The government's attitude toward foreign investment, based on its experience with Aramco, is favorable. Seeking to attract foreign capital and, especially, foreign technical know-how, the government has adopted a very liberal foreign investment policy. It encourages foreign companies to establish firms within Saudi

Arabia in order that the country may benefit from the entrepreneurial knowledge and initiative of experienced foreign businessmen and thereby achieve more rapid economic development.

Foreign investment is governed by a new Foreign Capital Investment Code, which was promulgated by royal decree in February 1964 and replaced the Foreign Capital Investment Code of 1957. The code covers all investment of foreign capital in projects which contribute to economic development, excepting mineral and petroleum projects or any that are covered by special agreement. Foreign investors apply to a Foreign Capital Investment Committee composed of five members drawn from the Ministries of Finance and National Economy, Agriculture and Water, Petroleum, Commerce and Industry, and the Planning Organization, with the minister of commerce and industry as chairman. Once approved, the investments are entitled to the same privileges as those granted to Saudi enterprises under the Regulation for the Protection and Encouragement of National Industries—exemption from customs duties for machinery, equipment, primary raw materials and semifinished products necessary for the establishment of the enterprise; land provided by the state at nominal or no rent for the construction of factories and living quarters for employees; and some degree of tariff protection (see ch. 24, Monetary and Financial System).

Whereas the previous Foreign Capital Investment Code stipulated that Saudi participation be no less than 51 percent of total capital of the firm, the new code indirectly limits the minimum Saudi participation. It stipulates that Saudi ownership must be no less than 25 percent in order for the investment to qualify for a 5-year exemption from income taxes, to which firms having non-Saudi capital are subject by law.

Until recently, the only contracts with large foreign investment were those with Aramco and with the Saudi Arabian Mining Syndicate which exploited gold deposits during 1939 to 1954. The lack of conditions and resources, except for oil, which would support profitable enterprise prevented further major investment in the country. This situation has, however, been changing. The government's adoption of a positive policy toward economic development is resulting in the gradual improvement of the economic infrastructure and in increased economic activity throughout the country (see ch. 20, Industry). Opportunities for investment, both domestic and foreign, have opened up, and the Foreign Capital Investment Committee has received several applications from foreign companies for setting up new industries. The applications include many from Pakistan and from Japan. In April 1965 a

Procter and Gamble soap factory was inaugurated in Jidda, and negotiations are in progress regarding several other firms.

The General Petroleum and Mineral Organization, established in November 1962, is playing an important role in stimulating both local and foreign investment in new industrial activities. In June 1965 it signed an agreement with a subsidiary of the Italian petroleum company Ente Nazionale Idrocarburi (ENI) for the establishment of a polyvinyl chloride plant, which calls for an Italian investment of 30 percent of the $55 million investment.

In addition to investments in major development projects, there are, according to official data, several small enterprises which have been set up by approximately 1,012 non-Saudi Arabs in Jidda, Riyadh, Mecca and in cities in Eastern Province. Over 75 percent of them are from the regions bordering Saudi Arabia on the south, and 143 are from the Persian Gulf region; the rest are Palestinian refugees, Jordanian, Syrian, Egyptian, Lebanese and Sudanese. Their businesses include groceries, haberdasheries, tailor shops, hotels and restaurants. They are all required to have a Saudi partner.

CHAPTER 24

MONETARY AND FINANCIAL SYSTEM

The monetary and financial system was brought into being by monetary and budgetary reforms carried out in 1960 to restore and maintain economic stability, which had been seriously threatened by a severe financial crisis beginning in 1956. The reforms fixed the rate of the official currency, the Saudi riyal, at SR4.50 to US$1, and replaced the bimetallic currency with paper money, fully backed by gold and foreign exchange. Fiscal controls were established for the first time over the annual government budget.

Since the reforms were carried out, annual state budgets have been prepared by the Ministry of Finance and National Economy and approved by the Council of Ministers and by the king. The concept of the budget as an instrument of financial policy has been accepted, thereby permitting a more carefully planned utilization of the country's vast oil revenue.

Oil revenues in the form of royalties, taxes and direct payments provided over 83 percent of total revenue in 1965. Customs duties accounted for approximately 4.6 percent of government receipts. Other receipts are from income taxes imposed on foreigners, but not on Saudi Arabs, from various indirect taxes imposed by the government for revenue purposes and from the *zakat,* a small traditional Moslem tax originally established to fulfill the Koranic requirement that Moslems give alms to support the needy. The size of the oil income has made it unnecessary to impose heavy tax burdens on the people.

The government's expenditure pattern has been changing since 1958 under the influence of Faisal Ibn Abd al-Aziz al-Faisal al-Saud, first as prime minister and since 1964 as king. There have been sharp decreases in expenditures for the royal family and increasing expenditures for agriculture, education, communications and other development activities, and for defense.

Increased government spending for economic development since the early 1960's has led to an expansion of the monetized sector of the economy, which until then had been based largely on trade in imported goods. The Saudi Arabian Monetary Agency (SAMA), created in 1952 as a modified central bank, plays a key role in assisting the government to adjust the monetary system to the changing economy. Its responsibilities include issuing the currency, holding the government's account and controlling fluctuations in local currency and foreign exchange.

The commercial banking system was still relatively underdeveloped in 1965, but greater economic activity and monetary stability had resulted in an increase in the number of banking institutions and in the use of banking facilities by private citizens. Larger numbers of Saudi Arabs have begun to deposit their funds in the banks and to demand credit from the banks for financing imports and investment activities. The system lacks specialized credit institutions; one, the Agricultural Bank, was created in 1963, and an industrial bank has been proposed but as of 1965 had not been established. The government, aware of the important role that sound banking practices play in the developing economy, was considering various means of regulating and improving the banking structure.

BACKGROUND

The first coin issued by the Saudi Government was a copper and nickel coin called the quirsh, issued in 1925 in the name of Abd al-Aziz Ibn Saud, "King of the Hejaz and Sultan of Nejd." It circulated with the silver riyal and copper quirsh struck by the Hashemite Government of the Hejaz. Other coins in circulation in the area included the British gold sovereign, the Turkish silver majidi, the Maria Theresa dollar, the Indian rupee and the gold dinar.

In 1928 the government established a bimetallic currency system. It issued the Saudi riyal, a silver coin using the British gold sovereign (1 sovereign then equaled US$4.87) as its standard base, with a value of 1 sovereign to SR10. The riyal was divided into 22 quirsh darij. The all-metal currency commanded the confidence of the people, who traditionally relied on the intrinsic metal content of money. A disadvantage of the system was the necessity of carrying heavy weights of metal and counting large quantities of coins for any sizable transactions. More important were the problems of instability and speculation presented by the bimetallic system.

Fluctuations in the values of the two currencies were determined primarily by the international supply and demand for gold and silver. The strong feeling, held by religious authorities, that Islamic law forbade fiduciary coins, that is, coins which circulate at a value above that of their metallic value content, made it necessary to use "full weight" silver riyals. Any significant rise in the world price of silver made it profitable to export the riyal or melt it down for use as silver bullion. The value of the internationally used British sovereign could not be controlled by Saudi Arabs. Neither government restrictions on the import and export of silver and gold nor the issuance in 1935 of a new silver riyal of smaller weight and size solved the problem.

It was extremely difficult to maintain a fixed rate between the riyal and the British gold sovereign. The public found it necessary to pay rates of exchange which covered the profits of the moneychangers of the banks—profits that were high enough to compensate for the risk of fluctuating exchange rates.

Until 1948 banking institutions were very limited; the only commercial bank was the Netherlands Trading Society, established in 1926. There was no central bank. Until 1932 a government-operated "General Finance Agency" handled some of the functions of a treasury and a central bank, including the collection and channeling of public revenues, minting of coins, handling of all official purchases and management of the public debt. The Ministry of Finance, established in 1932, took over the functions of the General Finance Agency.

In 1948 the French Banque de l'Indochine established a branch and the first two Saudi banking firms were created: the Partnership of Kaki and Mahfouz, which handled most of the government's local transactions, and the Bank Ibrahim Zahran. In 1950 the Jordanian Arab Bank, the British Bank of the Middle East, and the National Bank of Pakistan established branches in Jidda. The Egyptian Bank Misr also opened an office during this period, but operated on a sporadic basis.

Since the monetized sector of the economy was based almost entirely on import trade, commercial banking activities were generally limited to short-term financing of imports and, to a lesser extent, the financing of enterprises catering to pilgrims. The taking of interest has been interpreted by the religious authorities as unlawful gain, condemned by Koranic teachings and is therefore prohibited; the prohibition has restricted the development of banking as a savings and credit institution.

Saudi Arabians other than merchants preferred to hold their funds in the form of cash rather than in bank deposits. Savings of the great majority of Bedouin were invested in additional livestock; savings of the settled cultivators were kept in cash or invested in land if possible. Credit was sought by the majority from individual moneylenders or from family members. The banks earned their profits by charging commissions on credit, which they gave in the form of overdrafts on customers' current accounts, and by engaging in commercial dealings in jewelry.

Moneychangers centering in Jidda, the financial center, and in other large cities supplemented the moneychanging functions of the banks. After 1931 the government required the moneychangers to register, but their operations were not supervised or controlled except for an occasional requirement to adhere to officially fixed rates of exchange for certain currencies. Until 1952 there was no agency responsible for the regulation of monetary policy, and government interference in money matters went no further than attempts to control exchange rates between the riyal and the British gold sovereign.

The inadequacies of the currency and banking system became especially pronounced as oil revenues increased, providing a huge source of revenue in the form of foreign exchange. Revenue from oil had to be converted into riyals and sovereigns before it could be used locally; wide fluctuations in the value of the currency made conversion expensive and were harmful to foreign trade. For a country so dependent on imports, reduced foreign trade meant a lower standard of living.

The problems were aggravated by outmoded methods of handling of finances. Until World War II the pattern of income, expenditures and financial administration had remained essentially unaltered since the eighteenth century.

The first Saudi budget was published for fiscal year 1947–48, but subsequent budgets were published only irregularly. The budgets contained only rough estimates and were not used as an instrument of fiscal policy. The king's financial obligations included the financing of a small government machinery, the maintenance of charitable institutions, religious administration, gifts to the tribes, costly burdens of almost boundless generosity and hospitality, his personal requirement and the expenses of the royal household.

Before the growth in oil revenue, government income was small. It has been estimated that in 1932, for example, revenues amounted to the equivalent of approximately $2.5 million. Pilgrimage fees provided the major source of foreign exchange. The government charged the pilgrims fees fixed at the equivalent of about $56 and quarantine fees equivalent to about $14 per pilgrim. Customs duties in the 1930's were levied uniformly on all imports at an ad valorem rate of 8 percent.

The rapid increase in oil revenues after 1944, and especially after the end of World War II, led to a too-optimistic attitude toward oil as an infinitely large, never-ending source of revenue, which was translated into great expenditures by the government. The great importance that the Islamic religion attaches to charity and generosity influenced the expenditure pattern. Expenditures for religious endowments, hospitality and royal patronage reached unprecedented heights, allocations for social and economic development failed to match them.

By 1951 the government was becoming aware that if the revenue from oil was to be used for the development of the country, it was imperative to handle this huge source of revenue efficiently within an improved system of government financing. The government lacked the means to carry out effective currency measures and handle foreign exchange transactions.

An important step toward the modernization of the monetary and financial system was taken in 1951 when Minister of Finance Sheikh Abdullah al-Sulayman asked Arthur N. Young, of the United States Technical Cooperation Administration, for advice on some form of control over currency and fiscal affairs. A report subsequently submitted by Young proposed a plan for a "modified central bank." It was approved by King Abd al-Aziz, Crown Prince Saud, the minister of finance and other officials after they had made sure that it would not contravene Islamic law, and it became the basis for the charter of the SAMA.

The SAMA began operations in October 1952 with headquarters in Jidda. Later, branches were opened in Mecca, Medina, Dammam, Riyadh and Taif. Its monetary functions included stabilizing and maintaining the internal and external value of the currency; operating monetary reserves for purely monetary purposes; buying and selling gold and silver coins and bullion for government account; advising the government on all new coinage; procuring and issuing all coins; regulating commercial banks and moneychangers. Its fiscal functions included aiding the Ministry of Finance in centralizing the government receipts and expenditures by maintaining deposit accounts for the government and its agencies as directed by the Ministry of Finance, and acting as an agent of the government in paying out funds for purposes authorized by the government.

The SAMA was placed under the control of a board of directors comprising a president, a vice president, a governor and two other members. All members were appointed by royal decree upon nomination of the minister of finance. The first board of directors consisted of the minister of finance as president, the deputy minister of finance as vice president, and the governor and vice governor of the SAMA and two members representing commercial banks. The government supplied the initial capital of the equivalent of approximately $6 million.

During its first few years, the SAMA introduced several improvements into the monetary system. The government retained the bimetallic currency standard, but replaced the British gold sovereign by a national gold currency in the dual system, thereby permitting greater control over the value of the currency. In October 1952, Minister of Finance Sheikh al-Sulayman announced the introduction of the Saudi gold sovereign (SS). The Saudi sovereign was of the same size, weight and fineness as the British sovereign. The exchange rate between the Saudi riyal and the sovereign was set at 40 to 1 and was to be maintained unless changes in the world prices of gold and silver rendered it impractical. No fixed foreign exchange parity was set, but the sovereign was not to exceed $11. The SAMA was required to keep a special currency reserve fund of United States dollars and/or gold to maintain the value of the Saudi sovereign. By the end of 1953 good imitations of the Saudi sovereign, minted abroad and sent to Saudi Arabia, appeared in circulation and eventually led to the withdrawal of the Saudi sovereign in 1954.

The SAMA initially established a stabilization rate for the riyal at about 3.69 per $1. In November 1954 the official rate was set at 3.75. For 2½ years there was price and exchange stability in a market free of controls of exchange or trade, as the world price of silver was maintained relatively constant.

Although SAMA was not authorized to issue paper currency, it issued notes in 1953 called Pilgrims' Receipts, a form of paper currency printed in various languages and issued to facilitate currency transactions for the pilgrims traveling to Mecca. Because they lacked intrinsic value, the Receipts were not considered legal tender, but being initially fully backed with gold and foreign exchange, they were accepted throughout the country. They served to give flexibility to the currency during periods of seasonal fluctuations and eventually to replace riyals which were smuggled out of the country when the world price of silver began to rise in 1955.

In regard to the regulation of commercial banks, SAMA required all commercial banks to register with it and to make monthly reports concerning purchases and sales of foreign currencies. Commercial banking expanded in the early 1950's in response to the increasing need for banks and to the high profits accruing to the banking business. In 1955, SAMA requested all new branches of foreign banks in Saudi Arabia to submit applications to the Agency. The applications were then referred to the Ministry of Finance with SAMA's recommendations. Before approval, the banks' officers had to sign "bank guarantees" promising to abide by domestic laws and regulations. Moneychangers had to submit statements on capital and annual volume of business.

In fiscal matters, SAMA's powers were gradually curtailed. In 1953 a Ministry of National Economy was established and subsequently joined to the Ministry of Finance. In 1954 the Ministry of Finance and National Economy was given the responsibility of insuring closer government adherence to official budgets. It was empowered to supervise the accounts of the other ministries, which were requested to deposit their collected revenues with SAMA and to withdraw them only by means of checks which were countersigned by the Ministry of Finance and National Economy for purposes authorized by the budget. Any surplus accrued by a particular ministry was to be placed in a general reserve fund. All revenues and expenditures were to be audited by the Ministry of Finance and National Economy.

The constitution of the Council of Ministers, approved by King Saud in 1954, outlined the powers of the Council, including those relating to the financial matters of the state. The approval of the Council of Ministers was made necessary for the annual budget, the year-end balance sheet of the state, all new appropriations, and various other financial matters. An Office of the Comptroller General of State Accounts was attached directly to that of the prime minister. It possessed auditing powers over the accounts of all government agencies and could submit any critical or commendatory findings to the Council of Ministers.

There was, nevertheless, a severe economic imbalance which began in 1956. No precise statistical information exists for the period, but the primary cause of the economic imbalance was the inflationary deficit financing of government expenditures. Rapid increases in government expenditures which had accompanied equally rapid increases in oil revenues were not arrested when oil revenues leveled off between 1956 and 1958. The deficit was financed with external and internal loans, the latter coming mostly from SAMA, which in 1955 had been empowered to extend credit to the government. Deficit financing meant an increase in purchasing power, which was quickly translated into an increase in demand for imports and increasing difficulties in the balance of payments.

The exchange value of the riyal declined steadily from a free market rate, which had been approximately the same as the official rate of SR3.75 to $1, to SR6.18 by November 1957. The rapid depreciation raised prices and the cost of living. Capital flight due to loss of confidence aggravated the balance-of-payment problem.

By late 1957 the government's indebtedness to SAMA reached SR700 million, and, in early 1958, SAMA reserves for the backing of the currency were down to 14 percent of the currency in circulation, which was estimated at SR600 million. The government had discontinued the minting of gold and silver coin in 1955, and most of the currency in circulation was in the form of Pilgrims' Receipts. Despite the imposition of licensing controls on imports and capital export controls, the free market value of the riyal continued to decline; by early 1958 it had dropped to 6.25 to $1.

In June 1958 the government announced a stabilization program. On advice from consultants from the International Monetary Fund (IMF) and the International Bank for Reconstruction and Development (IBRD), temporary emergency measures were quickly applied to check the deterioration of the riyal and settle the public debt.

The controls restricted imports by requiring importers of nonessential goods to purchase foreign exchange at the free market rate; only the importers of foodstuffs and essentials were financed by the government at the official rate of SR3.75 to $1. Some price controls were established on essential goods. Taxes were imposed on such items as gasoline and automobiles, and higher duties were levied on luxury items.

In accordance with IMF advice, SAMA's regulations were revised. It was given greater control over commercial banks. Every bank had to maintain a fixed percentage of its deposits on reserve with the Agency. The power to grant loans to the government was withdrawn from the Agency. Its board of directors was henceforth to consist of a chairman and a vice chairman and three members who were not to be government employees. Since all decisions of the board were to be made by majority vote, SAMA was made independent of direct government control.

The new statute of the Council of Ministers, promulgated by royal decree in May 1958 contained a number of the financial reforms proposed by the IMF consultants. It provided for annual budgets to be approved by the Council of Ministers and the king. It strengthened controls over spending, borrowing and for auditing procedures.

The aim of the stabilization program in regard to budgetary matters was to restrict government spending in order to end deficit financing. In fact, surpluses were to be created for a number of years in order to repay the government debt. Expansion of expenditures was to be allowed only when the financial system was considered by the government to be out of crisis.

As a result of the successful implementation of the emergency stabilization program and government austerity, the value of the riyal appreciated. By July 1959 the free market rate of the riyal was down to SR4.75 per $1; it leveled off at the rate of SR4.5 per $1 by December 1959. It had been estimated that wholesale prices fell by about 15 to 20 percent during this period. Strict adherence to the budgetary controls led to substantial budgetary surpluses and the repayment of the internal debt to SAMA by 1960.

The government's definitive reform program, announced in December 1959, went into effect in January 1960. The rate of the Saudi riyal was officially set at SR4.50 to $1. The SAMA was given the power to issue official legal tender notes—that is, paper money—for the first time in the country's monetary history, but was required to back its issue fully with gold and foreign currencies. Pilgrims' Receipts were withdrawn in exchange for the agency's new notes. The gold sovereign was redeemed for SR40 per sovereign. SAMA was required to publish a fortnightly statement and an annual report of its operations, and was empowered to sell and purchase gold and foreign exchange in the market for the purpose of stabilizing the national currency.

The reforms of 1958–60 were generally well received, both at home and abroad. Providing the basis for a substantially improved system of monetary and financial administration, they paved the way for a better utilization of the ample oil revenues for social and economic development.

MONEY SUPPLY

Monetary developments are generally determined by foreign trade and the level of domestic spending. The monetized sector of the economy is primarily based on the production and exportation of oil, but government spending of the oil revenues on economic development projects since 1962 has resulted in increased economic activities on a broad front. As the economy developed, the monetized sector expanded and the money supply increased.

Relatively complete monetary data have been provided by SAMA since 1960 and indicate the changes in the size and composition of the money supply in Saudi Arabia (see table 12). The money supply, representing currency in circulation and private demand deposits, has been increasing. The rate of increase has largely depended on the level of government spending and the flow of imports. In 1963, for example, the money supply was 21 percent above the 1962 level because of a steep rise in government spending and a lag in imports. In 1964 government spending was more modest and imports increased; the rate of monetary expansion was only 7 percent.

Table 12. Money Supply in Saudi Arabia, 1960–64[1]
(in millions of riyals[2])

Year	Currency in Circulation	Demand Deposits	Total Money Supply
1960	514.53	398.22	912.75
1961	625.88	373.85	999.73
1962	672.52	408.67	1,081.19
1963	847.10	462.27	1,309.37
1964	893.00	510.40	1,403.40

[1] Calendar years 1960–64 are roughly approximate to Moslem fiscal years 1380–84 A.H. (*anno hegirae*).
[2] SR4.50 equal US$1.
Source: Adapted from Saudi Arabian Monetary Agency, *Annual Report 1383–84 A.H.*, p. 17.

Currency in circulation in 1965 represents still over 60 percent of the money supply as a result of the relative lack of use of banking facilities, but the use of demand deposits has been increasing. Demand deposits accounted for 37.4 percent of the money supply in 1961 and 37.8 percent in 1962. Although in 1963 their proportion of the money decreased to 35.2 percent, the absolute increase of SR54 million in demand deposits was the largest recorded since the stabilization program. In 1964 demand deposits increased more sharply than did currency in circulation, raising their proportion to 36.3 percent of the money supply.

BANKING AND CREDIT

Increased economic activity necessitated the expansion of banking facilities and has encouraged the establishment of banks in the country. Of the 12 commercial banks operating in Saudi Arabia at the end of 1964, 9 were foreign owned and 3—the National Commercial Bank, Riyadh Bank and Bank Ibrahim Zahran—were locally owned. Twenty-nine branches have been established through the country.

The greater confidence in the monetary system which resulted from the implementation of the reforms of 1958–60 has encouraged more people to use the banking facilities. Both demand deposit accounts and time and savings deposits increased sharply after 1960. In 1964 total deposits reached SR784 million. The IMF reported in 1965 that the Saudi-owned banks accounted for about 60 percent of total deposits.

Commercial banks have increased the number of loans and advances to the private sector since the early 1960's. In 1965 private demand for credit was still largely determined by the demand for imports, but bank credit increasingly was being utilized for various investment activities, particularly in the residential and commercial construction business. Credit to the private sector rose modestly in 1962 and 1963; in 1964 it rose sharply (17.7 percent) to reach a level of SR737 million by the end of the year (see table 13). The rate of the commission charged by the banks for their credit services is reportedly equivalent to approximately 6 percent.

Table 13. Commercial Bank Operations in Saudi Arabia, 1961–64[1]
(in millions of riyals[2])

	1961	1962	1963	1964
Cash in hand and with Saudi Arabian Monetary Agency	125	146	182	164
Net foreign assets (+) or liabilities (−)	−53	−57	+59	+83
Loans and advances to the private sector	565	642	625	737
Total deposits (excluding interbank transactions)	528	597	685	784

[1] Calendar years 1961–64 are roughly approximate to Moslem fiscal years 1381–84 A.H. (anno hegirae).
[2] SR4.50 equal US$1.

Source: Adapted from Saudi Arabian Monetary Agency, *Annual Report 1383–84 A.H.*, p. 18.

The identification of interest with usury, which is proscribed by Islamic law, precludes the use of the interest rate as a regulator of credit extension. The power of the commercial banks to extend credit is limited only by the requirement that they keep a certain percentage of their deposits on reserve with SAMA. In July 1962 the reserve requirement was lowered from 15 percent to 10 percent, thereby increasing their potential lending ability.

In spite of minimum control over the operations of commercial banks, SAMA reported in 1965 that credit extension had not been excessive. In part this was because banks had found it profitable to invest a portion of their liquid assets abroad. A draft of a Banking Control Law, intended to guard against possible dangers of inflation, was pending before the Council of Ministers in 1965.

The SAMA took steps to ensure that banking activities continue to spread and to improve in order to keep pace with the kingdom's economic development. It established a committee to report on the banking situation and on ways of increasing the appeal of banking services among the people.

SAMA has also shown an awareness of the need for specialized credit institutions. The only specialized credit bank, the Agricultural Bank, was established in April 1963, with its head office in Riyadh. It was established with an intial capital of SR30 million and was authorized to grant credit to individuals, groups, institutions and organizations working in agriculture, and to guarantee loans made to agriculture from other sources. It may issue short-term credit for up to 12 months, medium-term credit for up to 5 years, and long-term credit for between 15 and 20 years. The Bank began operations in the summer of 1963, and by the end of that summer it had reportedly received 10,000 credit application forms. In April 1965 it was reported that 262 short-term loans, totaling SR1.3 million, in the form of such agricultural equipment as tractors, pumps and fertilizers, had been extended to farmers in 11 areas. An industrial bank has been proposed; funds were allocated for its establishment, but by the end of 1965 they had not been utilized.

FISCAL ADMINISTRATION

The financial affairs of the state are under the authority of the Council of Ministers. Since the reforms of 1958–60 there has been an official separation between the general budget and allocations for the royal family.

All government receipts enter the account of the Ministry of Finance and National Economy and are administered by SAMA and its branches. The receipts can be disbursed only in accordance with the annual budget, which is intended to provide control over government expenditures. The central government budget is prepared by the budget department of the Ministry of Finance and National Economy after it has received the estimates of expenditures from the various ministries. The budget is submitted to the Council of Ministers at least 1 month before the beginning of the new fiscal year, which begins on the first day of the seventh month, Rajab, of the lunar year. The Council then approves it sector by sector. In its deliberations the Council of Ministers may be advised by the Ministry of Finance and National Economy, by committees especially set up by the Council to deal with various economic questions, and by the SAMA. After it is approved by the Council of Ministers, the budget is submitted to the king for his ratification. Since King Faisal is also Prime Minister and thus chairs the Council of Ministers, his approval as king is automatic.

Any expenditure not provided for in the budget must be approved by the Council. No transfers from one category of the budget to another can be made without that body's approval. No transfers from one subcategory to another can be made without the approval of the minister of finance and national economy.

Although the Ministry of Finance and National Economy is responsible for the collection of *zakat*, income taxes and custom duties, the Council of Ministers must approve all taxes, or the incurrence of government debt. In addition, the Council's approval is necessary for the granting of monopolies and concessions, the sale, usufruct or lease of state property, and for all salaries and compensations, utilizing state funds.

Until fiscal year 1966 a development budget was prepared separately from the general budget, but the two were published at the same time. Until 1965 the Supreme Planning Council, established in 1961, was responsible for preparing the development budget and allocating among various projects the funds provided for economic development in the general budget. It functioned as a ministerial subcommittee; its members consisted of the ministers concerned with various aspects of economic development and it was presided over by the prime minister. The Supreme Council's staff planned and supervised the implementation of projects.

A royal decree in January 1965 replaced the Supreme Planning Council with the Central Planning Organization, assigning to it the technical aspects of planning and followup, but leaving to the Ministry of Finance and National Economy the responsibility for the financial aspects of the earlier council's responsibilities. The Organization consists of 12 economic advisers with a supporting staff, and is headed by a president with ministerial rank. In addition, planning units established by the various ministries are to function in cooperation with the Central Planning Organization.

Tasks of the Central Planning Organization include the preparation of the economic development plans which are submitted to the Council of Ministers for its consideration. It assists the Ministry of Finance and National Economy by estimating the costs of projects, and it aids the ministries and independent agencies in their economic planning. In addition, it is to give technical advice to the king and to prepare economic reports on the progress and possibilities of economic development in the country. The Organization was working in 1965 on a detailed report that would form the basis of a 5-year plan which the government intends to complete as soon as possible (see ch. 18, Character and Structure of the Economy).

The reorganization of the planning machinery is part of the government's general effort to reorganize the entire administrative system and indicates the importance which the government gives to economic development in its policy considerations.

BUDGET

The general budget for fiscal year 1964–65 amounted to SR3,112 million, representing a 15.9 percent increase over the 1963–64 budget which amounted to SR2,686 million. It is financed entirely from internal sources, the largest of which is oil revenue.

The schedule of expenditures in the general budget is divided into four major categories: Chapter I, consisting of salaries and emoluments; Chapter II, consisting of the expenditures by the ministries, departments and other governmental branches for their general operations, including those dealing with development; Chapter III, including allocations to the private treasury of the royal family, a special allocation for national defense, government contributions for pensions, grants to organizations, subsidies for essential commodities, *hadj* (pilgrimage) and hospitality expenses, and additional allocations to various ministries; and Chapter IV, covering the government's development projects included in the general budget. In the general budget for 1964–65, Chapter I accounted for approximately 35.7 percent of the total (SR1,112 million); Chapter II accounted for approximately 20.3 percent (SR633 million); Chapter III, for 19.5 percent (SR606 million); and Chapter IV, for 24.5 percent (SR762 million).

In 1964 allocations to the development budget totaled SR1,205 million; they included the entire SR762 million allocation for projects—that is, Chapter IV expenditures—in the general budget, an allocation of SR321 million from the Economic Development Fund made in previous years, but expected to materialize only in the current year, and new allocations from the General Reserve and Economic Development Funds amounting to SR122 million. As the general budget included expenditures for development, as well as for current operations, the distinction between the two budgets is not clear. It appears that the general budget included only current expenditures on development, whereas the development budget covered longer term projects for which allocations are made each year.

Expenditure Pattern

Some changes have occurred in the pattern of expenditures in the general budget during the years following the 1960 financial reforms. Expenditures for the private royal treasury have decreased substantially in both relative and absolute terms. In 1961 these expenditures amounted to SR248 million, or 14.4 percent of the budget. By 1965, however, they were down to SR173 million, or 5.5 percent of total expenditures (see table 14). On the other hand, allocations to the National Guard and to the Ministry of Defense and Aviation, excluding those for civil aviation, amounted in 1961 to SR243 million, or about 14 percent of total expenditures. By 1965 they had reached SR543 million, representing 17.4 percent of the total expenditures (see ch. 25, The Armed Forces).

The sharpest increase has been in expenditures in the general budget for capital projects, reflecting the greater emphasis now being given to development. In 1961 the allocation for projects of SR291 million was already almost three times larger than the allocation for that purpose for the previous year. By 1965 it had increased to SR762 million, constituting 24.5 percent of the general budget.

Since part of the general budget allocations to the ministries is spent on development purposes, the Ministry of Finance and National Economy has estimated that SR1,792 million, or 58 percent of total budgeted expenditures for 1965, are actually related to development as compared to the parallel proportion of 45 percent (SR1,200 million) for 1964.

Less complete data are available on the actual spending of the government, but SAMA has reported substantial shortfalls. For example, actual government expenditures during 1963 amounted to SR2,195 million compared to the expenditures estimated in the general budget of SR2,686 million.

Expenditures in the development budget were dominated by those for transportation and communication, which in fiscal year 1965 amounted to SR417.7 million, or 34.7 percent of the budget. These expenditures reflect the governmental concern in providing an adequate communications network to connect the major areas of the country (see ch. 22, Domestic Trade). Also of major significance were the allocations for projects geared to improving the living conditions in the municipalities. In 1965 estimated expenditures for municipalities amounted to SR197.2 million, or 16.4 percent of the development budget (see table 15).

Significant changes in the expenditure pattern of the development budget in recent years have been sharp increases in the spending for projects related to the development of agriculture, livestock, and water and for those related to petroleum and mineral resources. Expenditures for education are also significant; they have fluctuated in relative terms in recent years, but have increased substantially in absolute terms.

Table 14. *Estimated Expenditures in the General Budgets of Saudi Arabia, 1964 and 1965*[1]
(amounts in millions of riyals[2])

	1964		1965	
	Amount	Percent	Amount	Percent
Private royal treasury	183	6.8	173	5.5
Royal Cabinet	10	0.3	6	0.2
Council of Ministers	11	0.4	14	0.5
Ministry of Defense and Aviation[3]	384	14.3	441	14.2
National Guard	134	5.0	146	4.7
Royal Body Guard	22	0.8		
Ministry of Foreign Affairs	39	1.5	49	1.6
Ministry of Labor and Social Affairs	55	2.0	62	2.0
Ministry of Interior	228	8.5	276	8.9
Ministry of Education[4]	292	10.8	329	10.6
Ministry of Communications[5]	144	5.4	119	3.7
Ministry of Agriculture and Water	58	2.2	67	2.2
Ministry of Finance and National Economy	61	2.3	63	2.0
Ministry of Petroleum and Mineral Resources	11	0.4	12	0.4
Ministry of Health	103	3.9	117	3.8
Ministry of Commerce and Industry	10	0.4	11	0.3
Ministry of Pilgrimage and Religious Foundations	32	1.2	34	1.1
Ministry of Justice	24	0.9	25	0.7
Ministry of Information	17	0.6	22	0.7
Religious organizations	14	0.5	15	0.5
Emirates of provinces	28	1.1		
Emergency expenses	60	2.2	60	1.9
Projects	550	20.5	762	24.5
Other expenditures	186	6.9	279	9.0
Cost increases and subsidies resulting from devaluation of the riyal	30	1.1	30	1.0
Total	2,686	100.0	3,112	100.0

[1] Calendar years 1964 and 1965 are roughly approximate to Moslem fiscal years 1384 and 1385 A.H. (*anno hegirae*).

[2] SR4.50 equal US$1.

[3] Includes allocations for civil aviation of SR38 million in 1964 and SR44 million in 1965.

[4] Includes other expenditures for education not administered by the Ministry of Education, most of which are administered by the Grand Mufti's office.

[5] Includes government subsidies of SR87 million in 1964 and SR57 million in 1965 to Saudi Government Railroad, Saudi Arabian Airlines and Posts, Telephone and Telegraph, to cover their operating deficits and capital investments.

Source: Adapted from Saudi Arabian Monetary Agency, *Annual Report 1383–84 A.H.*, pp. 38, 39.

Table 15. Estimated Development Budgets of Saudi Arabia, 1963–65[1]
(amounts in millions of riyals[2])

	1963 Original Allocations	1963 Percent	1964 Original Allocations	1964 Percent	1965 Original Allocations	1965 Percent
Transport and communications	178.5	32.5	196.9	28.1	417.7	34.7
Agriculture, livestock and water	34.3	6.2	86.6	12.3	149.0	12.4
Petroleum and minerals	7.5	1.4	23.3	3.3	94.7	7.8
Industry and commerce	1.8	0.3	8.7	1.2	7.9	0.7
Labor and social affairs	12.4	2.3	6.2	0.9	14.4	1.2
Education	35.4	6.4	60.8	8.7	74.1	6.1
Health and Red Crescent Society	11.6	2.1	16.0	2.3	23.5	1.9
Municipalities	87.8	16.0	110.4	15.7	197.2	16.4
Mosques	40.0	7.3	40.0	5.7	65.9	5.5
Pilgrimage affairs	3.4	0.6	1.9	0.3	15.6	1.3
Others	137.3	24.9	150.8	21.5	145.2	12.0
Total	550.0	100.0	[3]701.6	100.0	[4]1,205.2	100.0

[1] Calendar years 1963–65 are roughly approximate to Moslem fiscal years 1383–85 A.H. (anno hegirae).
[2] SR4.50 equal US$1.
[3] Including SR550 million allocated from the State Budget and SR151.6 million allocated from the Economic Development Fund.
[4] Including SR762 million allocated from the State Budget, SR122 million additional allocations from the General Reserve and Reserve Fund and SR321 million previous allocations from the Economic Development Fund for projects under execution.

Source: Adapted from Saudi Arabian Monetary Agency, *Annual Report 1383–84 A.H.*, p. 8.

Significant shortfalls are especially characteristic of development expenditures because of a lack of adequately planned projects ready for implementation. In 1963, for example, estimated expenditures in the development budget totaled SR550 million, but the actual expenditures reached only SR436.8 million.

The general budget for fiscal year 1966, published in October 1965, marked a record high of SR3,961 million—an increase of 27 percent over the general budget for 1965. It reflected the government's continuing concern with economic and social development, as greatest increases in estimated expenditures were for development projects. Allocations for the development projects were for the first time spelled out in Chapter IV (Projects), of the general budget, rather than in separately prepared development budget. The allocations under Chapter IV amounted to SR1,402 million, compared to SR762 million in 1965; those under Chapters I, II,

III, covering current expenditures, totaled SR2,559 million, compared to SR2,113 million in 1965.

Ordinary revenues, again derived mostly from oil, were estimated at SR3,614 million. Allocations of SR100 million from the Economic Development Fund and SR247 million from the General Reserve Fund, which were used toward financing economic development projects, brought the total revenue to SR3,961 million to balance the budget. With an additional SR259 million, consisting of funds from the Economic Development Fund, which were allocated but not spent in the previous year, total funds available for development added up to SR1,662 million, compared to SR1,205 million in the previous year.

The changes in the organization of the new budget rendered difficult the comparison of its expenditures for specific sectors with those in previous years. Statements by the Ministry of Finance and National Economy indicated, however, the major items in the budget. The largest expenditures are for communications, which include the construction of highways, the expansion of ports, the extension of the automatic telephone network, and the improvement of the Saudi Arabian Airlines. The allocation for the Ministry of Communications amounted to SR736 million, or 18.7 percent of total expenditures.

It was followed in importance by the allocation for defense, including the National Guard, which totaled SR731 million, or 18.6 percent of the budget. The third largest allocation was that for the Ministry of Education, which received SR515 million, or 13.0 percent. Other major allocations included those for Ministry of Agriculture and Water, SR288 million, or 7.3 percent; municipalities, SR280 million, or 7.1 percent; Ministry of Health, SR162 million, or 4.1 percent; Ministry of Petroleum and Mineral Resources, SR119 million, or 3.0 percent; Ministry of Labor and Social Affairs, SR97 million, or 2.4 percent; and Ministry of Information, SR75 million, or 1.9 percent.

Sources of Revenue

Oil is by far the largest source of revenue. In recent years it has accounted for between 70 and 90 percent of total government receipts in the form of royalties, income taxes and various direct payments, which are handled by the Ministry of Finance and National Economy. In 1965 oil revenues totaled SR2,592 million, constituting 83.2 percent of total revenues. Of this, SR813.4 million was derived from royalties and SR1,779 million from income tax and other minor fees and taxes.

Other sources of revenue are small in comparison to that derived from oil. Customs duties accounted for 4.6 percent, almost SR142 million, of the 1965 budget. Other revenue items included road taxes and fees for government services, such as railroad, airport, postal, telephone and telegraph fees. Transfers from the Economic Development Fund and General Reserve Fund added SR150 million to the total revenues (see table 16). The General Reserve is a fund which holds any additional revenue and savings from expenditures as estimated in the budgets, and is used as a balancing item.

Table 16. Estimated Revenues in the General Budgets of Saudi Arabia, 1964 and 1965[1]
(amounts in millions of riyals[2])

	1964 Amount	1964 Percent	1965 Amount	1965 Percent
Oil royalties	721.4	26.9	813.4	26.1
Income tax[3]	1,563.0	58.2	1,793.1	57.6
Tapline transit fees	18.5	0.7	1.8	0.1
Customs duties	136.0	5.1	141.8	4.6
Municipal fees	8.0	0.3	9.0	0.3
Port fees	9.5	0.4	10.0	0.3
Public service fees	10.0	0.4	15.0	0.5
Railroad, airport and posts, telephone and telegraph fees	31.5	1.2	30.0	1.0
Service payments by investment companies	5.8	0.2	5.8	0.2
Residence permits, passports and nationality booklets	3.5	0.1	4.0	0.1
Automobile fees	4.0	0.1	5.6	0.2
Road tax	35.0	1.3	38.0	1.2
Sale and rental of state property	6.0	0.2	6.5	0.2
Miscellaneous revenues	73.8	2.7	88.0	2.8
Transfers from Economic Development Fund			50.0	1.6
General reserve	60.0	2.2	100.0	3.2
Total	2,686.0	100.0	3,112.0	100.0

[1] Calendar years 1964 and 1965 are roughly approximate to Moslem fiscal years 1384 and 1385 A.H. (*anno hegirae*).

[2] SR4.50 equal US$1.

[3] Almost entirely from oil companies.

Source: Adapted from Saudi Arabian Monetary Agency, *Circular on Saudi Arabian Budget Estimates for 1384–85 A.H.*, p. 4.

Oil Revenue

Revenue from the three oil companies operating under concession agreements with the Saudi Arabian Government, the Arabian American Oil Company (Aramco), Getty Oil Company, and the Japanese Arabian Oil Company, amounted to SR455 million in 1963. This is the source of the government's foreign exchange. Aramco provided over 92 percent of the total revenue, Getty Oil provided 5 percent, and the Japanese Arabian Oil Company provided approximately 2.8 percent.

On the basis of the original concession agreement with Aramco in 1933, payment was initially in the form of loans, deductible from future royalties and taxes, and rental charges. Aramco undertook to pay a royalty of 4 gold shillings per ton of crude oil produced, less the petroleum used by the company or supplied to the government. The royalty could be paid in gold or its equivalent in sterling or dollars. A royalty on natural gas was set at 12.5 percent of sales receipts. Until 1950 Aramco was exempted from all local taxes and trade duties.

In December 1950, after prolonged discussions, Aramco signed an agreement with the government which called for a 50–50 profit-sharing arrangement. Henceforth, the government would receive a sum equal to half of the company's annual gross income after deducting operating, exploration and development expenses, depreciation and initially foreign taxes. The half-share would include the fixed royalties, the miscellaneous fees and levies and income taxes paid by the company to the government. The payments could be made in any proportion that currency bore to total receipts of the company.

Since 1950 there have been several agreements which have affected the company's payments to the government. In 1954, Aramco agreed to discontinue the practice of granting bulk discounts on takeoff oil to its parent companies. It paid to the government a retroactive settlement of $70 million for the discounts it had allowed between December 1951 and October 1953. In 1956, Aramco agreed to subject the profits earned at the refinery at Ras Tanura to the equal profit-sharing agreement.

In March 1963 an important agreement concluded between the government, Aramco and the Trans-Arabian Pipeline Company (Tapline) further affected Aramco's tax payments to the government. The tax payments are based on posted prices as set by the company, rather than actual prices at which sales are made. Until the time of the agreement, the posted prices at Ras Tanura on the Persian Gulf were used as the basis for the calculation of the government's share of profits. The new arrangement called for the recalculation of profits on oil delivered through Tapline to Zahrani, the Mediterranean terminal, near Sidon, Lebanon, on the basis of the higher prices posted at Sidon. This meant higher calculated profits for Aramco and therefore higher revenue for the government. The agreement was made retroactive to October 1953 and, according to the Saudi Arabian minister of petroleum and mineral resources, involved a sum equivalent to over $160 million, which was credited to the specially created Economic Development Fund.

In January 1965 another agreement was made modifying the profit-sharing arrangement. It provided that certain royalties would be considered an expense deductible rather than a subtraction from the income tax imposed on Aramco's operating income. In addition, it provided for specified discounts on posted prices on oil sold to Aramco nonaffiliates. The increase in revenues resulting from this agreement is also credited to the Economic Development Fund.

The Getty Oil Company was granted a concession in 1949, covering the Saudi half-interest in the Saudi-Kuwait Neutral Zone, and began exporting oil in 1954. In 1965 it provided revenue to the government through royalties set at $.55 a barrel of net crude oil, payable in dollars, and at 12.5 percent of gross receipts from the sale of natural gas. It also paid the government 20 percent of net profits from the sale of refined products and 25 percent from the sale of crude products before the deduction of foreign taxes.

The Japanese Arabian Oil Company obtained in 1957 a concession covering the Saudi share of the offshore area in the Saudi-Kuwait Neutral Zone. The terms of the agreement assign 56 percent of the company's total net profits to the government. The assigned share is to be paid in royalties set at 20 percent of annual production, including taxes and the production of asphalt and gas. If the payment falls short of the 56 percent, the company is to make a direct payment to the government, covering the difference.

In 1965 a concession agreement was concluded between the government and the French owned Auxiliaire de la Regie Autonome des Petroles (AUXIRAP) for oil exploitation in the Red Sea coastal area. Under this agreement the government will receive a 15 percent royalty which will be increased to 20 percent if production exceeds 80,000 barrels a day. Other payments are bonuses amounting to $5.5 million, $4 million of which was payable only when production reaches the level of 70 barrels of crude oil a day for 90 consecutive days, and rental charges ranging from $5 per square kilometer for the first 5 years to $500 during the last 5 years of a 30-year period. In addition the company will pay a 40 percent income tax (see ch. 20, Industry; ch. 23, Foreign Economic Relations).

Income Tax

The first income tax law was issued by royal decree in November 1950. It imposed income taxes on corporation profits and on all personal income in excess of SR5,000. Since a strict interpretation of Islamic law forbids the imposition of any direct tax other than the *zakat* (alms tax) on Moslems, the former minister of finance, Sheikh Abdullah al-Sulayman, attempted to justify the income tax on the basis of the need to capitalize the economy by obtaining revenue from sources which were noncommercial and therefore otherwise untaxable. The tax on Saudi Arabian nationals was abandoned in 1956 under the pressure of the ulema. Only those companies having non-Saudi capital pay corporate income taxes. The law provides that all non-Saudi Arabs pay tax on personal income derived from salaries, wages, fees, or compensation for any work done within the kingdom, and on income derived from invested capital. The law, including subsequent amendments, allows an exemption of SR6,000 for both personal and profit income.

The tax rates applying to an individual's income are 5 percent on total taxable income up to SR20,000; 10 percent on income between SR20,000 and SR50,000; and 20 percent on income in excess of SR50,000. Tax rates on net profits of corporatism having non-Saudi capital are 20 percent on profits up to SR100,000; 30 percent on profits ranging from SR100,000 to SR500,000; 35 percent on profits ranging from SR500,000 to SR1 million; and 40 percent on profits exceeding SR1 million. Total revenue from income taxes in fiscal 1964–65 amounted to SR1,793 million, or 57.6 percent of total government receipts, consisting mostly of income taxes paid by the oil companies.

Zakat

A third source of revenue is *zakat*, a traditional tax which is required of every Moslem. *Zakat* is an outgrowth of the Koranic command to the faithful to give alms and reflects the Islamic viewpoint that the surplus wealth of the rich should be distributed among the needy. Historically, however, payment of *zakat* acquired a political meaning. Among the Bedouin, especially, it has signified a recognition of the temporal sovereignty of the ruler under whose authority it is collected, in return for reciprocal benefits of protection.

As a source of revenue, *zakat* has always been relatively insignificant. The tax was fixed at 2.5 percent of an individual's capital or an established proportion of all his property in the form of livestock, agricultural produce, gold and silver, and merchandise. The government collected only one-half of the 2.5 percent on the premise that the difference will be used by the taxpayer for charity, accountable only to God. It is probable that the only people who pay *zakat* regularly are large property owners and the employees of the larger organizations and the government which keep regular accounts. Nomadic tribes increasingly felt that they had a right to subsidies from the king and felt less and less obligation to pay any taxes.

Zakat has traditionally been collected by two groups. One has been responsible for collecting the tax on merchandise, trade, gold, silver and agricultural produce in the villages. These collectors normally are residents of the villages and are appointed by local administration and paid on a commission basis. After the sale of produce the receipts are forwarded to the government. The other group collects the taxes on livestock; the collectors meet with the tribes of nomads at customary watering places at previously established times to estimate and collect the *zakat* from each individual. A taxpayer's testimony usually is accepted as sufficient proof of the extent of his property. The tax is collected immediately if possible, in cash or in kind, although cash is becoming more common. The receipts are taken to the emir under whose jurisdiction the tribe falls and are then forwarded by him to the Department of Zakat and Income Tax of the Ministry of Finance and National Economy.

SECTION IV. NATIONAL SECURITY

CHAPTER 25

THE ARMED FORCES

The armed forces in late 1965 numbered about 40,000, including the Royal Saudi Army, the small Royal Saudi Air Force and the very small Royal Saudi Navy under the Ministry of Defense and Aviation, and the National Guard—frequently referred to as the White Army—under the personal control of the king. The regular army and the National Guard each numbered about 20,000 men. The former Royal Guard, an elite force of some 4,000 officers and men directly controlled by the king, was incorporated into the regular army as an infantry regiment in the spring of 1964.

MILITARY BACKGROUND

Saudi Arabia was created between 1902 and 1926 through the conquests of Abd al-Aziz Ibn Saud. The first step in the process was taken in January 1902, when Abd al-Aziz (then 22 years old), with a small band of followers, recaptured Riyadh, the former seat of the Saudi emirate, which had been taken in 1891 by rival tribes under the Rashid family. Thereafter, he followed the aggressive policy which steadily won to his side the tribes first of the Nejd, and later of Al-Hasa (now Eastern Province), Hejaz and Asir (see ch. 3, Historical Setting).

The forcefulness of Abd al-Aziz's personality and the attraction for the Bedouin (nomadic) tribes of the militant puritanism of the orthodox Islamic sect founded by Mohammed Ibn Abd al-Wahhab in the early eighteenth century gained the Saudi leader the personal loyalty of an increasing number of the Nejdi tribes and permitted him to go from victory to victory in his struggle with the Rashids for control of the Nejd. By 1906 the Saudi forces had regained the central Nejd.

Realizing that his position depended upon the sometimes uncertain loyalty of the tribes and towns under his rule, Abd al-Aziz sent Wahhabi missionaries to the tribes to promote the establishment of Ikhwan (religious brotherhood) communities of mixed tribal composition. To these settlements he issued seed, farm tools and money as well as arms and ammunition. In each settled community, mosques, schools and homes were built and religious teachers were provided.

The Ikhwan villages grew rapidly in number and provided Abd al-Aziz with thousands of fighting men to support his campaign to unite the peninsula. It was reported that the Ikhwan could be completely mobilized within 96 hours, with 25,000 men under arms, although not more than 5,000 were normally called upon to take part in action. These troops were first used in putting down a revolt of the Mutayr tribe and in forcing the Turks out of eastern Arabia in 1913. These victories gave Abd al-Aziz access to the Persian Gulf coast between Kuwait and Qatar (see ch. 3, Historical Setting).

In October 1914, Abd al-Aziz found himself on the side of the British, who declared war on Turkey on October 31, 1914. The Rashids allied themselves with the Ottomans, and with their assistance attacked deep within the Saudi territory. In January 1915 a battle was fought northeast of Burayda with indecisive results; both sides withdrew and claimed victory. Negotiations with the British resulted in a treaty signed in December 1915 by which the British gave recognition of Saudi independence and the territorial integrity of the Nejd as well as a gift of 1,000 rifles, a supply of ammunition and £20,000 in cash. A later agreement in late 1916 gave Abd al-Aziz a monthly subsidy of £5,000 and a gift of 3,000 rifles with ammunition in exchange for his promise to keep 4,000 men in the field in his war with the Rashids. The Rashidi capital of Hail finally surrendered to the forces of Abd al-Aziz on November 2, 1921. He assumed the title of Sultan of Nejd and its Dependencies with the endorsement of the British. By the end of 1922 the Ikhwan forces were in control of the desert from the Fertile Crescent in the north to Rub al-Khali (Empty Quarter) in the south.

The greatest success of the Ikhwan came with the conquest of the Hejaz. After World War I, when Husein, the Hashemite king of the Hejaz, undertook defense negotiations with the Rashidi leaders, Abd al-Aziz's reaction was swift and harsh. He sent Ikhwan raiding parties against Hail, which was captured in 1921. Emboldened by their successes, the Ikhwan disregarded Abd al-Aziz's orders not to cross into Transjordanian territory. They raided and plundered several key oases in Transjordan, arousing the British allies of the Hashemite King of Transjordan to counterattack with aerial support and to decimate the Ikhwan raiders.

After Husein, whose control over the Hejaz had been gradually weakening for several years, laid claim to the Caliphate of Islam in 1924, Abd al-Aziz announced his intention of invading the Hejaz despite British warnings against such action. The undisciplined Ikhwan forces pillaged Taif and massacred several hundred of its inhabitants before Abd al-Aziz reasserted his control over them. During the next 15 months his forces occupied Mecca and laid siege to Jidda and Medina, which finally surrendered in December 1925.

For the next 2 years, Abd al-Aziz was occupied with creating the governmental organization to rule the vast, disparate territory which he had conquered. He began to build up an army and forbade the Ikhwan to continue their raiding. As a result, many Ikhwan leaders felt betrayed and sought the king's ouster. They led the Mutayr and Ajman tribes in rebellion against Abd al-Aziz and embarked on a program of indiscriminate raiding, including incursions into Iraq, Transjordan and Kuwait, which were all under British protection.

Despite a 1922 treaty between the British and Abd al-Aziz, which had established boundaries between Iraq and the Wahhabi state with the understanding that no military forts would be built on either side, the British High Commissioner in Iraq secretly agreed to the building of a series of forts along the Iraq-Nejd frontier. In late 1927 the tribal Ikhwan in the vicinity took matters in their own hands and massacred those engaged in the building of the forts. The British Air Force retaliated by bombing the tribal camps across the border. Undeclared warfare broke out along the border, and the Ikhwan forces raided into Iraq and Kuwait territory.

After conferring with the rebel leaders and demanding their surrender, Abd al-Aziz mobilized his regular troops to put down the rebellious Ikhwan. While he was in the Hejaz, Abd al-Aziz had negotiated for the purchase of four military airplanes and employed British pilots to fly them. In addition, the king had acquired a fleet of some 200 automobiles and trucks, which he used to good advantage. He took the field in person, and by the end of January 1930 the rebels were soundly defeated in battle. The Ikhwan movement was consigned to slow but certain oblivion.

A series of incidents in 1931-32 on the border with Yemen resulted in Yemeni forces occupying Najran, which lay in Saudi territory. The invaders were thrown back in the spring of 1932, but fighting continued along the mountainous border. Negotiations for a settlement continued until April 1934, when King Abd al-Aziz permitted two army columns to cross the frontier into Yemen. Emir Saud Ibn Abd al-Aziz commanded the desert column which was based on Abha and Najran; Emir Faisal Ibn Abd al-

Aziz al Faisal al-Saud commanded the column moving along the coastal route to the south. After substantial gains, both columns were ordered to hold their positions while a treaty was concluded at Taif (see ch. 3, Historical Setting).

Thereafter, the Saudi armed forces saw little military action. During the 1930's a regular army was slowly built up along European lines. The independent National Guard, formed of levies from the noble tribes of the Nejd as the Ikhwan had been, and the Royal Guard were created. These forces were little used except to maintain internal security; the harsh penalties meted out under the strict legal code enforced by the regime under the influence of the Wahhabi sect kept public disorders at a minimum.

During the early years of World War II, Saudi Arabia remained neutral although King Abd al-Aziz's personal feelings were with the Allies. In February 1945, Saudi Arabia declared war on Germany and Japan, but made no contribution of troops to the war effort.

The Saudi armed forces have had no real combat experience, although as a member of the Arab League Saudi Arabia made a token contribution of a single battalion to the Egyptian section of the Arab Army during the Palestine war of 1948.

After the outbreak of the Yemeni civil war in 1962, units of the National Guard and the regular army were posted near the Yemen border where, except for occasional conflict with raiding tribes, they avoided open conflict with Egyptian and Yemeni forces (see ch. 14, Foreign Relations).

MISSION AND ORGANIZATION

The armed forces have the conventional mission of safeguarding the integrity of the national boundaries by protecting the country against invasion. In times of internal disorders, the army has the added mission of assisting in restoring the internal security of the kingdom.

The National Guard, a paramilitary force, has the mission of supporting and assisting those forces responsible for the maintenance of internal security. In times of grave national danger the National Guard has the added mission of assisting the armed forces in repelling an invasion. The National Guard also has the mission of suppressing military insurgencies.

Position in the Government

The armed forces exert little or no influence on the government or the regime. Few officers are in a position to be called upon for or to give advice on military matters. Senior commanders of the army and the National Guard are chosen from among members of the royal family with unfailing loyalty to the king, but they probably have little effect in military policies. The regular armed forces are forbidden by royal decree governing the armed forces issued on March 20, 1960, "to express political opinions, engage in politics, or attend societies or organizations with political doctrines and inclinations."

The king, because of his position as Chief of State, is Commander in Chief of the Armed Forces. He has regularly named a senior member of the royal family as minister of defense and aviation. In 1965 this post was held by Prince Sultan Ibn Abd al-Aziz, a brother of King Faisal.

The minister of defense and aviation exercises supervision and operational control over the army, the navy and the air force as well as control of all civil aviation. He is assisted by two deputy ministers, one for the armed forces and one for civil aviation.

The National Guard is under the personal control of the king through a commander personally selected and appointed by him. As of the end of 1965, the commander was Prince Abdullah Ibn Abd al-Aziz.

The High Defense Council was established by royal decree on July 25, 1961, to draw up a long-range defense policy and to strengthen and uphold the standards of the armed forces. Members are the king, the ministers of defense and aviation, interior, finance and national economy, communications and foreign affairs, and the chief of staff.

Within the Ministry of Defense and Aviation a chief of staff (an army officer) is directly responsible to the minister for the supervision of the activities of the army, navy and air force. He is assisted by four staff directors responsible for personnel (G–1), intelligence (G–2), operations and training (G–3) and logistics (G–4).

Territorial Organization

Territorially, Saudi Arabia is divided into nine area commands, the boundaries of which are not clearly defined. Area commands provide intermediate headquarters between the Ministry of Defense and Aviation and units in the field.

Saudi army troops are garrisoned near the major cities. The largest garrisons are located near Jidda, Dammam, Taif, Al-Kharj and Riyadh.

In October 1962, shortly after the outbreak of civil war in Yemen, Saudi troops were sent to the Yemen border. Saudi and Jordanian forces under the command of Prince Khalid Ibn Abd al-Aziz were concentrated near Jizan and Najran. In January 1963 the government dispatched several squadrons of aircraft to airfields near the border and moved antiaircraft batteries to Najran. In August 1965 it was reported that 5,000 national guardsmen and an unspecified number of army troops were in positions along the Yemen border.

Navy personnel are located at the navy base at the port of Dammam; the Saudi air force is divided between the two principal airfields, located at Jidda and Dhahran.

THE MILITARY ESTABLISHMENT AND THE NATIONAL ECONOMY

Of the 1965 estimated population of 3.3 million, about 800,000 are males between the ages of 15 and 49, of whom 50 percent could be assumed to be physically fit for service in the armed forces (see ch. 2, Geography and Population). The total strength of the armed forces represents about 1.2 percent of the total population. Manpower requirements for the military can be met without causing adverse effects on industry or agriculture (see ch. 21, Labor).

Of the 1964–65 budget of expenditures totaling SR3,112 million (SR4.50 equal US$1), the defense share, excluding civil aviation (handled by the Ministry of Defense and Aviation) but including the National Guard, was somewhat over SR543 million, or roughly 17.5 percent, and constituted the largest single item in the budget (see table 17).

In mid-July 1965 the minister of defense and aviation announced a long-range plan for the modernization and development of the armed forces to cost about SR3,000 million over several years. The minister stated that of this amount, the air force would receive about SR1,200 million for the purchase of new planes and equipment, the establishment of new airbases, the creation of an air force academy, and the training of pilots abroad. The army would receive over SR1,600 million, including about SR450 million for the construction of army bases. The navy's share was to be SR156 million.

FOREIGN INFLUENCE

Saudi Arabia must depend on foreign sources for all its modern weapons, heavy ammunition and transport as well as for training in their use. The size and character of its armed forces are thus strongly influenced by the source and type of military assistance available. Since World War II the United States has supplied

Table 17. Defense Budget of Saudi Arabia, 1961–65[1]

Year	Total Budget[2]	Defense and National Guard Allocation[2]	Percent of Total Budget
1961	1,720	243	14.1
1962	2,085	322	15.4
1963	2,365	414	17.5
1964	2,686	519	19.5
1965	3,112	587	18.9

[1] Calendar years 1961–65 are roughly approximate to Moslem fiscal years 1381–85 A.H. (*anno hegirae*).
[2] In millions of riyals; SR4.50 equal US$1.
Source: Adapted from Saudi Arabian Monetary Agency, *Annual Report, 1383–84 A.H.*, pp. 38, 39; and *ibid.*, *Circular on Saudi Arabian Budget Estimates, 1384–85*, pp. 5–8.

more materiel and guidance for the Saudi armed forces than either the United Arab Republic or Great Britain, which had previously been the other major sources for military assistance. The country has received no Soviet assistance in equipping the armed forces, and no influence on the armed forces has been exerted by the Soviet Union or any of the Communist-bloc countries.

A 1947 agreement with the United States established a training base at the Dhahran airbase. In the same year the British established a military training mission and undertook the training of a mechanized division patterned after the British-trained Jordanian Arab Legion. In 1951 the United States and Saudi Arabia signed a mutual defense assistance agreement by which the United States would sell arms and defense materials and provide military training in their use in exchange for the continued use of the Dhahran airbase by the United States. In 1952 the United States took over from the British training mission and established the United States Training Mission to instruct the Saudi army. The Saudi Government agreed in April 1957 to a 5-year extension of the United States lease on the Dhahran airbase in return for the agreement of the United States Government to train the Saudi navy and air force and expand its training program for the Saudi army. In 1962 the Saudi Government declined to renew the United States lease on the Dhahran airbase and took over full operation of the base; the United States Military Training Mission (formerly, the United States Training Mission), however, was continued.

Military relations with other Arab countries have varied greatly from time to time. Saudi Arabia helped found the Arab League in March 1945. It furnished a battalion of troops for the invasion of Palestine by the Arab League armies. On July 17, 1950, Saudi Arabia joined other Arab League members in an Arab League Security Pact for joint defense in case of armed aggression against any member nation. In 1951 an Egyptian training mission was attached to the Saudi air force.

On October 27, 1955, Saudi Arabia and Egypt established a mutual defense pact which provided for joint command of the armed forces in both war and peace. Two and one-half years later, as an expression of his opposition to Nasser's formation of the United Arab Republic, King Saud terminated the arrangement under which, since 1951, Egypt had supplied a training mission attached to the Saudi air force.

On November 6, 1962, Saudi Arabia broke diplomatic relations with the United Arab Republic after Egyptian aircraft had attacked five Saudi Arabian villages and three Egyptian destroyers had bombarded a coastal village. At about the same time, Saudi Arabia and Jordan announced that a military alliance had been agreed upon and a joint defense council established. United States jet fighters carried out demonstration flights over Jidda and Riyadh, and a United States warship was sent to Jidda as a warning against further United Arab Republic attacks on Saudi Arabia.

In March 1964 diplomatic relations between Saudi Arabia and the United Arab Republic were reestablished, despite the continuation of the Yemeni war. Near the end of August 1965, an agreement for a cease-fire in Yemen was signed by King Faisal and President Nasser as supporters of the two warring factions which had begun the Yemeni civil war in September 1962.

As of late 1965 the United States exerted far greater influence on the Saudi Arabian armed forces than any other country. The organization and tactical doctrine of the armed forces were patterned after those of the United States, from the organization of the general staff to the units in the field. The extensive holdings of United States materiel and the long-continued assistance in training in the use of this materiel by the United States Military Training Mission have influenced the thinking of the military planners of Saudi Arabia. Extensive use of United States military schools has left a decided impression on young Saudi officers who are anxious to have a more modern, professional-type of army, navy and air force.

QUALITY AND SOURCE OF MANPOWER

Manpower resources are more than sufficient to meet the needs of the armed forces. Those born of Saudi parents are preferred for the armed forces, but provision has been made for the recruitment of naturalized citizens (see ch. 4, Ethnic Groups and Languages).

Saudi Arabs are generally short in stature, wiry, tough and courageous. Being accustomed to the harsh climate of their own country, they make effective desert fighters; they endure hardships stoically, accepting them as the "will of Allah."

The nomads, who make up half of the population, lived for centuries by raiding and tribal warfare. In order to survive, the tribesman had to become a superior rider on camel and horse and be able to use his gun and dagger with great skill. Fighting and raiding were highly respected among the men, whereas manual labor was left to the women. After Abd al-Aziz suppressed tribal warfare in the early decades of the twentieth century, the martial spirit of the tribes was lessened, but they have continued to take pride in their ability to exist in the desert and consider themselves superior to those who lead sedentary lives.

Recruitment

The government does not resort to conscription for recruits for the armed forces. All service is voluntary and recruits enlist for 3-year periods. Recruiting is done at specified locations in the larger cities and towns, and notices are sent out to tribal villages when necessary.

Recruiting for the regular armed forces is done on a nationwide basis and is not restricted to any particular region. As a result, army personnel constitute a fairly representative cross section of the population. In contrast, the National Guard is recruited on a tribal or area basis, and units stationed at various locations are recruited from the tribes in those areas. Units of the National Guard stationed near Mecca and Medina consist of men from the tribes of Hejaz; those stationed near Riyadh are composed of the tribes of Nejd (see ch. 4, Ethnic Groups and Languages).

Officers

A military career as an officer in the armed forces is open to any young man who is able to meet the requirements for a commission. To become an officer a man is required to have been a naturalized citizen for at least 5 years, but those who are Saudi Arabs by birth are greatly preferred and it is unlikely that many naturalized citizens have become officers. The candidate must be at least 18 years of age and qualified physically as well as mentally. He must be of good reputation and not previously subject to any *sharia* (Islamic law) penalty or imprisonment for a felony within the previous 5 years.

The bulk of the newer military officers are graduates of the Royal Military College in Riyadh; they are commissioned as second lieutenants. Graduates of technical schools who desire to become officers can also obtain commissions as second lieutenants. Graduates with science degrees from the university or the specialized colleges are commissioned in a rank determined by the number of years of study as compared with the 3 years of study in the Royal Military College (see ch. 9, Education). Warrant officers who are technically qualified by graduation from a technical school of the air force and who have served with the technical cadre of the air force may be promoted to second lieutenants of the air force. Noncommissioned officers may be promoted to second lieutenants for heroism in combat by order of the commander in chief.

Seniority is determined from the date of appointment or graduation standing in his class at the Royal Military College. If the original commission was a rank higher than second lieutenant, seniority is determined from the date of appointment but below that of regular promotions of the same date.

Newly appointed second lieutenants serve on probation for 2 years; if their performance has been unsatisfactory, they are transferred to another unit for an additional probationary period of 1 year. If they are still considered to be unsatisfactory officers, those commissioned from a warrant officer or noncommissioned grade revert to their former rank, and others are separated from the service.

Personnel files are kept on all officers at their units and are transferred with them to their new units. Efficiency reports are rendered by commanding officers every 6 months on second lieutenants on probation and once every year on all others up to the rank of brigadier general. An officer who receives an unsatisfactory efficiency report is informed of that fact and given 2 weeks in which to submit his rebuttal or explanation. The matter is then referred to the officers' committees, which have been established within the Ministry of Defense and Aviation for the handling of personnel affairs.

The officers' committees are responsible for appointment and promotion, retiring and recalling from active duty, recommending the granting of awards and decorations, appointments to key positions, transfers, selection of officers for chiefs of military schools, selection of candidates for military missions and the granting of educational leaves. There is no naval officers' committee; however, one could be established by a decision of the Council of Ministers. As of late 1965 the army officers' committees took care of the personnel affairs of naval officers.

TRAINING

Training in the Saudi armed forces is patterned after that of the United States Armed Forces and is a function of the training section of the G–3 (Operations and Training) Office in the Ministry of Defense and Aviation. Since 1943 the Saudi army has depended on foreign countries for its training guidance in the use of the modern weapons it has acquired since World War II. Great Britain, Egypt and the United States have all assisted at various times in the reorganization and training of the regular armed forces, but as of the end of 1965 the United States was the only country giving such assistance. The National Guard, on the other hand, was being assisted by the British.

The objective of the United States Military Training Mission is to equip and train a modern, well-balanced Saudi army, navy and air force. United States personnel advise and supervise the training programs of the army, navy and air force; Saudi officers and noncommissioned officers conduct the actual training.

The military school system comprises a number of service schools under the direction of the Army School Command. The schools known to be in operation are for the following services: infantry, artillery, armored vehicles, communications, physical training, ordnance (field maintenance), engineering, military police, nursing and military music. Most service schools offer basic and advanced courses for both officers and noncommissioned officers as well as basic courses for qualified privates. As the number of United States-trained Saudi officers increases, the effectiveness of the instruction offered at service schools will increase. Service schools are frequently operated below capacity because of a shortage of qualified students resulting from the generally low level of education which prevails in the army.

The government operates a number of basic military schools located in the larger cities offering a free education in elementary and intermediate subjects to prepare young men for service in the armed forces. The Military Preparatory School at Riyadh is open to young men who agree to enter the Royal Military College to become officers. While attending the military schools, students are given free board, lodging and uniforms, plus a small monthly allowance in cash.

The Royal Military College is the Saudi Arabian counterpart of the United States Military Academy at West Point, New York. The school offers a 3-year course of instruction, including academic and military subjects. About 60 students were graduated and commissioned as second lieutenants in July 1965.

PAY AND ALLOWANCES

In addition to a monthly base pay, members of the armed forces receive certain allowances which make them as well or better paid than any other government service. It has been reported that both officers and enlisted men are the best paid of any military personnel in the Arab countries. In addition, members of the armed forces and their dependents are given free medical and dental care and hospitalization at military installations, a few of which have special military hospitals (see ch. 11, Health and Welfare).

Periodic pay increases are provided every 2 years for all officer grades from second lieutenant to colonel, until a maximum for the grade is reached at which the officer remains until promoted. All officers receive a living allowance, servant allowance, clothing allowance and a housing allowance. Additional allowances are provided for officers who are in certain positions of command or who perform hazardous duties. Officers normally do not receive more than two of these allowances.

Warrant officers receive a cash living allowance, a clothing allowance and an annual housing allowance. Noncommissioned officers and privates may qualify for special allowances, which are classified into 16 pay categories according to skills.

ARMS AND EQUIPMENT

The armed forces are adequately supplied with modern weapons purchased chiefly from the United States. Infantry weapons include M1 rifles, 30-caliber carbines, 30- and 50-caliber machineguns, 3.5-inch rocket launchers, recoilless rifles, and 60-mm., 81-mm. and 4.2-inch mortars. Artillery weapons include both 105-mm. and 155-mm. howitzers. A limited number of tanks, including light M-41 and M-41A1 tanks, medium M-47 tanks and M-8 armored cars, are part of the arsenal of weapons. Motor transport vehicles have been purchased from the United States, the United Kingdom and West Germany.

In mid-December 1965 the government contracted with British concerns to purchase 40 British Lightning 3-jet interceptors, 25 BAC Provost jet trainers and a number of Marconi air defense radar installations. The initial cost was estimated to be about £100 million (about $280 million). At the same time, the government contracted to purchase about $70 million worth of United States Hawk antiaircraft missiles. The deal with the British includes spare parts and training through the next 10 years and will amount to the equivalent of about $500 million.

LEAVE

Leave policy for officers appears to be quite generous. Each officer is entitled to 45 days' regular leave each year; an occasional leave of 10 days may be granted for emergencies. Sick leave is granted in accordance with rules governing the leave of civil employees of the state. Field leave not to exceed 60 days a year may also be granted at the rate of 15 days a quarter. In addition, emergency leave of not more than 1 month per year may be granted to officers who have used up their regular leave.

The official leave policy established for noncommissioned officers and privates provides for regular leave, sick leave, field leave and emergency leave. Regular leave accrues at the rate of 1 month per year, plus a maximum of 10 days for extreme emergencies; it is not available for 11 months of the year in which the enlisted man becomes eligible for the leave. Sick leave is granted at varying rates of pay depending on whether illness or injury was incurred in the line of duty and on the length of time needed for recovery. Field leave not to exceed 30 days per year and emergency leave of not more than 15 days per year may also be granted under certain conditions.

AWARDS AND DECORATIONS

According to the Saudi Arabian regulations for the award of medals and decorations, all military awards are classified as decorations, achievement medals and medals. Decorations carry a monetary award which is paid to the recipient for the rest of his life, both active and retired.

Decorations include the King Abd al-Aziz Ibn Saud Decoration, the King Saud Star and the National Military Decoration. Achievement medals include the Efficiency Medal, the Medal of Merit and the Appreciation Medal. Medals include the Long Service and Good Example Medal, the Exceptional Promotion Medal, the War Wounded Medal and the Palestine Medal.

All military decorations and medals are awarded by approval and order of the king. The same approval is required for the acceptance of a foreign decoration by a member of the armed forces.

MILITARY JUSTICE

The Code of Military Justice for the Royal Saudi Army published by the Ministry of Defense in 1947 is the Saudi equivalent of the United States Uniform Code of Military Justice. It is applicable to all members of the armed forces, all retired military personnel and all civilians connected with the army who commit crimes or offenses of a military nature.

Punishable offenses are classified as felonies, misdemeanors and disobediences. Felonies and misdemeanors are subject to trial by a military court and, upon conviction, are punishable by severe or disciplinary punishments as prescribed. Disobediences are offenses of a less serious nature and are punishable administratively.

Military felonies include high treason against the kingdom and disloyalty against the country or the armed forces. Severe punishments are meted out to those found guilty of such offenses. The king alone has the right to execute the sentences of the court or to dismiss, commute or mitigate punishment in conformity with the laws.

Military misdemeanors meriting the imposition of disciplinary punishment include such acts as misbehavior in wartime, misuse of authority, misuse of military funds or equipment, agitating for leaving the service, or violation of military regulations and directives. Disciplinary punishments include imprisonment for up to 18 months and forfeiture of pay from 1 to 3 months.

Disobediences or failure to obey orders are punished administratively. Punishments, which range from forfeiture of 1 day's pay and imprisonment of from 24 hours to a maximum of 45 days, are scaled according to the seriousness of the offense.

Military trial courts have jurisdiction over offenses of a military or political nature committed by persons subject to military law. Religious crimes committed by military personnel are under the jurisdiction of the *sharia* law courts.

Military trial courts are appointed from among officers in good standing and consist of a president and four voting members, a legal adviser, a recorder and a recorder representing the accused. The president is the highest ranking member of the court and must be of higher rank than the accused or senior in grade if of the same rank.

Trial procedures are simple and direct and conducted so as to give the benefit of doubt to the accused. A case is brought to trial only after a thorough and impartial investigation and the submission of a complete report. The court's decision may be invalidated or commuted by the minister of defense and aviation or the commander in chief for irregularities, omissions, evidence of prejudice or pressure brought to bear. The commander in chief or the minister of defense and aviation has the sole right of review of sentences imposed by the trial court. Judgments of the trial court are final upon approval of the commander in chief in cases involving severe punishment and by the minister of defense and aviation for lesser offenses.

BIBLIOGRAPHIES

Section I, Social

RECOMMENDED FURTHER READING

Among the sources consulted in the preparation of this section, the following are recommended as additional reading on the basis of quality and general usefulness.

Arabian American Oil Company. *Aramco Handbook*, by Roy Lebkicher, George Rentz, Max Steineke, *et al.* Dhahran: Aramco, 1960.

Dequin, Horst. *Die Landwirtschaft Saudisch-Arabiens und ihre Entwicklungs-möglichkeiten.* (Series: Zeitschrift für ausländische Landwirtschaft.) Frankfurt: DLG-Verlags-GMBH, 1963.

Emam, Hani Shafeek. "The Economy of Saudi Arabia and the 1956–1960 Crisis." Unpublished Master's thesis, Columbia University, 1963.

Rentz, George. *The Arabian Peninsula: A Sketch.* Dhahran: Arabian American Oil Company, 1954.

――――. "Saudi Arabia: The Islamic Island," *Journal of International Relations*, XIX, No. 1, 1965, 77–86.

Sourdel, Dominique. *L'Islam.* Paris: Presses Universitaires de France, 1962.

Tomiche, Fernand J. *L'Arabie Séodite.* Paris: Presses Universitaires de France, 1962.

Twitchell, Karl Saben. *Saudi Arabia.* (3d ed.) Princeton: Princeton University Press, 1958.

U.S. Department of Labor. Bureau of Labor Statistics. *Labor Law and Practice in Saudi Arabia.* (BLS Report No. 269.) Washington: GPO, 1964.

Vidal, Federico S. *The Oasis of Al-Hasa.* Dhahran: Arabian American Oil Company, 1955.

Wolf, Eric R. "The Social Organization of Mecca and the Origins of Islam," *Southwestern Journal of Anthropology*, VII, Winter 1951, 329–353.

World Health Organization. Regional Office for the Eastern Mediterranean. "Report on a Health Survey of Saudi Arabia," by Chu, C.K.; Djazzar, S.K.; and Adham, M.H. (EM/PHA/110.) Alexandria, Egypt: WHO, 1963. (mimeo.)

OTHER SOURCES USED

Abercrombie, Thomas J. "Saudi Arabia: Beyond the Sands of Mecca," *National Geographic,* CXXIX, January 1966, 1–53.

"Arabia," *Encyclopaedia Britannica* (11th ed.), II, 1911, 254–276.

Arabian American Oil Company. "Closing in on Malaria," *Aramco World,* March 1961, 3–5.

———. *Report of Activities 1964: Arab Industrial Development Department.* Dhahran: Aramco, 1965.

Atiyah, Edward. *The Arabs.* Middlesex: Penguin Books, 1955.

Awad, Mohamed. "Settlement of Nomadic and Semi-Nomadic Tribal Groups in the Middle East," *International Labour Review,* LXXIX, January-June 1959, 25–56.

Baer, Gabriel. *Population and Society in the Arab East.* New York: Praeger, 1964.

Benoist-Mechin, Jacques. *Le Roi Saud.* Paris: Editions Albin Michel, 1960.

Caskel, Werner. "The Bedouinization of Arabia," *American Anthropologist,* LVI, No. 2, Pt. 2 (Memoir No. 76), April 1954, 36–46.

Christian Science Monitor, "School for Girls in Saudi Arabia," May 16, 1964.

Dickson, Harold Richard Patrick. *The Arab of the Desert: A Glimpse into Badawin Life in Kuwait and Saudi Arabia.* New York: Macmillan, 1949.

The Economist Intelligence Unit, Ltd., and the Cartographic Department of the Clarendon Press. *Oxford Regional Economic Atlas: The Middle East and North Africa.* London: Oxford University Press, 1960.

Ellis, Harry B. *Heritage of the Desert.* New York: Ronald Press, 1956.

Elphinstone, W.G. "The Future of the Bedouin of Northern Arabia," *International Affairs,* XXI, July 1945, 370–375.

Fisher, Sydney N. *The Middle East.* London: Routledge and Kegan-Paul, 1960.

Fisher, William Bayne. *The Middle East.* New York: Dutton, 1956.

Food and Agriculture Organization. *Report to the Government of Saudi Arabia on Pasture Development and Range Management,* by Marvin Klemme. (Report No. 1993.) Rome: FAO, 1965.

———. Agriculture Division. Program Analysis Service. *Characteristics and Problems of Agriculture in Saudi Arabia,* by N.A. Lateef. (Background Country Studies, No. 4.) Rome: FAO, 1956.

Gaury, Gerald de. *Rulers of Mecca.* London: Harrap, 1951.

Gibb, H.A.R. *Arabic Literature.* (2d ed., rev.) Oxford: Clarendon Press, 1963.

―――. *Mohammedanism: An Historical Survey.* (2d ed.) New York: Oxford University Press, 1962.

Gibb, H.A.R., and Kramers, J.H. (eds.). *The Shorter Encyclopaedia of Islam.* Ithaca: Cornell University Press, 1953.

Great Britain. Naval Staff. Naval Intelligence Division. *Western Arabia and the Red Sea.* (Geographical Handbook Series, BR 527.) London: HMSO, 1946.

Haddad, Edmonde Alex. "Saudi Arabia and Oil." Unpublished Master's thesis, Columbia University, n.d.

Hamady, Sania. *Temperament and Character of the Arabs.* New York: Twayne, 1960.

Haywood, J.A., and Nahmad, H.M. *A New Arabic Grammar of the Written Language.* Cambridge: Harvard University Press, 1962.

Hazard, Harry W. *Atlas of Islamic History.* (3d ed., rev.) Princeton: Princeton University Press, 1954.

―――. (ed.). *Saudi Arabia.* (Human Relations Area Files Subcontractor's Monograph.) New Haven: HRAF Press, 1956.

Helaissi, A.S. "The Bedouins and Tribal Life in Saudi Arabia," *International Social Science Bulletin,* XI, No. 4, 1959, 532–538.

Herdman, Thomas. "Geography, Exploration, Topographical and Related Details," *Encyclopaedia Britannica* (14th ed.), II, 1958, 168–176.

Hitti, Philip K. *History of the Arabs.* London: Macmillan, 1956.

Hogarth, D.G. *Arabia.* Oxford: Clarendon Press, 1922.

Hoskins, Halford L. *The Middle East.* New York: Macmillan, 1957.

Hottinger, Arnold. *The Arabs: Their History, Culture and Place in the Modern World.* Berkeley: University of California Press, 1963.

Howarth, David. *The Desert King, Ibn Saud and His Arabia.* New York: McGraw-Hill, 1964.

Kamal, Ahmad. *The Sacred Journey: Being Pilgrimage to Makkah.* New York: Duell, Sloan and Pearce, 1961.

Kelly, J.B. "Mehemet Ali's Expedition to the Persian Gulf 1837–1840, Pt. 1," *Middle Eastern Studies,* I, July 1965, 350–381.

Kirk, George. *Contemporary Arab Politics.* New York: Praeger, 1961.

―――. *A Short History of the Middle East.* New York: Praeger, 1957.

Laqueur, W.Z. *The Middle East in Transition.* New York: Praeger, 1958.

Lenczowski, George. *The Middle East in World Affairs.* Ithaca: Cornell University Press, 1962.

Longrigg, Stephen H. *The Middle East: A Social Geography.* London: Duckworth, 1963.

Meulen, D. van der. *The Wells of Ibn Saud.* New York: Praeger, 1957.

Nolte, Richard H. "A Tale of Three Cities: I: Dhahran." (AUFS Reports Service, Saudi Arabia, RHN-4-'57.) New York: American Universities Field Staff, April 1957.

Patai, Raphael. "The Middle East as a Culture Area," *Middle East Journal,* VI, Winter 1952, 1–21.

Philby, H. St. John. "Riyadh: Ancient and Modern," *Middle East Journal,* XIII, Spring 1959, 129–141.

Philby, H. St. John; Hitti, Philip K.; and Kirk, George E. "Wahhabi Movement," *Encyclopaedia Britannica* (14th ed.), II, 1958, 179–181.

Quarterly Education Review, "Higher Education in Saudi Arabia," July-October 1961.

Saudi Arabia. Meteorological Service. *Annual Climatological Report.* Jidda: 1959.

Saudi Arabia. Ministry of Education. *Brief Report on Educational Development and Other Progress and Relations Between the Saudi Ministry of Education and UNESCO.* Paris: 1964.

———. *A Brief Report on the Ministry of Education for the Year 1964–1965.* Geneva: 1965.

———. *Education in Saudi Arabia.* Jidda (?): 1962 (?).

———. *Programmes du Cycle Secondaire, 3ème Série.* Jidda (?): 1960.

———. Department of Special Education. *Report on the Conditions of the Blind in the Kingdom of Saudi Arabia and the Area of the Middle East.* Jidda (?): 1965.

Saudi Arabia. Ministry of Information. *Education for Girls.* Jidda (?): 1963 (?).

———. *Education in Saudi Arabia.* Jidda (?): 1964 (?).

———. *Health in Saudi Arabia.* Jidda (?): 1964 (?).

———. *Saudi Arabia: Land of Achievement.* Jidda: 1964 (?).

———. *Social Welfare.* Jidda (?): 1963 (?).

Saudi Arabia. Permanent Delegation of the Kingdom of Saudi Arabia to the United Nations. *The Buraimi Dispute.* New York: 1956 (?).

Shouby, E. "The Influence of the Arabic Language on the Psychology of the Arabs," *Middle East Journal*, V, Summer 1951, 284–302.

Shwadran, Benjamin. *The Middle East, Oil and the Great Powers*. New York: Praeger, 1955.

Silvert, K.H. (ed.). *Expectant Peoples: Nationalism and Development*. (American Universities Field Staff.) New York: Random House, 1963.

Simmons, James Stevens; Whayne, Tom F.; Anderson, Gaylord W.; Horack, Harold Maclachlan; and Thomas, R.A. *Global Epidemiology: A Geography of Disease and Sanitation*. Philadelphia: Lippincott, 1954.

Sweet, Louise E. "Samel Raiding of North Arabian Bedouin: A Mechanism of Ecological Adaptation," *American Anthropologist*, LXVII, No. 5 (Pt. 1), October 1965, 1132–1134.

Thatcher, Griffiths Wheeler, and Hitti, Philip K. "History," *Encyclopaedia Britannica* (14th ed.), II, 1958, 176–179.

Thesiger, Wilfred. *Arabian Sands*. New York: Dutton, 1959.

United Nations, Department of Economic and Social Affairs. *Administrative Problems of Rapid Urban Growth in the Arab States*. (Technical Assistance Programme.) New York: 1964.

U.S. Department of Commerce. Office of Climatology. Weather Bureau. Foreign Area Section. *An Annotated Bibliography on the Climate of the Arabian Peninsula*, by Annie E. Grimes. Washington: 1960.

U.S. Department of Defense. Military Assistance Institute. *Saudi Arabia*. Washington: 1959.

U.S. United States Information Agency. Research and Reference Service. *Arabian Peninsula: A Communications Fact Book*. (R–156–64.) Washington: 1964.

University of Riyadh. *Calendar*. Riyadh: 1964.

Wahba, Sheikh Hafiz. "Wahhabism in Arabia, Past and Present," *Journal of the Central Asian Society*, XVI, 1929, 458–467.

World Health Organization. *Trends in the Study of Morbidity and Mortality*. (Public Health Papers, No. 27.) Geneva: WHO, 1965.

Yale, William. *The Near East: A Modern History*. Ann Arbor: University of Michigan Press, 1958.

(The following sources were also used in the preparation of this section: *Keesing's Contemporary Archives* [London], from January 1958 through December 1965; *Middle East Journal* [Washington], from January 1958 through December 1965; *News from Saudi Arabia* [Jidda] [formerly *Saudi Weekly Newsletter*], from

February 1961 through December 1965; and *Saudi Arabia Today* [New York], from March 1964 through December 1965.)

The following additional sources were used in the preparation of the original *Area Handbook for Saudi Arabia*, published in 1958.

Albright, William Foxwell. "In Defense of the American Foundation for the Study of Man," *Middle East Journal*, VI, Winter 1952, 111, 112.

Allen, Theodore E. "Health Problems and Arabian American Oil Company Activities in Saudi Arabia," *Harvard Public Health Alumni Bulletin*, May 1951.

"Arabia: Arabic Dialects," *The Encyclopaedia of Islam*, I, 1913, 394–402.

Arabian American Oil Company. "Report of Operations 1953 to the Saudi Arab Government." Dhahran: 1954.

―――. "Report of Operations 1954 to the Saudi Arab Government." Dhahran: 1955.

―――. "Report of Operations 1955 to the Saudi Arab Government." Dhahran: 1956.

―――. "Report of Operations 1956 to the Saudi Arab Government." Dhahran: 1957.

―――. Department of Local Government Relations. *The Royal Family Officials of the Saudi Arabian Government and Other Prominent Saudi Arabs*. Dhahran: 1952.

Arabian American Oil Company. Industrial Relations Department. *Foreman's Guide to Personnel Administration*. Dhahran: 1954.

Arabian Oil Headlines, August 1955.

Armstrong, H.C. *Lord of Arabia*. London: Barker, 1934.

Arnold, T.W. *Painting in Islam: A Study of the Place of Pictorial Art in Muslim Culture*. Oxford: Clarendon, 1928.

Ayim, M. Abdal. "Bilharziasis Survey in Some Countries of the Eastern Mediterranean Region." World Health Organization Regional Office for the Eastern Mediterranean, May 1951. (Unpublished manuscript.)

Barber, Noel. "I Learned Slavery Isn't Dead," *Saturday Evening Post*, CCXXX, November 30, 1957, 27.

"Becoming a Nurse in Saudi Arabia," *The American Journal of Nursing*, June 1956.

Benoist-Mechin, Jacques. *Arabian Destiny*. (Trans., Denis Weaver.) London: Elek, 1957.

Brockelmann, Carl. *History of the Islamic Peoples*. London: Routledge and Kegan-Paul, 1949.

Burkhardt, John Lewis. *Travels in Arabia*. London: Colburn, 1829.

Butler, S.S. "Baghdad to Damascus via El Jauf, Northern Arabia," *Geographical Journal*, XXXIII, 1909, 517–535.

Carruthers, Douglas. "A Journey in Northwestern Arabia," *Geographical Journal*, XXXV, 1910, 225–248.

Carver, John L. (pseud.). "Slavery's Last Stronghold," *United Nations World*, II, June 1948, 24–27.

Chaglassian, H.T.; Bustani, N.; and Anderson, H.H. "Endemic Treponematosis (balash or bejel) in Saudi Arabia," *American Journal of Tropical Medicine and Hygiene*, September 1952.

Cheney, Michael S. *Big Oil Man from Arabia*. New York: Ballantine, 1958.

Cooke, Hedley V. *Challenge and Response in the Middle East: The Quest for Prosperity, 1919–1951*. New York: Harper, 1952.

Coon, Carleton Stevens. *Caravan: The Story of the Middle East*. New York: Holt, 1951.

———. "The Nomads." In Sydney Nettleton Fisher (ed.), *Social Forces in the Middle East*. Ithaca: Cornell University Press, 1955, 23–42.

———. "Operation Bultiste: Promoting Industrial Development in Saudi Arabia." In Howard M. Teaf, Jr., and Peter G. Franck (eds.), *Hands Across Frontiers: Case Studies in Technical Cooperation*. Ithaca: Cornell University Press, 1955, 307–361.

———. *The Races of Europe*. New York: Macmillan, 1939.

Crary, Douglas D. "Recent Agricultural Developments in Saudi Arabia," *The Geographical Review*, XLI, 1951, 366–383.

Dickson, Harold R.P. *Kuwait and Her Neighbors*. London: Allen and Unwin, 1956.

Dickson, Violet. "Artistic House-Decoration in Riyadh," *Man*, XLIX, 1949, 76, 77.

Dowson, V.H.W. "The Date and the Arab," *Journal of the Royal Central Asian Society*, XXXVII, Pt. 1, January 1949.

Editor and Publisher International Yearbook, 1957, XC, February 28, 1957.

Farid, M.A. "The Pilgrimage and Its Implications in a Regional Malaria Eradication Program," World Health Organization, April 9, 1956. (Unpublished manuscript.)

Field, Henry. *Ancient and Modern Man in Southwestern Asia*. Coral Gables, Florida: University of Miami Press, 1956.

Field, Henry, and Glubb, John Bagot. *Yezidis, Sulubba and Other Tribes of Iraq and Adjacent Regions*. ("General Series in Anthropology," No. 10.) Menasha, Wisconsin: Banta, 1943.

Fisher, William Bayne. *The Middle East: A Physical, Social, and Regional Geography*. (2d ed.) New York: Dutton, 1952.

Gaury, Gerald de. *Arabia Phoenix*. London: Harrap, 1946.

El Ghoroury, A.A. "The Syphilis Problem in Asir Province, Saudi Arabia," *Bulletin of the World Health Organization*, X. Geneva: World Health Organization, 1954.

Gill, James P., and Golz, Harold H. "A Health Survey of the Student Body of the Jebel School." Dhahran: Arabian American Oil Company, 1949.

Glubb, John Bagot. "The Bedouins of Northern Arabia [misprinted as Iraq]," *Journal of the Royal Central Asian Society*, XXII, 1935.

──────. "Ignoble Tribes of Southwestern Asia." In Henry Field and John Bagot Glubb, *Yezidis, Sulubba and Other Tribes of Iraq and Adjacent Regions* ("General Series in Anthropology," No. 10). Menasha, Wisconsin: Banta, 1943, 14–16.

──────. *The Story of the Arab Legion*. London: Hodder and Stoughton, 1956.

Goeje, Michael Jan de. "Arabia: Ethnology," *The Encyclopaedia of Islam*, I, 1913, 372–377.

Great Britain. Board of Trade. *Markets in the Middle East: Report of the United Kingdom Trade Mission to Iraq, Kuwait, the Lebanon, Syria and Saudi Arabia, November-December 1953*. London: HMSO, 1954.

Great Britain. Geographical Section of the Naval Intelligence Division, Naval Staff, Admiralty. *A Handbook of Arabia*, I. London: HMSO, 1920.

Harrison, Paul W. *The Arab at Home*. New York: Crowell, 1924.

──────. *Doctor in Arabia*. London: Hale, 1943.

──────. "Slavery in Arabia," *Moslem World*, XXIX, April 1939, 207–209.

Hartley, John G. *The Political Structure of Saudi Arabia*, May 21, 1956. (Unpublished manuscript not available for distribution.)

Harvard School of Public Health. *Industry and Tropical Health*. (Proceedings of the Second Conference of Industrial Council for Tropical Health, II.) Boston: 1955.

"Health Center in Saudi Arabia," *Aramco World*, January 21, 1956.

Hitti, Philip K. "Arabic," *Encyclopedia Americana* (6th ed.), II, 123, 124.

Ibn-al-Kalbi, Hisham. *The Book of Idols; being a Translation from the Arabic of the Kitab al-Asnam*. (Trans., Nabih Amin Faris.) Princeton: Princeton University Press, 1952.

Inayatullah, Sheikh. *Geographical Factors in Arabian Life and History*. Lahore: Shaikh Muhammad Asharf, 1942.

Johns Hopkins University. *Area Handbook on Iraq*. HRAF Subcontractor's Monograph, 1956.

Jong, Garrett E. de. "Slavery in Arabia," *Moslem World*, XXIV, April 1934, 126–144.

Kimbal, Solon T. "American Culture in Saudi Arabia," *Transactions of the New York Academy of Sciences*, XVIII, No. 5, March 1956.

Kuntz, Robert E. "Schistosoma Mansoni and S. Haemstobrium in the Yemen, S.W. Arabia," *Journal of Parasitology*, February 1952.

Lammens, Henri. "L'attitude de l'Islam Primitif en Face des Arts Figurés," *Journal Asiatique*, II Serie, VI, 1915, 239–279.

Landau, Rom. *The Arabesque: The Abstract Art of Islam*. San Francisco: The American Academy of Asian Studies, 1955.

Lateef, N.A. *Characteristics and Problems of Agriculture in Saudi Arabia*. (Background Country Studies, No. 4.) Prepared in the Program Analysis Service, Agriculture Division, Food and Agriculture Organization of the United Nations, October 1956.

Lebkicher, Roy. "The Training of Saudi Arab Employees: Arabian American Oil Company." Reprinted from *The Yearbook of Education*, 1954. London: Evans, 1954.

Lebkicher, Roy; Renty, George; and Steineke, Max. *The Arabia of Ibn Saud*. New York: Moore, 1952.

Lengyel, Emil. "Social Tensions in the Middle East," *Annals of the Academy of Political and Social Sciences*, CCLXXVI, July 1951.

Lewis, Bernard. *The Arabs in History*. London: Hutchinson, 1954.

Longrigg, Stephen Hemsley. *Oil in the Middle East; Its Discovery and Development*. New York: Oxford University Press, 1954.

Margoliouth, D.S. "Wahhabiyya." In H.A.R. Gibb and J.H. Kramers (eds.), *The Shorter Encyclopaedia of Islam*. Ithaca: Cornell University Press, 1953.

Marett, William C. "Some Medical Problems Met in Saudi Arabia," *United States Armed Forces Medical Journal*, IV, January 1953.

The Middle East—1957. London: Europa Publications, 1957.

Montagne, Robert. *La Civilisation du Désert*. Paris: Librairie Hachette, 1947.

Morris, James. *Islam Inflamed*. New York: Pantheon, 1957.

Muksam, H.V. "Fertility and Reproduction of the Bedouin," *Population Studies*, IV, March 1951, 354–363.

Musil, Alcis. *The Manners and Customs of the Ruwala Bedouins*. ("Oriental Explorations and Studies," No. 6.) New York: American Geographical Society, 1928.

———. *The Northern Hejaz: A Topographical Itinerary*. ("Oriental Explorations and Studies," No. 1.) New York: American Geographical Society, 1926.

Nicholson, Reynold A. *A Literary History of the Arabs.* Cambridge: Cambridge University Press, 1956.

Omar, Wasfy. "The Mecca Pilgrimage; its Epidemiological Significance and Control," *Postgraduate Medical Journal,* May 1952.

Page, R.C., and Daggy, R.H. "Arabian American Oil Company's Preventive Medicine Program." A paper presented at the Persian Gulf Medical Society annual meeting at Kuwait, December 8, 1955.

Philby, H. St. John B. *Arabia.* London: Benn, 1930.

―――――. *Arabia of the Wahhabis.* London: Constable, 1928.

―――――. *Arabian Days.* London: Hale, 1948.

―――――. *Arabian Highlands.* Ithaca: Cornell University Press, 1952.

―――――. *The Empty Quarter: Being a Description of the Great South Desert of Arabia Known as Rub' al Khali.* New York: Holt, 1933.

―――――. *Forty Years in the Wilderness.* London: Hale, 1957.

―――――. *The Heart of Arabia.* London: Constable, 1922.

―――――. *Saudi Arabia.* London: Benn, 1955.

Polin, Clair C.J. *Music of the Ancient Near East.* New York: Vantage, 1954.

Raswan, Carl R. "Tribal Areas and Migration Lines of the North Arabian Bedouins," *The Geographical Review,* XX, 1930, 494–502.

Rentz, George. "Muhammad ibn Abdal-Wahhab (1703/04–1792) and the Beginnings of the Unitarian Empire in Arabia." Unpublished Doctoral dissertation, University of California, August 1948.

―――――. "Notes on Dickson's 'The Arab of the Desert'," *Moslem World,* XLI, 1951, 49–64.

Richards, J.M. "Desert City—an Account of Hail in Central Arabia," *The Architectural Review,* CV, January 1949, 35–41.

Rubissow, Helen. *Art of Asia.* New York: Philosophical Library, 1954.

Rutter, Eldon. *The Holy Cities of Arabia.* 2 vols. New York: Putnam, 1928.

―――――. "Slavery in Arabia," *Journal of the Royal Central Asian Society,* XX, 1933, 315–332.

Sanger, Richard H. *The Arabian Peninsula.* Ithaca: Cornell University Press, 1954.

Saudi Arabia. "Jiddah Quarantine Station," April 3, 1956. (Unpublished manuscript.)

―――――. "Ministry of Health," March 1956. (Unpublished manuscript.)

———. Government Relations Department. Arabian Research Division. "Ministry of Health Circular, Number 1." Dammam: March 29, 1955.

Saudi Arabia. Ministry of Finance. *Labor and Workman Regulations.* (Trans., Arabian American Oil Company, Relations Department.) Dhahran: 1948.

Saudi Arabian News (Washington), *passim.*

"Saudi Arabians and Foreign Education," *Moslem World,* XLV, October 1955, 386.

Seligmann, C.G. "The Physical Characters of the Arabs." *Journal of the Royal Anthropological Institute of Great Britain and Ireland,* XLVII, 1917, 214–237.

Shaffer, Robert. *Tents and Towers of Arabia.* New York: Dodd, Mead, 1952.

Shah, Sayid Idris. *Destination Mecca.* London: Rider, 1957.

Shanklin, William M. "Anthropology of the Akeydat and Maualy Bedouin," *American Journal of Physical Anthropology,* XXI, 1936, 217–252.

———. "Blood Groupings of the Maualy and Akeydat Bedouin," *American Journal of Physical Anthropology,* XXI, 1936, 39–48.

Smith, Sidney. "Events in Arabia in the Sixth Century A.D.," *BSOAS,* XVI, No. 3, 1954, 425–468.

Smith, Wilfred C. *Islam in Modern History.* Princeton: Princeton University Press, 1957.

Southern, I.W. "Ras Tanura: The Story of a Middle East Refining Community and Its Preventive Sanitation Program," *Modern Sanitation,* August 16, 1955.

Stauffer, Thomas B. "The Industrial Worker." In Sydney Nettleton Fisher (ed.), *Social Forces in the Middle East.* Ithaca: Cornell University Press, 1955, 83–98.

Stoddard, Phillip. *An Economic Survey of Saudi Arabia.* Typescript in Princeton University library, May 1951.

Tannous, Afif I. "The Arab Tribal Community in a Nationalist State," *Middle East Journal,* I, 1947, 5–17.

———. "Land Reform: Key to the Development and Stability of the Arab World," *Middle East Journal,* V, Winter 1951, 1–20.

Thesiger, Wilfred Patrick. "Across the Empty Quarter," *Geographical Journal,* III, 1948, 1–21.

Mountains," *Geographical Journal,* CX, July-September 1947,

———. "The Badu of Southern Arabia," *Journal of the Royal Central Asian Society,* XXXVII, 1950, 53–61.

———. "A Journey Through the Tihama, the Asir, and the Hijaz 188–200.

Thomas, Bertram. *Arabia Felix.* New York: Scribner's, 1932.

Trial, George T., and Winder, R. Bayly. "Modern Education Saudi Arabia," *History of Education Journal*, I, No. 3, 1950, 121–133.

Twitchell, Karl Saben. "Water Resources of Saudi Arabia," *Geographical Review*, XXXIV, 1944.

Twitchell, Karl Saben, and Jurji, Edward J. *Saudi Arabia: With an Account of the Development of its Natural Resources.* (2d ed.) Princeton: Princeton University Press, 1953.

United Nations Education, Scientific and Cultural Organization. Compulsory Education in the Arab States. (Studies on Compulsory Education, XVI.) Paris: 1956.

———. *World Communications: Press, Radio, Film, Television.* (3d ed.) New York: 1956.

———. *World Survey of Education, Handbook of Educational Organization and Statistics.* Paris: 1955.

Uthman, Haafiz. "The Prophet Muhammad's Mosque," *Islamic Review*, February 1957, 19–23.

Viardot, Louis. "Quelques Notes sur la Peinture et la Sculpture chez les Mussulmans," *Gazette des Beaux Arts*, 2 periods, I, 1869, 556–559.

Vidal, F.S. "Date Culture in the Oasis of Al-Hasa," *Middle East Journal*, VIII, 1954, 417–428.

"What is Islam," *Islamic Review*, January 1957.

Winder, R. Bayly. "A History of the Su'udi State from 1233/1818 until 1308/1891." Unpublished Doctoral dissertation, Princeton University, 1950.

World Health Organization. *The Work of WHO, 1954.* Annual Report of the Director-General to the World Health Organization Assembly and the United Nations. Geneva: March 1955.

———. *Proposed Programme and Budget Estimates for the Financial Year, January 1-December 31, 1957.* Geneva: 1955.

———. "Weekly Epidemiological Record," 1950–1956.

Worthington, Edgar B. *Middle East Service: A Survey of Subjects other than Agriculture.* London: Oxford University Press, 1946.

Al-Yamamah, No. 5, January 1955.

Zahra, Muhammad Abu. "Family Law." In Majid Khadduri and Herbert J. Liebesny (eds.), *Law in the Middle East.* Washington: Middle East Institute, 1955, 132–178.

Section II, Political
RECOMMENDED FURTHER READING

Among the sources consulted in the preparation of this section, the following are recommended as additional reading on the basis of quality and general usefulness.

Lenczowski, George. *The Middle East in World Affairs.* Ithaca: Cornell University Press, 1962.

Rentz, George. "Saudi Arabia: The Islamic Island," *Journal of International Affairs,* XIX, No. 1, 1965, 77–86.

"Saudi Arabia: The New Statute of the Council of Ministers," *Middle East Journal,* XII, Summer 1958, 318–323.

"Transfer of Powers from H.M. King Saud to H.R.H. Amir Faisal," *Middle East Journal,* XVIII, Summer 1964, 351–354.

OTHER SOURCES USED

Al-Idhaa (Jidda), November 1964.

Anshen, Ruth Nanda (ed.). *Mid-East: World Center.* New York: Harper, 1956.

Arabian American Oil Company. *Aramco Handbook,* by Roy Lebkicher, George Rentz, Max Steineke, *et al.* Dhahran: Aramco, 1960.

Benoist-Mechin, Jacques. *Le Roi Saud.* Paris: Editions Albin Michel, 1960.

Brown, E. H. *The Saudi Arabia-Kuwait Neutral Zone.* (Middle East Oil Monographs, No. 4.) Beirut: Middle East Research Publication Center, 1963.

Davis, Helen (ed.). *Constitutions, Electoral Laws, Treaties of the States in the Near and Middle East.* Durham: Duke University Press, 1953.

Deadline Data on World Affairs, 1964, *passim.*

Dimbleby, David. "Britain and King Faisal," *New Statesman,* LXIX, April 23, 1965, 632, 633.

Eddy, William A. "King Ibn Saud: 'Our Faith and Your Iron,'" *Middle East Journal,* XVII, Summer 1963, 257–263.

"Exchange of Letters Between President John F. Kennedy and Amir Faisal, Premier and Foreign Minister of Saudi Arabia," *Middle East Affairs,* XIV, February 1963, 47, 48.

Gibb, H.A.R., and Kramers, J.H. (eds.). *The Shorter Encyclopaedia of Islam.* Ithaca: Cornell University Press, 1953.

Harrington, Charles W. "The Saudi Arabian Council of Ministers," *Middle East Journal,* XII, Winter 1958, 1–19.

Hoskins, Halford L. "Background of the British Position in Arabia," *Middle East Journal,* I, April 1947, 137–147.

Howard, Bushrod, Jr. "Buraimi: A Study in Diplomacy by Default," *Reporter,* XVIII, January 23, 1958, 13–16.

Kelly, John B. *Eastern Arabian Frontiers.* New York: Praeger, 1964.

Khadduri, Majid, and Liebesny, Herbert J. (eds.). *Law in the Middle East,* I. Washington: Middle East Institute, 1955.

Levy, Reuben. *The Social Structure of Islam.* (2d ed.) Cambridge: Cambridge University Press, 1957.

Liebesny, Herbert J. "International Relations of Arabia: The Dependent Areas," *Middle East Journal,* I, April 1947, 148–168.

The Middle East and North Africa, 1964–65. London: Europa Publications, 1964.

"Ministerial Statement of 6 November 1962 by Prime Minister Amir Faisal of Saudi Arabia," *Middle East Journal,* XVII, Winter-Spring 1963, 161, 162.

Nallino, Carlo Alfonso. *L'Arabia Saudiana.* Rome: Instituto per l'Oriente, 1939.

Nolte, Richard H. "Faisal Takes Over in Saudi Arabia," *Reporter,* XVIII, May 1, 1958, 7–10.

―――. *The Modern Middle East.* New York: Atherton Press, 1963.

―――. "The Rule of Law in the Arab Middle East," *The Muslim World,* XLVIII, October 1958, 4.

―――. "A Tale of Three Cities: I, Dhahran; II, Riyadh; III, Jedda and the King." (AUFS Reports Service, Saudi Arabia, RHN-4-'57, RHN-6-'57, and RHN-7-'57.) New York: American Universities Field Staff, 1957.

Polk, William R. *The United States and the Middle East.* Cambridge: Harvard University Press, 1965.

Saudi Arabia. Ministry of Information. *Saudi Arabia: Land of Achievement.* Jidda: 1964.

Schacht, Joseph. *An Introduction to Islamic Law.* Oxford: Clarendon Press, 1964.

Schmidt, D.A. "Faisal Modernizes, But With Caution," *New York Times Magazine,* November 1, 1964, 38.

Sharabi, H.B. *Government and Politics in the Middle East in the 20th Century.* Princeton: Van Nostrand, 1962.

Sheean, Vincent. "King Faisal's First Year," *Foreign Affairs,* XLIV, January 1966, 304–313.

Silvert, K.H. (ed.). *Expectant Peoples: Nationalism and Development.* (American Universities Field Staff.) New York: Random House, 1963.

Stevens, Georgiana G. (ed.). *The United States and the Middle East.* (The American Assembly, Columbia University.) Englewood Cliffs: Prentice Hall, 1964.

Twitchell, Karl Saben. *Saudi Arabia.* (3d ed.) Princeton: Princeton University Press, 1958.

United Nations. Department of Economic and Social Affairs. "Urban Administration in the Kingdom of Saudi Arabia." In *Administrative Problems of Rapid Urban Growth in the Arab*

States. (Technical Assistance Programme.) New York: 1964, 128–130.

U.S. Department of Labor. Bureau of Labor Statistics. *Labor Law and Practice in Saudi Arabia.* (BLS Report No. 269.) Washington: GPO, 1964.

U.S. Department of State. Historical Office. Bureau of Public Affairs. "Saudi Arabia." In *Foreign Relations of the United States, Diplomatic Papers, 1944.* Washington: GPO, 1965, 658–773.

U.S. Information Agency. Research and Reference Service. *Arabian Peninsula: A Communications Fact Book.* (R–156–64.) Washington: 1964.

Voice of America. *Program Schedule to Middle East,* May-July 1965.

Von Grunebaum, G.E. "Islam: Essays in the Nature and Growth of a Cultural Tradition," *American Anthropologist,* LVII, No. 2, Pt. 2 (Memoir No. 81), April 1955, 127–140.

Yassin, Hassan Youssef. "The Saudi Arabian State: Historical, Social and Political Aspects," Unpublished Master's thesis, University of California (Berkeley), 1963.

Yearbook of the United Nations, 1963. New York: UN, 1964.

(The following sources were also used in the preparation of this section: *Al-Nadwa* [Mecca], from January 1965 through December 1965; *The Economist* [London], from January 1958 through December 1965; *Keesing's Contemporary Archives* [London], January 1958 through December 1965; *Middle East Journal* [Washington], from December 1947 through December 1965; *News from Saudi Arabia* [Jidda] [formerly *Saudi Weekly Newsletter*], from February 1961 through December 1965; and *Saudi Arabia Today* [New York], from March 1964 through December 1965.)

The following additional sources were used in the preparation of the original *Area Handbook for Saudi Arabia,* published in 1958.

Ali, Maulana Muhammad. "Penal Laws of Islam," *Islamic Review,* XXXVII, June 1949, 7–11.

Anderson, H.N.D. "Homicide in Islamic Law," *Bulletin of the School of Oriental and African Studies,* XIII, 1951, 811–828.

The Arab Information Center. *Basic Documents of the League of Arab States.* New York: 1955, 40.

Arabian American Oil Company. *Handbooks for American Employees,* II, Dhahran: 1952.

Arbitration for the Settlement of the Territorial Dispute Between Muscat and Abu Dhabi on One Side and Saudi Arabia on the

Other; Memorial of the Government of Saudi Arabia. 3 vols. Cariro: Al-Maaref Press, 1956.

Armstrong, H.C. *Land of Arabia.* Beirut: Ichayat's College Book Cooperative, 1934.

———. *Lord of Arabia.* London: Barker, 1934.

Ashkenazi, Touvia. "The Anazah Tribes," *Southwestern Journal of Anthropology*, IV, 1948, 222–239.

Benoist-Mechin, Jacques. *Arabian Destiny.* (Trans., Denis Weaver.) London: Elek, 1957.

Caroe, Olaf. *Wells of Power.* London: Macmillan, 1951.

"Changing Arabia: Significant Factors in the Impact upon Saudi Arabian Life and Economy of Oil Developments," *Petroleum Press Service Bulletin*, XX, August 1953, 288.

Cheney, Michael S. *Big Oil Man from Arabia.* New York: Ballantine, 1958.

"Council of Ministers," *Middle East Journal*, XII, No. 2, 1958.

Davis, Rodger P. *The Organization of the Government of Saudi Arabia.* (Report No. 3.) Jidda: 1948. (Microfilmed typescript.)

Dickson, Harold R.P. *The Arab of the Desert: A Glimpse into Badawin Life in Kuwait and Saudi Arabia.* London: Allen and Unwin, 1949.

———. *Kuwait and Her Neighbors.* London: Allen and Unwin, 1956.

Doughty, Charles M. *Travels in Arabia Deserts.* New York: Random House, 1946.

Ellis, Harry B. *Heritage of the Desert.* New York: Ronald Press, 1956.

Gaury, Gerald de. *Arabia Phoenix.* London: Harrap, 1946.

Glubb, John Bagot. *A Soldier with the Arabs.* New York: Harper, 1957.

———. *The Story of the Arab Legion.* London: Hodder and Stoughton, 1956.

Harrison, Paul W. *The Arab at Home.* New York: Crowell, 1924.

Hart, Parker T. "Application of Hanbalite and Decree Law to Foreigners in Saudi Arabia," *George Washington Law Review*, XXII, December 1953, 165–175.

Hartley, John G. *The Political Structure of Saudi Arabia*, May 21, 1956. (Unpublished manuscript not available for distribution.)

Hazard, Harry W. (ed.). *Saudi Arabia.* HRAF Subcontractor's Monograph, 1956.

Hurewitz, J.C. *Diplomacy in the Near and Middle East.* 2 vols. Princeton: Van Nostrand, 1956.

Jones, Catesby Thomas. "A Comparative Study of Northern and

Southern Pastoral Nomadism in Asia." Unpublished Doctoral dissertation, John Hopkins University, 1952.

Kheirallah, George. *Arabia Reborn*. Albuquerque: University of New Mexico Press, 1952.

Kirkpatrick, Evron M. (ed.). *Year of Crisis; Communist Propaganda Activities in 1956*. New York: Macmillan, 1957.

Lebkicher, Roy; Rentz, George; and Steineke, Max. *The Arabia of Ibn Saud*. New York: Moore, 1952.

Longrigg, Stephen Hemsley. *Oil in the Middle East; its Discovery and Development*. New York: Oxford University Press, 1954.

Meulen, D. van der. *The Wells of Ibn Saud*. New York: Praeger, 1957.

The Middle East—1957. London: Europa Publications, 1957.

The Middle East, a Political and Economic Survey. (2d ed.) London: Royal Institute of International Affairs, 1954.

"Miscellanea," *Muslim World*, XLV, 1955, 387, 388.

Montagne, Robert. *La Civilisation du Desert*. Paris: Librairie Hachette, 1947.

"Morality and Law in Arabia," *Moslem World*, XLIV, 1954, 68, 69.

Morris, James. *Islam Inflamed*. New York: Pantheon, 1957.

Peaslee, Amos J. *Constitutions of Nations*. (2d ed.) III. The Hague: Nijhoff, 1956.

Philby, H. St. John B. *Arabia*. London: Benn, 1930.

―――――. *Forty Years in the Wildnerness*. London: Hale, 1957.

―――――. "The New Reign in Saudi Arabia," *Foreign Affairs*, XXXII, 1953–54, 446–458.

―――――. *Saudi Arabia*. London: Benn, 1955.

"Phoenix; A Brief Outline of the Wahhabi Movement," *Journal of the Central Asian Society*, XVII, 1930, 401–416.

Sanger, Richard H. *The Arabian Peninsula*. Ithaca: Cornell University Press, 1954.

Saudi Arabian News (Washington), *passim*.

Shaffer, Robert. *Tents and Towers of Arabia*. New York: Dodd, Mead, 1952.

Smalley, W.F. "The Wahhabis and Ibn Saud," *Moslem World*, XXII, July 1932, 227–246.

The Times (London), 1955, *passim*.

Twitchell, Karl Saben, and Jurji, Edward J. *Saudi Arabia: With an Account of the Development of Its Natural Resources*. (2d ed.) Princeton: Princeton University Press, 1953.

Yearbook of the United Nations, 1955. New York: Columbia, 1956.

Yearbook of the United Nations, 1956. New York: Columbia, 1957.

Section III, Economic
RECOMMENDED FURTHER READING

Among the sources consulted in the preparation of this section, the following are recommended as additional reading on the basis of quality and general usefulness.

Arabian American Oil Company. *Aramco Handbook*, by Roy Lebkicher, George Rentz, Max Steineke, et al. Dhahran: Aramco, 1960.

Dequin, Horst. *Die Landwirtschaft Saudisch-Arabiens und ihre Entwicklungs-möglichkeiten.* (Series: Zeitschrift für ausländische Landwirtschaft.) Frankfurt: DLG-Verlags-GMBH, 1963.

U.S. Department of Labor. Bureau of Labor Statistics. *Labor Law and Practice in Saudi Arabia.* (BLS Report No. 269.) Washington: GPO, 1964.

OTHER SOURCES USED

Anwar, Ali, and Hitti, Said. "Monetary Experience of an Oil Economy," *Finance and Development*, II, December 1965, 223–229.

Arabian American Oil Company. *Report of Activities 1964: Arab Industrial Development Department.* Dhahran: Aramco, 1965.

Baer, Gabriel. *Population and Society in the Arab East.* New York: Praeger, 1964.

Cressey, George B. *Crossroads; Land and Life in Southwest Asia.* New York: Lippincott, 1960.

Emam, Hani Shafeek. "The Economy of Saudi Arabia and the 1956–1960 Crisis." Unpublished Master's thesis, Columbia University, 1963.

Farmer, Richard N., and Richman, Barry M. "A Day in the Life of an American Manager of a Saudi Business Enterprise." In *Comparative Management and Economic Progress.* Homewood: Irwin, 1965, Appendix A.

Finnie, David H. *Desert Enterprise: The Middle East Oil Industry in Its Local Environment.* Cambridge: Harvard University Press, 1958.

Food and Agriculture Organization. *Production Yearbook 1963*, XVII. Rome: FAO, 1964.

──────. *Report to the Government of Saudi Arabia on Grazing Resources and Problems*, by Harold Heady. (Report No. 1614.) Rome: FAO, 1963.

──────. *Report to the Government of Saudi Arabia on Pasture Development and Range Management*, by Marvin Klemme. (Report No. 1993.) Rome: FAO, 1965.

———. *Report to the Government of Saudi Arabia on the Organization of Fisheries Operations on the Red Sea,* by Odd Mevatne. (Fisheries Reports No. 16.) Rome: FAO, 1964.

———. *Water Laws in Moslem Countries,* by Dante A. Caponera. Rome: FAO, 1954.

———. Agriculture Division. Program Analysis Service. *Characteristics and Problems of Agriculture in Saudi Arabia,* by N.A. Lateef. (Background Country Studies, No. 4.) Rome: FAO, 1956.

"France's RAP Enters Saudi Oil Scene," *Middle East Economic Survey* (Special Issue) (Beirut), April 5, 1965.

Great Britain. Naval Staff. Naval Intelligence Division. *Western Arabia and the Red Sea.* (Geographical Handbook Series, BR 527.) London: HMSO, 1946.

Haddad, Edmonde Alex. "Saudi Arabia and Oil." Unpublished Master's thesis, Columbia University, n.d.

Harrington, Charles W. "The Saudi Arabian Council of Ministers," *Middle East Journal,* XII, Winter 1958, 1–19.

International Petroleum Institute. *World Petroleum Legislation.* New York: IPI, 1964.

Issawi, Charles, and Yeganeh, Mohammed. *The Economics of Middle Eastern Oil.* New York: Praeger, 1962.

Khadduri, Majid, and Liebesny, Herbert J. (eds.). *Law in the Middle East,* I. Washington: Middle East Institute, 1955.

Lenczowski, George. *Oil and State in the Middle East.* Ithaca: Cornell University Press, 1960.

Longrigg, Stephen H. *Oil in the Middle East: Its Discovery and Development.* London: Oxford University Press, 1961.

Organization of the Petroleum Exporting Countries. *Background Information.* N. pl.: n. pub., n.d.

———. *Exporting Countries and International Oil,* by Francisco R. Parra. (EC/64/I) London: 1964.

Pauling, N.G. "Labor Separation in an Undeveloped Area: Saudi Arabia," *American Journal of Economics,* XXIII, October 1964.

Saudi Arabia. *Labor and Workmen's Regulations.* (Trans., Arabian American Oil Company.) N. pl.: 1958.

———. Division of Planning, Programming, Traffic and Statistics. *Road Transportation Statistics.* (No. 11/126.) N. pl.: March 15, 1964.

Saudi Arabia. Laws, Statutes, etc.

"Legislation Concerning the General Budget for 1384–85 A.H." (Royal Decree No. 4.) Jidda: Saudi Arabian Monetary Agency, 1964.

Regulations for the Protection and Encouragement of National Industries, May 27, 1962. (Royal Decree No. 50.)

Saudi Arabia's New Foreign Capital Investment Code, February 25, 1964. (Royal Decree No. 35.)

Saudi Arabia. Ministry of Agriculture. *Annual Report 1382–83.* Jidda (?) : 1964.

Saudi Arabia. Ministry of Information. *Prince Faisal Speaks.* Jidda (?) : 1963.

———. *Saudi Arabia: Land of Achievement.* Jidda: 1964 (?).

———. *Social Welfare.* Jidda (?) : 1963 (?).

———. *Trade and Industry.* Jidda (?) : 1963 (?).

Saudi Arabia. Ministry of Petroleum and Mineral Resources. *Mineral Resources of Saudi Arabia: A Guide for Investment and Development.* (Bulletin No. 1.) Jidda: 1965.

Saudi Arabia. Saudi Arabian Monetary Agency. *Annual Report 1381–82 A.H. (1962).* Jidda: 1963.

———. *Annual Report 1382–83 A.H. (1963).* Jidda: 1964.

———. *Annual Report 1383–84 A.H. (1964).* Jidda: 1965.

———. *Circular on the Saudi Arabian Budget Estimates for 1384–85 A.H.* (No. 3920/26/14/10.) Jidda: 1964.

———. *Statistical Summary,* I, Nos. 1 and 2. Jidda: 1963 and 1964.

"Saudi Arabia: An Ancient Land with a Promising Future," *New York Times,* Section 11, January 12, 1964.

"Saudi Arabia: The New Statute of the Council of Ministers," *Middle East Journal,* XII, Summer 1958, 318–323.

"Saudi Arabia Moves Ahead," *Herald Tribune,* October 25, 1964.

"Saudi Arabian Decree on Devaluation of the Riyal and the Establishment of a Paper Currency," *Middle East Journal,* XIV, Spring 1960, 203–205.

Twitchell, Karl Saben. *Saudi Arabia.* (3d ed.) Princeton: Princeton University Press, 1958.

United Nations. *To Accelerate the Industrial Growth of Saudi Arabia,* by Erwin S. Penn. New York: 1965.

U.S. Department of Commerce. Bureau of Foreign Commerce. *Income Tax Law of Saudi Arabia.* (World Trade Information Service: "Economic Reports," Pt. 1, No. 57–62.) Washington: GPO, January 1957.

———. *Law on the Investment Code of Foreign Capital in Saudi Arabia.* (World Trade Information Service: "Economic Reports," Pt. 1, No. 57–75.) Washington: GPO, September 1957.

U.S. Department of Commerce. Bureau of International Commerce. *Basic Data on the Economy of Saudi Arabia.* (Overseas Business Reports: "Economic Reports," OBR 64–40.) Washington: GPO, 1964.

_____. *Saudi Arabia: A Market for U.S. Products*, by Albert N. Abdo. Washington: GPO, 1962.

_____. "World Customs Data," *International Commerce*, August 2, 1965.

_____. "Worldwide Import Rules," *International Commerce*, August 9, 1965.

Vidal, Federico S. *The Oasis of Al-Hasa*. Dhahran: Arabian American Oil Company, 1955.

World Petroleum Report (New York), March 15, 1965.

Young, Arthur N. "Financial Reforms in Saudi Arabia," *Middle East Journal*, XIV, Autumn 1960, 466–469.

_____. "Saudi Arabian Currency and Finance, *Middle East Journal*, VII, Summer 1953, 361–380; Autumn 1953, 539–556.

(The following sources were also used in the preparation of this section: *Keesing's Contemporary Archives* [London], from January 1958 through December 1965; *Middle East Economic Survey* [Beirut], from January 1962 through December 1965; *Middle East Journal* [Washington], from January 1958 through December 1965; *News from Saudi Arabia* [formerly *Saudi Weekly Newsletter*] [Jidda], from March 1961 through December 1965; *Petroleum Press Service* [London], from January 1960 through December 1965; *Quarterly Economic Review: Middle East Oil and the Arabian Peninsula* [London], March 1964 through October 1965; *Review of Operations* [Aramco], from 1960 through 1964; and *Saudi Arabia Today* [New York], from March 1964 through December 1965.)

The following additional sources were used in the preparation of the original *Area Handbook for Saudi Arabia*, published in 1958.

Arab News and Views (Washington), June 20, 1957; July 5, 1957; August 5, 1957; August 20, 1957; October 1957; November 20, 1957; December 20, 1957; January 1958.

Arabian American Oil Company. "Report of Operations 1953 to the Saudi Arab Government." Dhahran: 1954.

_____. "Report of Operations 1954 to the Saudi Arab Government." Dhahran: 1955.

_____. "Report of Operations 1955 to the Saudi Arab Government." Dhahran: 1956.

_____. "Report of Operations 1956 to the Saudi Arab Government." Dhahran: 1957.

"Arabic Seoudite: Naissance d'une opinion," *L'Express*, V, April 17, 1958, 11.

Barrows, Gordon H. (ed.). *World Petroleum Report, 1957; An*

Annual Review of International Oil Operations, III. New York: Mona Palmer, 1957.

Bowen, Richard Lebaron, Jr. "Marine Industries of Eastern Arabia," *Geographical Review*, XLI, 1951.

Cooke, Hedley V. *Challenge and Response in the Middle East: The Quest for Prosperity, 1919–1951.* New York: Harper, 1952.

Coon, Carleton Stevens. "The Nomads." In Sydney Nettleton Fisher (ed.), *Social Forces in the Middle East*. Ithaca: Cornell University Press, 1955, 23–42.

Coon, Carleton Stevens. "Operation Bultiste: Promoting Industrial Development in Saudi Arabia." In Howard M. Teaf, Jr. and Peter G. Franck (eds.), *Hands Across Frontiers: Case Studies in Technical Cooperation*. Ithaca: Cornell University Press, 1955, 307–361.

Dickson, Harold R.P. *The Arab of the Desert; A Glimpse into Badawin Life in Kuwait and Saudi Arabia.* London: Allen and Unwin, 1949.

——————. *Kuwait and Her Neighbors.* London: Allen and Unwin, 1956.

The Economist Intelligence Unit, Ltd. *Annual Supplement, Iraq,* August 1957.

——————. *Three-Monthly Economic Review; Iraq and Arabian Peninsula,* No. 7, November 1957. London: 1957.

——————. *Three-Monthly and Annual Reports on Iraq and the Arabian Peninsula,* 1956–1957, 1958, *passim*.

Ellis, Harry B. *Heritage of the Desert.* New York: Ronald Press, 1956.

Erdman, Donald S. "Fishing in Arabia," *Scientific Monthly*, LXX, 1950.

Federal Reserve System. Board of Governors. *Federal Reserve Bulletin*, XLIV, March 1958.

Food and Agriculture Organization. *Agriculture in the Near East; Development and Outlook.* Rome: November 1953.

——————. *Report to the Government of Saudi Arabia on Agricultural Extension.* (Report No. 518.) Rome: August 1956.

——————. *Yearbook of Fisheries Statistics 1948.* Rome: 1950.

Food and Agriculture Organization. Agriculture Division. Program Analysis Service. *Characteristics and Problems of Agriculture in Saudi Arabia,* by N.A. Lateef. New York: 1956.

Gordon, Nathanial. "The Strangest Railroad on Earth," *Saturday Evening Post*, CCXXVI, No. 20, 1953–54.

Great Britain. Board of Trade. *Markets in the Middle East: Report of the United Kingdom Trade Mission to Iraq, Kuwait, the Lebanon, Syria and Saudi Arabia, November-December 1953.* London: HMSO, 1954.

Great Britain. Geographical Section of the Naval Intelligence Division, Naval Staff, Admiralty. *A Handbook of Arabia*, I. London: HMSO, 1920.

Hale, William Harlan. "Troubled Oil in the Middle East," *The Reporter*, XVIII, January 23, 1958.

Hall, Harvey P. (ed.). "Middle East Resources, Problems and Prospect." (A series of addresses presented at the eighth annual conference on Middle Eastern Affairs by the Middle East Institute, March 19–20, 1954.) Washington: Middle East Institute, 1954.

Harrison, Paul W. *The Arab at Home*. New York: Crowell, 1924.

Hazard, Harry W. (ed.). *Saudi Arabia*. HRAF Subcontractor's Monograph, 1956.

Heyworth-Dunne, J. "Report from Saudi Arabia," *Jewish Observer and Middle East Review*, IV, January 14, 1955, 13, 14.

Inayatullah, Sheikh. *Geographical Factors in Arabian Life and History*. Lahore, India: Shaikh Muhammad Ashraf, 1942.

"Inside Saudi Arabia; Visit with the Ruler of Vital Oil-Rich Desert Land," *Newsweek*, XLV, March 7, 1955, 44–46.

International Monetary Fund. *Eighth Annual Report, Exchange Restrictions*. Washington: 1957.

———. *International Financial News Survey*, X, No. 9, August 30, 1957.

———. *International Financial Statistics*, XI, No. 1, January 1958.

———. *Seventh Annual Report, Exchange Restrictions*. Washington: 1956.

Jones, K. Westcott. "The Romance of Saudi Arabia's Oilfields; Changes in Arab Way of Life," *Great Britain and the East*, LXVIII, February 1952, 21–23.

Kheirallah, George. *Arabia Reborn*. Albuquerque: University of New Mexico Press, 1952.

Lebkicher, Roy. "The Training of Saudi Arab Employees: Arabian American Oil Company." Reprinted from *The Yearbook of Education, 1954*. London: Evans, 1954.

Lebkicher, Roy; Rentz, George; and Steineke, Max. *The Arabia of Ibn Saud*. New York: Moore, 1952.

Longrigg, Stephen Hemsley. "The Liquid Gold of Arabia," *Journal of the Royal Central Asian Society*, XXXVII, Pt. 1, January 1949.

Maunsell, F.R. "One Thousand Miles of Railroad Built for Pilgrims and Not for Dividends," *National Geographic Magazine*, XX, 1909.

Meulen, D. van der. *The Wells of Ibn Saud*. New York: Praeger, 1957.

The Middle East—1957. London: Europa Publications, 1957.
The Middle East, a Political and Economic Survey. (2d ed.) London: Royal Institute of International Affairs, 1954.
Mikesell, Raymond F. "Monetary Problems of Saudi Arabia," *Middle East Journal,* I, April 1947, 169–179.
Mikesell, Raymond F., and Chenery, Hollis B. *Arabian Oil; America's Stake in the Middle East.* Chapel Hill: University of North Carolina Press, 1949.
"Ministry of Finance Reorganized," *Saudi Arabian News,* II, January 1957.
National Commercial Bank. "World Wide Banking Services." (Balance Sheet as at end of Safar 1374 Hijrieh year the 27th October 1954.) Beirut: Azar Press, n.d.
New York Times, April 4, 1958.
"Oil and Social Change in the Middle East," *The Economist,* CLXXVI, July 2, 1955.
Patai, Raphael. "The Middle East as a Culture Area," *Middle East Journal,* VI, Winter 1952, 1–21.
Philby, H. St. John B. *Arabian Highlands.* Ithaca: Cornell University Press, 1952.
———. *Forty Years in the Wilderness.* London: Hale, 1957.
———. "The Land of Sheba," *Geographical Journal,* XCII, 1938.
———. "The New Reign in Saudi Arabia," *Foreign Affairs,* XXXII, 1953–54, 446–458.
———. *Saudi Arabia.* London: Benn, 1955.
"Royal Decree Approves Budget for New Fiscal Year," *Saudi Arabian News,* III, January 1958, 4.
Sanger, Richard H. *The Arabian Peninsula.* Ithaca: Cornell University Press, 1954.
Shamma, Samir. *The Law of Income Tax and Zakat in the Kingdom of Saudi Arabia.* Beirut: Dar al-Ahad, August 1951.
Shwadran, Benjamin. *The Middle East, Oil and the Great Powers.* New York: Praeger, 1955.
———. "Oil in the Middle East Crisis," *Middle Eastern Affairs,* VII, April 1957, 126–134.
Statistisches Bundesamt, Wiesbaden. *Der Aussenhandel der Bundesrepublik Deutschland, Ergänzungsreihe: Der Aussenhandel des Auslandes, Nr. 41: Saudisch-Arabien* (Zusammengestellt nach Angaben der Aussenhandelsstatistiken der Partnerländer im Handelsverkehr mit Saudisch-Arabien und der Bundersrepublik Deutschland). Stuttgart and Cologne: W. Kohlhammer, January 1957.
Tannous, Afif I. "Land Reform: Key to the Development and

Stability of the Arab World," *Middle East Journal*, V, Winter 1951, 1–20.

Thesiger, Wilfred Patrick. "A Journey Through the Tihama, the Asir, and the Hijaz Mountains," *Geographical Journal*, CX, July-September 1947, 188–200.

Twitchell, Karl Saben. "Water Resources of Saudi Arabia," *Geographical Review*, XXXIV, 1944.

Twitchell, Karl Saben, and Jurji, Edward J. *Saudi Arabia: With an Account of the Development of its Natural Resources.* (2d ed.) Princeton: Princeton University Press, 1953.

United Nations. Department of Economic and Social Affairs. *Economic Developments in the Middle East, 1955–1956* (Supplement to World Economic Survey, 1956). New York: 1957.

United Nations Statistical Office, International Monetary Fund, and International Bank for Reconstruction and Development. *Direction of International Trade, Annual Issue, Annual Data for the Years 1938, 1948, and 1953–1956.* (Statistical Papers, Series T, VIII, No. 7.) N.pl.: October 16, 1957.

U.S. Congress. 82d. Senate. *The International Petroleum Cartel.* (Staff Report to the Federal Trade Commission submitted to the Subcommittee on Monopoly of the Sebet Committee on Small Business, United States Senate.) Washington: 1952.

U.S. Department of Agriculture, Foreign Agriculture Service. *The Agricultural Resources of the Arabian Peninsula,* by Henrietta M. Holm. Washington: 1955.

―――. *Notes on the Agricultural Economy of Saudi Arabia.* Washington: Summer 1957.

U.S. Department of Commerce, Bureau of Foreign Commerce. *Economic Development in Saudi Arabia 1954.* (World Trade Information Service: Economic Reports, Pt. 1, No. 55–58.) Washington: June 1955.

―――. *Licensing and Exchange Controls . . . Saudi Arabia.* (World Trade Information Service: Operations Reports, Pt. 2, No. 57–119.) Washington: November 1957.

U.S. Department of the Treasury. Office of the Director of the Mint. *Annual Report of the Director of the Mint for Fiscal Years Ended June 30, 1954 and 1956; Including a Report on the Production and Consumption of Gold and Silver for the Calendar Years 1953 and 1955.* Washington: 1955 and 1957.

Vidal, F.S. "Date Culture in the Oasis of al-Hasa," *Middle East Journal*, VIII, 1954, 417–428.

Washington Post and Times Herald, November-December 1957, passim.

Yeganeh, Mohammed. "Investment in the Petroleum Industry of the Middle East," *Middle East Journal*, VI, Spring 1952, 241–246.

Section IV, National Security

Arabian American Oil Company. *Aramco Handbook*, by Roy Lebkicher, George Rentz, Max Steineke, *et al.* Dhahran: Aramco, 1960.

Deadline Data on World Affairs, 1964, *passim*.

Ellis, Harry B. *Heritage of the Desert*. New York: Ronald Press, 1956.

Fisher, Sydney N. *The Middle East*. London: Routledge and Kegan-Paul, 1960.

Philby, H. St. John. *Saudi Arabia*. London: Benn, 1955.

Saudi Arabia. Saudi Arabian Monetary Agency. *Circular on the Saudi Arabian Budget Estimates for 1384–85 A.H.* (No. 3920/26/14/10.) Jidda, 1964.

U.S. Department of Defense. Military Assistance Institute. *Country Study—Saudi Arabia*. Washington: MAI, 1963.

(Also used in the preparation of this section were: *Keesing's Contemporary Archives* [London], from January 1958 through December 1965; *New York Times*, from January 1958 through December 1965; and *Saudi Arabia Today* [New York], from March 1964 through December 1965.)

The following additional sources were used in the preparation of the original *Area Handbook for Saudi Arabia*, published in 1958.

Armstrong, H.C. *Land of Arabia*. Beirut: Ichayat's College Book Cooperative, 1934.

Caroe, Olaf. *Wells of Power*. London: Macmillan, 1951.

Dickson, Harold R.P. *The Arab of the Desert; A Glimpse into Badawin Life in Kuwait and Saudi Arabia*. London: Allen and Unwin, 1949.

Longrigg, Stephen Hemsley. *Oil in the Middle East; its Discovery and Development*. New York: Oxford University Press, 1954.

Meulen, D. van der. *The Wells of Ibn Saud*. New York: Praeger, 1957.

Morris, James. *Islam Inflamed*. New York: Pantheon, 1957.

Sanger, Richard H. *The Arabian Peninsula*. Ithaca: Cornell University Press, 1954.

Shaffer, Robert. *Tents and Towers of Arabia*. New York: Dodd, Mead, 1952.

INDEX

Abd al-Aziz Ibn Rashid: 33, 34, 36, 37
Abd al-Aziz Ibn Saud: 2–6, 11, 25, 37, 59, 136; and Bedouins, 50, 56, 144; and foreign policy, 162, 164, 170, 172, 173; and government, 139–140; as king, 138, 153, 158, 198, 329; and public order, 189 *ff*.; unification, 7, 37–40, 133, 201, 321–324; and *zakat*, 129
Abd ar-Rahman: 33, 34
Abdullah Ibn Abd ar-Rahman: 157
Abdullah, Prince Ibn Abd al-Aziz: 325
Abdullah al-Sulayman: 301
Abha: 215; and dam, 239
Abqaiq: 15, 21
Aden: 11, 170
Adnan: 48, 61
agriculture (*see also* irrigation, land tenure, pastoralism): 6–7; 46, 213–240; and Bedouin Tribes, 56–57; cooperatives, 226; credit, 236–237, 298, 308; crops, 13, 22, 208, 214, 217, 220, 227–230, 238, 239, 279; cultivation, 9, 208, 215, 216 (fig. 6); economy, 5; and education, 97–98; experimental farms, 211, 238, 293; and government projects, 211, 237; and labor force, 226–227, 258; practices, 230–232; production, 211, 214, 227–230
air force: 321
air transportation: 5, 41, 274–275, 279, 314
Ajman tribe: 39, 49 (fig. 4), 323
Akrama dam: 239
Alflag: 14
Algeria: 43, 162, 163, 165, 167, 170, 278
Al-Hasa: 146; cultivation, 18, 227, 229, 232; and description, 15, 19, 38, 89, 97, 226; history, 2, 7, 29, 30, 33–36, 170; and irrigation, 17, 215

Al-Kharj: 14, 33, 248; and agriculture, 227, 230, 231 *ff*.; and experimental farms, 211, 238, 293; and irrigation, 17, 215, 218; and livestock, 233 *ff*.
Al-Khobar: 21, 126; description of, 235, 243, 286; and labor force, 259; and oil terminal, 259
Ali: 28, 29, 88, 110
Anaza tribe: 49 (fig. 4), 64
animal husbandry (*see also* livestock): 14, 50, 56, 213, 232–235, 258
Arab Federation: 44, 161, 166
Arab Industrial Development Department (AIDD): 252
Arab League: 8, 41–42, 55, 93, 161, 164, 167, 324, 328
Arabian American Oil Company (Aramco): 174, 268, 285–286, 288–294, 316–317; and agreement; 165, 172–173, 210; and concessions; 207, 245, 246 (fig. 7), 247; deposits, 40; and economy, 241; and educational facilities, 7, 92–93, 97, 101, 103, 181, 184–185; and exports, 282; and labor force, 4–5, 21, 51, 55, 57, 67, 259–261, 263, 265–266; and port facilities, 41, 275; and railroad, 4, 41, 173, 250, 273; and strikes, 42, 151; and water resources, 17; and welfare activities, 120, 125–126, 131–132; and Western culture, 4, 83, 88, 159
Arabian Peninsula: 1, 9, 11–12, 28, 37, 161, 235
Arafat: 115
armed forces: 321–326, 327 (table 17), 328–335; and the king, 134; and military justice, 334; and political power, 151
army: 321
Asia: 282
Asir: 37, 112, 128, 146; climate, 9, 16–17, 214; description, 12–13, 89, 219–235, 239, 258; and history, 2, 30–32, 36, 40, 167; and population, 5, 18, 19, 47, 49, 52

363

associations and interest groups: 60, 63, 65, 151
Badiet ash-Sham: 15-16
Baghdad: 1, 29; and Pact, 43, 165, 169
Bahrein: boundaries, 171; history, 32, 170; oil shipment, 247-248
balance of payments: 283, 284 (table 11), 285-286, 303
balance of trade: 212
Bani Khadir tribe: 48, 49 (fig. 4)
banditry: 189-190, 329
banks: 5, 297-298, 299, 302, 306, 307 (table 13), 308; Agricultural Credit Bank, 236-237, 298, 308
Basic Law: 135-137
Bedouin tribes: diet, 120; encampments, 22; and government, 144; history, 1-2, 29, 30, 31, 34, 35, 201; and king, 133, 138; language, 54; lineages, 61; livestock, 232 ff., 299; marriage and divorce, 73; as nomads, 14, 15, 49-51, 208; population, 5; religion, 112; resettlement, 213-214; social practices, 3, 6, 70, 76; social values, 47, 79, 80
birth rate: 18
boundaries: x (fig. 1), 1, 9-11, 324
budget: 211, 277, 297, 300, 308-312, 313 (table 15), 314
Buraimi Oasis: 11, 43, 161, 165, 171, 172
Burayda: 14, 34, 65, 97, 215, 226, 227, 322

capital: flight, 43, 209, 303; foreign, 254, 285, 293-294; and government, 254
Carmathiaus: 29
cement: 212, 279; and plants, 250, 253
censorship: 178, 187
census: 9, 18
Central Planning Organization: 210-211, 309
Christianity: 27, 55, 105
cities: population, 18, 19, 20-23; and government, 149, 150
citizenship: 55, 56, 144
climate (see also rainfall): 16-17, 9, 215, 232
collective bargaining: 151, 264

communications facilities: 46, 201, 241, 248, 276, 314
communism: 169; and Eisenhower Doctrine, 44; and Islam, 106; radio broadcasts, 187; and suspected subversion, 199
Communist states: 327; relations with, 8, 161, 163, 164; trade with, 282, 283
Constantinople: 29, 30
construction industry: 252-253; and imports, 279-280
cooperatives: 226, 270
copper mines: 242, 243
Council of Ministers: 7, 42, 44, 46, 138, 139-141, 142 (table 3), 143, 156; and the budget, 142, 297, 303, 304, 308, 309; and education, 93; and history, 136-137; and the king, 133; and political reforms, 154, 155; and provincial government, 146-149
courts: 194-196
credit institutions: 277, 299, 306-308
crime: 189, 190, 191, 196-198
Cox, Sir Percy: 36, 37, 39
currency: 208, 297-298, 300 ff., 305, 306 (table 12)

Dahna: desert, 9, 12, 14, 218; and oil concessions, 245
Damascus: 1, 28, 29, 31
Dammam: 17, 325; description, 127, 129, 235, 243, 254, 255, 261, 269, 286, 287, 293, 301; oil industry, 4, 10, 21, 207, 245, 247, 249; port, 41, 275; railroad, 4, 41, 173, 250, 273
Dariya: 30, 31, 33
dates: cultivation, 15, 17, 227-228; export, 278; irrigation, 5
death rate: 18
decree law: 193-194
deserts (see also Dahna Nafud and Rub al-Khali): 10 (fig. 2), 14-15
Dhahran: 15, 42, 100, 126; airfield, 41, 43, 44, 45, 165, 170, 173, 174, 205, 274, 292, 327; description, 21, 243, 265; and oil industry, 246
Dibdiba: 15; and oil exploration, 250
diet: 120-121, 228, 229, 260
disease: 119, 121-124, 220
divorce: 74, 75

364

Eastern Province: 47, 112, 128, 135, 152; and agriculture, 215, 217, 218, 229; and culture, 83, 89; description, 5, 22, 219, 220, 224, 225, 231, 232, 250, 253, 254, 269, 293; history, 7, 25; labor force, 258, 259; local government, 145, 157; oil industry, 4, 207, 241, 244, 247; population, 21, 51, 55, 63, 67; public security, 192, 193; trade, 267; welfare facilities, 126, 131

Economic Development Fund: 210, 310, 315

education (*see also* Ministry of Education): 91-94, 95 (table 1), 96-104; modernization 6, 42, 46, 77-78, 91-92; students abroad, 43, 67, 102, 203; TV programs, 184-185

Egypt: 41, 169, 328, 331; relations with, 8, 43, 44, 153, 164 *ff*.

electric power: and companies, 243; in Haradh Valley, 239, 293; in urban areas, 21, 128, 177, 243

emir: and the king, 133; and public security, 192; in village hierarchy, 64, 145, 150

employment: (*see also* Arabian American Oil Company, oil industry) 4, 261-264

Europe: 280, 281

expenditure, government, 310, 311, 312 (table 14), 313-314

exports: 278, 279 (table 7), 281 (table 9), 282, 284, 287, 304

Faisal Ibn Abd al-Aziz al-Faisal al-Saud: 6, 7; Basic Law, 135-137; education, 100; foreign policy, 8, 44, 163, 166 *ff*., 170, 173, 174; government of Hejaz, 39; and intellectual expression, 87; as king, 45-46, 134, 138-139, 156, 158-159, 204; and local government, 144, 145; as prime minister, 42; and reform program, 45-46, 152, 193; resignation, 44; as ruler, 139, 151, 204; as spiritual leader, 116; and Yemen war, 323-324

farms (*see also* land tenure, agriculture): 208-209, 214, 225-226, 229

Fatima: 28

Federation of South Arabia: 170

Fertile Crescent: boundaries, 38, history, 1, 2, 322; relations with, 164

festivals: 113, 114, 115

films: 177, 186

fiscal system (*see also* expenditure, government; budgets, government): 5, 208, 297

fishing industry: 235-236; and exports, 278

Five-Year Plan: 256

Food and Agriculture Organization (FAO): 175, 233, 238, 239, 292

foreign aid: 293; medical programs, 126; military 326 *ff*., 331, 332; technical, 212, 228, 254, 291-292

foreign exchange: and balance of trade, 212; and financial crisis of 1956-57, 287; and hadj, 285; and oil industry, 207, 251, 277, 300

foreign investment: 254, 293-295

foreign population: (*see also* immigration): 55-56; attitude toward, 205; employment, 143-144; and taxes, 143

foreign relations (*see also* country entries): 8, 161-177

foreign trade: 277-288, 305

forestry: 235

France: 37; and oil concessions 247, 291, 317; relations with, 43, 165, 170; trade, 281 (table 9)

General Petroleum and Mineral Organization: creation, 242; iron and steel project, 255, 256; and oil industry, 250, 291, 293, 295

Germany: 36; relations with, 170, 324; trade with, 282; World War II, 41

gold: 242, 243, 294, 299

governor general: 146, 147, 151

government (*see also* king): 6, 7, 133-140, 141 (fig. 5), 142-150; and employees, 143-144, 263

Grand Mufti: and education, 93, 94, 100; and government, 116, 133, 155, 156, 194; and police force, 189, 193

365

Great Britain: and Buraimi Oasis, 43, 161; history, 32, 34, 35, 36, 37 ff.; and lend-lease assistance, 291; and military assistance, 327, 331; and oil interests, 38, 161; relations with, 43, 165, 170–172, 322–324
Great Rift: 11–12
gross national product: 251

Hadith: 108, 134; and family matters, 69; and intellectual expression, 84
hadj (pilgrimage): 117, 163, 173, 302; and budget, 310; health problems, 123–124; and immigration, 52; and Islam, 106, 108, 112, 114–115, 164; and trade, 270–271, 277, 285, 300
Hail: agricultural area, 215; capital of Shammar district, 13; history, 33, 322; Rashidi capital, 36, 37
Hanbalites: 35, 112, and inheritance, 71; and jurisprudence, 109, 112, 193
handicrafts: 243–244, 257
Hanifite school: 109, 112, 135
Haradh: 249; experiment station, 17, 21, 293; settlement project, 239
Harb tribe: 49 (fig. 4), 226
Hashemites: 28, 30, 39, 133, 168; and Hejaz, 25, 36–38, 322
Hejaz: 17, 41, 47, 89, 128, 133; and climate, 16, 214, 215; description, 7, 12–13, 59, 219, 221, 225, 226, 231–232, 235; and government, 136, 139, 145, 193, 194; history, 1, 2, 26, 29–33, 36–38, 163, 170, 190, 322–324; irrigation, 17, 215, 217; labor force, 259; population, 19, 21, 52, 65; as province, 146; public order, 193; and religion, 112, 135
Hofuf: agricultural production, 229; description, 15, 19, 65, 235, 237, 239, 243, 253; natural gas, 250; and religion, 112
hospitals: 124–127, 172, 253
housing: 128
Husein: 36–38, 322

Ikhwan warriors: 35; battle between Husein and Abd al-Aziz, 37, 38; end of use by Abd al-Aziz, 40; history, 2, 321–324; and settlement of Bedouins, 56, 190

ikta land: 219–220, 221, 224
imam: history, 111; and the king, 3, 116, 133, 135; as religious leader, 27
immigration: 47, 51, 52, 105
imports: 212, 214, 277, 279 (table 7), 280 (table 8), 282 (table 10), 283, 285, 287, 299, 300, 304
income tax: 289, 290, 318
industrialization: under Faisal, 46; and social mobility, 60, 66
industry: 252–254; construction, 252–253; and legislation, 211–212, 241–242, 254; maritime, 244
infant mortality: 18, 70
International Atomic Energy Agency (IAEA): 175
International Bank for Reconstruction and Development (IBRD): 18, 175, 210, 276, 278, 292, 304
International Civil Aviation Organization (ICAO): 175
International Monetary Fund (IMF): 175, 209, 277, 278, 292, 304, 306
International Telecommunications Union (ITU): 175
Iran: 8, 162, 165, 290
Iraq: boundaries, 38, 39; history, 1–2, 11, 37, 290, 323; relations with, 163, 165 ff.
iron: deposits, 243, 256; and steel plants, 242, 255
irrigation: 214, 215–218, 231, 238, 239; in Al-Hasa, 15; in Nejd, 14; systems, 211; and water regulations, 224–225
Islam: 105–113, 114 (table 2), 115–117; central role, 1, 2, 8; history, 25, 27; and Saud family, 6; schools of law, 134–135; values, 3, 4, 5, 47, 78, 79, 81, 82
Israel: 8, 169, 175, 204, 288
ITALCO: 239–240

Jabrin: 215, 218, 220, 227
jahad: 108
Japan: 294; relations with, 324; trade with, 278, 282
Jawf: 16
Jebel Shammar: 13, 36, 226
Jews: 47, 55, 105

Jidda: 112, 325; conquest by Abd al-Aziz, 38; description, 236, 243, 250, 286, 287, 293, 295, 300, 301; and education, 97, 101, 102, 103; and government, 136, 149, 162; history, 32, 166, 168 323, 328; labor force, 259, 261; medical facilities, 124, 126, 172; modernization, 42, 90, 152; population, 18, 19, 52; and sea traffic, 13, 275
Jiluwi family: 7, 145, 157, 192
jinns: 115, 116
Jizan: agricultural production, 215, 237; history, 3, 26; ports, 13
Jordan: boundaries, 11; history, 1, 2, 26, 37; relations with, 43, 163, 165 ff., 328
journalism (*see also* newspapers): 178
judicial system: 194 ff.

Kaaba: 27, 29; holy shrine at Mecca, 26, 106, 113, 114-115; and pilgrimage, 108
Khalid Ibn Abd al-Aziz al-Saud: 325-326; Council of Ministers, 155; crown prince, 156, 157; deposition decree, 46; deputy prime minister, 45
Khalid tribe: 49 (fig. 4), 226
Khaybar: 13, 52, 213; agricultural area, 215, 217-218, 220, 229
Khurma: 37
king: 133-134, 136, 138-139; attitude toward, 203-205; powers, 158-159, 203; and provincial government, 144-150; sheikh of sheiks, 145, 203
kinship: and family, 69, 70; nomads, 60-62; relations with king, 145; and social status, 66; and tribal structure, 3, 5, 6, 203; villages, 62-64
Koran: 2, 27, 30, 108 ff., 113; and classical Arabic, 53; and family matters, 69; and intellectual expression, 84, 85; and radio, 182, 183; and *sharia* law, 134, 135, 193; and social values, 79
kuttab: 23, 92-93
Kuwait: boundaries, 38, 171; history, 1, 11, 32, 33, 34, 36, 322 323; and neutral zone 247, 251, 317; and oil resources, 169, 242, 244, 245, 246, 290

Labor Code: 261-262, 264
labor force (*see also* Arabian American Oil Company, skilled labor): in government, 258-259; in maritime industry, 244
labor relations: 264-266
labor unions: 7, 42, 151
land tenure: 218-225; and conservation, 213; and Islamic law, 208-209; and social status, 68
land use: 19, 214-215
language: 52-54; Arabic, 47, 79; in education, 96; foreign, 53; non-Arabic, 52
legal system: 194
libraries: 253
literacy: 42, 102-103, 153, 177, 188
livestock: 222, 232-235, 238, 267, 268, 278, 299
living conditions: 8, 119, 127-128, 300; and government programs, 42
locust control: 237

majlis: and tribal government, 6, 62, 63, 144, 145, 204; and village headman, 204
Malekite school: 109, 112, 135
marriage: 70
Mecca: 55, 87, 124; conquest by Abd al-Aziz, 38-39; description, 12, 22, 119, 130, 215, 217, 243, 269, 286, 287, 295, 301; education, 97, 99, 104; government, 149; history, 26, 27, 29-32, 112, 323; holy city, 1, 105, 106, 108, 123; modernization, 41-42, 90; population, 18, 19, 56
medical services: 21, 124-127
Medina: 97, 124; conquest by Abd al-Aziz, 38; description, 13, 22, 130, 215, 217, 226-227, 229, 237, 243, 269, 286, 301; and government, 149; history, 27-31, 323; holy city, 3, 105, 106, 115, 123, 135; and intellectual expression, 87, 89, 90; population, 18, 19, 56
Middle East: 1, 8, 36, 166; relations with, 161, 162, 165; trade, 282
minerals: 212, 242, 243, 255
Ministries of: Agriculture and Water, 142, 181, 229, 233, 235, 237, 239, 294, 314; Commerce and Industry, 140, 142, 254, 287; Communications, 140, 142, 273, 276,

314, 325; Defense and Aviation, 45, 103, 142, 156, 157, 275, 321, 326, 330, 331, 334; Education, 88, 91 ff., 102, 103, 126, 130, 140, 142, 181, 185, 260, 314; Finance and National Economy, 51, 131, 140, 142, 154, 157, 210, 223, 237, 261, 265, 294, 297, 299, 301 ff., 308, 309, 311, 314, 318–319; Foreign Affairs, 140, 142, 162, 163, 325; Health, 119–120, 124, 126, 127, 140, 142, 172, 314; Information, 7, 140, 142, 178, 181, 184 ff., 239; Interior, 140, 142, 146 ff., 156, 157, 181, 189, 191, 192, 198, 325; Justice, 137, 140, 142, 190, 194; Labor and Social Affairs, 65, 129 ff., 142, 226, 261–262, 264, 270, 314; National Defense and Aviation, 140, 142, 325; Pilgrimage and Religious Foundations, 117, 142, 223; Petroleum and Mineral Resources, 100, 142, 154, 212, 241, 314

miri land: 219, 221, 222, 223

modernization: 159, 201–204; and government, 41–43; and Islam, 116–117; and oil industry, 67

Mohammed: 26–28, 48, 89, 105 ff., 201; and classical Arabic, 53; founder of Islam, 1; and justice, 193; Koran, 85, 134; pilgrimage, 3; and social status, 66; and water rights, 223

Mohammed Ali: 31, 32, 33

Mohammed Ibn Abd al-Wahhab: and Bedouin following, 31; and Hanbalite school, 109, 112, 135; and puritanic Islamic movement, 2, 30, 321

Mohammed Ibn Rashid: 13, 33

Mohammed Ibn Saud: 30–31, 47

monarchy: 133, 138, 203–204

Moslem World League: 162

mosques: 64, 65, 111, 117, 322; in cities, 22, 23

mountains: 9, 10 (fig. 2), 12–13

mulk land: 220, 221, 222

Municipal Regulations (1938): 145, 149

Musaad Ibn Abd ar-Rahman: 155, 157

Muscat: 11, 161, 170

mushaa land: 220, 226

Mutayr tribe: 35, 39, 49 (fig. 4), 226, 322, 323

Nafud: 9, 12, 13, 14, 218

Najran: 11; agricultural area, 215; bombed by UAR, 174; boundaries, 9; history, 323, 326; Treaty of Taif, 40

Nasser, Gamal Abdul: 153; relations with, 43, 164, 165; and socialism, 181, 203; Suez crisis, 8, 44; Yemen civil war, 166, 168, 328

national consciousness: 2–3, 201–203

National Guard: 321, 325, 329, 331; and budget, 155, 311, 314, 326; creation, 190, 324; and public order, 189, 191, 192

national income: 211, 279

National Police: 189, 191, 192

national symbols: 202

natural gas: 242, 249–250

navy: 321, 326

Negroes: 52

Nejd: 67, 112, 128, 135, 136; climate, 16; cultivation, 17, 18, 215, 217, 225–232, 258; description, 12, 13, 14, 22, 219, 220, 234; and government, 136, 139; history, 2, 7, 30–39; oil industry, 245, 248; as province, 146; and tribes, 20, 25

newspapers: 7, 177, 178, 179 (table 4), 180–181

news services: 178, 181

nomads: 2, 5, 6, 9, 49, 60–62, 208, 209; and crime, 191; employment, 67; and family, 69; history, 25, 329; pastoralism, 213; and resettlement, 20, 35, 190, 211, 239

Northern Frontier Province: 146

oil industry (*see also* Arabian American Oil Company): 3, 21, 38, 244–252; and companies, 244–247, 251, 285, 316, 317; concessions, 244–247; discovery, 3, 4, 25, 277; employees, 251; exports, 5, 208; fields, 169, 242, 249, 250, 251; and foreign relations, 161, 288–291; and modernization of country, 42, 59, 66, 67, 152; production, 41; refineries, 4, 242; revenues, 5, 43, 66, 117, 136, 207, 209, 210, 297, 300, 301, 314–317; transportation, 173

Oman: boundary dispute, 11, 161, 170, 172, 174; history, 32, 33

Onassis, Aristotle: 173, 289
Organization of Petroleum Exporting Countries (OPEC): 290, 291
Ottoman Empire: 1, 30, 31, 33–36, 322

Palestine: relations with, 43, 161, 164, 165; war, 8, 41, 328
Pan-Arab nationalism: 203
pastoralism: 213, 232, 241, 257, 267
paternalism: 204, 257, 264
periodicals: 7, 177, 179 (table 4)
Persian Gulf: 9, 10; and agriculture, 218, 230, 236; description, 15; history, 29, 30, 32, 35, 322; maritime industry, 244; oil industry, 4, 12, 171, 245, 247; ports, 41, 275, 286
pilgrimage: *see* hadj
police force: 192; reforms, 152–157; system, 153
polygamy: 70–71, 73
population: 1, 2, 5, 18–19, 20 (fig. 3), 21–23
press: 177–181
prime minister: 140, 146, 308
prisons: 197–198
Protectorate of South Arabia: 170
provinces: and government, 144–150, 159; number of, 146
public health service: 124–126

qadis: 63, 64; and education, 96; and family matters, 69, 73, 75; and government, 150; and judicial system, 194 *ff.*
Qahtan: 48, 61
Qasim: 19, 33, 34, 97, 217, 226
Qatar: 290; boundaries, 11, 171; history, 32, 322
Qatif: agricultural areas, 215, 227, 232, 239; oil fields, 249; and population, 20, 21
qiyas: 134
Quraysh tribe: 26, 28, 48, 49 (fig. 4)

radio: 21, 166, 170, 177, 178, 182, 184, 188; and intellectual expression, 84, 85; government-operated, 7, 269; and stations 183 (table 5)
railroads: 32, 271, 272 (fig. 8), 273–274; between Dammam and Riyadh, 4, 41, 250, 293

rainfall: 5, 9, 13, 16, 17, 214–216, 224
Ramadan: 3, 77, 79, 86, 107, 112, 113, 114, 193
Ras Tanura: 126, 127; description, 15, 119, 291; and labor force, 259; and oil industry, 21, 207, 247–249, 289, 291, 316; seaport, 275
Rashid tribe: 33, 34, 36, 37, 321–322
recreation: 60, 65, 82
Red Crescent Society: 126, 129
Red Sea: 9–14, 52; description, 215, 224, 230, 236, 286; history, 1, 30; oil exploration, 170, 247, 317; seaport, 275
revenue, government: 207, 241, 246, 252, 267, 277, 300, 301, 303, 314, 315 (table 16), 316–319
Riyadh: 14, 33, 172; and armed forces, 325; description, 9, 12, 22, 119, 125, 126, 127, 129, 130, 170, 208, 211, 215, 237, 250, 253, 254, 286, 287, 295, 301, 308; and education, 97, 99, 100, 103; and government, 136; history, 7, 31, 34, 39, 321, 328; modernization, 5, 42, 90, 152; population, 18, 19, 21, 65, 261; railroad, 18, 19, 41, 173, 250, 273; and religion, 35, 112
riyal (SR): 208, 209, 277, 287, 297–300, 302–304
roads: 5, 248, 271, 272 (fig. 8), 273
Royal Cabinet: 139
Royal Guard: 155, 156, 324
Rub al-Khali: description, 9, 12, 14–15, 218; history, 2, 322; and oil industry, 250

sabotage: 198–199
Sakaka: 16
Saud family: 133, 144, 157–158; history, 25, 30–33, 203; political activity, 7, 151; rivalry, 153–157
Saud Ibn Abd al-Aziz: 6, 31, 42–46, 138; and Bedouins, 144; deposed, 134, 204; and foreign policy, 162–163, 165, 166, 168, 169, 173, 174; heir to throne, 42; as king, 153–158; opposition, 153; and reform, 152; as ruler, 138–139
Saud Ibn Abdullah Ibu Jiluwi: 145
Saud Ibn Rashid: 36
Saudi Arabian Airlines: 101–102

369

Saudi Arabian Mining Syndicate: 242, 278, 298
Saudi Arabian Monetary Agency (SAMA): 209–210, 283–286, 292, 297, 301–308
Saudi-Kuwait Neutral Zone: 10, 11, 247, 251, 317
seaports: 13, 275–276
Semites: 25, 47, 53
sewerage facilities: 119
Shafite school: 109, 135
shahada: 106
Shammar tribes: 13, 33
Sharart tribe: 48, 49 (fig. 4)
sharecroppers: 68, 221–222, 226
sharia: 3, 6, 64, 107, 109, 116–117, 136, 330; and education, 96, 99, 100; and family matters, 69; inheritance, 218–219; and justice, 190, 193 *ff.*; and king, 133–134, 135, 138; and labor relations, 264; and Ministry of Justice, 140; and modern legal problems, 137; and nomads, 189; and provinces, 146; and subversion, 198–199
sheikhs: 61–62, 65, 129, 133; and government, 144, 150, 190–191; king, 138, 203; and land ownership, 220; and social status, 67
Shiites: 28, 29, 110, 113; and culture, 89; discrimination against, 55; location, 51; numbers, 51; religious practices, 63, 88
shorfa: 66
silver: 242, 243, 299
skilled labor: 59, 67, 205, 257, 259, 260–262
slavery: 45, 47, 59, 159
social and economic reforms (*see also* modernization): 159
social security: 119, 128, 129, 130–131
social status: 59, 60, 74; and mobility, 60
social structure: 3, 4, 56, 58–68, 159–160
social welfare services: 65, 119, 128, 129, 159
socialism: 106, 155, 181, 203, 266
Société Auxiliaire de la Régie Autonome des Petroles (AUXIRAP): 247, 291, 317

soil erosion (*see also* irrigation): 231
Soviet Union: 163–166, 173, 327
strikes: 151, 261, 265–266
subversion: 198–199
Sudayri family: 157
Suez crisis in 1956: 8, 170, 172
Sufis: 110
suk: 22, 23, 64, 65, 267–268, 271
Sulaba tribe: 48, 49 (fig. 4), 88
sunna: 108–109, 134
Sunni: 28, 29, 109–110, 113; and discrimination, 55; numbers, 50, 112; and religious practices, 63
Syria: 8, 169; relations with, 163, 165, 166

Taif: 325; agricultural area, 215, 226, 229; description, 239, 243, 301; history, 30, 37, 38, 213, 323, 324; modernization, 90; and population, 18, 19
Talal Ibn Abd al-Aziz, Prince: 44, 45, 137; and constitutional reform, 152, 153–155
tariffs: 212, 287, 294; liberal structure, 277
Tariqi, Abdullah Ibn Hammud: 154, 155
taxes (*see also zakat*): 212, 290
technical training programs: 5
television: 4, 46, 88, 152, 177, 185–186; and education, 103, 184; government operated, 7
Tihama coastal plain: 12, 215, 216, 229, 230, 232, 233
Tihama mountains: 9, 16–17, 19
trade, domestic: 208, 267–276
Trans-Arabian Pipeline Company (TAP): 125, 127, 234, 248, 249, 272, 286, 291; and settlements, 17, 20, 21, 57; and special agreement, 210, 316–317
transportation network: 6, 50, 208, 211; in agriculture, 214, 227; development, 241, 279; and equipment, 278–280
tribes (*see also* Bedouins): 49 (fig. 4); and armed forces, 329; and family groups, 70, 203; power of chiefs, 151; and raiding, 189, 190
Trucial Oman: 32, 171
Tuwaiq mountains: 12, 14, 17

ulema: 6, 45–46, 66, 87, 111, 112, 116, 151–152, 182; and education, 92; and executive powers, 156, 157; and *fetwa*, 143, 156; and justice, 193 *ff.*; and monarchy, 133, 138
Umayad family: 28, 29, 87
Unayza: 14, 33, 34, 215, 227
United Arab Republic (*see also* Nasser, Gamal Abdul): 266, 327; attitude toward, 204–205; relations with, 8, 44, 45, 161–164, 167–169, 174, 175, 202, 203
United Nations: 167, 168, 170, 175; aid, 278, 292; and Communist China, 164; member, 8, 41, 42, 161, 175; Observation Mission, 175; Oman dispute, 172, 174; Relief and Works Agency for Palestine Refugees (UNRWA), 175; Special Fund, 239, 292; Yemen dispute, 167, 168
United Nations Educational, Scientific and Cultural Organization (UNESCO): 100, 128, 175
United Postal Union (UPU): 175
United States (*see also* Arabian American Oil Company): 126, 205, 242, 292; airbase at Dhahran, 43–44, 45; and Eisenhower Doctrine, 165, 173; lend-lease program, 41, 173, 291, 292; military assistance, 326, 327, 328, 331, 332; relations with, 44, 45, 165, 170, 172–174; technical assistance, 163, 228, 239, 254, 291–292; trade with, 278, 282
universities: 92, 99–101, 104

vocational education: 5, 97–98
Voice of America (VOA): 188

Wadi Fatima: 215, 217, 229, 232
wadis: 12–18, 215–218, 227, 231
Wafrah: 246–247
wages: 263 (table 6), 264, 265
Wahhabi movement (*see also* Islam): 34, 37, 39, 47, 109, 112, 115, 116, 135, 182, 189, 323, 324; and missionaries, 35, 190, 321; and puritanism, 33, 152, 193
waqf land: 129, 219, 220–221, 223, 257
water (*see also* irrigation): conservation, 17, 238–239; development projects, 248, 293; rights, 223–225; supplies, 21, 23, 119, 128, 208, 211, 215, 218, 232, 234
women: 18–19, 67, 77, 80, 127; and education, 77–78, 91–92, 93, 94, 98–99, 101, 152; marriage and divorce, 67, 70, 73–75; and values, 81–82; veiling and seclusion, 69, 71, 73
World Health Organization (WHO): 120, 122, 125, 126, 127, 128, 175
World Meteorological Organization (WMO): 175
World War II: 5, 21, 324

Yemen: 41, 198; boundary, 9, 11, 323; civil war, 45, 155, 166–168, 174, 175, 203, 325–326, 328; history, 25, 26, 29–33, 40; relations with, 161, 163, 164

Zakat: 35, 107, 111, 129, 131, 171, 297, 309, 318–319

PUBLISHED AREA HANDBOOKS

550-65	Afghanistan	550-69	Ivory Coast
550-98	Albania	550-30	Japan
550-44	Algeria	550-34	Jordan
550-59	Angola	550-56	Kenya
550-73	Argentina	550-50	Khmer Republic (Cambodia)
550-169	Australia	550-81	Korea, North
550-170	Belgium	550-41	Korea, Rep. of
550-66	Bolivia	550-58	Laos
550-20	Brazil	550-24	Lebanon
550-168	Bulgaria	550-38	Liberia
550-61	Burma	550-85	Libya
550-83	Burundi	550-163	Malagasy Republic
550-166	Cameroon	550-45	Malaysia
550-96	Ceylon	550-161	Mauritania
550-159	Chad	550-79	Mexico
550-77	Chile	550-76	Mongolia
550-60	China, People's Rep. of	550-49	Morocco
550-63	China, Rep. of	550-64	Mozambique
550-26	Colombia	550-35	Nepal, Bhutan and Sikkim
550-67	Congo, Dem. Rep. of (Zaire)	550-88	Nicaragua
550-91	Congo, People's Rep. of	550-157	Nigeria
550-90	Costa Rica	550-94	Oceania
550-152	Cuba	550-48	Pakistan
550-22	Cyprus	550-46	Panama
550-158	Czechoslovakia	550-156	Paraguay
550-54	Dominican Republic	550-92	Peripheral States of the Arabian Peninsula
550-155	East Germany		
550-52	Ecuador	550-42	Peru
550-150	El Salvador	550-72	Philippines
550-28	Ethiopia	550-162	Poland
550-167	Finland	550-160	Romania
550-29	Germany	550-84	Rwanda
550-153	Ghana	550-51	Saudi Arabia
550-87	Greece	550-70	Senegal
550-78	Guatemala	550-86	Somalia
550-82	Guyana	550-93	South Africa, Rep. of
550-164	Haiti		
550-151	Honduras	550-95	Soviet Union
550-165	Hungary	550-27	Sudan, Dem. Rep. of
550-21	India	550-47	Syria
550-154	Indian Ocean Territories	550-62	Tanzania
550-39	Indonesia	550-53	Thailand
550-68	Iran		
550-31	Iraq	550-89	Tunisia
550-25	Israel	550-80	Turkey

550-74	Uganda	550-71	Venezuela
550-43	United Arab Republic (Egypt)	550-57	Vietnam, North
		550-55	Vietnam, South
550-97	Uruguay	550-99	Yugoslavia
		550-75	Zambia